FASHIONING THE CANADIAN LANDSCAPE

Essays on Travel Writing, Tourism, and National Identity in the Pre-Automobile Era

Fashioning the Canadian Landscape

Essays on Travel Writing, Tourism, and National Identity in the Pre-Automobile Era

J.I. LITTLE

UNIVERSITY OF TORONTO PRESS
Toronto Buffalo London

Toronto Buffalo London
utorontopress.com

ISBN 978-1-4875-0021-4

Library and Archives Canada Cataloguing in Publication

Little, J. I. (John Irvine), 1947–, author
Fashioning the Canadian landscape : essays on travel writing, tourism, and national identity in the pre-automobile era / J.I. Little.

Includes bibliographical references and index.
ISBN 978-1-4875-0021-4 (cloth)

1. Travel – Canada – History – 19th century. 2. Tourism – Canada – History – 19th century. 3. Travelers' writings, British – History and criticism. 4. Travelers' writings, American – History and criticism. 5. National characteristics, Canadian – History – 19th century. 6. Picturesque, The, in literature. 7. Landscapes in literature. 8. Canada – In literature. 9. Canada – Description and travel. I. Title.

FC72.L58 2018 917.104'5 C2017-906709-5

University of Toronto Press acknowledges the financial assistance to its publishing program of the Canada Council for the Arts and the Ontario Arts Council, an agency of the Government of Ontario.

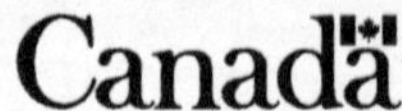

Fashion (verb): "to change (something) so as to make it suitable for a new use or situation"; "to bring into being by combining, shaping, or transforming materials." http://www.merriam-webster.com/thesaurus/fashion%5Bverb%5D. Viewed 7 January 2015.

Landscape (noun): "all the visible features of an area of countryside or land, often considered in terms of their aesthetic appeal." https://www.google.ca/?gws_rd=ssl#q=landscape+definition. Viewed 7 January 2015.

Contents

Illustrations

Preface

> If the Canadian people are to find their soul, they must seek for it ... in the little ports of the Atlantic provinces, in the flaming autumn maples of the St. Lawrence Valley, in the portages and lakes of the Canadian Shield, in the sunsets and relentless cold of the Canadian prairies, in the foothill, mountain and sea of the west and in the unconquerable vastness of the north. From the land, Canada, must come the soul of Canada.
>
> A.R.M. Lower, *Colony to Nation*, 1946, p. 560.

Colony to Nation was the text book for my freshman course in Canadian history, so perhaps Arthur Lower played a role not only in my choice of career, but in my decision to focus on rural history as well as in my longstanding interest in Canada's national identity.

But had I become aware of Roderick Nash's *Wilderness and the American Mind* soon after it was first published in 1968 (the year I graduated), my research might well have taken a much earlier turn towards the subject of the essays in this volume. Environmental history was late in coming to Canada, however, so late that when I began teaching a seminar on the subject in the 1990s I had difficulty finding enough Canadian publications to complete the syllabus. Canadian historians have more than made up for lost time since then, and it has been a great pleasure to witness and share in the enthusiasm of this latest generation of young scholars. This volume does not pretend to capture the Canadian "mind," à la Nash, but it does attempt to shed light on why and how Canada became so closely identified with its physical landscape.

Collected here are revised versions of eight essays published since 2003, as well as two that appear here for the first time. I wish to thank the journals listed in the credit section for permission to republish, and to acknowledge once again the editors and readers for their invaluable advice and encouragement. I also benefited from the able assistance of three student researchers, in particular – Sean Wilkinson, Alice Huang, and Liam O'Flaherty – whose employment was made possible by a research grant from the Social Sciences and Humanities Research Council. Gratefully acknowledged, as well, is the generous grant from Simon Fraser University's Publication Fund. I'm also very grateful to UTP editor Len Husband for having faith in this collection, and I wish to thank associate managing editor Frances Mundy for her supportive role in its production, as well as Anne Fullerton for her excellent copy editing. And thanks, above all, to Andrea for the continuing support and for ensuring that I do not become completely submerged by my work now that I've entered my "retirement" years.

My first trip across Canada was with my undergraduate friend Lloyd Perkins in his old VW Beatle in the summer of 1970. We generally followed the Trans-Canada highway as we headed West, but we did get close to nature, for my vivid memories of that trip include being chewed by mosquitoes in our moth-eaten pup tent in northern Ontario; listening to whooping cranes nesting outside our cabin at a Ducks Unlimited sanctuary somewhere in Manitoba; battening down in a gale-force wind in a Saskatchewan roadside camp-site; seeking shelter from a late June snowstorm in a Jasper hostel; and being awakened on the Pacific coast's Long Beach by the biggest and brightest moon I've ever seen, and with the high tide washing over our sleeping bags. Lloyd stayed fit enough to live to a hundred but he died this year, and I dedicate this book to his memory as a brilliant and generous friend, as well as to the memory of another friend from Bishop's University days who was also recently taken by cancer. Peter Anderson inspired me with his cheerful passion for life to the very end as a professional ski instructor, fly-fishing guide, and free spirit.

Bowen Island, BC
1 September 2016

FASHIONING THE CANADIAN LANDSCAPE

Essays on Travel Writing, Tourism, and National Identity in the Pre-Automobile Era

Introduction

Although there are no towering firs on the prairies, no majestic mountains in Nova Scotia, no forbidding icebergs in Vancouver, and no tidal flats in Ontario, we relate to the ... natural aspects of our country as being part of who we are as Canadians. We are mostly an urban people now, yet we think of ourselves in terms of our geography.

David Silcox, *The Group of Seven and Tom Thomson*, 2003, p. 49.

Due to the work of Anthony D. Smith, among many others, we are now quite familiar with the distinction between a genealogical "ethnic" national identity based on a community of descent, and a territorial "civic" national identity based on common institutions. Smith insists, nevertheless, that all national identities are consciously characterized by both a historical and a geographical heritage.[1] The balance between the two obviously varies from country to country, but the above citation from Silcox would suggest that geographical heritage plays a particularly strong role in Canada, at least outside Quebec where the historical heritage dominates.[2] It is telling, after all, that the original French lyrics to "O Canada" open with "terre de nos aïeux" and refer to the country's history as "une épopée des plus brilliant exploits," while the official English lyrics refer to "Our home and native land" and "The True North, strong and free." In fact, historian W.L. Morton suggested long ago that "The ultimate and the comprehensive meaning of Canadian history is to be found where there has been no Canadian history: in the North."[3]

Morton was not the first historian to stress the role of geography in Canadian history, for in the 1930s A.R.M. Lower's work on the forest frontier was influenced by Frederick Jackson Turner, and Harold Adams Innis's staples thesis associated the country's evolution with the exploitation of a series of raw materials – fish, furs, timber, wheat – thereby inspiring Donald Creighton's Laurentian thesis. In historian Carl Berger's words, "The feeling that pervaded Creighton's narrative had much in common with that evoked by the paintings of the Group of Seven. The landscapes of a northern terrain, for the most part without human figures, moulded the national character. What the painters had only implied, Creighton (and Innis) documented historically. The landscape of rivers, lakes and Shield was the matrix of Canadian institutions, economics, and national hopes."[4] By the 1950s, Berger notes, political biography had become the dominant form of historical writing,[5] but the influence of the staples and Laurentian theses persisted into the 1960s and beyond.

The process of nationalizing the landscape, historian Orvar Löfgren has pointed out, was particularly prevalent in countries "that saw themselves as marginal to the grand narrative of western civilization – the Scandinavian countries, the United States, and, later, Canada."[6] According to cultural geographer Brian Osborne, it was the nationalizing state that created what he refers to as Canada's geography of identity.[7] The studies in this collection reveal, however, that Canada's identification with the landscape has roots that predate its creation as a nation state, roots that extend to Great Britain and, to a lesser extent, the United States. What developed into what Osborne refers to as Canada's "patriotic topography" is, rather ironically, largely a product of the country's colonial legacy, as reflected in the hundreds of narratives published by upper-middle-class British travellers between the late eighteenth and early twentieth centuries. Those narratives focus on the landscape largely because of the British assumption that Canada, outside Quebec, had little of historical or cultural interest to offer. Furthermore, what was described was not objectively viewed geographical space, for – as Simon Schama has noted – landscapes "are culture before they are nature; constructs of the imagination projected onto wood and water and rock."[8]

Schama, among many others, has written about how landscape painting, which originated in fifteenth-century Italy with the discovery of the centralized perspective, allowed for the pictorial representation of three dimensions on a flat surface, thereby creating the illusion of looking into an actual scene that was frozen in time. As Denis Cosgrove explains, "in an important, if not always literal, sense the spectator *owns* the view because all of its components are structured and directed towards his eyes only."[9] It is not difficult to understand, then, why colonial environments came to be depicted as landscapes.[10] Even the military draftsmen had been trained to some extent in the landscape tradition.[11] Furthermore, the colonializing British gaze was drawn particularly to the picturesque, a perspective that had emerged in the late eighteenth century as a reaction against the rapid expansion of the cultivated English landscape.

The origin of the English picturesque is accredited particularly to the Reverend William Gilpin, followed by Sir Uvedale Price and Richard Payne Knight. As defined by them, the picturesque view fell between the Burkean duo of the sublime which was associated with that which awes or terrifies, and the beautiful, associated with that which calms or pleases. The term picturesque applied to scenes that embodied roughness and irregularity while accentuating the harmony between human beings and nature.[12] Historian I.S. MacLaren has noted that the picturesque is a way of seeing nature that is especially appropriate to the geography of England where the diverse landforms of moderate size can readily be organized into the unity of foreground, middle ground, and background, and outlines are blurred and colours softened by the moist atmosphere.[13] Applied to the colonies, Australian historian Simon Ryan claims, the picturesque tamed the landscape's "threatening vastness and unfamiliarity," as well as "proving the transportability and universal validity of European visual taste."[14]

As for the travel writers from south of the border, they too had a colonializing perspective for they were particularly attracted to what they saw as distinctive about their own country, namely the rugged sublime. We should note, however, that judgment of what made a particular landscape beautiful, picturesque, or sublime was somewhat subjective, for these were not air-tight categories. Thus, Canadian art historian Marylin McKay observes a certain hybridity between all three categories in the painting as well as writing produced by several members of the colonial Canadian elite. She also states that in the latter half of the nineteenth century Canadian artists began to reject such formulaic compositions in favour of more Romantic styles reflecting a more personal and intimate engagement with Nature.[15] Whatever the aesthetic category, however, Canada's landscape remained a prominent theme, even for early twentieth-century writers such as the English poet Rupert Brooke who deeply personalized their travel accounts.

Most historical studies of the Canadian landscape have focused either on painting and photography,[16] or poetry and fiction,[17] and explorers have also received some attention,[18] but interest in the popular and certainly influential genre of travel writing was quite limited until recently.[19] As late as 2002, in fact, the introduction to *The Cambridge Companion to Travel Writing* claimed that travel writing was "a vast, little-explored area."[20] Social scientists such as geographer Stephen Daniels had become aware, however, that "Landscape imagery is not merely a reflection of, or distraction from, more pressing social, economic or political issues; it is often a powerful mode of knowledge and social engagement."[21] And historian Catherine Hall, among others, has argued that colonization was achieved not only through political and economic means, but also through images.[22] The advantage of prose descriptions, as David Arnold has pointed out, is that they communicate even more powerfully than visual representations the sense of a place being scrutinized and appraised by outsiders.[23] Canadian scholars certainly have a rich archive of travel narratives at their disposal, for literary scholar Elizabeth Waterston has catalogued approximately 700 English-language Canadian travel books for the period prior to 1900 alone, and there were also a good many newspaper and magazine articles. Waterston claims, in fact, that "For contemporary readers, these reported perceptions became 'Canada.'"[24] It should also be noted that during the 1880s, Canada was finally "rediscovered" by travellers from France, though, as Sylvain Simard demonstrates in *Mythe et reflet de la France*, French interest in Canada declined once again after 1890.[25]

Rather than attempting a comprehensive survey of how Canada came to be identified in the English-speaking world with its geography – agricultural and small town as well as wilderness – this volume consists of a series of detailed studies on how various parts of the country were described not only by travel and tourism literature, but also by recently-arrived genteel settlers, most of whom were birds of passage. The main focus is, inevitably, on those who viewed the landscape and its people from the outside rather than the inside, but one chapter will examine the Canadian nationalist perspective of the young country.

The visual image of Canada is commonly associated with the Group of Seven's modernist landscape paintings of the 1920s, but the temporal focus of this collection is on the sailing ship and steamship/railway eras when an earlier landscape image was being forged. Rather than following the travel narratives from the Atlantic to the Pacific, the chapters are organized in a rough chronological fashion. We begin in chapter 1 at the place that early British and American travellers were most attracted to, Quebec City, viewed as the most European and the most historical of North American cities. Quebec City was distinctive within Canada insofar as its appeal to travellers and tourists was based largely on its association with the French Regime and the British Conquest, but the British were also impressed by the apparently impregnable position of the fortification atop Cape Diamond, and by the commanding picturesque view of the St Lawrence and beyond. Chapter 2 examines how picturesque imagery was also employed to promote British settlement southwest of Quebec City where the Eastern Townships was viewed as an ideal region for the gentlemanly pursuit of pastoral farming.

With chapter 3 the focus shifts to the West coast and the journals written by young British men attracted to the Fraser River gold rush, as well as those produced by British agents of the colonial government. Rather surprisingly, these men described the rugged mountainous terrain in distinctly picturesque terms, demonstrating how entrenched that colonializing perspective was among the well-educated British middle class. We then return to the Eastern Townships with chapter 4, the first of the four chapters to examine the rather neglected topic of American tourists and travel writers in Canada. To the Americans who flocked to Lake Memphremagog during the railway era, the area north of the forty-fifth parallel was a natural, though less developed and more sublime, extension of their own northern New England resort landscape.

In chapter 5 we find a small group of American tourists in search of an indisputably sublime landscape, namely that of the Labrador coast, which served as an imaginative outpost of their own country. The interpreter is the New England Transcendentalist, David Atwood Wasson, who was the guest of an artist in search of icebergs during the summer of 1864, and whose magazine articles describe the landscape as well as its Inuit inhabitants as elemental nature. Two decades later, in the mid-1880s, another American writer, Charles H. Farnham, was also attracted to the Labrador coast. Before arriving there, however, he spent extended periods of time on the lower St Lawrence, describing what he viewed as the last remnants of the Montagnais (today's Innu), but focusing more sympathetically on the "folk" customs of the French-Canadian habitants. In Farnham's articles, the subject of chapter 6, the province of Quebec as a whole is associated with the economically marginal lower St Lawrence region, and with the struggle for survival in a cold and barren land. As we shall see in chapter 7, much the same construction was applied to the Maritimes, for American travel writers – including

Farnham – were particularly drawn to isolated and rugged Cape Breton Island and what they described as the romantic folk culture of the Highland Scots population.

Like their American counterparts, British and Canadian travel writers assumed that national character was fashioned by geography, but they tended to focus on the more economically promising areas, and to have less interest in "folk" cultures. Chapter 8 examines the vision of Canada promoted by the popular *Picturesque Canada*, published as two volumes in 1882 and 1884. The editor was one of the country's leading nationalists, the Reverend George Monro Grant, who also wrote several of the volumes' chapters. *Picturesque Canada*, which was aimed partly at the American tourist market, not only reflects the western expansionist impulse of the post-Confederation era, but also how doggedly Canadian writers clung to the picturesque in contrast to the American sublime, as reflected in the two-volume *Picturesque America* (1872, 1874).

The later nineteenth century also saw a renewal of British interest in the former colonies of settlement as – in the words of imperial historian Duncan Bell – "the ocean-going steamship and submarine telegraph … allowed what had seemed unbridgeable distances to be overcome."[26] In his descriptions of his visits to Canada, the famous imperialist author Rudyard Kipling – the subject of chapter 9 – expressed less interest in the rural landscape as viewed from the window of his private rail car than in the towns and the people he observed, but he did wax eloquent about the opportunities offered by the wide-open Prairie region to England's "surplus" working-class population. As we shall see in chapter 10, the outlook of the romantic young English poet Rupert Brooke contrasted sharply with that of Kipling, for Brooke expressed considerable pessimism about the benefits of economic progress when he travelled by rail across Canada in 1913. Like Kipling, however, he was most interested in the Prairies, though as a still relatively unspoiled Eden that would inevitably be ruined by philistinism and greed. In short, Brooke's rather morbid gothic imagery represents the acme of the Romantic tradition in Canadian travel writing.[27]

The Canada described by the American travel writers was, for the most part, not that of the British and Canadian writers, but all who are examined in this volume were romantic – whether they were describing Quebec City as a medieval outpost, the Eastern Townships as an Arcadian paradise, colonial British Columbia as a wilderness garden, Labrador as primeval Nature, Quebec habitants and Cape Breton Scots as folk remnants, or Canadians as a virile northern race. This was a different image of Canada than the one fashioned by the Group of Seven, with their paintings of the Canadian Shield's small lakes and scrub-like trees, paintings that have stamped the country's image as an uninhabited northern wilderness.[28] Nor was it the British Columbia of Emily Carr's iconic paintings depicting a dark and somewhat foreboding coastal forest landscape, also largely devoid of Aboriginal or settler presence.[29] These modernist artists self-consciously set out to depict a Canada that was distinct from Britain and Europe, as well as the United States, and Northrop Frye followed by Margaret Atwood projected that image of settlers feeling overwhelmed by a hostile Canadian wilderness back to the nineteenth century. Thus, in his very influential *The Bush Garden* (1971), Frye suggested that in contrast to the United States where "one could choose to move out to the frontier or to retreat from it back to the seaboard," Canadian settlers sailing down the St Lawrence and into the Great Lakes feared being engulfed and swallowed by Nature.[30] A year later Atwood wrote in *Survival* that Canadian stories "are likely to be tales not of those who made it but of those who made it back, from the awful experience – the North, the snowstorm, the sinking ship – that killed everyone else."[31] That interpretation is still commonly accepted by literary scholars, but, as we shall see, the Canadian landscape that emerges from the travel narratives and tourism brochures examined in this volume was – on the whole – a much more inviting place, and certainly not one whose inhabitants were incapable of adapting to isolation or the cold climate.[32]

As a collection of sharply focused essays rather than a broad overview,[33] this volume does have significant gaps in coverage, the first one being that none of the chapters focus exclusively on women travel writers in Canada. Historian Françoise LeJeune has, however, recently published a comprehensive study on the topic, and the picturesque landscape perspective of earlier writers such as Anna Jameson, Catharine Parr Traill, and Susanna Moodie is well known.[34] In addition, there are obvious gaps in geographic coverage, for neither Ontario nor the Prairies is the focus of an individual chapter, though both regions do receive considerable attention in the chapters on *Picturesque Canada*, Rudyard Kipling, and Rupert Brooke. Those three chapters are all focused on the post-Confederation era, but pre-Confederation travellers' views of Upper Canada and Rupert's Land have already been fully examined in Patricia Jasen's path-breaking *Wild Things: Nature, Culture, and Tourism in Ontario, 1790-1914*, and in Greg Gillespie's *Hunting for Empire: Narratives of Sport in Rupert's Land, 1840-70*, respectively.[35]

Put briefly, Jasen describes tourism in Upper Canada / Ontario as "a search for wilderness and wildness," and Gillespie argues that descriptions of big-game hunting in the northwestern prairies were "situated within picturesque and sublime landscape imagery."[36] The implication in both studies is that the sublime perspective was as common as the picturesque,[37] but Jasen admits that a tamed Niagara Falls, picturesque Thousand Islands, and equally picturesque Muskoka district attracted most of Ontario's tourists and day-trippers. Likewise, Gillespie states that the big-game hunters he examined produced "non-threatening consumable images and suggested that sublime landscapes merely required settlement and colonization to transform sublime wilderness into picturesque colonial landscapes."[38]

As a particularly popular tourist mecca with a unique landscape as far as Canada is concerned, Prince Edward Island also deserves special attention, but, once again, this ground has been covered to a considerable extent, for historians Alan MacEachern and Edward MacDonald have each published studies on nineteenth-century travellers' perceptions of the small province.[39] Not only is the PEI landscape uniformly picturesque and even beautiful in the Burkean sense, but the island was described and promoted as a picturesque facsimile of Old England.[40] Whether long-settled or largely empty space, then, Canada was largely defined by its landscape, as it still is today, but it was only at the dawn of the automobile era – when most of the arable land had finally been settled – that the country was mature enough to embrace a northern wilderness vision, and it is only in more recent years that Aboriginal Canadians have been incorporated into that vision.

NOTES

1 Anthony D. Smith, *National Identity* (Reno: University of Nevada Press, 1991).

2 Marilyn J. McKay points out that the landscape tradition did not take root among Quebec's French-speaking artists until the 1880s, and that it was characterized by a distinctively sedentary concept of territory. *Picturing the Land: Narrating Territories in Canadian Landscape Art, 1500–1950* (Montreal and Kingston: McGill-Queen's University Press, 2011), 7. On the challenges of shaping a national Canadian identity through heritage commemoration, see J.E. Tunbridge and G.J. Ashworth, *Dissonant Heritage: The Management of the Past as a Resource in Conflict* (Chichester, UK: John Wiley and Sons, 1996), chapter 7.

3 W.L. Morton, "The 'North' in Canadian Historiography," *Transactions of the Royal Society of Canada*, Series IV, 8 (1970): 40.

4 Carl Berger, *The Writing of Canadian History: Aspects of English-Canadian Historical Writing: 1900 to 1970* (Toronto: Oxford University Press, 1976), 214. See also John H. Wadland, "Great Rivers, Small Boats: Landscape and Canadian Historical Culture," in John S. Marsh and Bruce W. Hodgins, eds, *Changing Parks: The History, Future, and Cultural Context of Parks and Heritage Landscapes* (Toronto: Natural Heritage / Natural History, 1998), 1–11.

5 Berger, *The Writing of Canadian History*, 160–1.

6 Orvar Löfgren, *On Holiday: A History of Vacationing* (Berkeley, CA: University of California Press, 1999), 35. See also, Eric Kaufman, "'Naturalizing the Nation': The Rise of Naturalistic Nationalism in the United States and Canada," *Comparative Studies in Society and History* 40, no. 4 (1998): 666–95.

7 Osborne, "Landscapes, Memories, Monuments."

8 Simon Schama, *Landscape and Memory* (New York: Knopff, 1995), 61.

9 Denis E. Cosgrove, *Social Formation and Symbolic Landscape* (London: Croom Helm, 1984), 9–10, 26–7. The quote is from p. 26. See also, Malcolm Andrews, *Landscape and Western Art* (Oxford: Oxford University Press), 1999, chapters 1–4.

10 Leo Marx suggests that it was no coincidence that landscape painting emerged as an independent genre "with the establishment of the first permanent European colonies in North America." Leo Marx, "Foreward," in Mick Gidley and Robert Lawson-Pebbles, eds, *Views of American Landscapes* (Cambridge and New York: Cambridge University Press, 1989), xvi–xvii. See also W.J.T. Mitchell, *Landscape and Power* (Chicago: University of Chicago Press, 1994); Andrews, *Landscape*, chapter 7; and John Crowley, "'Taken on the Spot': The Visual Appropriation of New France for the Global British Landscape," *Canadian Historical Review* 86 (2005): 1–28.

11 Helen Bergen Peters, *Painting During the Colonial Period in British Columbia, 1845–1871* (Victoria: Sono Nis Press, 1979).

12 See Keith Thomas, *Man and the Natural World: Changing Attitudes in England, 1500–1800* (London: Allen Lane, 1983), 261–2; Anne Bermingham, *Landscape and Ideology: The English Rustic Tradition, 1740–1860* (Berkeley and Los Angeles: University of California Press, 1986), 1, 10, 13–14, 66; and Susan Glickman, *The Picturesque and the Sublime: A Poetics of the Canadian Landscape* (Montreal and Kingston: McGill-Queens University Press, 1998), 9–12.

13 I.S. MacLaren, "The Limits of the Picturesque in British North America," *Journal of Garden History* 1 (1985): 97.

14 Simon Ryan, "Exploring Aesthetics: The Picturesque Appropriation of Land in Journals of Australian Exploration," *Australian Literary Studies* 15, no. 4 (1992): 282.

15 See McKay, *Picturing the Land*, 48, 58–63, and chapter 3, especially 72–3, 85–6.

16 See, for example, Ronald Rees, "Images of the Prairie: Landscape Painting and Perception in Canadian Art," *Canadian Geographer* 20 (1976): 259–78; Maria Tippett and Douglas Cole, *From Desolation to Splendour: Changing Perceptions of the British Columbia Landscape* (Toronto: Clarke, Irwin, 1977); Dennis Reid, *'Our Own Country Canada': Being an Account of the National Aspirations of the Principal Landscape Artists in Montreal and Toronto, 1860–1930* (Ottawa: National Gallery of Canada, 1979); I.S. MacLaren, "The Grandest Tour: The Aesthetics of Landscape in Sir George Back's Exploration of the Eastern Arctic, 1833–1837," *English Studies in Canada* 10, 4 (1984): 436–56; Brian Osborne, "The Iconography of Nationhood in Canadian Art," in D. Cosgrove and S. Daniels, eds, *The Iconography of Landscape* (Cambridge, UK: Cambridge University Press, 1992); Colin Coates, "'Like the Thames towards Putney': The Appropriation of Landscape in Lower Canada," *Canadian Historical Review* 74 (1993): 317–44; Lynda Villeneuve, *Paysage, mythe et territorialité: Charlevoix au XIXe siècle.* (Sainte-Foy, QC: Les Presses de l'Université Laval, 1999); Alain Parent, *Entre empire et nation: les représentations de la ville de Québec et des ses environs, 1760–1833* (Sainte Foy, QC: Presses de l'Université Laval, 2005); Crowley, "'Taken on the Spot'"; Joan M. Schwartz, "Photographic Reflections: Nature, Landscape, and Environment," *Environmental History* 12, no. 4 (2007): 966–93; J. Keri Cronin, *Manufacturing National Park Nature: Photography, Ecology, and the Wilderness Industry of Jasper* (Vancouver: UBC Press, 2011); and McKay, *Picturing the Land*.

17 See, for example, Gaile McGregor, *The Wacousta Syndrome: Explorations in the Canadian Langscape* (Toronto: University of Toronto Press, 1985); S.J. Squire, "Ways of Seeing, Ways of Being: Literature, Place, and Tourism in L.M. Montgomery's Prince Edward Island," in Paul Simpson-Housley and Glen Norcliffe, eds, *A Few Acres of Snow: Literary and Artistic Images of Canada* (Toronto: Dundurn Press, 1992); W.J. Keith, *Literary Images of Ontario* (Toronto: University of Toronto Press, 1992); Margaret Atwood, *Strange Things: The Malevolent North in Canadian Literature* (Oxford, UK: Oxford University Press, 1995); and Glickman, *The Picturesque and the Sublime*. For one study that examines both graphic art and literature, see William J. Berg, *Literature and Painting in Quebec: From Imagery to Identity* (Toronto: University of Toronto Press, 2012).

18 See, for example, Daniel Clayton, *Islands of Truth: The Imperial Fashioning of Vancouver Island* (Vancouver: UBC Press, 2000); and the articles by I.S. MacLaren, including "David Thompson's Imaginative Mapping of the Canadian Northwest, 1784–1812," *Ariel* 15, no. 2 (April 1984): 89–106; "Retaining Captaincy of the Soul: Response to Nature in the First Franklin Expedition," *Essays on Canadian Writing* 28 (1984): 57–92; "Samuel Hearne and the Landscape of Discovery," *Canadian Literature* 103 (1984): 27–41; and "The Aesthetic Mapping of Nature in the Second Franklin Expedition," *Journal of Canadian Studies* 21, no. 1 (1985): 39–57. On fur traders' perceptions of the landscape, see Elizabeth Vibert, *Traders' Tales: Narratives of Cultural Encounters in the Columbia Plateau* (Norman, OK: University of Oklahoma Press, 1997), chapter 3.

19 Examples include E.J. Hart, *The Selling of Canada: The CPR and the Beginnings of Canadian Tourism* (Banff, AB: Altitude, 1983); R. Douglas Francis, "From Wasteland to Utopia: Changing Images of the Canadian West in the Nineteenth Century," *Great Plains Quarterly* 7, no. 3 (Summer 1987): 178–94; I.S. MacLaren, "Creating Travel Literature: The Case of Paul Kane," *Papers of the Bibliographic Society of Canada* 27 (1988): 80–95; Patricia Jasen, *Wild Things: Nature, Culture, and Tourism in Ontario, 1790–1914* (Toronto: University of Toronto Press, 1995); Kevin Flynn, "Destination Nation: Nineteenth-Century Travels Aboard the Canadian Pacific Railway," *Essays on Canadian Writing* 67 (Spring 1999): 190–222; Nicole Neatby, "Meeting of Minds: North American Travel Writers and Government Tourist Publicity in Quebec, 1920–1955," *Histoire sociale – Social History* 36, no. 72 (2003): 465–95; Jeffrey McNairn, "Meaning and Markets: Hunting, Economic Development, and British Imperialism in Maritime Travel Narratives to 1870," *Acadiensis* 34, no. 3 (2005): 3–25; Diane Newell, "Belonging – Out of Place: Women's Travelling Stories from the Western Edge," in Katie Pickles and Myra Rutherdale, eds, *Contact Zones: Aboriginal and Settler Women in Canada's Colonial Pasts* (Vancouver: UBC Press, 2005); Wendy Roy, *Maps of Difference: Canada, Women, and Travel* (Montreal and Kingston: McGill-Queen's University Press, 2005); Jeffrey L. McNairn, "'Everything was new, yet familiar': British Travellers, Halifax and the Ambiguities of Empire," *Acadiensis* 36, no. 2 (2007): 28–54; Greg Gillespie, *Hunting for Empire: Narratives of Sport in Rupert's Land, 1840–70* (Vancouver: UBC Press, 2007); Joan Sangster, "Constructing the 'Eskimo' Wife: White Women's Travel Writing, Colonialism, and the Canadian North, 1940–1960," in Joan Sangster, ed., *Through Feminist Eyes:*

Essays on Canadian Women's History (Edmonton: AU Press, 2011); Françoise LeJeune, *How Canada is Described in the Writings of Nineteenth-Century Canadian Women: The Feminine Experience in the Margins of the British Empire* (Lewiston, NY: Edwin Mellen Press, 2012); Jacinthe Archambault, "Much more than a few hundred miles of land or water ... témoignages du voyage autour de la peninsula gaspésienne (1929–1950)," *Cahiers de Géographie du Québec* 57, no. 162 (2013): 479–502; and Faye Hammill and Michelle Smith, *Magazines, Travel, and Middlebrow Culture: Canadian Periodicals in English and French, 1925–1960* (Edmonton: University of Alberta Press, 2015).

20 Peter Hulme and Tim Youngs, "Introduction," in *The Cambridge Companion to Travel Writing* (Cambridge, UK: Cambridge University Press, 2002), 1.

21 Stephen Daniels, *Fields of Vision: Landscape Imagery and National Identity in England and the United States* (Princeton, NJ: Princeton University Press, 1993), 8.

22 Catherine Hall, "Introduction: Thinking the Postcolonial, Thinking the Empire," in Catherine Hall, ed., *Cultures of Empire: Colonizers in Britain and the Empire in the Nineteenth and Twentieth Centuries* (Manchester: Manchester University Press, 2000).

23 David Arnold, *The Tropics and the Traveling Gaze: India, Landscape, and Science, 1800-1856* (Seattle and London: University of Washington Press, 2006), 24.

24 Elizabeth Waterston, *The Travellers: Canada to 1900* (Guelph, ON: University of Guelph, 1989), 379.

25 Simard identified more than 700 French-published books and brochures, as well as 643 articles, dealing in whole or in part with Canada between 1850 and 1919. Twenty-three per cent of the books and brochures, and 50 per cent of the articles were published in the 1880s. While travel narratives were the largest category, however, they represented only 19 per cent of the total number of books and brochures. Sylvain Simard, *Mythe et reflet de la France: L'image du Canada en France, 1850–1914* (Ottawa: Les Presses de l'Université d'Ottawa, 1987), 12, 14, 16, 20.

26 Duncan Bell, *The Idea of a Greater Britain: Empire and the Future of World Order, 1860–1900* (Princeton: Princeton University Press, 2007), 29. Françoise LeJeune is therefore mistaken when she states that the fascination of British travel writers with Canada dissipated between Confederation and the First World War. See her *How Canada*, 507–8. See also, R.G. Moyles and Doug Owram, *Imperial Dreams and Colonial Realities: British Views of Canada, 1880–1914* (Toronto: University of Toronto Press, 1988).

27 Glendening argues that even in the eighteenth century travel writers were essentially romantic inasmuch as they were seeking "something that seemed more real and substantial, and thus more moving, than what they had known in their increasingly tense and disrupted lives." John Glendening, *The High Road: Romantic Tourism, Scotland, and Literature, 1720–1820* (New York: St Martin's Press, 1997), 3.

28 See McKay, *Picturing the Land*, chapters 8 and 9; and Jonathan Bordo, "Jack Pine - Wilderness Sublime or the Erasure of the Aboriginal Presence from the Landscape," *Journal of Canadian Studies* 27, 4 (1992–3): 93–128.

29 See Gerta Moray, "Wilderness, Modernity or Aboriginality in the Paintings of Emily Carr," *Journal of Canadian Studies* 33, no. 2 (1998): 43–65; and Bruce Braun, *The Intemperate Rainforest: Nature, Culture, and Power on Canada's West Coast* (Minneapolis: University of Minnesota Press, 2002), chapter 5.

30 Northrop Frye, *The Bush Garden: Essays on the Canadian Imagination* (Toronto: Anansi, 1971, republished 1995), 219, 222.

31 Margaret Atwood, *Survival: A Thematic Guide to Canadian Literature* (Toronto: Anansi, 1972), 33.

32 For one example of a study strongly influenced by Frye's "garrison" thesis, see McGregor, *The Wacousta Syndrome*. For a trenchant critique of this interpretation, see Mary Lu MacDonald, "The Natural World in Early Nineteenth-Century Canadian Literature," *Canadian Literature* 111 (Winter 1986): 48–65. But for more recent discussions that assume its acceptance, see Rob Shields, *Places on the Margin: Alternative Geographies of Modernity* (London: Routledge, 1991), 184–5; and Eva Mackey, *The House of Difference: Cultural Politics and National Identity in Canada* (Toronto: University of Toronto Press, 2002), 43–9.

33 Other articles I have written on landscape and/or tourism history include: "The Naturalist's Landscape: Philip Henry Gosse in the Eastern Townships, 1835–38," *Journal of Eastern Townships Studies* 20 (Spring 2002): 59–74; "Life without conventionality: Social Reformers as Summer Campers on Lake Memphremagog, 1878–1905," *Journal of the Gilded Age and* Progressive *Era* 9, no. 3 (July 2010): 281–311; "Vancouver's Playground: Leisure and Sociability on Bowen Island, 1902–57," *BC Studies* no. 171 (Autumn 2011): 37–67; "In Search of the Plains of Abraham: Viewing a Symbolic Landscape, 1793–1913," in Phillip Buckner and John Reid, eds, *Remembering 1759: The Conquest of Canada in Historical Memory* (Toronto: University of Toronto Press, 2012); "Views from the Deck: Union Steamship Cruises on Canada's Pacific Coast, 1889–1958," in Ben Bradley, Colin Coates, and Jay Young, eds, *Moving Natures: Mobility and Environment in Canadian History* (Calgary: University of Calgary Press,

2016); and "The Tourism/Ecology/Heritage Triangle: Developing Bowen Island's Crippen Regional Park, 1981–2005," *BC Studies*, no. 194 (Summer 2017): 119–48.

34 LeJeune, *How Canada*. On Upper Canada, see also Edward H. Dahl, *'Mid Forests Wild': A Study of the Concept of Wilderness in the Writings of Susanna Moodie, J.W.D. Moodie, Catharine Parr Traill and Samuel Strickland, c. 1830–1855* (Ottawa: National Museum of Man, 1973); F.K. Stanzel, "Innocent Eyes? Canadian Landscape as Seen by Frances Brooke, Susanna Moodie and Others," *International Journal of Canadian Studies* 4 (fall 1991): 97–109; Glickman, *The Picturesque*, chapter 4; and Roy, *Maps of Difference*, chapter 1. McKay (*Picturing the Land*, 9–10) notes that women of the British middle and upper-middle classes "were taught to represent the landscape in much the same way as men."

35 Because Jasen's *Wild Things* extends beyond the colonial era, it examines not only the Thousand Islands and the Niagara area, but also the Muskoka and upper Great Lakes regions.

36 Jasen, *Wild Things*, 3; Gillespie, *Hunting for Empire*, 11.

37 For a materialist interpretation of the nineteenth-century English sublime, see Cosgrove, *Social Formation*, chapter 8.

38 Gillespie, *Hunting for Empire*, 90.

39 See Alan Andrew MacEachern, "Discovering an Island: Travel Writers and Tourism on Prince Edward Island," *The Island Magazine* 29 (1991): 8–16; and Edward MacDonald, "A Landscape … with Figures: Tourism and Environment on Prince Edward Island," in Claire Campbell and Robert Summerby-Murray, eds, *Land and Sea: Environmental History in Atlantic Canada* (Fredericton: Acadiensis Press, 2013), 61–77.

40 MacEachern, "Discovering an Island," 11; MacDonald, "A Landscape," 64.

1 "Like a fragment of the old world": The Historical Regression of Quebec City in Travel Narratives and Tourist Guidebooks, 1776–1913

Prior to the 1960s the stereotypical image of French-speaking Quebec was of a profoundly Catholic society that placed religious faith and family ahead of the individualism and materialistic values of Anglo-Protestant North America. That land-based image, which was fostered by the priests who wrote most of the province's early histories and trained its historians,[1] also appealed to the romantic sensibility that drew English-speaking artists, writers, and tourists to the province in search of the traditional and the picturesque. Historians and literary scholars examining this phenomenon have focused on rural areas such as Charlevoix County,[2] but it was not only the countryside that was seen as out of step with modernizing society. This chapter will examine how, as the nineteenth century progressed, tourism promoters increasingly depicted the very heart of the province, Quebec City itself, as a medieval outpost in the rapidly evolving New World.

The earliest and most numerous sources describing Quebec City are the memoirs published by British and American travellers, most of which are referred to in this chapter, but we shall also examine descriptions by British officers stationed in the garrison town for a period of time, and by genteel colonists who passed through en route to Upper Canada. As historian W.H.A. Williams notes, British travellers had an acute visual orientation, and the ability to describe the landscapes they encountered was considered a mark of social distinction.[3] Tourism, on the other hand, has generally been associated with tasteless consumerism, but it was Quebec City's historic character that made it a uniquely popular urban tourist destination as early as the 1830s. While, to the outsider, Montreal represented the modern English-speaking face of the province, Quebec City epitomized its traditional French-speaking face, frozen in historical time. What influence this image had on the provincial capital's economic development is impossible to judge, and historians are divided as to whether tourism is essentially a positive or negative force, but, as architectural historian Marc Grignon has pointed out, images are not innocent for they help to define reality rather than simply re-presenting it.[4]

British Views

In the fall of 1776, a British army officer wrote that, due to the American siege of the previous winter, Quebec City no longer conformed to "the beautiful description given by that elegant writer Mrs Brookes in her Emily Montague, for many houses were destroyed for fuel, others to prevent harbouring the enemy, and shot and shells continually defacing and burning the rest … greatly contribute to destroy all ideas of regularity."[5] Even after the damage had been undone, however, it would not be the city itself but its defensive capabilities and the wide-sweeping views from its Citadel that would impress the first upper-middle-class British travellers as they sought to enlighten their fellow countrymen about the colonies they visited.[6] Like those who visited colonial Halifax, the diversity of their political and religious affiliations did not prevent them from sharing a remarkably common perspective,[7] that perspective being that Quebec City was the military and later the symbolic key to the North American empire.

The colonial capital's shipbuilding and timber export economy boomed as a result of the Napoleonic Wars, but the early British visitors were unanimous in their expressions of disgust with the mud, stench, and crowded conditions of working-class Lower Town, which lies at the base of Cape Diamond. After opening with a description of how he had jumped from his ship into a mud hole surrounded by a herd of swine, the pseudonymous Jeremy Cockloft focused in 1811 on the port's insalubrious market places and uncomfortable lodgings.[8] Although Quebec City ranked third as a North American port in 1830,[9] Irish-born emigration proponent Edward Talbot was one of the few observers to describe its commercial sector in Lower Town, and his vivid image is telling: "The granaries, warehouses, and dwellings, though generally very lofty, are frowned upon by the impending rocky projections of Cape Diamond, which, in some directions, seem to threaten them with instant destruction."[10] A more concrete example of the anti-commercial bias of the genteel travellers is the observation in 1833 by Thomas Hamilton, retired

Scottish officer and gentleman, that "It is in this quarter that merchants do most congregate; and here are the exchange, the custom-house, the banks, and all the filth and circumstances of inglorious commerce."[11] The only visitor to demonstrate much interest in Quebec's commerce was the self-styled "mercantile man," James Lumsden, who wrote in 1844 of Pollock, Gilmour, and Company's operations in Wolfe's Cove that "the quantity of timber afloat in the booms and lying in their ship-building yards astonished me not a little."[12]

But mercantile men had little time or inclination to publish travel accounts, and the main focus of such narratives in the early nineteenth century was on Quebec's defensive strengths. British historians have concentrated on the empire's so-called "swing to the East" after the loss of the Thirteen Colonies, and neither Quebec City nor the rest of the country are mentioned in John Mackenzie's survey of British imperial guidebooks published in the nineteenth and early twentieth centuries.[13] The fact remains, however, that the scores of British travellers who passed through Quebec City were certainly not prepared to relinquish the part of the North American continent that remained under British rule. Anglo-Irish travel writer Isaac Weld wrote in 1799, for example, that the approach from the St Lawrence was "so strongly guarded by nature, that it is found unnecessary to have more than very slight walls" on that side. Weld's painting of a very steep Cape Diamond topped by a rather diminutive fortress clearly illustrates his point, but he added that "On the land side, the town owes its strength solely to the hand of art, and here the fortifications are stupendous."[14]

Eight years later, George Heriot's *Travels Through the Canadas* also included an artist's view of the city from across the St Lawrence that made the city's defences appear to be impregnable (see figure 1.1).[15] John Lambert, who spent the winter of 1807 in Quebec and returned briefly in 1809, was a rare exception, for he referred to the site of the fortress as "a heap of ruins and rubbish; a heterogeneous collection of old wooden log-houses and broken-down walls."[16] The situation had clearly changed by 1824 when Talbot wrote that the fortifications were "kept in excellent repair, and new defences are added whenever they may be deemed necessary."[17] Similarly, John Morison Duncan described how, as one approached by steamboat, "first are seen two of the Martello towers, which like gigantic sentinels keep watch over the celebrated plains; then the redoubts around the citadel on the summit of Cape Diamond, slowly develop their strength; embrasures, cannon, and loop holes, successively presenting themselves."[18] Finally, there is

1.1 *Quebec from Pointe Levis, S.W.*, by George Heriot. Library and Archives Canada, C-12751.

Susanna Moodie's recorded impression as an immigrant en route to Upper Canada in 1832: "Canadians! - as long as you remain true to yourselves and her, what foreign invader could ever dare to plant a hostile flag upon that rock-defended height, or set his foot upon a fortress rendered impregnable by the hand of Nature?"[19]

As the military value of the fortifications declined, the Citadel and Quebec City were increasingly viewed from an aesthetic and symbolic perspective. Reflecting what art historian Albert Boime refers to as the northern European "reverential gaze,"[20] Edward Thomas Coke described in 1833 how "The bold craggy rocks of Cape Diamond, crowned with the impregnable fortress, stand in bold relief against the sky." That same year, Thomas Hamilton wrote that even "the most obtuse traveller" could not mistake Quebec for "a mere commonplace and vulgar city. It towers with an air of pride and of menace – the menace not of a bully, but of an armed Paladin prepared for battle."[21] To Charles Dickens, writing in 1842, Quebec City was the "Gibraltar of America, its giddy heights, its citadel suspended, as it were in the air."[22] These descriptions clearly challenge the thesis of architectural historians Noppen and Morriset that the British image of Quebec City was internally focused (the city as the "sum of its private domains") as opposed to the externally focused French image of the "king's city" in the pre-Conquest era.[23]

Much to her disappointment, Susanna Moodie was unable to disembark at Quebec because of the cholera epidemic, but, if the view of Cape Diamond from the river assured British travellers that their country's grip on the trans-Atlantic colonies rested on a solid base, they were even more enthusiastic about the prospect from atop that cliff. Its fading military value aside, the Citadel was an excellent site for what Boime refers to as the "magisterial gaze," one that embodied the "desire for dominance."[24] Boime associates this perspective with American "manifest destiny," and the views of the mid-nineteenth-century paintings he examines are generally from a wilderness elevation towards the "improved" landscape, sometimes including a city – in short, from the past to the future. In contrast, the view from Cape Diamond was, necessarily, from the city to the wilderness, but this was a fitting perspective for an Old World power that was expanding its influence on the New World frontier. The magisterial gaze was not as distinctly American as Boime assumes, for, as literary historian Mary Louise Pratt states, the "monarch-of-all-I-survey" trope favoured by British explorers was an imperialist one that served to "naturalize" the domination of colonized spaces by visualizing them as landscapes (see figure 1.2).[25]

Whereas the view of Cape Diamond from below, on the St Lawrence, evoked the awe-inspiring sublime, with its sense of an overpowering Nature, that from the top of the cliff invariably conformed to the more domesticated picturesque. In England, the ideal perspective was from a low elevation, allowing for the intimate sense of being enveloped by the landscape,[26] which could explain why Isaac Weld felt overwhelmed by "the vastness of the scene" from the top of Cape Diamond, where he felt he was "looking at a draft of the country more than the country itself." But Weld simply moved lower down to the upper battery where he still had a commanding view. From this perspective, the southern bank of the St Lawrence appeared to be "indented fancifully with bays and promontories," while the opposite shore was "one uninterrupted village, seemingly, as far as the eye can reach," with the houses appearing to be built on the sides of mountains that "rose directly out of the water."[27]

The rules of the picturesque were becoming looser in the early nineteenth century because of the influence of romanticism, and other British observers expressed no discomfort with the high elevation of Cape Diamond when painting their picturesque images. Thus, Hugh Gray claimed in 1809 that the view from there surpassed that from the Rock of Gibraltar, the pass of Bellegarde in the Pyrenees, the Cintra near Lisbon, or even Kingsweston near Bristol! What particularly appealed to Gray was the picturesque "blending of art and nature," by which he meant the combination of "villages, country houses, cottages, and

1.2 *View from near the Officer's* [sic] *Barracks Citadel, Quebec – Cap Tourment, Island of Orleans and Point Levi* by Milicent Mary Chaplin. Library and Archives Canada, C-812

corn fields" with "primeval woods, fine rivers, beautiful islands, magnificent waterfalls, towering hills, and lofty mountains."[28] Similarly, J.C. Morgan of the Royal Marines wrote in 1824:

> however much we may feel gratified in contemplating this noble entrepót [*sic*] of our North American possessions, the eye turns with more pleasing satisfaction to the wild and romantic scenery which surrounds it. The celebrated fall of Montmorenci, the numberless cascades rushing through the woods and tumbling down the rocks, together with the little village of Point Levi, with its whitened cottages scattered amongst the green foliage of the trees, presents a scene upon which the contemplative mind will dwell with incessant delight.[29]

As the number of British travel narratives reached its peak in the early 1830s, the magisterial gaze swept ever wider, reminding us that in North America the concept of landscape was not confined to land modified for permanent human habitation.[30] Rather than having the single focal point of a formal landscape painting, most of these literary views unfolded like a panorama as the eye swept in a circle, but, as Simon Ryan has pointed out, the panorama was also an imperial perspective.[31] In 1834, for example, the barrister Henry Tudor painted a scene in words that included

> all the objects of a perfect landscape; a river unsurpassed in beauty and crystal clearness – the lovely island of Orleans in the centre of its channel – extensive plains and chains of mountains stretching away, in various directions, to the northward; the distant wilderness of forests, untouched by the hand of man, and untrodden by human foot, except by that of the Indian hunter roaming in pursuit of game through its almost impervious wilds, and which sweep along, in boundless extent, to the shores of Hudson's Bay.[32]

The allusion to the lone Indian hunter was a romantic one, but the implication was that this vast space, as unknown as central Africa, according to Sir James Edward Alexander, was there to be explored.[33] Any sense of independence for the Natives was undermined by the many descriptions of the Hurons of nearby Lorette as a domesticated and degenerate people.

The magisterial gaze also extended southward to the still-contested American border. Thus, the former medical officer John J. Bigsby wrote that the opposite shore of the St Lawrence was "rugged and high, occupied with dwellings, and farms near at hand, while the more distant region, the valley of the Chaudière chiefly, is a sea of undulating forests, extending within sight, I verily believe, of the frontiers of the United States."[34] A few years later, the panoramic sweep of James B. Brown also ended imaginatively in "the dim mountains of the States of Maine and Vermont."[35] One might assume that imperialists would focus on colonial improvements, but the early nineteenth-century picturesque convention clearly inspired a fascination with unspoiled nature.[36]

If the view of and from Quebec City was exotic yet familiar insofar as it could be described in picturesque terms, the city itself was also felt to be familiar as the most European of North American cities yet exotic in its romantic Catholicism and *ancien régime* history. Thus, John M'Gregor expressed his fascination in 1832 with the "imposing grandeur" of the city's Catholic cathedral, including its High Mass with "the loud solemn tones of the organ; the kneeling crowds; the silver censers; the incense; the splendour which surrounds the altar." M'Gregor also noted approvingly that the French-speaking gentry "retain the courteous urbanity of the French school of the last century."[37] On a similar note, the English artist David Wilkie proclaimed of Quebec in 1837 that "This ancient city was the only spot of real historical interest" that he had discovered in North America. Wilkie sought out Wolfe's Cove "and the sacred spot, too, on the Plains, where this short-lived hero breathed his last," but he was most interested in the Chateau St Louis, the old seat of the Quebec government that had burned to the ground three years earlier. Reflecting the English fascination with their own country's monastic ruins, which symbolized a return to the state of nature, Wilkie suggested that "visitors to Quebec look with more interest upon the smoked ruins of the castle of St Lewis, than they do perhaps upon many of the natural wonders to be seen over the face of the continent."[38]

The Irish actor Tyrone Power was also drawn to the ruins of the Chateau St Louis in the mid-1830s, and Dickens wrote a few years later that "Apart from the realities of this most picturesque city, there are associations clustering about it which would make a desert rich in interest."[39] Quebec City was presumably becoming too familiar by the 1840s – a decade of mass British emigration through the port – to appeal to the market in travellers' memoirs, for the number that described the old city dropped significantly. Furthermore, as Britain swung towards free trade and the province of Canada towards self-government, the few mentions that were made tended to be less than complimentary. In 1843 the Oxford chemist Charles Daubeny simply dismissed Quebec as, "for the most part, a congeries of second-rate or mean looking houses." Eleven years later, the Scottish publishing figure, William Chambers, referred to it as "a curious old city," then assured potential emigrants that they would soon be able to take the railway to destinations further west.[40]

American Views

Meanwhile, though far fewer in number than their British counterparts, American travel writers had also begun to visit Quebec City in the early nineteenth century. Not surprisingly, they tended to be less enthusiastic than the British about Quebec's role as a bastion of British imperialism.

Joseph Sansom, who in 1817 claimed to be the first American to write an account of Canada, complained about the inconveniences caused by the zigzag pattern of Upper Town's fortifications, which were swarming with sentries. As a veteran of the War of 1812, Sansom left Quebec with the "confirmed opinion" that "its citadel, reputed the strongest fortification in North America, with its hundreds of heavy cannon, and its thousands of well disciplined troops," would "cost infinitely more than it could be worth" were Americans disposed to take it.[41] Thirty-two years later, in 1849, the southerner J.C. Myers also expressed a fascination with the city's fortifications, noting how an officer had shown him the "small impressions made by cannon shot … for the purpose of getting the impression abroad that the walls could not be effectually reached, even with the heaviest guns." But Myers clearly felt less threatened than Sansom, for he described how from the top of the tallest building in the Citadel, "and under the folds of the British flag, I viewed with astonishment one of the most splendid prospects in the world." This was "the great key by which the British hold their power in America," one that "would never be taken by storm, so long as the garrison remained true to their trust."[42]

As one would expect of a proponent of civil disobedience, Henry David Thoreau was less impressed by the fortifications when he visited Quebec City in 1850. After complaining that he was forced to zig-zag in a "ditch-like road, going a considerable distance to advance a few rods," Thoreau stated that the artillery on the cliff was "faithfully kept dusted by officials, in accordance with the motto 'In time of peace prepare for war'; but I saw no preparations for peace: she was plainly an uninvited guest." Thoreau likened the "frowning citadel" to "the beak of a bird of prey," but he also reassured his American readers that it was "a 'folly' – England's folly, – and, in more senses than one, a castle in the air."[43] To Thoreau, Quebec was less an imperial garrison than a medieval city, for he wrote of the Citadel that "Such structures carry us back to the Middle Ages, the siege of Jerusalem, and St. Jean d'Acre, and the days of the Bucaniers." The first French builders of the fortress, Thoreau claimed, were already "behind their age; and those who now inhabit and repair it are behind their ancestors or predecessors." Associating the Catholic Church with backwardness, as well, Thoreau added that all large stone structures "rather oppress than liberate the mind," with the result that the citizens of Quebec were "suffering between two fires, the soldiers and the priesthood."[44]

Thoreau's rather negative assessment to the contrary, Quebec City's historic character had begun serving as a powerful draw for romantic

Americans who felt that their own cities had little to offer in this respect.[45] Thus the Methodist clergyman, James Dixon, commented in 1849 that "The ecclesiastical buildings of all sorts – cathedrals, (for there are two, Popish and Protestant,) churches, convents, hospitals, *Hôtels de Dieu*, and all the rest – are seen to predominate over everything secular." Dixon did not share Thoreau's pacifist views, but he added that "This feature, together with the military air of the place, causes Quebec to wear an aristocratic and feudal appearance, perfectly dissimilar to the trading and commercial aspect of all other places in America, whether belonging to the States or to Great Britain."[46] From this perspective Quebec City was of interest to the American traveller not only because of its exoticism, but because it was a tangible reminder of how Catholicism had stalled the enlightened progress made by their own Anglo-Protestant society.

One can also detect a condescending tone in the 1865 assessment by Charles F. Browne (posing as the uneducated Artemis Ward) that Quebec was "old fogeyish, but chock full of interest."[47] But the famous American novelist Henry James was unreservedly enthusiastic, writing in 1871 that "if Quebec is not the most picturesque city in America, this is no fault of its incomparable site." As one approached the city by rail, James enthused, "The old world arises in the midst of the new in the manner of a change of scene on the stage." The cosmopolitan James was even nostalgic about the British Empire, reflecting on how the "idle ramparts" were but "a shadowy image of that great English power, the arches of whose empire were once built strong on foreign soil."[48]

Historians once made a sharp distinction between the solitary traveller driven by intellectual curiosity and the tourist viewed as consumer of a packaged commodity,[49] but it was the Old World image of Quebec that ensured its inclusion as early as 1828 on what was known as the northern tourist circuit. That was the year that G.M. Davison's *The Fashionable Tour*, published in Saratoga Springs, New York, offered a "methodical plan of excursion" through the old city. Davison complained that much of the town was "taken up with the religious and military establishments, which, with their courts and gardens, leave the streets very irregular, and uneven, and give rather an unfavorable impression of the taste and elegance of its inhabitants," yet he assured his readers that "it presents much to gratify the curiosity of the stranger."[50] And, while Theodore Dwight's *The Northern Traveller* dismissed Lower Town in 1830 as "crowded and dirty" with "no decent public houses," it also went so far as to suggest that "no scene in Canada, or the United

States, can boast of a combination of objects comparable in variety and magnificence to those here presented to view."[51] In 1850 the American-produced *Appleton's Northern and Eastern Traveller's Guide* noted that the city's trade was extensive, and that "vessels from all parts of the world may be seen riding at anchor in its capacious harbour," but it claimed that "The citizens of Quebec are less enterprising than those of Montreal, and there is a greater spirit of improvement in the latter city than in the former."[52] Like the British travellers in Catholic Ireland, then, American tourists who flocked to Quebec City as the railway drew near were "clarifying and justifying the values of the industrial capitalist culture" that was remaking their own country.[53]

Canadian Views

Meanwhile, Quebec's early promoters – in striking contrast to those of Halifax[54] – had begun to publish books that demonstrated their eagerness to capitalize on their city's historic character by attracting American tourists, though without sacrificing capital investment. As early as 1829 George Bourne's *The Picture of Quebec* described the views from various vantage points and outlined a historic walking tour of the city, but it also depicted Quebec as a bustling commercial centre that would greatly benefit, "as the natural emporium of Canadian traffic," from "the proposed wharves across the mouth of the St. Charles." Bourne argued, as well, that because the crowded conditions of Lower Town were damaging business what was needed was a major landfill project to allow expansion onto the tidal flats.[55] Similarly, although the illustrated guidebook produced by the topographic artist and commander of the Quebec garrison, Lieutenant-Colonel James Patterson Cockburn, painted a more romantic picture of the city in 1831, it did not ignore the local industries. Cockburn recommended to "our American friends" that they visit the modern sawmills that Peter Patterson had built at the base of nearby Montmorency Falls, and he even included a partial view of them in one of his illustrations.[56] But such attractions would fade more and more into the background as the focus of the local promotional publications shifted increasingly towards attracting tourists in search of historic sites.

On the basis that history rendered "every spot in this remarkable city a sort of consecrated ground," *Hawkins's Picture of Quebec with Historical Recollections*, published in 1834, included six chapters on Quebec's past, as well as describing the historical significance of all its major public attractions.[57] Similarly, the anonymously-written *The Hand-book of Quebec*, which appeared in 1850, informed tourists that Quebec was "the only fortified city in North America," and that interesting sights included the Seminary garden, Place d'Armes, Theatre St Lewis, Durham Terrace, the Old Chateau St Louis, the Governor's garden, and the Plains of Abraham.[58] In 1857, three years after the rail link was forged with the United States, the *Travellers Hand-book of the City of Quebec and its Environs* declared that "There is no city on this continent in which so many varied attractions to the sight-seer are accumulated as in Quebec, and more especially is this true of the American Traveller." At the risk of offending the very people it was aiming to attract, the *Travellers Handbook* ventured that "The cities of America, – Boston to some small extent excepted, – afford nothing of historical interest." Quebec being "the emporium of the lumber trade," the timber coves were said to be "an object of decided interest," yet Lower Town was "a place every stranger will escape as soon as possible" because it was "an overcrowded depot of commerce."[59]

Quebec: As It Was and As It Is, published by local journalist Charles Roger in 1857, also made brief reference to the modern side of the city, claiming that "with moderate opportunities for advancement, it must become one of the greatest cities of the new world in respect of learning, arts, commerce and manufactures." But Roger's guidebook was essentially a history of Quebec, and his self-professed aim was to entice tourists to spend more time exploring "this Old Cabinet of Curiosities."[60] Ten years later *Chisholm's All Round Route and Panoramic Guide of the St Lawrence,* which was published in Montreal, made little attempt to depict Quebec as in any way modern. Claiming that the plateau on which the city stood had "for thoroughfares the identical Indian paths of Stadacona or the narrow avenues and approaches of its first settlers in 1604," the guidebook added that "it would be vain to hope for regularity, breadth and beauty in streets, such as modern cities can glory in. It is yet in its leading features a City of the 17th century – a quaint, curious, drowsy, but healthy location for human beings, a cheap place of abode."[61] Such descriptions were clearly effective, for the *Quebec and Montreal Travellers' Free Guide* observed in 1872 that "During summer months Quebec is largely visited by strangers specially [*sic*] Americans who take much interest in viewing the many historical scenes and objects connected with it."[62]

Particularly devoted to promoting the romantic image was the city's own prolific naturalist and antiquarian, James MacPherson LeMoine, who published *The Tourists' Notebook* in 1876.[63] Raised on his grandfather's seigneurie, LeMoine claimed that Quebec City was replete with relics "of the mysterious past that has hallowed these with all the mystic interest that attaches to antiquity, great deeds, and beautiful memories. To see all these, a tourist requires at least two days' time." One of those tourists was the influential American clergyman and social reformer Henry Ward Beecher, whom LeMoine quoted approvingly from the New York *Ledger*. "It is a shame," Beecher wrote, "when Quebec placed herself far out of the way, up in the very neighbourhood of Hudson's Bay, that it should be hunted and harassed with new-fangled notions, and all the charming inconveniences and irregularities that narrow and tortuous streets, that so delight a traveller's eye, should be altered to suit the fantastic notions of modern people."[64]

LeMoine was determined that tangible reminders of the past be preserved by defending the walled city from the forces of "improvement" that were inspired by Baron Haussman's urbanist vision for Paris. Deploring the fact that four of the city's gates had been destroyed since 1871, the year that the British military had withdrawn and the modern-styled provincial parliament building and post office had been built,[65] LeMoine played on the Canadian nationalist theme by arguing that Quebec's ramparts were "very costly monuments of national history, unequalled on the continent." Quebec was not only "where the foundation of civilized society in Canada was first firmly laid," but – equally important – it was where "the protracted duel between France and England for dominion on this continent was decisively fought to a conclusion destined to become the basis of our future Canadian nationality." It followed, therefore, that the idea "of destroying the walls of Quebec, and utilizing the ground occupied by them and their outworks for building purposes, was not only a mistake as regards the welfare of the city itself, but was also a contemplated wrong to the people of this country generally." Quoting Beecher again, LeMoine concluded: "The place should always be kept old. Let people go somewhere else for modern improvements."[66]

Lemoine was not averse, however, to seeing the old city's attractions embellished for the benefit of tourists. To take advantage of the view, he suggested that a "continuous promenade" be built around the Citadel and the walls (in fact, the walls were lowered in strategic places), and that every monument and historic site be developed in order to inspire "sentiments of historical renown and national honour." What he had in mind was turrets and bridges to "enhance the antique effect of the gates and walls."[67] LeMoine's ideas were inspired to some extent by Governor-General Lord Dufferin who was also steeped in the romanticism of the era. Classifying Quebec as one of the three most beautiful cities in the world, Dufferin had initiated a campaign in 1874 not only to preserve but also to embellish its historic attractiveness "on behalf of civilization and the inhabitants of the whole American continent."[68] The result was the creation within the next few years of what historian Martine Geronomi refers to as "une pure fantaisie romantique et moderniste magnifiant un passé indéfini."[69]

With the intensification of Canadian nationalism in the 1880s, landscape artists from Montreal and Toronto turned to Quebec City as a symbol of the country's historical continuity.[70] This was the decade that saw the appearance of overtly nationalist publications such as *Picturesque Canada* whose editor, George Monro Grant, paid tribute to LeMoine's "Boswell-like consciousness in chronicling everything connected with the sacred spot."[71] While – as we shall see in chapter 9 – *Picturesque Canada* includes modern images of Montreal, such as a close-up illustration of a towering Victoria Bridge and the unloading of steamers by electric light, the focus of the Quebec City illustrations is almost exclusively on the military fortifications and the view of and from the Citadel, as well as on Catholic institutions and street scenes within the walled part of the city. Not surprisingly, then, Agnes Maule Machar's chapter on Quebec City focuses mostly on the many expansive views and the historical background of the more notable sites.[72]

As a romantic, however, Machar was outshone by Toronto's Reverend William H. Withrow, whose *Our Own Country Canada* appeared in 1889. Withrow, whom historian Kenneth Winsor refers to as "the cultured and industrious editor of the *Canadian Methodist Magazine*,"[73] described how, as he approached Quebec at sunrise, "The numerous spires and tin roofs of the city caught and reflected the level rays of the sun like the burnished shields of an army hurling back the javelins of an enemy. The virgin city seemed like some sea-goddess rising from the waves with a diamond tiara on her brow; or like an ocean-queen seated on her sapphire-circled throne, stretching forth her jewelled hand across the sea and receiving tribute from every clime." Quebec City's virginity, in Withrow's overwrought imagination, did not preclude its antiquity: "The historic associations that throng around it, like the sparrows round its lofty towers, the many reminiscences that beleaguer it, as once did the hosts of the enemy, invest it with a deep and abiding interest. But its greatness is of the past. The days of its feudal glory have departed. It is interesting rather on account of what it has been than for what it is."[74]

Two years later, in 1891, the considerably more talented Canadian writer, Charles G.D. Roberts, produced a rare modern literary image of Quebec City for his American audience: "The waterfront of the city is thronged with ships whose masts and funnels obscure the warehouses. Ships are anchored thickly mid-channel, and between them dodge the puffing tugs and the high two decker ferries making their hasty way to the lofty and huddling town of *Point Lévis*, whose heights resound all day to the shrieks of locomotives."[75] Roberts then shifted, however, to the more static picturesque imagery characteristic of the earlier British travel writers:

> The picture is one whose sublime lines and masses are brought out to the full by the fresh coloring that plays over it. Under the vivid and flawless blue come out sharply the pale gray of the citadel, the duller gray of the cliff-face streaked with rust-color and splashed with light green, the black guns bristling on the ramparts and batteries, the brown streets, roofs of shining tin, and gilded steeples, with here and there a billow of thick foliage, the blue-green flood of the St. Lawrence, the white and emerald of the tributary farms and villages, and the sombre purple setting of the remote surrounding hills.[76]

Rather paradoxically, the guidebooks distributed by the railway companies at this time made even less reference than did Roberts to the modern features of Quebec City. The Quebec Central's *Car Window Glimpses*, published in New York in 1887, declared that "Quebec stands like a fragment of the old world – like a creation of the contentious feudal ages stranded upon the shores of a new continent."[77] Six years later, *An Intercolonial Outing Along the Shores of the Lower St. Lawrence* declared that "Other places anticipate the future: Quebec clings fondly to the past. It is well that it should be so, for, in this practical and prosaic age, but few cities retain the halo of romance that surrounded them in their early years. New York may afford to grow wealthy and forget New Amsterdam, but the Quebec of to-day reminds one at every turn of the Ancient Capital as it was in the centuries that are dead and gone."[78]

Yet another railway publication, the Canadian Pacific's *The Ancient City of Quebec*, published in 1894, was equally close to LeMoine's book in spirit. This is hardly surprising given that the CPR depended on tourists to occupy its recently erected Chateau Frontenac, strategically located to take advantage of the view and designed by an American architect to evoke the Renaissance castles of the Loire.[79] Rather than becoming more modern with time, the guidebook claimed, Quebec City was becoming more ancient, with "Its tortuous thoroughfares, its huge fortifications, its old-world buildings – aye, and its inhabitants, so many of whom speak the quaintest of French dialects – all these breathe out the charm of dead centuries saturated with Indian traditions, the traditions of Brittany and Normandy, and of the France and England of days gone by."[80]

Quebec City's factory-based industries, such as shoe manufacturing, had expanded as its shipbuilding industry had declined, but its population grew very little between 1861 and the end of the century, by which time even the locally published guidebooks were denying the city's commercial and industrial character.[81] Thus, Chambers' *Guide to Quebec*, published in 1895, declared that the city stood "at the very threshold of this strong and impatient New World, in this age of progressive activity and enterprise, like a little patch of mediaeval Europe, transplanted, it is true, upon a distant shore, but shutting out by her mural surroundings the influences that the whole surrounding continent has failed to exercise upon her."[82] In fact, Chambers claimed, "the absence of commercial turmoil and competition, and the story of her glorious past, are alike the objects of her pride."[83]

As for the French Canadians, they still favoured religious pilgrimages over secular ones,[84] but the romantic image of Quebec City conformed nicely with the conservative ultramontane ideology of French-Canadian nationalists. Thus, in 1904, Judge Adolphe-Basile Routhier published the lengthy *Quebec: A Quaint Medieval French City in America at the Dawn of the XXth Century*. With unbridled enthusiasm, Routhier proclaimed that "Quebec is for all lovers of the ideal, a casket of precious stones; a shrine of historical relics, which if approached by sacrilegious hands, would call forth from all sides, a cry of protest." While the city might be "entering upon an era of material progress," Routhier wrote, he felt confident that it would not simply be "of a commercial, industrial and maritime nature. Its artistic and monumental developments will be so great, that it will be considered as the most beautiful city on the American continent."[85] Travellers from France also described Quebec as an essentially medieval city, though they were more enthused by the fact that English was rarely heard in its streets than by its conservative, religious character.[86]

Later Imperialist Views

By the time of Routhier's publication, British imperialism was revived and Quebec City had been rediscovered by romantic British imperialists such as the wife of the Governor-General, Lady Aberdeen, who wrote in her travel memoir of 1893: "It is strange that the emigrant to the New World should make acquaintance with it first in this old-world city, full of associations and traces of the past – its very inhabitants seeming to transport you to a France of two or three centuries ago." Ignoring the city's industries, Lady Aberdeen described how LeMoine had guided her and her husband up the cliffs scaled by Wolfe's army and to the scene of the famous battle.[87] In a similar vein, Douglas Brooke Wheeton Sladen declared in his *On the Cars and Off* that "He must be strangely constituted whose heart does not beat a trifle quicker when, turning a sharp corner on the mighty St. Lawrence, he suddenly beholds looking up before him the Rock of Quebec, with its fantastic pile of steeples and ramparts bristling with old-fashioned cannon ... and, high over all, the banner of England – an old shot-rent Union Jack."[88]

Sladen mourned the destruction of the city's gates as "an act of vandalism" not in any way warranted by the subsequent increase in business, but his picture of the city was still a romantic one, with references to the story of "le Chien d'Or" which had inspired William Kirby's novel of the same name, as well as to Horatio Nelson's attempted elopement with a local barmaid. Lower Town, once disparaged for its dirt and confusion, was now "most interesting with its queer stores, where the hardy sailors of the St. Lawrence buy their fishing and boating outfits," and its market-place "where the time-honoured quack with his vegetable medicines, and the Indian corn-doctor with his long hair, who used to drive about drawn by four white horses, still excite the profoundest faith, conducting their professions in the midst of a medley of dried tobacco leaves, maple-sugar cakes, black puddings, blocks of frozen milk in winter, rubbishy haberdashery and sabots, which the habitants, in their coarse blue home-made serges of old Breton fashions, come to sell or buy."[89]

Prior to this point, the common people of the city had not been subjected to what sociologist John Urry refers to as the tourist gaze, but Sladen's description was strictly in keeping with the conventional picturesque focus on English gypsies and beggars.[90] The famous English poet, Rupert Brooke, whose travel dispatches were published in the *Westminster Gazette* in 1913 (see chapter 10), was also fascinated by the local inhabitants, writing that he felt that he was in "a foreign land for the people have an alien tongue, short stature, the quick, decided cinematographic quality of movement, and the inexplicable cheerfulness, which mark a foreigner." Racialized as this image was, the romantic young Brooke claimed that he did not feel out of place in the "mediaeval, precipitous, narrow, winding, and perplexed streets" of old Quebec.[91]

Conclusion

The reverse shift in the representation of Quebec City from imperial bastion to medieval town was not a sudden one, especially as those images were more complementary than mutually exclusive. But it did tend to follow the decline of British interest in the North American colonies and the rise of American tourism in the railway era. If the earlier British travel writers sought out the picturesque as an aesthetic link to the imperial centre, the message of the tourism promotional literature was even more romantic. Admittedly, tourism was strongly linked to commerce and consumption, as illustrated by the increased number of advertisements for Quebec City's hotels and other establishments in the guidebooks of the 1880s.[92] In 1912, Ella G. Farrell's *Among the Blue Laurentians* went so far as to imbed such a promotion in the text by advising its American readers to visit "the large fur store of Holt, Renfrew, & Co.," a "wonderful firm" whose capital was one million dollars. Here, where the "magnificence and variety can scarcely be surpassed by Paris," customers would be regaled by "quaint stories of the customs of the Indian," for the employees "deal directly with the primitive people in purchasing their goods."[93] A fur coat purchased at Holt, Renfrew was not only a luxury consumer item, then, it was also evidence that middle-class tourists were anxious to display their cultural distinction.

Farrell was clearly addressing a well-to-do audience, as were most of the writers of travel memoirs, but the romantic imagery of the tourist guidebooks and railway brochures suggests that less wealthy tourists were also attracted by the opportunity to demonstrate their respectability and cultivation, as Jill Steward has noted.[94] What made Quebec so unique as a North American city was not only its French Catholic character, but also its dramatic history as the site of the first permanent European settlement in Canada as well as of the famous battle of 1759. It was those two historical turning points that were commemorated by the momentous tercentenary celebration in 1908, an event that reflected the revival of British imperialism (as demonstrated by the renewed interest of British travel writers) while also attracting thousands of American tourists.[95]

Four years later, the city's publicity bureau finally admitted that Quebec's "picturesque location, its romantic and chivalrous history has so captured the imagination of the tourist, traveller and writer, that they have lost sight of the fact, that it is also a great industrial centre; a city of mammoth factories, the products of which are sent to all parts of the civilized world."[96] Tourism was, of course, an important source of income for a city that was falling well behind Montreal and Toronto in commercial and industrial growth, as the railway companies and municipal authorities were well aware.[97] But the Old World image would do little to serve the larger goal of attracting outside economic investment, as tourism promotion was doing in cities such as Halifax and Vancouver.[98] In fact, it may have had the reverse effect, as suggested by the observation of the English-Canadian poet and journalist, A. Ethelwyn Wetherald, in 1888: "Quebec is the Old World of America. Its claims to distinction depend not upon any trustworthy hopes of future greatness; they rest with confidence of assurance upon an unforgettable and richly dowered past."[99]

NOTES

1 See Serge Gagnon, *Quebec and its Historians: 1840 to 1920* (Montreal: Harvest House, 1982).

2 See, for example, James Murton, "La 'Normandie du Nouveau Monde': la société Canada Steamship Lines, l'antimodernisme et la promotion du Québec ancien," *Revue d'histoire de l'Amérique française* 55, no. 1 (2001), 3–44; and Nathalie Duhamel, "Coordonner tourisme et artisanat, ou comment mettre en valeur le visage pittoresque du Québec, 1915–1960," *Histoire sociale – Social History* 34 (May 2001), 97–114.

3 William H.A. Williams, *Tourism, Landscape, and the Irish Character: British Travel Writers in Pre-Famine Ireland* (Madison, WI: University of Wisconsin Press, 2008), 21.

4 Marc Grignon, "Comment s'est faite l'image d'une ville: Québec du XVIIe au XIXe siècle," in Lucie K. Morriset, Luc Noppen, and Denis Saint-Jacques, eds, *Ville imaginaire, ville identitaire: échos de Québec* (Quebec: Éditions Nota Bene, 1999), 101. Most histories of tourism are critical of its impact, but for a different perspective see John A. Jakle, *The Tourist: Travel*

in Twentieth-Century North America (Lincoln, NB: University of Nebraska Press, 1985).

5 An Officer, *Travels Through the Interior Parts of America: In a Series of Letters*, vol. 1 (London: William Lane, 1789), 50. Frances Brooke's novel, *The History of Emily Montague*, was published in 1769.

6 Williams, *Tourism*, 13.

7 Jeffrey L. McNairn, "'Everything was new, yet familiar': British Travellers, Halifax and the Ambiguities of Empire," *Acadiensis* 36, no. 2 (Spring 2007): 34.

8 Jeremy Cockloft, *Cursory Observations Made in Quebec Province of Lower Canada in the Year 1811* (Bermuda: Edmund Ward, n.d., reprinted Toronto: Oxford University Press, 1960), 15, 30, 36–7. On the question of Cockloft's identity, see Donald Fyson, "Jeremy Cockloft's Cursory Observations," *Society Pages* 20 (Summer 2008): 3–5.

9 N. Giroux, "Québec dans les récits de voyage (1830–1850)," in Serge Courville and Robert Garon, eds, *Québec: Ville et Capitale* (Sainte-Foy: Les Presses de l'Université Laval, 2001), 155.

10 Edward Allen Talbot, *Five Years' Residence in the Canadas*, vol. 1 (London: Longman, Hurst, Rees, Orme, Brown and Green, 1824), 45–6.

11 Thomas Hamilton, *Men and Manners in America* (Edinburgh and London: William Blackwood and Sons, 1843), 424. The introduction states that the first edition appeared in 1833. On Hamilton's travel narrative, see the numerous references in Christopher Mulvey, *Anglo-American Landscapes: A Study of Nineteenth-Century Anglo-American Travel Literature* (Cambridge: Cambridge University Press, 1983), and esp. 197–200, 215–18, 224–5.

12 James Lumsden, *American Memoranda by a Mercantile Man, During a Short Tour in the Summer of 1843* (Glasgow: Bell and Bain, 1844), 47–8.

13 John Mackenzie, "Empires of Travel," in John K. Walton, ed., *Histories of Tourism* (Clevedon, Buffalo, Toronto: Channel View Publications, 2005). Recent Canadian publications are beginning to address this oversight. See, for example, Phillip Buckner, ed., *Canada and the British Empire* (Oxford: Oxford University Press, 2008).

14 Isaac Weld, Jr, *Travels Through the States of North America and the Provinces of Upper and Lower Canada During the Years 1795, 1796, and 1797* (London: John Stockdale, 1799), 197. The original of Weld's "Vue du Cap-Diamant," painted in 1802 or 1803, is in the John Carter Brown Library at Brown University, and may be viewed online.

15 George Heriot, *Travels Through the Canadas* (London: Printed for Richard Phillips by T. Giller, 1807), 64–6. Trained as a topographical artist, Heriot

served as deputy postmaster-general of the colony from 1800 to 1816. See Gerald E. Finley, "Heriot, George," *Dictionary of Canadian Biography Online.*

16 John Lambert, *Travels Through Lower Canada, and the United States of North America, in the Years 1806, 1807, and 1808* (London: Richard Phillips, 1810), 21, 41. On Lambert, see Jacqueline Roy, "Lambert, John," *Dictionary of Canadian Biography Online*; and Mulvey, *Anglo-American Landscapes*, 138, 153, 173–4, 185.

17 Talbot, *Five Years' Residence*, vol. 1, 46.

18 John Morison Duncan, *Travels Through Part of the United States and Canada in 1818 and 1819*, vol. 2 (New Haven: Howe and Spalding; New York: W.B. Gilley, 1823), 182.

19 Susanna Moodie, *Roughing it in the Bush*, ed. Michael Peterman (New York: W.W. Norton, 2007), 25–6.

20 Albert Boime, *The Magisterial Gaze: Manifest Destiny and American Landscape Painting c. 1830–1865* (Washington: Smithsonian Institution, 1991), 21–2. On the transition to the aesthetic view, see Judith Adler, "Origins of Sightseeing," *Annals of Tourism Research*, 16 (1989), 18–24.

21 E.T. Coke, *A Subaltern's Furlough: Descriptive Scenes in Various Parts of the United States, Upper and Lower Canada, New Brunswick, and Nova Scotia, During the Summer and Autumn of 1832* (London: Saunders and Otley, 1833), 68; Hamilton, 424.

22 Charles Dickens, *American Notes for General Circulation*, vol. 2 (London: Chapman and Hall, 1842), 202. On Dickens' views of the United States, see Mulvey, *Anglo-American Landscapes.*

23 Luc Noppen and Lucie K. Morriset, "The Architecture of Old Quebec, or the History of a Palimpsest," *Material History Review* 50 (Fall 1999): 14–15.

24 Boime, *The Magisterial Gaze*, 21, 23.

25 Mary Louise Pratt, *Imperial Eyes: Travel Writing and Transculturation* (London: Routledge, 1992), 213.

26 Andrews states that "The repudiation of the high viewpoint in late-eighteenth-century Picturesque theory suggests a failure of confidence," while Ousby claims that the bird's-eye view is rare in the early travel descriptions of England's Lake District because it flattened the landscape. Malcolm Andrews, *The Search for the Picturesque: Landscape Aesthetic and Tourism in Britain, 1760–1800* (Aldershot, UK: Scolar Pres, 1989), 61–3; Ian Ousby, *The Englishman's England: Taste, Travel and the Rise of Tourism* (Cambridge, UK: Cambridge University Press, 1990), 156–7.

27 Weld, *Travels*, 203–4.

28 Hugh Gray, *Letters From Canada, Written During a Residence There in the Years 1806, 1807, and 1808* (London: Longman, Hurst, Rees, and Orme, 1809), 64–7.

29 J.C. Morgan, *The Emigrant's Notebook and Guide* (London: Longman, Hurst, Rees, Orme, and Brown, 1824), 95. See also, Lieutenant Francis Hall, *Travels in Canada and the United States, in 1816 and 1817*, second edition (London: Longman, Hurst, Rees, Orme, and Browne, 1819), 59.

30 See Leo Marx, "Foreward," in Mick Gidley and Robert Lawson-Peebles, eds, *Views of American Landscapes* (Cambridge: Cambridge University Press, 1989), xix–xx.

31 Simon Ryan, *The Cartographic Eye: How Explorers Saw Australia* (Cambridge: Cambridge University Press, 1996), 90–100.

32 Henry Tudor, *Narrative of a Tour in North America*, vol. 1 (London: James Duncan, 1834), 307–8. For another example, see Adam Fergusson, *Practical Notes Made During a Tour in Canada* (Edinburgh: William Blackwood; and London: T. Cadell, 1831), 77–8. On Tudor's comments on the United States, see Mesick, *The English Traveller*.

33 Sir James Edward Alexander, *Transatlantic Sketches Comprising Visits to the Most Interesting Scenes in North and South America, and the West Indies* (London: R. Bentley, 1833), 200.

34 John J. Bigsby, *The Shoe and Canoe or Pictures of Travel in the Canadas*, vol. 1 (London, 1850; reprinted New York: Paladin Press, 1969), 1, 12, 24.

35 James B. Brown, *Views of Canada and the Colonists Embracing the Experience of Eight Years' Residence*, second edition (Edinburgh: Adam and Charles Black, 1851), 14–15. See also Charles Lenman, *Adventures of an Angler in Canada, Nova Scotia and the United States* (London: R. Bentley, 1848), 160–1.

36 Andrews, *The Search*, 64–6, 236.

37 John M'Gregor, *British America*, vol. 2 (Edinburgh: W. Blackwood; London: T. Cadell, 1832), vol. 2, 477.

38 Andrews, *The Search*, 45–50; Ousby, *The Englishman's England*, 126; David Wilkie, *Sketches of a Summer Trip to New York and the Canadas* (London: Berwick, 1837), 248, 250–62. Alan Gordon suggests that the loss of the Chateau St Louis to fire in 1834 may have been what precipitated interest in the city's history. Alan Gordon, "'Where Famous Heroes Fell': Tourism, History, and Liberalism in Old Quebec," in Phillip Buckner and John Reid, eds. *Remembering 1759: The Conquest of Canada in Historical Memory* (Toronto: University of Toronto Press, 2012), 71.

39 Tyrone Power, *Impressions of America; During the Years 1833, 1834, and 1835*, vol. 2 (Philadelphia: Sherwood, Gilbert, and Piper, 1837), 313, 317, 322; Dickens, *American Notes*, 167.

40 Charles Daubeny, *Journal of a Tour Made Through the United States and Canada* (Oxford: T. Combe, 1843), 28; William Chambers, *Things As They*

Are in America (1854, reprinted New York: Negro Universities Press, 1968), 81, 89–91. On Chambers, see McNairn, "Everything was new," 28, 39.

41 Joseph Sansom, "Travels in Lower Canada, 1820," in James Doyle, ed., *Yankees in Canada: A Collection of Nineteenth-Century Travel Narratives* (Toronto: University of Toronto Press, 1980), 44, 49–52. On the inconveniences and public dangers caused by the gates and the labyrinth of passageways, see André Charbonneau, Yvon Desloges, and Marc Lafrance, *Québec The Fortified City: From the 17th to the 19th Century* (Ottawa: Parks Canada, 1982), 433–8.

42 I have assumed that Myers was a southerner because his book was published in Virginia. J.C. Myers, *Sketches on a Tour Through the Northern and Eastern States, the Canadas and Nova Scotia* (Harrisonburg, VA: J.H. Wartmann, 1849), 205–9. Also pro-British was the London-published travel narrative by Yale College's Dr Benjamin Silliman. See his *A Tour to Quebec in the Autumn of 1819* (London: Sir Richard Phillips and Co., 1822). On Silliman in England, see Mulvey, *Anglo-American Landscapes*, 38–40, 67, 94, 122–3.

43 Henry David Thoreau, *A Yankee in Canada* (1866, reprinted Montreal: Harvest House, 1961), 39, 92, 97–8.

44 Thoreau, *A Yankee*, 99, 103, 107, 110.

45 Ian McKay and Robin Bates, *In the Province of History: The Making of the Public Past in Twentieth-Century Nova Scotia* (Montreal and Kingston: McGill-Queen's University Press, 2010), 60–1; Catherine Cocks, *Doing the Town: The Rise of Urban Tourism in the United States, 1850–1915* (Berkeley: University of California Press, 2001), chapter 1.

46 James Dixon, *Personal Narrative of a Tour Through Part of the United States and Canada* (New York: Lane and Scott, 1849), 147. See also, "Major Jones's Sketches of Travel: Comprising the Scenes, Incidents, and Adventures, in his Tour from Georgia to Canada (1848)," in Doyle, ed., *Yankees in Canada*, 53, 61–2; and *The Journal of Richard Henry Dana, Jr.*, ed. Robert F. Lucid (1968), in Doyle, 89.

47 Charles F. Browne, *Artemis Ward: His Travels (1865)*, in Doyle, ed., *Yankees in Canada*, 109, 112. On "Artemis Ward" in England, see Mulvey, *Anglo-American Landscapes*, 79–80.

48 Henry James, "Quebec," 1871, in Doyle, ed., *Yankees in Canada*, 125, 128–9. On James's observations on England and the United States, see Mulvey, *Anglo-American Landscapes*.

49 For a critique of this view, see Ousby, *The Englishman's England*, 6–8.

50 G.M. Davison, *The Fashionable Tour: An Excursion to the Springs, Niagara, Quebec, and Through the New England States* (Saratoga Springs, NY: G.M. Davison, 1828), 202–3, 296–305.

51 Theodore Dwight, *The Northern Traveller, and Northern Tour, With the Routes to the Springs, Niagara & Quebec, and the Coal Mines of Pennsylvania* (New York: J. and J. Harper, 1830), 221, 227. Michael Broadway is mistaken, then, in stating that prior to the later 1880s tourists simply used Canadian cities as transportation hubs to scenic locations in the surrounding countryside. Michael J. Broadway, "Urban Tourist Development in the Nineteenth-Century Canadian City," *American Review of Canadian Studies* 26, no. 1 (1996), 83–99.
52 W. Williams, *Appleton's Northern and Eastern Traveller's Guide* (New York: D. Appleton, 1850), 187–8. On Appleton's guides, see Cocks, 27.
53 Williams, *Tourism, Landscape*, 198.
54 McKay and Bates, 54, 61–2.
55 George Bourne, *The Picture of Quebec* (Quebec: D. and J. Smillie, 1829), 12, 32, 34. The English-born Bourne had emigrated to the United States in 1804, then become the first minister of Quebec's Congregational church in 1824. He wrote, at least in part, several scurrilous anti-Catholic publications, including *Lorette: The History of Louise, Daughter of a Canadian Nun* (1833), and the *Awful Disclosures by Maria Monk, of the Hotel Dieu Nunnery of Montreal* (1836). See Karen Stanworth, *Visibly Canadian: Imaging Collective Identities in the Canadas, 1820–1910* (Montreal and Kingston: McGill-Queen's University Press, 2014), 32–43; and Carole Gerson, *A Purer Taste: The Writing and Reading of Fiction in English in Nineteenth-Century Canada* (Toronto: University of Toronto Press, 1989), 112.
56 *Quebec and Its Environs; Being a Picturesque Guide to the Stranger* ([Quebec]: Thomas Cary, 1831), 4. On this guidebook, see Martine Geronimi, "Québec dans les discours des guides touristiques, 1830–1930," *Canadian Folklore Canadien* 18, no. 2 (1996), 72. For a useful analysis of Cockburn's Quebec City paintings, see Alain Parent, *Entre empire et nation: les représentations de la ville de Québec et des ses environs, 1760–1833* (Quebec: Les Presses de l'Université Laval, 2005), 197–238.
57 *Hawkins's Picture of Quebec with Historical Recollections* (Quebec: Neilson and Cowan, 1834), 462. Hawkins also produced *The Quebec Directory and Stranger's Guide to the City and Environs, 1844–5* (Quebec: Printed for A. Hawkins by W. Cowan, 1844), 27, 40, 69. On Hawkins, see Dorothy E. Rider, "Hawkins, Alfred," *Dictionary of Canadian Biography Online*.
58 *The Hand-book of Quebec. A Compendium of Information for the Use of Strangers Visiting the City and its Environs* (Quebec: T. Cary, 1850), A2, 17. The 1852 edition of the *Strangers' Guide* also provided brief descriptions of points of interest such as the Durham Terrace and the Citadel. Robert W. Stuart Mackay, *The Strangers' Guide to the Cities of Montreal and Quebec* (Montreal: R. and A. Miller, 1852).

59 *Travellers Hand-book of the City of Quebec and its Environs* (Quebec: G.T. Cary, 1857), 3, 4, 7.
60 Charles Roger, *Quebec: As It Was and As It Is, or, A Brief History of the Oldest City in Canada, From Its Foundation to the Present Time*, fifth edition (Quebec: printed for the proprietor, 1867), v–vi; Kenneth N. Winsor, "Historical Writing in Canada to 1920," in *Literary History of Canada*, second edition, vol. 1 (Toronto: University of Toronto Press, 1976), 230. Part of Roger's preface was cribbed by the author of *The American House Traveller's Guide for River St. Lawrence, and the Cities of Montreal, Quebec & Ottawa* (Montreal: D. Rose, 1868), 26.
61 *Chisholm's All Round Route and Panoramic Guide of the St Lawrence* (Montreal: Chisholm and Co., 1867), with images from *Hunter's Panoramic Guide from Niagara Falls to Quebec* (Boston: J.P. Jewett; Cleveland: H.P.B. Jewett, 1857), was republished in 1868, 1870, and 1871. The quotes are from the 1870 edition, p. 95.
62 *Quebec and Montreal Travellers' Free Guide: Containing Interesting Information for Tourists* (Montreal: E. Senecal, 1872), 82–3.
63 On LeMoine, see Carol W. Fullerton, "LeMoine, Sir James MacPherson," *The Canadian Encyclopedia Online*; and Guy Mercier and Yves Melançon, "A Park in the City, 1830–1910," in Jacques Mathieu, *Plains of Abraham: The Search for the Ideal* (Sillery, QC: Septentrion, 1993), 181, 187–8.
64 J.M. LeMoine, *The Tourists' Notebook* (Quebec: F.X. Garant, 1876), 13–14, 16.
65 Martine Geronimi, *Québec et la Nouvelle-Orléans: Paysages imaginaires français en Amérique du Nord* (Paris: Éditions Belin, 2003), 84–5. For details on the demolition and reconstruction, see Charbonneau, Desloges, and Lafrance, *Quebec*, chapter 15.
66 LeMoine, *The Tourists' Notebook*, 14, 16, 38. *Holiwell's New Guide to the City of Quebec*, whose sixth edition appeared in 1888, also presented a critical view of the modernizing pressures upon the city. Its author lamented that "Much that is interesting and ancient in Quebec has in the last few years disappeared. The old gates, which excited the wonder and curiosity of the traveller, have been levelled, and the fortifications and walls of the city, which then bristled with cannon and were patrolled night and day by vigilant sentinels, have changed their warlike appearance to peaceful promenades." Thos. J. Oliver, *Holiwell's New Guide to the City of Quebec*, sixth edition (Quebec: C.E. Holiwell, 1888), 5–6, 43.
67 Oliver, *Holiwell's*, 40; Grignon, "Comment s'est faite l'image," 114.
68 Quoted in Geronimi, *Québec*, 127.

69 Geronimi, *Québec*, 131. See also Christina Cameron, "Lord Dufferin contre les gothes et les vandales," *Cap-aux-Diamants* 2, no. 2 (1986), 39–41; and Mercier and Melançon, "A Park," 188–9.
70 Dennis Reid, *'Our Own Country Canada': Being an Account of the National Aspirations of the Principal Landscape Artists in Montreal and Toronto, 1860–1890* (Ottawa: National Gallery of Canada, 1979), 277.
71 George Monro Grant, ed., *Picturesque Canada; The Country As It Was and Is* (Toronto: Belden [1882]), vol. 1, 1.
72 Grant, *Picturesque Canada*, vol. 1, 33–61, 104–43.
73 Winsor, "Historical Writing," 232.
74 W.H. Withrow, *Our Own Country Canada: Canada, Scenic and Descriptive* (Toronto: W. Briggs, 1889), 169–70.
75 According to a recent art history study, vessels largely disappeared from the paintings depicting Quebec from the river between 1890 and 1920. See Deborah Anne Arsenault, "Visual Imagery of the Saint Lawrence River – Landscape as an Historical Discourse" (PhD diss., Concordia University, 2006), 72.
76 Charles G.D. Roberts, *The Canadian Guide-Book: The Tourist's and Sportsman's Guide to Eastern Canada and Newfoundland* (New York: Appleton, 1891), 83.
77 *Car Window Glimpses. En Route to Quebec by Daylight via Quebec Central Railway* (New York: Leve and Aldent's Publication, 1887), 17.
78 *An Intercolonial Outing Along the Shores of the Lower St. Lawrence and Through the Provinces By the Sea* [St John, NB? 1893?], 7.
79 Geronimi, "Québec dans les discours," 81, 85. See also Marc Vallières et al., *Histoire de Québec et de sa région, tome 2, 1792–1939* (Quebec: Les Presses de l'Université Laval, 2008), 1193–4. According to Gowans, Gothic revival became the Canadian national style. Alan Gowans, "The Canadian National Style," in W.L. Morton, ed., *The Shield of Achilles: Aspects of Canada in the Victorian Age* (Toronto: McClelland and Stewart, 1968), 208–18.
80 *The Ancient City of Quebec*, Issued by the Canadian Pacific Railway Company (Copyrighted by the Chateau Frontenac Co., 1894), 1, 5. Quebec was also described as a mediaeval city by yet another railway company, the Grand Trunk. *Montreal, Quebec and Ottawa: Three Interesting Cities in Canada* (Passenger Department, Grand Trunk Railway System, 1910), 13–28.
81 On the economy, see Vallières et al., *Histoire de Québec*, chapter 13.
82 *Souvenir, Union Meeting, Canadian Divisions, Brotherhood of Locomotive Engineers, Quebec, 18–20 June 1907* [no page numbers].
83 E.T.D. Chambers, *The Guide to Quebec* ([Quebec]: Quebec Morning Chronicle [1895]), 5–7.

84 Roger Brière, "Les grands traits de l'évolution du tourisme au Québec," *Bulletin de l'association des géographes de l'Amérique française* 11 (September 1967), 93; Christine Hudon, "La sociabilité religieuse à l'ère du vapeur du rail," *Journal of the Canadian Historical Association* ns 10 (1999), 129–47. The only guidebook for French-Canadian tourists that I discovered was the brief and prosaic Eugène Gingras, *Guide de Québec* (Quebec: L.J. Demers et Frère, 1880). Geronimi ("Québec dans les discours," 78) also refers to a bilingual guidebook written by L.W.T. Frechet.

85 A.B. Routhier, *Quebec. A Quaint Mediaeval French City in America at the Dawn of the XXth Century* (Montreal: Montreal Printing and Pub., ca 1904), 2, 38, 389.

86 See Sylvain Simard, *Mythe et reflet de la France: L'image du Canada en France, 1850–1914* (Ottawa: Les Presses de l'Université d'Ottawa, 1987), 121–33, 313–16.

87 The Countess of Aberdeen, *Through Canada with a Kodak* (Edinburgh: W.H. White and Co., 1893), 11–12, 16–17.

88 Douglas Brooke Wheeton Sladen, *On the Cars and Off: Being a Pilgrimage Along the Queen's Highway, From Halifax in Nova Scotia to Victoria in Vancouver's Island* (London and New York: Ward, Lock [189_?]), 35. Sladen, who had published nine books, was commissioned by the editor of *Queen's Magazine*, which targeted the "upper 10,000" to write a series of articles on Canada. Jill Steward, "'How and Where To Go': The Role of Travel Journalism in Britain and the Evolution of Foreign Tourism, 1840–1914," in Walton, ed., *Histories of Tourism*, 48–9; E.J. Hart, *Trains, Peaks and Tourists: The Golden Age of Canadian Travel* (Banff, AB: Summerthought, 2000), 60–1. On travellers, tourists, and the Plains of Abraham, see J.I. Little, "In Search of the Plains of Abraham: Viewing a Symbolic Landscape, 1793–1913," in Buckner and Reid, *Remembering 1759*.

89 Sladen, *On the Cars*, 38–47. British travellers described the Halifax market much the same way. See McNairn, "Everything was new," 49–50. Aside from writing a chapter on the Battle of Quebec, Sladen (*On the Cars*, 49–50) also suggested that the Citadel could still serve a military purpose, and included an evocative example of the magisterial view.

90 John Urry, *The Tourist Gaze: Leisure and Travel in Contemporary Societies* (London: Sage, 1990); Andrews, *The Search*, 59–60.

91 Rupert Brooke, *Letters From America* (Toronto: McClelland, Goodchild, and Stewart, 1916), 64–5. See also, Joseph Adams, *Ten Thousand Miles Through Canada* (London: Methuen, 1912), 19–20.

92 Geronimi, "Québec dans les discours," 80.

93 Ella G. Farrell, *Among the Blue Laurentians, Queenly Montreal, Quaint Quebec, Peerless Ste. Anne de Beaupré* (New York: Kenedy [1912]), 32. On the link between romance and consumerism in general, see Colin Campbell, *The Romantic Ethic and the Spirit of Consumerism* (Oxford: Oxford University Press, 1987).

94 Steward, "How and Where To Go," 40–1. Catherine Cocks argues, however, that the rise of urban tourism reflected the displacement of the "ideology of refinement" by "consumption and leisure in defining meaningful participation in the social order." Cocks, *Doing the Town*, 1–5, 14.

95 See H.V. Nelles, *The Art of Nation-Building: Pageantry and Spectacle at Quebec's Tercentenary* (Toronto: University of Toronto Press, 1999); and Ronald Rudin, *Founding Fathers: The Celebration of Champlain and Laval in the Streets of Quebec, 1878–1908* (Toronto: University of Toronto Press, 2003) chapter 4.

96 *Quebec, Canada* (Quebec: Publicity Bureau of Quebec City, [1912]), 3.

97 During the summer of 1928, when Quebec City's population was still under 130,000, it received over half a million visitors, making tourism its second most important industry. Vallières et al., *Histoire de Québec*, 691, 1304; Geronimi, "Québec dans les discours," 72, 78.

98 McKay and Bates, *In the Province*, 62–5; Michael Dawson, *Selling British Columbia: Tourism and Consumer Culture, 1890–1970* (Vancouver: UBC Press, 2004), 33–4, 43.

99 Quoted in Gerson, *A Purer Taste*, 110. On the current tension between what he refers to as "patrimoine et territoire" in Old Quebec, see Guy Mercier, "La territorialité des lieux de mémoire: à qui appartient le Vieux-Québec," in Anne Gilbert, Michel Bock, and Joseph Yvan Thériault, eds, *Entre lieux et mémoire: l'inscription de la francophonie dans la durée* (Ottawa: Les Presses de l'Université d'Ottawa, 2009), 173–91.

2 Canadian Pastoral: Promotional Images of British Colonization in Lower Canada's Eastern Townships during the 1830s

In the spring of 1836, three years after she and her husband Edmund had settled near the small town of Sherbrooke in Lower Canada's Eastern Townships (see figure 2.1), Lucy Peel wrote in her letter diary: "Pray do not for a moment suppose I am tired of Canada, it would be a dreadful change to leave a house & farm of our own, give up horses, Cows, and carriages, for a humble cottage in Wales; No, dearest Mamma, though sometimes half frozen in the winter, I am very happy, and get more attached to this place every day." Lucy's tone had changed by the fall, however, after the wheat crop had failed and prices for produce were inflated by the arrival of settlers attracted by the newly established British American Land Company (BALC). She now wrote: "Edmund is, after four years hard labour, convinced that nothing is to be done by Farming in Canada; the land here produces too little to pay for the labour requisite to cultivate it."[1] In December the Peels decided to return to England where Edmund – the nephew of former and future Conservative Prime Minister Sir Robert Peel – would resume his career as a naval officer.

As a romantic newly married couple, the Peels had been seduced by the age-old dream of living in harmony with a domesticated nature. Even the stones and stumps did not dampen Lucy's enthusiasm during their first year as settlers, for she wrote in November 1833: "I am sure you would like to ramble with us over our rude and romantic *Estate*, the greater part as nature formed it, with here and there, such stones as would even defy the power of Sampson to dislodge from their deep, snug, and mossy bed; and large stumps of trees which have been cut down, gradually and slowly mouldering away, and enriching the earth as they scatter themselves around."[2] This pastoral fantasy – invariably

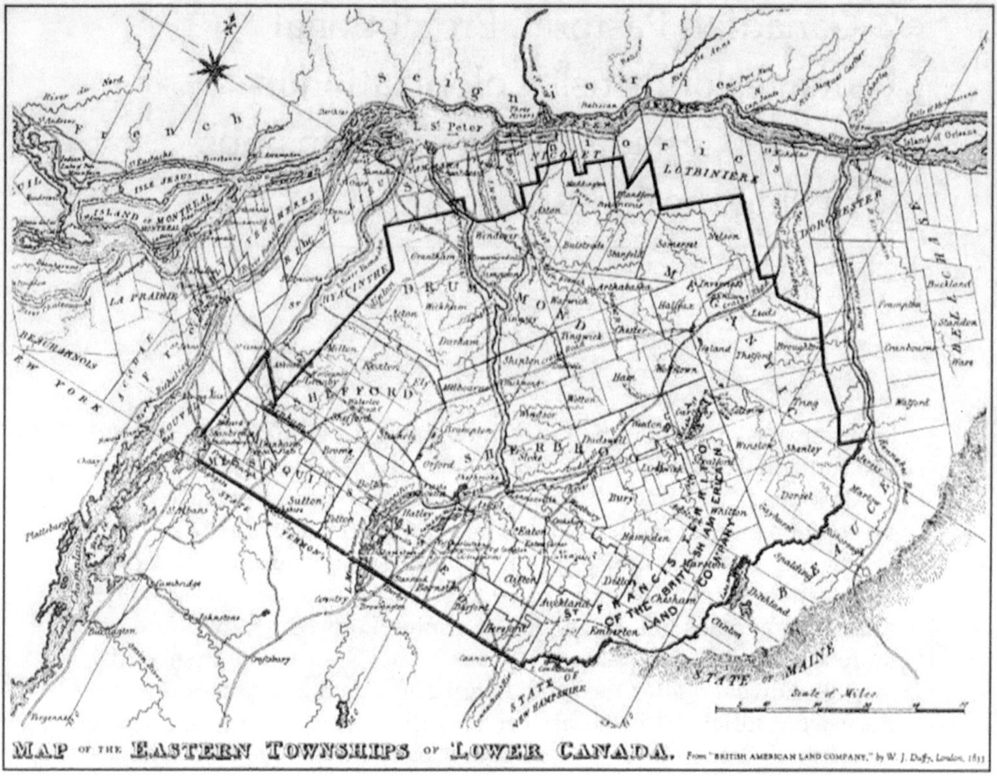

2.1 *The Eastern Townships of Lower Canada in the 1830s.* W.J. Ruffy, *British American Land Company* (London, 1833).

associated with a golden age of the past – was particularly alluring to members of the upper middle class who hoped to escape the increasing commercial pressures and popular unrest in Britain by recreating a genteel society on the colonial frontier. Lying south of the old St Lawrence valley seigneuries, the natural features of the rolling northern Appalachian plateau known as the Eastern Townships made it particularly well-suited to promoters of such an Arcadian dream, as illustrated by the picturesque imagery not only in Lucy Peel's letters but in the publications funded at least in part by the London-based BALC.[3] The effectiveness of this landscape imagery in holding the genteel settlers and attracting those of more limited means was another matter. The Eastern

Townships would remain a largely American-settled region during the first half of the nineteenth-century, with the British-born representing only 23 per cent of the 58,203 English-speaking inhabitants in 1851, when 35 per cent of Upper Canadians were from Great Britain.[4]

A Colonial Landscape

When the Eastern Townships region – lying North of the Vermont/New Hampshire border – was finally opened to settlement in 1792, it attracted many land-hungry Americans who had little concern about national allegiance. The colonization process was relatively slow, however, largely because access to external markets was hampered by the lack of navigable tributaries flowing into the St Lawrence River.[5] Exports in the pre-railway era were mostly confined to potash or the more refined pearl ash, frozen meat, salt pork, butter, and potato whiskey, all of which could be transported over snow-packed roads during the winter. Cattle were also herded to market in the fall.[6]

Hilly as the Eastern Townships region was, its soil was sufficiently fertile and its climate sufficiently benign to allow farmers to produce most of what they needed, and for a small minority to operate at a highly commercial level.[7] Still, the population in 1831 was only 37,000, and, during the following years of heavy British immigration to North America, the vast majority continued to bypass the region. The BALC was established in 1833 to address that problem by directing British colonists to the 250,000 acres of crown reserves and the 600,000-acre unsurveyed block known as the St Francis Tract (see Figure 2.1). But the energetic colonization efforts of the BALC ultimately made little impact on immigration to the region, largely because of the financial difficulties caused by the outbreak of the Lower Canadian rebellion in 1837, as well as the company's misguided focus on recruiting parish-assisted emigrants to settle in the isolated and mountainous St Francis Tract rather than on the more fertile and accessible former crown reserves.[8] As early as 1834 the influential Edward Hale pointed to the political climate of the colony as the reason for refusing the BALC's request to write an account of his experiences settling near the future town of Sherbrooke, even though he had chosen the site because of the "fever and ague" on his father's extensive properties in Upper Canada.[9]

The physical appeal of the Eastern Townships – but also its limitations – was described by Dr James Marr Brydone the following year, in 1835. Brydone had been persuaded by the BALC to visit the region after delivering to Upper Canada a group of English settlers sponsored by the Petworth Emigration Committee. Unfortunately for the BALC, Brydone – who had been negotiating to send more settlers to the Canada Company's Huron Tract in Upper Canada – was not impressed with the economic potential of the hilly Lower Canadian region. He wrote to one of his colleagues: "was most pleased with the romantic pictoresque and (in many places) beautiful scenery on the banks of the St Francis, and although I think favourably of these townships, as combining a certain proportion of the useful with the ornamental, to gentlemen already possessed of a moderate independence, I do not consider them of half the agricultural value of the Upper Province ... to the poor man." Brydone repeated to the BALC's Nathaniel Gould that the Eastern Townships was clearly better suited for cattle and sheep pasture than for crop-based agriculture – for wealthy emigrants than for poor ones.[10] The company directors nevertheless continued to emphasize the region's picturesque scenery and malaria-free environment, as well as the opportunity it provided to engage in a pastoral economy, three themes that emerged repeatedly in the settlers' letters published in its promotional brochures, as we shall see.

An important reason for the gentlemen settlers' attraction to the pastoral economy was the belief by advocates of agricultural improvement that it was necessary to maintain soil fertility, not only by rotating crops and plowing back all stalks and stubble, but by feeding most of the harvest to livestock in order to produce manure for the arable land. Feed crops would also allow fields to recuperate from grains grown for the market. Based on what historical geographer Kenneth Kelley claims was an inappropriate old-world conception of soil exhaustion, early settlers' guides written by British travellers and immigrants accused Canadian farmers of being slovenly, lazy, and ignorant.[11] One settlers' guide to the Eastern Townships moralized as follows: "The man who lets his farm be unproductive, is analogous to the barren fig tree, so appositely alluded to in the Scripture. He is merely an encumbrance to the earth, and is fit, as he very soon must be, only for removal – he is a robber, not merely of man, but of God – for in a short time, he leaves his lands, which, with moderate care, might have been productive, a prey to weeds and thorns, etc., which injure even his very neighbours."[12] From this perspective it was almost a religious imperative to Anglicize this American-settled region.[13]

Ironically, much of the appeal of pastoral agriculture to the British gentility was that it provided more opportunity than did crop farming for leisure.[14] Most felt that worthwhile profit from a small farm was impossible even when the land was devoted to cash grains, therefore farmers should at least strive to live well.[15] In the pages of the British colonization booklets, the rolling countryside of the Eastern Townships was depicted as an emerging Arcadia, which in the classical world was the border between tilled land and wilderness, but which can also be defined as the balance between nature and culture.[16] Indeed, the British "cult of the countryside" was not only the product of an aesthetic sensibility, but an attempt to preserve a natural harmony that was under threat by urbanization and industrialization.[17] In short, the elucidation of the three themes of picturesqueness, salubrity, and pastoralism in the BALC's promotional material sheds light on the values and aspirations of a gentry society undergoing a crisis of confidence and authority in industrializing Britain during the early nineteenth century, yet eager to impose its cultural values and political influence on a colonial landscape.[18]

Immigrants' Letters

The correspondence published by the BALC appears to have been genuine enough, though some of the "letters" were lengthy essays whose publication was clearly subsidized by the land company.[19] Publishing settlers' correspondence was a technique used to considerable effect at this time by the Petworth Emigration Committee in its campaign to encourage pauper families from West Sussex and area to settle in Upper Canada.[20] But the difference as far as the Eastern Townships letters were concerned was that the BALC chose well-educated, recently arrived correspondents who shared the values and outlook of the landed gentry.[21] By presenting a positive interpretation of the most distinctive feature of the Eastern Townships, namely its hilly topography (which was actually exaggerated in the illustrations printed by the BALC in 1836 – see figure 2.2), these letters would help the region to compete with the physically unimpressive Upper Canada for those settlers who were imbued with the romantic sensibility of the early nineteenth century.[22] This was obviously a limited market as far as potential land purchasers were concerned, but the company undoubtedly hoped to benefit from the capital that the better-off immigrants would inject into the region's economy.[23] And, at a more subconscious level, the visualization of an American-settled frontier as an English-like landscape was a colonializing act in itself, one that reinforced subjective control over an objective environment.[24]

2.2 *View in the Eastern Townships, Lower Canada on the River St Francis*. Library and Archives Canada, C-114135. This lithograph originally appeared in the brochure titled *British American Land Company Views in Lower Canada* (London: 1836). It is attributed to Surveyor-General Joseph Bouchette.

While the identities of the correspondents are difficult to trace in most cases, Dr William Wilson was a man of some wealth who had reportedly left England because of his disgust with the Reform Act of 1832.[25] Wilson was more interested in becoming a farmer than in setting up a medical practice in Sherbrooke, which already supported two doctors. His published letter, written to a former neighbour in Yorkshire in January 1834, opened with a dramatic description of a prosaic topic, the previous week's weather. The temperature had been colder "than is recollected by the oldest inhabitant," he wrote. Indeed, at approximately "50 degrees below the freezing point," it was colder than Wilson's thermometer was capable of recording. Far from complaining, however, the doctor described how warm the interior of his plastered and stove-heated house was, while outdoors "My boys are in a state of great enjoyment, the polished face of the earth supplies them with constant diversion; and the chopping of wood, for our fires, is for them a wholesome exercise, and a useful employment. The snow is now so well tracked, that travelling is very easy and pleasant, when the cold is not too great."[26]

Wilson then painted a picture of plenty, with frozen meat and maple sugar for sale at reasonable prices, and fish and game available for the taking. Having leased a house in town for the year, Wilson was negotiating to purchase a 211-acre farm, with fifty acres under cultivation, "8 head of cattle, 12 sheep, 20 tons of hay, 80 bu. of potatoes, farming implements, some useful household furniture, iron boiler, and sugar utensils." In short, for the "moderate sum" of £450, Wilson hoped to "obtain a farm capable of producing every requisite for the use of my family except tea."[27] Growing a cash crop to purchase necessities or pay off a mortgage was clearly not a priority in Wilson's mind.

An excerpt from a subsequent letter reveals that Wilson did purchase the farm in question, and that he hired men to build a new house while his family remained in town: "My cottage fronts the west, and on this and the southern aspect, I have built verandahs. Here my little ones enjoy a shade or shelter in the open air, as the sun, wind, rain, or snow prevail, and here, how greatly should I enjoy the society of my good English friends."[28] Wilson's description illustrates how what was then known as a villa or cottage was designed to fuse architecture and landscape into a picturesque whole, with the verandah serving as a spatial bridge between interior and exterior space, as well as providing an ideal spot from which to enjoy the landscape vistas.[29] With its exotic colonial associations, the verandah that Wilson took care to mention doubtless also symbolized the British imperial presence in this northern settlement zone.

Wilson's intended audience was quite explicitly other immigrants with "a few hundred pounds to invest." He warned them not to do so in wild land because they would be "quite unfit for the operation of clearing, which department should be left to the Americans." With operating farms rapidly rising in price in Upper Canada, however, Wilson strongly advised settling in the Eastern Townships, adding that the "wholesomeness of this part is an important consideration, giving it the advantage over all the fertile regions in the United States as well as Upper Canada."[30]

The health issue was also a priority in the second letter published in the BALC's 1834 report. Dr. W. Robertson was a resident of Montreal but he wrote that he had taken his military lands in the Eastern Townships in preference to Upper Canada largely because "fevers or agues" were "seldom or never known" in the former region. Robertson added that "the fine hill and dale lay of the land, adapts them admirably for grazing farms, which, properly managed, remunerate the farmer well; and with less labour than any other kind of farming."[31] This was a message that would clearly appeal to any prospective gentleman farmer.

For the following year, 1835, the BALC published the statement of Frederick Templeton concerning his extended summer tour throughout the region. Templeton noted that, after leaving Drummondville in the lower St Francis Valley, the country "assumes a varied and picturesque appearance, and is well adapted for all purposes of husbandry; it is thickly settled, and amongst the inhabitants are to be found many highly respectable families." The link between topography and social class reappeared in Templeton's report where he noted that the scenery was "romantic, picturesque, and in many places beautiful about Lennoxville, Compton, and Stanstead; in which district are many improved and excellent farms, occupied by highly respectable proprietors."[32]

Another document from 1835, identified only as an "Extract of a Letter from a Gentleman resident at Sherbrooke," noted the abundance of the year's harvest, particularly wheat, which would find a "sure remunerating market." Other sources suggest that this was an exaggeration, though the region appears to have escaped the devastation by the wheat fly of that year's harvest in the seigneurial zone, which had also experienced several years of wheat blight.[33] "Gentleman" nevertheless placed more emphasis on raising livestock: "for grazing no country can be before this. Millions of sheep ought now to be kept, and I am confident wool will become a staple article here. The States of Vermont and New Hampshire are getting rich with their sheep, why not the Townships also?"[34]

By 1830 the New England hill country was, indeed, beginning to enjoy large returns from raising the long-haired Merino sheep that had been introduced from Spain,[35] and this was clearly the direction the BALC wanted the Townships to move in. It had acquired a woollen mill in Sherbrooke in 1834,[36] and it reprinted an article from the *Montreal Herald* recommending that much more attention be paid to the raising of sheep. The wolf problem was simply dismissed with the statement that "this evil is not half so serious as it is generally considered to be," though Phillip Henry Gosse later wrote that wolves would kill as many as ten of his neighbours' sheep in a night if they were left in a field.[37] Perhaps not surprisingly, Townships farmers failed to embrace sheep farming with the same enthusiasm as their Vermont neighbours.[38]

Two separate booklets of letters appearing in 1837 had no overt connection with the BALC, though it seems likely that the company at least subsidized their publication. The credibility issue was clearly a significant one, for W.G. Mack of Shipton Township prefaced his "letter" of twenty-six pages with the claim that he was "totally unconnected with any speculations either in land or commerce." He therefore could not "be suspected of having any sinister motives for lauding one part of America or depreciating another."[39] Mack stated that his original intention on leaving Scotland had been to clear a few acres and build a log house in the "far west" in order to live "a life of comparative solitude, with charming independence." He had travelled "along the banks of Lake Ontario, Lake Erie, and up the river St Clair, into Lake Huron, as far as Goderich, which at present is the Ultima Thule of British settlers in Canada." Here the soil "was almost always rich and highly productive," but this was the region's only strong point:

> I found roads wretched every where, except for a mile or two around such places as Toronto or Niagara; the country, with very few exceptions, flat and uninteresting, your view being always limited to the number of acres cleared around the unseemly-looking log houses; the black stumps and ragged patches of grain or potatoes giving the whole an air of desolation and discomfort, enough to dampen the hopes of a much more sanguine emigrant than myself.[40]

Mack admitted that he had also seen "very beautiful farms cleared of stumps, laid out into neat fields, with good frame houses and large barns upon them," but they were not owned by families who had arrived within the previous six or seven years. The fate of the more recent settlers, even those of "great respectability," was to live "packed like sheep" in small log cabins.[41] To purchase an improved farm of 150 to 200 acres in Upper Canada would cost at least £800, while the same could be had in the Eastern Townships for £500.[42]

Of the latter region, Mack wrote, "I could not help being much struck with the highly picturesque appearance of the country, contrasted with the tedious monotony of the flats and swamps of the Upper Province. Here you have something to relieve the eye; nay, I may safely say that the scenery which presents itself to the traveller is rarely surpassed in any country."[43] Environmental historian Roderick Nash has observed that the "enjoyment of wilderness was a function of gentility" in the mind of romantic writers,[44] but it is evident that only a certain kind of wilderness was appreciated by the British newcomers. That described by Mack, like the other correspondents, conformed closely to the conventions of the picturesque:

> From Durham to Sherbrooke the road winds for the greater part along the banks of the beautiful river St Francis, at every turn presenting new features for admiration; here it rushes in heavy rapids over its rocky bed, – there it expands itself into a broad and silent stream, enriching the meadows on its banks, and the numerous rich islands with which it is studded, and which are for the most part cultivated, and yield large crops of hay and corn. To increase the beauty of the vale of the St Francis, you feel that though enough of the ancient forest remains to give grandeur and wildness to the whole, still the numberless cleared farms around, sometimes placed high on the hill-sides in the most romantic situations, inform the traveller that he is in the midst of a thriving and populous country.

The picture Mack painted of the somewhat older townships of Compton, Eaton, and Stanstead was still more bucolic. There the traveller "will find whole tracts of country cleared in all directions, with stone-fenced fields, free of black stumps; neat white-washed houses surrounded with gardens and orchards, large herds of sheep and black cattle grazing in the fields, and flocks of geese and turkeys feeding along the road sides."[45] Mack admitted that "It may appear of little consequence to the settler whether he is situated upon a picturesque farm or not, provided it is of an excellent soil," but he insisted that natural beauty was "a great desideratum, and one which, if combined with other advantages, is not to be slighted."[46] As for the soil of the Eastern Townships, "except in its capabilities of raising heavy crops of wheat," it was "in all other respects equal" to that of Upper Canada, "and from the undulating surface of the country, and the innumerable streams and springs, it is infinitely superior as a grazing country." Furthermore, hay was "raised in great abundance, with the least possible labour."[47]

Even the long cold winters were seen as an advantage by Mack. Though he admitted to not having yet experienced one, he reported:

> instead of the severity of that season being looked forward to as a time of hardship of endurance, my neighbours hail its near approach with the greatest pleasure. Then it is, say they, we have good roads and bridges wherever we choose to go. Produce of all kinds is taken to Montreal, and supplies brought back at the cheapest prices; the grain is thrashed, firewood cut, and rails got out for the ensuing summer; and what makes it a pleasant season to all, is, that all the visiting between friends in any easy and hospitable way is then in its full force ... Surely such a winter as this, is much preferable to damps and thaws which occur more or less during an Upper Canadian winter; the latter cutting up the roads to such a degree, that they are rendered impassable, both for the sleigh and the waggon [*sic*].[48]

Furthermore, while Upper Canada's winter might be shorter by a couple of weeks, "their spring is ushered in ... by fevers and agues, rheumatisms, intermittent and lake fevers, in short by all the diseases which are necessarily engendered by a flat and marshy country, and which in the Eastern Townships are, from the very opposite character of the surface, totally unknown."[49] Indeed, the strongest objection Mack had to settling in Upper Canada or the "western" United States was their "sickly springs and autumns."[50] Like several of the other writers, Mack also stressed that "when the Cholera was raging in 1832 and 1834, in all other parts of both Provinces, not a single case occurred in the whole of this district."[51]

Mack failed to point out that the lack of cholera in the Eastern Townships illustrated how few Irish famine refugees were settling in the region, but, more explicitly than the other correspondents, he argued that the Eastern Townships had a distinct advantage over Upper Canada "in point of society." He explained:

> I do not mean to say that the people who have settled here, are at all superior to those who have gone "far west"; but we are closer together, so that instead of travelling a dozen or twenty miles to see our friends I can in a circuit of three miles find twenty ... Of the advantages of having a pleasant society around one, I need not here speak; suffice to say, that you will no where see in this part of the country, gentlemen with their beards a week old, wearing shoes that despise Warren, or sitting down to dinner

> without their jackets. The reason is obvious, – we are surrounded by people who retain the ideas of propriety with which they have been brought up in the "old country."[52]

Despite the strict class lines, Mack painted a rather utopian picture of pioneer socializing:

> There is … a natural feeling of fellowship among any set of people under our circumstances which leads us to look upon each other as the crew of a ship do upon their shipmates. We have all left our dear fatherland, to adopt a new, and a distant home, – our pursuits are the same, our toils, our pleasures, our interests are all alike; and as no one here pretends to riches, so no one attempts to eclipse his neighbour, and thus petty jealousies arising from envy are in a great measure unknown.[53]

The British gentleman's paradise would obviously have included a good deal of hunting and fishing,[54] but Mack's enthusiasm was uncharacteristically tempered on this topic. The reason was not a lack of game but that the practical goal of adding to the larder tended to eclipse the sporting aspects, particularly when "you must submit to the annoyance of being half devoured by mosquitoes, and black flies." There was no sport in hunting partridges, "for they very politely fly into the trees, and you may very deliberately shoot them all, for they seldom go far." As for deer, Mack described how hunters on snowshoes simply followed their dogs until their prey "sink deep, become fatigued, and are soon overtaken." Finally, the process of pursuing "moose deer" might involve several days of hard slogging which "would appear to be making a labour of a pleasure."[55] Fishing was passed over even more quickly, except for the advice not to bring tied flies from Britain because "American fish prefer, like Yankees, a bit of fat pork."[56]

Mack's distinctly unromantic descriptions of hunting and fishing lend an air of authenticity to his otherwise uncritical report, but he was obviously only pretending to write a letter. The second booklet to appear in 1837, on the other hand, contained what was evidently a genuine correspondence from an unnamed settler in Eaton Township, near the village of Cookshire, to his relatives in England. Titled *Extracts From Letters Written During a First Year's Residence in the Eastern Townships of Lower Canada*, this publication differed from the others only in its candour about the loneliness that the unmarried author felt in this American-settled community. The letters began while the author was still crossing the Atlantic in June 1836, and even then he complained about "the want of society on board, not having one person with whom I can converse with pleasure." Aside from a lieutenant who was "by no means a congenial companion," and an eighteen-year-old girl who was "a complete boarding-school miss," all of the approximately 150 passengers were "second-cabin or steerage."[57] The author was obviously a person of considerable connections, for he informed his mother that Peter McGill – the prominent Montreal merchant who was a commissioner of the BALC – had invited him to dine with the governor, Lord Gosford.[58]

Despite his elevated social status, this anonymous correspondent was – like Edmund Peel – eager to engage in manual labour. After purchasing a 200-acre farm, which he christened Woodcote Place, he began in July to plough as well as pile old logs for burning:

> My system is this: I rise at five o'clock, have my basin of bread and milk, and walk to my work. In the middle of the day, while the men and cattle are feeding, I do some little carpentering job. We work till half-past seven or eight, when I walk home and have my supper, generally consisting of a small piece of fried bacon, two eggs, and from six to eight cups of tea. I find this system enables me to endure much harder labour than if I fed in the day, and my health, thank God, is excellent.[59]

Having made himself "master of the theory of ploughing from books," by the end of the season the Eaton correspondent claimed to have "broken up fifteen or sixteen acres of old pasture land, which is destined for my wheat, oats, and potatoes."[60] The following winter he reported that he worked nearly every day in the woods, and boasted that he had become "an expert chopper, not fearing to engage a tree of any dimensions."[61]

While this gentleman-settler clearly attributed whatever success he enjoyed to his strong work ethic, he also possessed distinct advantages over the average newcomer to the colony, or even many of his long-established neighbours. He employed a Scottish domestic servant and two English farm labourers at the cost of twenty-one dollars a month, and he had been able to purchase "a most superior short-horned Durham bull and heifer, three cows, one pair of oxen, two working mares, and one for my own use, and a foal." Nor did he forget to mention that he had "a black cur-dog, for the cattle, and a beautiful spaniel of the Devonshire breed."[62]

Despite declaring that "The only thing for a man to do here is throw aside all affectation of superiority, and meet the Yankee on his own grounds," the Eaton correspondent reported that the local settlers "have no idea of doing more than support themselves ... Their farming is carried on in a most slovenly manner: the filth of their stable and farm buildings would disgrace a Hottentot, and they are always behind-hand."[63] According to him, British immigrants need not be concerned about the quality of the soil on the improved farms because the Yankees were "far too slovenly and careless farmers to exhaust the land when they have been on it ever so long."[64] As a result, they were "fast retiring before the tide of emigration, the more sagacious among them predicting the total ruin of the country from this irruption on their old haunts and habits. A few men of the same, or less means than myself, coming here would buy them out and make a delightful neighbourhood."[65]

In the meantime, in contrast to the active social scene described by Mack, the Eaton correspondent had to make the best of his self-described solitary situation: "it is not actual loneliness, for I have three besides myself in my family, and several neighbours, but it is the want of some one to whom to communicate my ideas. You will understand this when I tell you that I have not a single educated individual within fifteen miles, and at that distance, from the necessity of constant attention to home affairs, we seldom meet."[66] Like the other correspondents, who failed to mention local town meetings or political institutions of any kind, this self-described "high tory of the old school" scrupulously avoided involvement in public affairs. He clearly did not share the civic humanist philosophy which associated agrarian society with popular political virtue, for he argued that politics engendered "a spirit which, to say the least of it, is decidedly opposed to that inculcated by our Great Master and pattern."[67] The Eaton correspondent did take solace in attending church and conducting daily prayers with his household. And he was careful to ensure his readers that manual labour and social isolation need not imply cultural degeneration – his October letter described how "the domestics having retired to bed," he was seated "at a round birch-wood table before a comfortable wood fire, with my library and everything around me, with slippered feet, after a pretty good day's work, performed under the additional comfort of a fall of snow."[68]

The Eaton correspondent's comfortable five-bedroom "cottage" itself helped to compensate for his social isolation. He wrote proudly that it was such as "I have often pictured to myself in my waking dreams, with a verandah open to a garden in the front."[69] In November he informed his mother that "I know not where you can enjoy a more pleasing view of a fine sunset than from my verandah, nor listen on a brilliant moonlight night with more advantage to the soothing sound of a waterfall in the neighbouring river."[70] Here, then, were the requisite features of the picturesque landscape – an expansive view and a nearby body of water – without the need to design a costly and artificial landscape garden. The Eaton settler's correspondence ends on the positive note that "we have market for every kind of produce at our doors, as well as shops, or as they are called here stores, in every village." He had had to pay high prices for provisions "on account of the great influx of emigrants," but he anticipated that "next year I shall raise everything I require, and have a good deal of overplus to sell into the bargain."[71] It seems doubtful, however, that this anonymous correspondent would remain on his farm once the Rebellion of 1837 broke out and the economy deteriorated, along with the hope of a major influx of British immigrants.

The "Practical" Settlers' Guide

The BALC finally shifted its strategy somewhat after the rebellions by republishing William F. Buchan's *Remarks on Emigration* in or around 1842.[72] The well-travelled surgeon had only visited the Eastern Townships briefly, and he admitted that much of his information was obtained from the land company's Nathaniel Gould.[73] But he generally avoided appeals to romantic sensibilities, focusing instead on the physical and settlement geography of the region, as well as on the steps immigrants should take to settle there. Claiming that he was addressing "the class of persons with ... limited means, and labourers with none," Buchan actually disapproved of the fact that "in the circuit of a few miles, you may, at times, find a M.A., a M.D., or a W.S. chopping wood or digging potatoes."[74] He assured his readers, however, that the "forms and absurd refinements of a more settled country" were not to be found in the Eastern Townships.[75]

The main argument in Buchan's booklet was, nevertheless, the same as that in the early BALC publications. He stressed repeatedly that, as compared to Upper Canada, land and labour in the Eastern Townships were less expensive and markets were closer. He lamented that "A sort of delusion has sprung over the minds of Emigrants – a delusion which ignorance or private prejudices, and misrepresentations, have continued to increase, that either there was no south side of the St Laurence [*sic*], or that for useful purposes, it was unworthy notice [*sic*]."[76] As for the climate, Buchan claimed that its "salubrity is not to be surpassed by any yet known," and he attributed this fact to "the number of streams and rivers which intersect, and thoroughly drain it, – to the natural undulating character of the surface of the land, causing a rapid flow and discharge of their contents."[77] While he admitted that Upper Canada had a slightly shorter winter, Buchan argued, as had W.G. Mack, that the frequent thaws there made sleighing difficult. This was a serious disadvantage because snow-packed roads were needed by the settler to market produce, purchase supplies, carry logs to the saw-mill, draw firewood to the house, "and lastly the socialities of the season require him to be moving about among his friends."[78]

According to Buchan, the reputation of the Eastern Townships suffered from the fact that the intervening St Lawrence settlements were occupied by French Canadians "to whom farming (except for their own purposes – their immediate necessities) is a matter that receives no attention." The British immigrant should "consider his journey but begun" when he arrived at Drummondville on the lower St Francis River. From there the country "commences to be Anglicized, and a progressive improvement in its appearance continues as he may advance."[79] Nor was Buchan impressed by the agricultural capabilities of the American-origin settlers, whose "relation to farmers is much like that of a body of pioneers to an army, to clear away impediments to a free progress, by cutting down the forest. To make a clearing, build a hut, work up ashes, and get a crop or two of wheat, and then sell or sometimes leave the land, is the manner peculiar to them, – leaving the more regular details of farming to subsequent hands."[80] Buchan advised British settlers to purchase operating farms if possible, claiming that partly cleared lots "with decent houses, barns, etc. ... can be procured at a price generally less than the actual expense of clearing the land." Even though the cultivated portion may have been exhausted, "you generally find an abundance of old manure which has been accumulating for years and never applied to its proper purpose."[81]

Buchan stressed that the Eastern Townships was a better grazing country than Upper Canada, but claimed that "the rage for potash making, and raising wheat, and other grain crops, have had their due share of influence in retarding such pursuit."[82] He argued that, with proper attention, fall wheat could be grown successfully, but the grain he most favoured was barley because it could be used to fatten pigs "which fetch, as pork, a much higher price than any other meat." Another advantage of barley was "the great good it would effect in a moral point of view, as leading the inhabitants to make malt and drink beer, in lieu of the horrid trash called spirits, distilled here, and drunk to excess from the want of beer or cider."[83] Buchan also recommended the planting of Indian corn, pumpkins, potatoes, cabbages, and other vegetables, some of which were being introduced by British settlers.[84] Finally, the Eastern Townships provided an excellent opportunity to produce sugar, which "is obtained in abundance by simply tapping the maple tree, and boiling the liquid so obtained." While there was little market for maple sugar, it was produced at a time of year when little else could be done, and "is allied, as to pleasure and recreation, with English haymaking." It also provided the satisfaction of being "drawn from our own land, and not from a distance."[85] In short, for British settlers willing to work towards establishing an independent livelihood in harmony with a benign Nature, the Eastern Townships was the ideal location.[86]

Conclusion

The descriptive construction of a picturesque Eastern Townships landscape was clearly a colonializing act, one which the BALC had attempted to apply to its own commercial and hegemonic purposes, but the usefulness of the colonization brochures in attracting immigrants was largely limited to genteel romantics such as Lucy and Edmund Peel of Ascot Township, or the anonymous correspondent of neighbouring Eaton.[87] The vision of the region was pastoral in the literal sense of favouring a livestock economy, and also in the philosophical sense of tacitly repudiating the importance of economic criteria as the measure of a good society.[88] Buchan and the other commentators may have criticized French-Canadian and American-born farmers for failing to take full advantage of the market possibilities at hand, but they were more outraged by what they perceived to be an indifferent attitude towards the long-term productivity of the soil. The fact that economic growth was not a primary consideration in these pamphlets conforms with Michael Bunce's observation that "The British and especially the English countryside is valued primarily as a landscape aesthetic." Although it evolved within the framework of agricultural progress, being created by the process of enclosure, that was progress constrained by the entrenched hierarchical structure of a rural society in which agrarian objectives were often subordinated to the requirements of gentrification. In this landscape or countryside, leisure and aesthetic enjoyment were as important as agricultural productivity and rural trade.[89]

Needless to say, the social and political connotations of British colonial agrarianism were quite distinct from those of the egalitarian and democratic American version.[90] The English gentility of the Eastern Townships distinguished themselves from their American neighbours by virtue of their education and their social graces. They also employed servants and farm labourers, though the pride they expressed in their own physical labour ensured that their pastoralism was more authentic than the "rentier's vision" assumed by Raymond Williams for rural romantics in England.[91] The letters published by the BALC may have been authentic, but their value as settlers' guides was limited because they did not appeal to the large numbers of British immigrants who were arriving at Quebec in steerage rather than first-class cabins, and because they reflected only the initial impressions and early experiences of the genteel settlers who wrote them. W.G. Mack claimed that "the Yankees, who still hold lands in the townships, are all anxious to sell out, not because they are ill pleased with the country, but because they see a fair chance of making a few dollars – a consideration which far outweighs their love of home, a feeling which hardly finds place in a real American breast."[92] But, if farms were less expensive in the Eastern Townships than in Upper Canada, it was largely because economic prospects were brighter in the latter colony.[93] Thus, Lucy Peel wrote to her family in England in 1834: "I think the Mr. B_ are right to go to Upper Canada if they go out with the intention of making anything by farming, and can put up with eating at the same table with their helps ... at present this [the Eastern Townships] is only a country for a Gentleman who wishes to live quietly and cheaply, without an idea of accumulating money."[94] One suspects, however, that the Peels were far from the only members of the disappointed gentry who returned to England once they grew tired of labouring simply to survive.[95]

In short, the romantic promise of a life in civilized harmony with Nature would prove to be still more elusive than the imperialist strategy of imposing a British political and cultural hegemony over the Eastern Townships, a strategy that effectively ended with the Rebellions. The 1840s would see the victory of the modern liberal state accompanied by the rise of industrial capitalism and a largely American-born bourgeoisie that was more indifferent to the charms of an idealized Nature than the British gentry had been.[96] As for families to colonize its large landholdings, the BALC would turn to the French-speaking seigneuries before the end of the decade.[97] The British-inspired picturesque vision would, however, leave an idealizing mark on the perception of the Eastern Townships, as it did on Canada as a whole.

NOTES

1 J.I. Little, ed., *Love Strong as Death: Lucy Peel's Canadian Journal, 1833–36* (Waterloo, ON: Wilfrid Laurier University Press, 2001), 8.
2 Little, ed., *Love Strong as Death*, 83.
3 On the physical geography of the Eastern Townships, see Jean-Pierre Kesteman, Peter Southam, and Diane Saint-Pierre, *Histoire des Cantons de l'Est* (Sainte-Foy: Les Presses de l'IQRC, 1998), chapter 1.
4 J.I. Little, *Ethno-Cultural Transition and Regional Identity in the Eastern Townships of Quebec* (Ottawa: Canadian Historical Association, 1989), 13, table 2.
5 Kesteman *et al.*, *Histoire*, 157–60.
6 Francis A. Evans, *The Emigrant's Directory and Guide to Obtain Lands and Effect a Settlement in the Canadas* (Dublin: William Curry; London: Simpkin and Marshall; and Edinburgh: Oliver and Boyd, 1833), 55; *Information Respecting the Eastern Townships of Lower Canada* (London: W.J. Ruffy, 1833), 12–14; *Report of the Court of Directors of the British American Land Company to the Proprietors*, 19 June 1834 (London: W.J. Ruffy, 1834), 11–12; Philip Henry Gosse, *The Canadian Naturalist. A Series of Conversations on the Natural History of Lower Canada* (London: John Van Voorst, 1840; reprint Toronto: Coles, 1971), 31, 340, 353; Kesteman et al., *Histoire*, 140, 149, 152.
7 Kesteman et al., *Histoire*, 132–4, 141–5.
8 The BALC also purchased 60,000 acres in clergy reserves and 32,000 privately-owned acres. J.I. Little, *Nationalism, Capitalism, and Colonization in Nineteenth-Century Quebec* (Montreal and Kingston: McGill-Queen's University Press, 1989), chapter 2.
9 McCord Museum, Hale Papers, Peter McGill to E. Hale, Montreal, 14 October 1834; E. Hale to P. McGill, Orford, 27 November 1834; E. Hale to George Innes, 24 June 1840. On Hale, see Louis-Phillipe Audet, "Hale, Edward," *Dictionary of Canadian Biography*, vol. 10, 326–7.
10 Quoted in Little, *Nationalism*, 45. See also Wendy Cameron and Mary McDougall Maude, *Assisting Emigration to Upper Canada: The Petworth Project, 1832–1837* (Montreal and Kingston: McGill-Queen's University Press, 2000), 182.

11 Kenneth Kelley, "The Transfer of British Ideas on Improved Farming in Ontario during the First Half of the Nineteenth Century," *Ontario History* 63 (1971): 103–11.

12 William F. Buchan, *Remarks on Emigration: more particularly applicable to the Eastern Townships Lower Canada*, second edition. (Devonport and London: 1842), 64–5.

13 Colin Coates notes that "the intellectual principle justifying the Hale's [*sic*] appropriation of the seigneury [of Sainte-Anne] was the belief that they were improving it." See his "'Like The Thames towards Putney': The Appropriation of Landscape in Lower Canada," *Canadian Historical Review* 74 (1993): 339.

14 Charlotte Erickson, "Agrarian Myths of English Immigrants," in O. Fritiof Ander, ed., *In the Trek of the Immigrants* (Rock Island, Illinois: Augustana College Library, 1964), 78.

15 Similarly, Erickson ("Agrarian Myths," 74–7) found that British settlers in the American mid-west shared a belief in subsistence farming as a way of life, largely because of the great value they placed on independence.

16 Evan Eisenberg, *The Ecology of Eden: An Inquiry into the Dream of Paradise and a New Vision of our Role in Nature* (Toronto: Random House, 1998), xxii, 164. Marylin J. McKay makes the distinction between Arcadia, "as already perfect and readily available to the individual who seeks it out," and "postlapsarian Eden," which "involves a quest on the part of a group for a site that, through hard work, will eventually proved a homeland." See her *Picturing the Land: Narrating Territories in Canadian Landscape Art, 1500–1950* (Montreal and Kingston: McGill-Queen's University Press, 2011), 6–7.

17 Keith Thomas, *Man and the Natural World: Changing Attitudes in England, 1500–1800* (London: Allen Lane, 1983), 13–16, 243–54.

18 Linda Colley, *Britons: Forging the Nation, 1707–1837* (New Haven: Yale University Press, 1992), 149–55.

19 Historical analysis suggests that emigrant letters published to attract the poor to Upper Canada were written by actual settlers, but sometimes presented in a misleading fashion. See Terry McDonald, "'Come to Canada while you have a chance': A Cautionary Tale of English Emigrant Letters in Upper Canada," *Ontario History* 91 (1999): 111–30. On this theme, see also Wendy Cameron, Sheila Haines, and Mary McDougall Maude, eds., *English Immigrant Voices: Labourers' Letters from Upper Canada in the 1830s* (Montreal and Kingston: McGill-Queen's University Press, 2000), xxxv–xxxix.

20 This correspondence has been reprinted in Cameron *et al.*, *English Immigrant Voices.*

21 Contrast, as well, the testimonials of settlers who had spent several years in the Canada Company's Huron Tract, and which were published as J.J.E. Linton, *Letters from Settlers in the Huron District, C.W.* (London: n.p., 1843).

22 Like Craig, Dilley finds that British travellers in Upper Canada were not impressed by the scenery, apart from Niagara Falls. See Gerald M. Craig, ed., *Early Travellers in the Canadas, 1791–1867* (Toronto: Macmillan, 1955), xxvi; and Robert S. Dilley, "British Travellers in Early Upper Canada: A Content Analysis of Itineraries and Images," *Canadian Papers in Rural History* 5 (1986): 203, 219. The picturesque image of the Eastern Townships, on the other hand, was reinforced by the eighteen views of the region printed in William Henry Bartlett's popular *Canadian Scenery* in 1842. See Victoria Baker, "L'art et les artistes des cantons de l'est, 1800–1950," in *L'art des Cantons de l'est (1800–1950)* (Sherbrooke: Université de Sherbrooke, 1980), 10–12; and R.S. Dilley, "Establishing a Sense of Community: Early Representations of the Eastern Townships," *Journal of Eastern Townships Studies* 14 (1999): 23–5.

23 On the retarding influence of the lack of capital in the region at this time, see Kesteman *et al., Histoire*, 162–8.

24 On this theme, see Barrell, *The Idea of Landscape*; Denis E. Cosgrove, *Social Formation and Symbolic Landscape* (Madison, WI: University of Wisconsin Press, 1984, reprint 1998), 233–4; and MacLaren, "The Limits of the Picturesque," 97–111.

25 Little, *Love Strong as Death*, 47.

26 "Letters From the Eastern Townships," *Report of the Court of Directors*, 11.

27 "Letters From the Eastern Townships," 11–12.

28 Buchan, *Remarks on Emigration*, 42.

29 Janet Wright, *Architecture and the Picturesque in Canada* (Ottawa: Parks Canada, 1984), 17, 25–6, 34, 55–7. On the origins of the English country house, see Michael Bunce, *The Countryside Ideal: Anglo-American Images of Landscape* (London: Routledge, 1994), 77–9.

30 "Letters From the Eastern Townships," 13.

31 The extract from Robertson's letter is dated 16 May 1834. "Letters from the Eastern Townships," 14.

32 "Statement Made to a Special Court of the Directors of the British American Land Company, Held on the 3rd of February, 1836, by Frederick Templeton, Who Passed the Previous Summer in the Eastern Townships of Lower Canada," *Report of the Court of Directors*, 5–6.

33 Fernand Ouellet, *Economic and Social History of Quebec, 1760–1850: Structures and Conjonctures* (Ottawa: Institute of Canadian Studies, Carleton University, 1980), 339–42. Kesteman *et al., Histoire*, 137, states that the Eastern Townships wheat harvests of 1829, 1831, and 1835 were

damaged by rain and early snow, and that the wheat fly began to have an effect in 1833. The crop for 1836 was a failure, but that for 1837 gave a fair average return.

34 Extract of a Letter From a Gentleman Resident at Sherbrooke, in the Eastern Townships of Lower Canada. Dated, 12th November, 1835, *Report of the Court of Directors*, 8.

35 Harold Fisher Wilson, *The Hill-Country of Northern New England: Its Social and Economic History, 1790–1830* (New York: Columbia University Press, 1936), 76.

36 Kesteman et al., *Histoire*, 154.

37 Montreal *Herald*, 23 December 1835, in *Report of the Court of Directors*, 9–10; Gosse, *Canadian Naturalist*, 34–5. On the British naturalist's sojourn in the Eastern Townships, see J.I. Little, "The Naturalist's Landscape: Philip Henry Gosse in the Eastern Townships, 1835–38," *Journal of Eastern Townships Studies*, 20 (Spring 2002): 59–74.

38 Kesteman et al., *Histoire*, 142.

39 W.G. Mack, *A Letter From the Eastern Townships of Lower Canada* (Glasgow: David Robertson, 1837), iv.

40 Mack, *A Letter*, 6.

41 Mack, *A Letter*, 6.

42 Mack, *A Letter*, 15.

43 Mack, *A Letter*, 8–9.

44 Roderick Nash, *Wilderness and the American Mind*, third edition (New Haven: Yale University Press, 1982), 60.

45 Mack, *A Letter*, 9.

46 Mack, *A Letter*, 9–10.

47 Mack, *A Letter*, 11–12.

48 Mack, *A Letter*, 14.

49 Mack, *A Letter*, 14.

50 Mack, *A Letter*, 7.

51 Mack, *A Letter*, 14.

52 Mack, *A Letter*, 16–17. Craig, *Early Travellers*, xxxi, notes that some British travellers advised gentry immigrants to settle in remote sections of Upper Canada where they would find other newly arrived settlers with the education and refinement lacking among the native-born farmers.

53 Mack, *A Letter*, 17.

54 See Colley, *Britons*, 170–3.

55 See also, Gosse, *Canadian Naturalist*, 20–1, 57–8. According to Craig, *Early Travellers*, xxvi, British travellers were not impressed with the hunting in Canada.

56 Mack, *A Letter*, 18–19. Buchan stated simply that salmon, trout, bass, pike and other fish were "taken in prodigious quantities," and could serve "an important part in the maintenance of an emigrant's family." Hunting was not thought of "as a pastime ... no doubt on account of there being no game laws." Buchan, *Remarks*, 54.
57 *Extracts From Letters Written During a First Year's Residence in the Eastern Townships of Lower Canada* (London: J.L. Cox and Sons, 1837), 6.
58 *Extracts From Letters*, 9.
59 *Extracts From Letters*, 12. Compare the daily routine described by John Langton, the Cambridge graduate who settled in the Otonabee district of Upper Canada in 1833. Patrick Dunae, *Gentlemen Emigrants: From the British Public Schools to the Canadian Frontier* (Vancouver: Douglas and McIntyre, 1981), 22–3. On this theme, see also, J.I. Little, "Gender and Gentility on the Lower Canadian Frontier: Lucy Peel's Journal, 1833–1836," *Journal of the Canadian Historical Association* 10 (1999): 77.
60 *Extracts From Letters*, 22.
61 *Extracts From Letters*, 24–5.
62 *Extracts From Letters*, 16.
63 *Extracts From Letters*, 13, 21.
64 *Extracts From Letters*, 26.
65 *Extracts From Letters*, 8, 13.
66 *Extracts From Letters*, 14.
67 *Extracts From Letters*, 18. On civic humanism, see Louis-Georges Harvey, "The First Distinct Society: French Canada, America, and the Constitution of 1791," in Janet Ajzenstat and Peter J. Smith, eds., *Canada's Origins: Liberal, Tory, or Republican?* (Ottawa: Carleton University Press, 1995), 79–107.
68 *Extracts From Letters*, 15.
69 *Extracts From Letters*, 14.
70 *Extracts From Letters*, 20.
71 *Extracts From Letters*, 31.
72 The original edition appeared in 1834.
73 Buchan, *Remarks*, 4. A local settler wrote that Buchan had studied in London, was four years in Edinburgh, and afterwards in Paris. Little, *Love Strong as Death*, 109.
74 Buchan, *Remarks*, 9, 30.
75 Buchan, *Remarks*, 59–60.
76 Buchan, *Remarks*, 17–18.
77 Buchan, *Remarks*, 28.
78 Buchan, *Remarks*, 18–20.

79 Buchan, *Remarks*, 43–5. Craig, *Early Travellers*, xvi, notes that British travellers consistently accused the French Canadians of lethargy and poor farming techniques. On the recommendations made by British observers of French-Canadian agricultural practices, see Louise Dechêne, "Observations sur l'agriculture du Bas-Canada au début du XIXe siècle," in Joseph Goy and Jean-Pierre Wallot, eds., *Évolution et Éclatement du Monde Rural: France Québec XVIIe–XXe siècles* (Montreal: Les Presses de l'Université de Montréal, 1986), 196–8.

80 Buchan, *Remarks*, 45–6.

81 Buchan, *Remarks*, 40–1.

82 Buchan, *Remarks*, 44, 51–2. For his discussion of livestock production in the region, see Buchan, *Remarks*, 54–7.

83 Buchan, *Remarks*, 46–8. Buchan, *Remarks*, 57, also recommended growing apples, claiming that despite the need for a "refreshing drink" during "the great heat of summer … scarcely a ton of cider is made, and there is not a single brewery." Buchan's "Errata" on p. 75 did note, however, that breweries had been opened in Lennoxville and Stanstead.

84 Buchan, *Remarks*, 48–50.

85 Buchan, *Remarks*, 53.

86 On the importance of land and independence to the early nineteenth-century artisanal immigrant, see Michael Vance, "Advancement, Moral Worth and Freedom: Some Possible Meanings of Independence Among Early Nineteenth-Century Glasgow Emigrants to Upper Canada," in Ned C. Landsman, ed., *Nation and Province in the First British Empire* (Lewisburg, PA: Bucknell University Press: 2001).

87 The pastoral image of the Eastern Townships was less artificially constructed but also less commercially successful than the Edenic image exploited by land developers to sell apple orchards in British Columbia's Okanagan Valley at the turn of the twentieth century. See Jason Patrick Bennett, "Apple of the Empire: Landscape and Imperial Identity in Turn-of-the-Century British Columbia," *Journal of the Canadian Historical Association* 9 (1998): 63–92.

88 It is in this sense that the pastoral ideal differs from the agrarianism of the Physiocrats. W.J. Keith distinguishes between the rural and pastoral traditions by arguing that the latter is predominantly urban in character. See W.J. Keith, *The Rural Tradition: A Study of the Non-Fiction Prose Writers of the English Countryside* (Toronto: University of Toronto Press, 1974), 4.

89 Bunce, *The Countryside Ideal*, 34–5.

90 Leo Marx, *The Machine in the Garden: Technology and the Pastoral Ideal in America* (New York: Oxford University Press, 1964), 127.

91 Raymond Williams, *The Country and the City* (London: Chatto and Windus, 1973), 46–7.

92 Mack, *A Letter*, 26.

93 On the difficult transition of the Eastern Townships region's rural economy from 1831 to 1844, see Ouellet, *Economic and Social History*, 367–8.

94 Little, *Love Strong as Death*, 99–100. While he was the well-educated son of an English poet and translator, the letter of advice written by Charles Julius Mickle of Guelph, Upper Canada, suggests that he was one of those who preferred to accumulate money. See Terence A. Crowley, "'The site of paradise': A Settler's Guide to Becoming a Farmer in Early Upper Canada," *Canadian Papers in Rural History* 6 (1988): 266–78.

95 Though he was not a member of the landed gentry, the English naturalist Phillip Henry Gosse sold his Eastern Townships farm after less than three years of rather impractical agricultural experiments in the late 1830s. See J.I. Little, "The Naturalist's Landscape: Philip Henry Gosse in the Eastern Townships, 1835–38," *Journal of Eastern Townships Studies*, 20 (Spring 2002): 59–73. And, despite their minimal success as settlers, the disgraced George Stacey and his family remained on their Ascot Township farm only because George's father – the Ordnance Clerk in the Tower of London – refused to pay for their return to England. See Jane Vansittart, *Lifelines: The Stacey Letters, 1836–1858* (London: Peter Davies, 1976). Contrast the success of the versatile English farm labourers sent to Upper Canada by the Petworth Emigration Committee, or the Gaelic-speaking families cleared from the Isle of Arran who settled in Lower Canada's isolated Inverness Township. Cameron and Maude, *Assisting Emigration*, 195; J.I. Little, "From the Isle of Arran to Inverness Township: A Case Study of Highland Emigration and North American Settlement, 1829–34," *Scottish Economic and Social History* 20 (2000): 3–30.

96 See Kesteman *et al.*, *Histoire*, chapters 6–8; and J.I. Little, *State and Society in Transition: The Politics of Institutional Reform in the Eastern Townships, 1838–1852* (Montreal and Kingston: McGill-Queen's University Press, 1997), chapter 1.

97 The French-Canadian population increased from 23 per cent in 1844 to 36 per cent in 1851. Little, *Ethno-Cultural Transition*, 21, table 5. On French-Canadian colonization in the Eastern Townships, see Little, *Nationalism*.

3 West Coast Picturesque: Class, Gender, and Race in a British Colonial Landscape, 1858–1871

I shall call hills steep, which ought to be bold; surfaces strange and uncouth, which ought to be irregular and rugged; and distant objects out of sight, which ought only to be indistinct through the soft medium of a hazy atmosphere … I know nothing of the picturesque.

Jane Austen, *Sense and Sensibility* (Oxford University Press, 2004), 73.

Beginning in 1858, word of gold discoveries lured to the Fraser River of British Columbia more than 25,000 men, many of them veterans of the California gold rush, though others were young middle-class adventurers who arrived directly from Britain. One of the latter, Kinahan Cornwallis, published in 1858 a lengthy treatise titled *The New Eldorado; or British Columbia* which began with the remarkable statement that the colony

> stands alone and unparalleled in the long annals of the world. It has eclipsed California and outshone Australia; it has attracted by an almost magical influence, tens of thousands to its shores, and flashed upon the universe in alluring fascination. It has sprung into full life armed, as Minerva from the brain of Jove. That which, but a brief period gone, reposed a solitary yet riant wilderness, is now alive with the clamours of a rushing of men, and the foundations of cities are already laid far down the Rocky Mountains to Vancouver, that hilly and forest-clad isle of a thousand beauties and a nation's promise – the England of its ocean.[1]

Cornwallis was obviously engaging in promotional hyperbole, but his publication reflected the rapid transition that was already taking place on the West coast of British North America. Gold valued at more than $18,500,000 would be exported between 1858 and 1865, and the White population of approximately 1,000 in 1857 would increase tenfold by 1871, the year that British Columbia joined Confederation. By 1881 the Native population would decline by as much as 95 per cent to approximately 29,000.[2] In the words of Cole Harris, the province had rapidly passed "from the local worlds of fishing, hunting, and gathering peoples to a modern corner of the world economy."[3]

The story of this colonization process has been told many times and from many angles, with recent studies adopting a distinctly "postcolonial" theoretical perspective, namely one that insists that culture is not simply a reflection of the world, but, in the words of Derek Gregory, "a series of representations, practices, and performances that enter fully into the constitution of the world."[4] Daniel Clayton, for example, examines how the eighteenth-century explorations of James Cook and George Vancouver produced an "anticipatory geography" of colonialism by redefining Indigenous territory as empty crown land.[5] Curiously, though – given the nature of British Columbia's physical geography – Elizabeth Vibert's examination of narratives produced by fur traders in the Columbia Plateau, and Noel Elizabeth Currie's analysis of the various versions of Cook's Nootka Sound journal, are the only studies to pay close attention to the initial Euro-American perceptions of the wilderness landscape.[6] This chapter will shift the focus to the era of colonial government and settlement. It will also exploit the insights of Mary Louise Pratt and other postcolonialist scholars who have examined how the domination of colonized spaces was "naturalized" by explorers and travel writers who recorded their perceptions and interpretations of the physical environment as "landscapes." Further, it will demonstrate that even the most mountainous landscapes were described as picturesque rather than sublime, thereby implying that the colony was suitable for colonization, and that the "uncivilized" environment posed no threat to the cultured sensibilities of the genteel young men who produced what has been mistakenly interpreted as exclusively female imagery.

Class and Gender

British travel writers of the Victorian era may have been much less interested in North America than in the more exotic Latin America, Africa, Middle East, or Asia, but Britain clung to the Pacific coast as a base to facilitate access to the Orient. The surrender of Oregon to the

United States in 1846 was followed by the establishment of the colonies of Vancouver Island in 1849 and (in response to the Fraser River gold rush) British Columbia in 1858. These young colonies attracted highly literate explorers, naval officers, prospectors, and other agents of colonization, a number of whom wrote accounts of their experiences. As Margaret Hunt notes, it had long been "'the done thing' for perfectly ordinary travellers to keep travel journals or write up their journeys after the fact."[7]

While postcolonial studies tend to refer to the reports of British explorers as typical of the colonializing male perspective, this essay examines a wider spectrum of British newcomers to the West coast colonies. Only two could be characterized as explorers – Robert Brown and Colquhoun Grant – and the latter is referred to largely for comparative purposes since his report was produced in a slightly earlier era. My other primary sources include the personal letters of the well-connected Robert Burnaby, government official and merchant, as well as those of the naval lieutenant, Edmund Hope Verney to his equally influential family; the official journal of another naval lieutenant, E.A. Porcher; the memoirs of Commander R.C. Mayne, Captain C.E. Barrett-Lennard, and the naturalist, John Keast Lord; the private journal of the Anglican bishop, George Hills; and the gold-rush narratives of W. Champness, William Mark, John Emmerson, Harry Guillod, and the above-noted Kinahan Cornwallis. Many promotional pamphlets and articles were also printed during these years,[8] but only the Cornwallis document of those selected for our purposes comes close to fitting that description. As we shall see, the views expressed by these men towards their new environment were generally candid yet uniform in most respects despite the variety of their occupations, the different audiences they wrote for, and the different genres their narratives were written in – with editors playing a hidden role in those that were published.[9] These views were clearly those of the English upper-middle class who governed the colonies, though at least one of the men, Harry Guillod, came from a more middling background.

The fact that all the documents examined here were written by men reflects the composition of the non-indigenous population on the Northwest coast, particularly outside the towns.[10] Pratt argues that the colonializing gaze was distinctively male in any case, for she claims that "It is hard to think of a trope more decisively gendered than the monarch-of-all-I-survey scene. Explorer-man paints/possesses newly unveiled landscape-woman."[11] Other feminist writers have gone much further. According to Susan Morgan, "The language of sexual aggression, the erotic possibility of sexual experience, the rhetoric of virile masculine conquest of a supine and mysterious but finally penetrable and controllable feminine land, form the lineaments of an utterly familiar metaphor in Victorian men's travel accounts about the 'near' and 'far' east."[12] Cheryl McEwan writes, similarly, that British men employed "the language of penetration, conquest, and domination," and Anne McClintock states that "Knowledge of the unknown world was mapped as a metaphysics of gender violence ... In these fantasies, the world is feminized and spatially spread for male exploration."[13] Finally, referring to the American settlement frontier, Annette Kolodny states that "men sought sexual and filial gratifications from the land, while women sought there the gratifications of home and family relations."[14] Unfortunately, these studies – with their heavily charged male-as-rapist trope – focus largely on female travellers, making the assumption that the views of their middle-class male counterparts were essentially the same as those of a few famous explorers such as the much-quoted Henry Morton Stanley and Richard Burton. As we shall see, rather than being aggressively sexualized, the images produced in the narratives of the English male newcomers to colonial British Columbia conformed to the same picturesque convention adhered to by the female travel writers of their era.[15]

Given that the roughest English countryside was relatively tame in comparison to the rocky coastlines, dark forests of gigantic trees, and arid interior valleys of North America's Northwest coast, the visualization of these wilderness "landscapes" as picturesque can only be explained as the product of a colonializing perspective. The cult of the picturesque – with its cultured sensibility – was not clearly coded either male or female,[16] but it was certainly a signifier of British middle-class respectability. As Keith Thomas points out, "The ability to derive pleasure from scenes of relative desolation ... was more likely to be found among those who by virtue of their social and economic position could contemplate with equanimity the prospect of leaving land uncultivated which might otherwise have produced food."[17] The picturesque landscape also evoked "a sense of order and control, a cultivated wilderness already framed as if ready for a painting."[18] The "inherently appropriative" nature of this perspective will become clear when we examine how British Columbia's indigenous peoples were marginalized and denigrated by the same English newcomers.

Vancouver Island and the North Coast

It is commonly assumed that British travellers, while praising North American scenery in general terms, found it to be rather monotonous because of its lack of historical references such as ruined abbeys or feudal castles that would provide the narrative element that was thought to enhance the picturesque scene.[19] Christopher Mulvey notes, however, that what the English who began to go to America as tourists in 1815 were looking for was "the effects of the more rugged kind of English countryside."[20] This landscape would also be difficult to find on the northwest Pacific coast, for Maria Tippett and Douglas Cole describe how, as one sailed north from Puget Sound with its scenery reminiscent of the noble estates of Europe, "The foreshore of today's British Columbia disappeared as the mountains rose directly from the sea, creating steep cliffs around deep inlets. No longer were there gently ascending hills chequered with varied woodlands, but only conifer-clad mountains rising precipitously above the snowline. The scene lacked all the qualities of the familiar and beautiful."[21]

To support their argument that British Columbia's scenery was not truly appreciated until late in the nineteenth century, Tippett and Cole quote from an article written by W. Colquhoun Grant in 1852 complaining that the interior regions of Vancouver Island "are wild without being romantic, and … from the absence of any bold outline, never approach to the sublime or beautiful." Grant, a former military officer, was clearly influenced by his failure as (according to him) the island's first settler.[22] He stressed the lack of arable land on an island that, "if it contain not some unheard-of natural wealth, is really not worth the ink and paper which it would take to describe it."[23] But the men who arrived with the gold rushes beginning in 1858 were not interested in becoming farmers, nor were they emulating the British travellers who had begun seeking out sublime mountainous landscapes in order to stimulate a sense of awe or spirituality.[24] Rather, the images recorded in the writings examined by this essay – like the graphic illustrations produced by the colony's topographical artists and surveyors – were distinctly picturesque, an aesthetic more suitable to colonial expansion.[25]

The first stop for the newcomers was the small town of Victoria, Pacific headquarters of the Hudson's Bay Company since 1843, capital of the colony of Vancouver Island since 1849, and a "perfect Eden" in the eyes of Governor James Douglas.[26] In December 1858 the initial impression of the young newcomer from London, Robert Burnaby, was more domestic in nature than it was exotic. In his words it was "a broken, hilly country, covered with pines and very Scotch looking," and the bay was broken into inlets "dotted with white wooden houses." The description in Burnaby's second letter drew upon the picturesque features of colour, light, and shade: "I cannot tell you how very lovely Esquimalt Harbour looked in the moonlight last night, with the sharp points of the trees against the clear frosty sky, dark shadows on the deep waters of the bay, and lights twinkling here and there on the shore."[27] Similarly, the naturalist John Keast Lord, writing eight years later, claimed that the boundary commission's headquarters on a point of land near Victoria was "a pretty spot, very English-like in its general features, but in the rough clothing of uncultivated nature."[28]

Colquhoun Grant's negative assessment, noted above, was of the rugged wilderness beyond the southern tip of Vancouver Island, but in 1860 the first Anglican bishop of Vancouver Island and British Columbia, George Hills, was more favourably impressed as he sailed up Barkley Sound and Alberni Inlet on the island's rain-swept West coast. Like Grant, Hills did not find many good agricultural prospects to attract his eye, but, rather than resorting to Grant's negative imagery, he noted simply that the land "was undulating mountain ranges covered with interminable pine," while adding somewhat tentatively that "Here & there were openings where probably tracts of land may eventually be cultivated." And the bishop became quite excited while canoeing with some Aboriginal guides up the river that empties into the head of Alberni Inlet. Here, in a natural prairie meadow, he found the pastoral landscape that was so rare in British Columbia, yet so valued by the British gentility: "It contained about 500 acres of the choicest land, covered with grass & ready at once to be occupied with herds of cattle. Towards the end of it, nearer the main river, were occasional clumps of trees, as though planted & having the aspect of a cultivated park." From Hills' perspective, this was a virtual Arcadia: "Wild fowl flew around in abundance, geese, & ducks, innumerable. The river seemed to swarm with salmon which continually jumped out of the water in sizes which must have been from ten to twenty pounds weight. The gentle winding of the stream, its placid flow, the noble trees reminded us of the Thames between Richmond & Windsor."[29] Advocated as a means of landscape appreciation by Richard Payne Knight, associationism ensured that "'new' landscapes are never seen as new but as versions of previously known ones."[30]

Three years later, in 1863, Dr Robert Brown – a noted naturalist who had arrived under the auspices of the Edinburgh Botanical Society[31] – would venture beyond such navigable streams by leading the first Vancouver Island "Exploring Expedition" from the Cowichan Valley to the West coast. Brown set the scene by resorting to gothic imagery:

> There it stretched, wave after wave of forest-clad hill and valley – the sea of giant pine only broken by a quiet, glassy lake, or a fiery river rushing over its rocky bed in foaming cascades, or winding in tortuous course through the silent glades, like a shining silver thread. It is in vain that we ask for some clue to that interior, so near at hand, yet, in knowledge, so far off. Trappers and hunters know nothing of it. Searching for bear or for beaver, these knight-errants of the West have gone into it a little way, trusting to luck and their good rifle, and have come back telling strange tales. Indians know less, for they all live on the coast, and are scared when out of sight of their villages. In awe-controlled whispers the elk-hunter tells of the strange sight *he* has seen, or which some equally reliable friend of his told him, about the terrible things which lurk in that great forest and by the banks of those unsearched rivers.[32]

It soon becomes clear to the reader, however, that this is neither unknown nor particularly dangerous territory. Brown and his men are guided by the elderly Kakalatza, chief of the last village on the Cowichan River, and they take advantage of huts and canoes used by the West coast Nittinat people on their travels to the East coast of the island. Much of Brown's narrative focuses on the challenges he and his rain-soaked men overcome as they proceed up the densely forested valley, though it is interspersed with the tales and myths recounted by Kakalatza. Rather than describing a supine natural landscape, Brown depicts the men as dwarfed in forests "composed of gigantic firs, every tree fit for the spear of a Titan, or the 'mast of some great admiral.'" Nor does he resort to sexualized imagery when they reach the source of the Cowichan River, described as "a large and beautiful lake, stretching away among wooded hills in solitary grandeur." Here, where the expedition spent a week, "rambling all around the neighbouring country," Brown's narrative is at its most descriptive:

> The forests were fragrant with the piny odour; the large white flowers of the dogwood (*Cornus Nuttala*) were reflected in the little glassy bays of the lake; woodpeckers tapped the trees merrily; grouse drummed in

the woods; humming-birds (*Selasphorus rufus*) darted like winged gems of emeralds and rubies among the flowering currant bushes; while the lordly-looking bald-headed eagle (*Haliaetus leucocephalus*) sat perched on the topmost branch of some giant fir, now and then swooping down to a trout from the lake.[33]

This edenic scene is less a view, defined as a landscape depicted at a distance, than it is a vision, namely something that, in the words of Driver and Martins, "engages the imagination and turns the spectator into an active participant in the scene."[34] Pratt argues, however, that such forays into natural history, with their scientific, classificatory terminology, served much the same purpose as landscape descriptions because they "created a utopian, innocent vision of European global authority." Imperial and pre-bourgeois European expansionism had simply been succeeded by an androgynous "anti-conquest" conception.[35] Conforming to this conception was Brown's self-deprecatory comment that "so wonderful was the adventure, that he had hesitated to relate it before, in case the discovery of the source of the Nile and the descent of the Nittinat, all in one year, might upset the geographical world!"[36]

The naval gunboat commander, Lieutenant Edmund Hope Verney, who had dropped Brown's expedition off at the mouth of the Cowichan River, recorded his own impressions of the landscape as he proceed northward into Desolation Sound. This was the name chosen in 1792 by Captain Vancouver to reflect his jaundiced perception of the rocky coastline,[37] but Verney mocked Vancouver's log:

> Vancouver describes this as the most desolate inhospitable country the most melancholy creature could be desirous of inhabiting: (vol. 1. page 374): it was even too dreary and lonely for the mussels and cockles they had hitherto met with: can you not picture to yourself the solitary, used-up, misanthropic cockle watching for a fair tide, then slowly detaching himself from his boulder, and shaking the last grain of sand from his pediment, drift down the arm, bidding adieu for ever to this desolate and inhospitable country, and betake himself to join a society of gay and hospitable cockles on Vancouver Island. I dare say Vancouver was not here in the duck season.[38]

Heading still further north, Verney wrote: "Our course continues to lie through the most beautiful inland navigation, presenting fresh points of colour every hour: now it is some grand and lofty snow capped mountain, then some bold cliffs and precipices, then perhaps a sweet little valley, with a torrent rushing down and emptying itself in one broad foaming sheet into the water, or down the steep bare face of the rock comes a slender waterfall, streaming over the smooth water-worn surface, with many a sheer descent, or slightly off from crag to crag."[39] While this scene unfolds like a panorama (a masculine perspective, according to Ryan)[40] as Verney's ship sails northward, it still conforms to the picturesque convention because the eye moves from a distant perspective to an ever closer one, and the sublime elements of cliffs, precipices, torrents, and so on repeatedly give way to the beautiful, with adjectives such as "sweet," "slender," and "smooth." And, while the sweet little valleys penetrated by foaming sheets of water may be suggestive of the eroticized landscape for those inclined towards a Freudian interpretation, the scene more obviously conforms to the definition of the picturesque as a synthesis of the sublime and the beautiful.

Verney's perspective of the Northwest coast was not unique, even for a naval officer, for four years later – in 1867 – another gunboat commander, Lieutenant Edwin A. Porcher of the Sparrowhawk, described the same scenery as follows:

> Many of the archipelagoes passed through were of [*sic*] surprisingly beautiful, the scenery being almost of a highland character, the shores wooded close to the water's edge, numerous canals resembling a succession of inland lakes, dotted with many beautiful islets; the scenery ever-varying in shade and outline, and consisting of open glades and gently sloping activities, at others of snow clad peaks and mountains, cleft by deep ravines, down whose sides thundered impetuous mountain torrents.[41]

Porcher's watercolours, not surprisingly, combine the picturesque with the topographical.

Finally, as John Keast Lord's ship steamed through Johnstone's Strait, he described the scenery as incomparable, with bays and creeks that were "very Edens for wildfowl," Hardwicke Island "like a floating emerald," and, in the background, hills rising "sharp and conical crowned with snow." Having many times "threaded the intricate passages" of the St Lawrence River's Thousand Islands, Lord declared that "the scenery from Chatham Point to the mouth of the Nimkish river is wilder, bolder, and in every respect more beautiful, lovely as I admit the Canadian scenery to be."[42] Lord was more ambivalent a day or so later, however, claiming that "the ragged peaks of the Cascade Mountains, tinting with rosy light their snow-clad summits," had "a wild grandeur … that evoke feelings of awe rather than admiration." But his brief reference to "the fearful monotony of the interminable hills" was a rare admission that he did not feel that he was entirely in his element.[43]

The Lower Mainland

In 1859 Colonel Richard Moody, lieutenant governor of British Columbia and commanding officer of the Royal Engineers company that was building the new mainland capital of Queensborough, described the mouth of the Fraser River in distinctly picturesque pastoral terms:

> Everything is large and magnificent worthy of the entrance to the Queen of England's dominions on the Pacific Mainland. I scarcely ever enjoyed a scene so much in my life. My imagination converted the silent marshes into Cuyp-like pictures of horses & cattle lazily fattening in rich meadows in a glowing sunset. One cannot write prosaically of such scenes as these, so pray make allowances when I get into rhapsodies at any time about this most beautiful country.[44]

Robert Burnaby, who would spend his first year on the West coast as Moody's private secretary, was initially less enthusiastic. He complained to his mother that "You can scarcely conceive it, but what we in England would reckon the most sublime combination of mountain, wood, and water become actually tiresome and pall on the taste, so monotonous and endless are they. It is quite refreshing to think of a green field and a glimpse of Salisbury plain or the great Sahara would be a relief."[45] But he, too, soon began to express considerable interest in the local landscape, writing to his sister in June 1859:

> I can never tire of writing to you about the exquisite scenery which changes every day. The snow gradually leaving the mountains, which become a distant blue – the vast forests, piled in layers one over the other, with the most inimitable effects of *distances*, and presenting endless varieties of green tints, now that the summer shoots are out on the pines, the green leaves of the Maple and other deciduous trees are in all their glory. The big river, swollen with melted snow, rolls swiftly and muddily past – bearing great trees some 250 and 300 feet long, fantastic roots, and every variety of stick and snag on its bosom.[46]

In this colourful scene, the reader's imaginary view drops from the distant snow-capped mountain peaks to the green forested slopes, and, finally, to the muddy river in the foreground with the giant floating trees that stand in for gothic European ruins, a popular feature of the picturesque.

Pratt claims that such a presentation of the view as a painting ordered in terms of background and foreground, symmetries, and so forth is a characteristically masculine practice.[47] In McEwan's words, however, "a major feature of landscape description by white women travelers in west Africa was their recognition of order in the natural environment," as when the British explorer Mary Kingsley described the horizontal bands of colour that could be seen when approaching from the sea.[48] Burnaby's foregoing description of the scene from the banks of the lower Fraser River presents a similar sense of order, though one is struck by the movement in the foreground. Passive verbs change to active ones as the scene unfolds, and the swollen river "bearing great trees ... on its bosom" may evoke female nudity and pregnancy, but also power and even danger, thereby undermining the reassuring sense provided by the picturesque imagery.

But such hints of unease are rare in Burnaby's writing. Like Robert Brown at Lake Cowichan, his frequent focus on the foreground often results in a naturalistic Arcadian vision such as the following in which the forest literally comes alive:

> In the woods the wild flowers spring up in thousands, the delicious 'ribes' growing 7 and 8 feet high, full of bloom, wild raspberry with its bright pink flowers, mimulus, pansy, lily, some exquisite specimens all in trefoil, three leaves and trefoil flower growing between, perfectly white, dogtooth violets, purple flowers of the crocus tribe. The air is alive with the hum of bees, and humming birds chase each other in the sunshine, and as one walks through the woods, little squirrels run up stately cedars and peer at you with enquiring eyes, and you hear now and then the sharp rap of the woodpecker, a lovely bird brown and red.[49]

Such descriptions challenge the transferability of McEwan's assertion that it was only women travel writers who depicted Africa as a potential garden in need of cultivation, as well as Kolodny's statement that the garden metaphor was central and exclusive to women's fantasizing of the American frontier.[50]

Certainly, Burnaby was no masculine conqueror, for his most notable adventure was ascending a tributary of the Fraser River in the early spring of 1859 to the lake which would bear his name, now located in the centre of the city which also adopted his name. He was accompanied by the young English lawyer, Henry Pering Pellow Crease, as well as an old Canadian voyageur named Presse and two unnamed Natives to manage the canoe. Burnaby wrote to his sisters: "It was interesting to see an unexplored river opening up gradually, turning tortuously round about, with most exquisite vistas formed by the sloping banks. The Indians push the canoes through the narrowest and most unpromising spots where you must bend your head low down as you pass under the logs not an inch from your nose, in through rough branches overhanging the rapids."[51] Like the naturalist-collectors whom Pratt claims often portrayed themselves in infantile or adolescent terms in order to escape the guilt of European conquest (an emotion Burnaby was not burdened with),[52] Burnaby related anecdotes that revealed the helplessness of himself and Crease in this environment, as each in turn had to be rescued from the frigid water. Once at the campsite, old Presse quickly started a roaring fire while the two Englishmen occupied themselves with the more menial task of cutting red cedar branches for their beds.

Rather than expressing a sense of unease about his helplessness, Burnaby's narrative moves on to make the exotic familiar by adding that there were some nice specimens of this cedar tree "round the grass plot at Quorn, only here they grow to a tremendous size."[53] Such familiar frames of reference were clearly not as exclusively characteristic of female travel writers as has been claimed.[54] Nor – like Robert Brown's entry into Lake Cowichan – was the final "penetration" of the lake charged with sexual imagery, for Burnaby simply wrote that "by 12 o'clock we find the water deepening, widening and more still, and we gradually enter a noble lake about 3 miles long and more than a mile broad, all surrounded by hills and wooded down to the margin." Once again, Burnaby was more interested in the foreground, for he described how "All about us the vegetation is rich, cranberries, rhododendrons, wild raspberries and all sorts of fruits, looking dreary enough now but prolific no doubt a month or two hence."[55] The colonialist implications of Burnaby's "anti-conquest" perspective (to use Pratt's term) manifested themselves in the pride he expressed in helping to build what he felt would become a great city (though he thought the new name, New Westminster, absurdly pretentious). He also predicted presciently that Burrard Inlet (the future site of Vancouver) "will be one of the greatest naval rendezvous and centers of commerce on this side of the world."[56]

Further up the Fraser Valley, at the mouth of the Chilliwack River, John Keast Lord described the "open grassy prairie" stretching before him for three miles, a scene he depicted as a colourful and domesticated landscape:

> The Indian summer is drawing to a close; the maple, the cottonwood, and the hawthorn, fringing the winding waterways, like silver cords intersecting the prairie, have assumed their autumn tints, and, clad in browns and yellows, stand out in brilliant contrast to the green of the pine forest. The prairie looks bright and lovely; the grass, as yet untouched by the frost-fairy's fingers, waves lazily; wild flowers of various tints, peep out from their hiding-places, enjoying the last of the lingering summer.[57]

Lord did feel a sense of unease when lifting his gaze to the Cascade Mountains with "their craggy slopes split into chasms and ravines, so deep, dark, and lonesome, that no man's footfall has ever disturbed their solitudes," but we shall see that contemporary British narrators who actually penetrated that mountain range were more upbeat (see figure 3.1).

Ascending the Fraser from Hope to the Cariboo

The general attitude of British Columbia's early inland explorers towards the mountainous landscape they encountered was essentially the same as that of Cook and Vancouver on the coast. Descending the river that would bear his name, Simon Fraser wrote in 1808: "I scarcely ever saw any thing so dreary … and at present while I am writing this, whatever way I turn, mountains upon mountains, whose summits are covered with eternal snows, close to the gloomy scene."[58] The Scottish fur trade-factors who followed the explorers did respond to the British reading public's appetite for the picturesque when they wrote their memoirs or edited their journals for publication, but the prevailing image of the territory between the Rocky Mountains and the Coast Range in their view was that of a desert.[59] And even though Tippett and Cole admit that by the 1840s the mainland's mountains "were beginning to be appreciated by the few who came into contact with them," they add that this scenery "became the subject of conventionalized emotion and romantic exaggeration. No one in the Victorian era could write of mountains without resorting to rhetorical bombast."[60]

To support their point, Tippett and Cole cite as characteristic Commander Richard C. Mayne's description of trekking up the Fraser

3.1 *Yale, the Head of Navigation of the Fraser, 16 May 1867*, Edwin Augustus Porcher HMS Sparrowhawk Diary and Watercolour Drawings. Western Americana Collection, Beinecke Rare Book and Manuscript Library.

Canyon with its "precipitous cliffs" and "crags so steep that we had to clamber up them with our hands and feet, until we arrived breathless at the top of a projecting ledge, on which we were glad to halt a few minutes, to draw breath and gaze with wonder on the scene." "Clichéd and conventional" as such passages may be, the dominant vocabulary in the gold rush era was that of the picturesque and not what Tippett and Cole term the "conventional mountain sublime."[61] Thus, Commander Mayne described Hope, near the mouth of the steep-sided Fraser Canyon, as "perhaps the prettiest town on the Fraser."

> Behind it Ogilvie Peak rises abruptly to a height of 5000 feet: to the right stretches the valley of the Que-que-halla, through which the trail to the new gold districts in the Semilkameen country is cut; while in the front

> the river glides, its channel divided by a beautiful little green island, the hills upon its opposite bank rising gradually to a considerable height, and forming a charming background to the prospect.[62]

Much like the landscape art of this era, Mayne's hills and mountains form a picturesque backdrop to a scene featuring human habitation.

Tippett and Cole themselves note that in his *Travels in British Columbia* (1862) Captain C.E. Barrett-Lennard described the upper Fraser scenery as "romantically beautiful," comparing the mountains at Hope to the Scottish Highlands and suggesting that Harrison Lake was "quite Alpine in its character."[63] The same was true of Commander Mayne once he had passed through the Fraser Canyon, for his *Four Years in British Columbia* (characterized by the *Illustrated London News* as "a manly, sensible book")[64] describes the hillsides sloping to the Nicola River as "clothed with long, soft grass, and bright with numberless wild flowers which grow so luxuriantly in this country." Though in an arid zone, Lillooet was depicted by Mayne as "a very pretty site," and he claimed that the views of Kamloops and the Thompson River were also "very beautiful."[65]

Bishop Hills' diary also adheres to this picturesque convention even as it records his rather arduous journey on foot with Colonel Moody and members of his Royal Engineers to visit the Fraser Canyon gold mining camps in June and July, 1860.[66] On the first day, Hills wrote: "Towards the upper river the scenery became more beautiful. The mountains nearer, the river more rapid." At Hope, "The air was balmy & scenery entirely Swiss. You might have believed yourself in Chamouni [Chamonix] or by the upper Rhine, except that there are no glaciers shining in the clouds." In the nearby Coquihalla Valley the Brigade trail became "a walk winding through trees & flowers & where at times you might fancy yourself in the wilder parts of some cultivated domain in England. The scenery is a combination of Swiss & Scotch … About three miles brought us to Dallas Lake, a sweet spot where one felt one could live for ages." Hills stressed the domestic, even at Hill's Bar where "two miners were gathering roses & other flowers. Perhaps to adorn their huts for Sunday. Butterflies were abundant. Particularly the Swallow Tail & the Painted Lady."[67] Hills was less impressed with the "bare & dusty" townsite of Lytton where there was "not a tree near for some hundreds of yards." But eighteen miles further along there was "a group of beautiful mountains," and, nearing the upper end of his journey in early July, he declared the scenery to be "very beautiful, the view from Cayoosh [Lillooet] down the river with mountains on one side & green slopes & trees & the plateau which looks like a park on the other, [is] particularly pleasing."[68]

The many men attracted by the Fraser and Cariboo gold rushes had more materialist goals in mind than did the bishop, and they could not count on the assistance of the Royal Engineers in their encounters with the unforgiving mountainous environment. But the account written in 1858 by Kinahan Cornwallis is unfailingly positive in its description of his experience. To demonstrate that he had not been debased by the company of his American partners, "more engrossed by the consideration of where our camping-ground should be, and where and when we might be able to renew our stock of provisions than by the scenery which met our gaze," Cornwallis waxed eloquent about the natural beauties of the upper Fraser: "I must say, in justice to my own good taste, that, in spite of hope and danger, I dwelt with something like rhapsody on the picturesque region of mountain and forest which delighted my admiring, not to say astonished, gaze."[69] After spending a night where "the stars shone out like jets of fire, and the moon again, with steady light, silvered the landscape," Cornwallis and his companions woke at daybreak and "found gold everywhere." At the end of the first day, he claimed, they had collected seven nuggets varying from half an ounce to five ounces in weight, plus an average of four ounces of gold dust per man, worth approximately $64. But this did not satisfy Cornwallis's Yankee partners, and so they pressed on towards the Rocky Mountains, continuing to find ever larger quantities of the precious metal.[70]

Cornwallis's account was clearly aimed at young men of the middle class, for he wrote that "in too many cases the intellectual labourer may unceasingly toil in the vineyard of professional and daily life, and scarce eke out for himself the means of a bare subsistence." Such men were needed to improve "the future welfare, stability, and greatness" of the colony by diluting the influence of the "disorderly mass of the Americans" who "are republicans and democrats" while "we are supporters of a monarchy and an aristocracy."[71] But the Englishmen who were attracted to the Cariboo gold rush of 1862 by such fanciful accounts would find themselves woefully unprepared for the arduous 560-kilometre journey on foot through an extremely rugged mosquito-plagued terrain, as a number of their memoirs attest. In these narratives, Man does not conquer Nature but emerges bloodied and humbled by the encounter, though there is little evidence that the experience was deeply transformative. Rather, there is a sense of pride that they have not only survived the ordeal but maintained their civilized virtues and values in doing so. From this perspective, these ostensibly anti-colonial accounts (what Burnett would refer to as imperial countercurrents) conform for the most part to Pratt's colonializing anti-conquest paradigm, though not to the male-as-sexual-predator one.[72]

W. Champness of Southampton, for example, expressed considerable bitterness towards "the utter fallaciousness of certain writers who have sent home glowing reports of this land and its advantages."[73] The problem was not lack of gold, but the cost of extracting it, as well as the unpleasantness of labour "under the cold dripping of water from leaky flumes, and with clothes saturated with slush and water from head to foot," even if all such jobs were not already taken by experienced miners from Cornwall and California. Champness and his small party soon headed back to the coast, only to become hopelessly lost, forcing them to survive without food for three days as they were tormented by mosquitoes. Perhaps not surprisingly, under the circumstances, Champness was not particularly impressed with British Columbia's scenery, complaining that there were fewer flowers than in California or England, and that "Heavy, sombre, lofty pine and oak, together with mountain and gorge, are the chief features of the Columbian landscape." But he sang the praises of British rule, and concluded that "the climate of British Columbia is, on the whole, very favourable to English emigrants," with "A clear atmosphere, pure water, generally cloudless skies, and a varied landscape of mountain and forest."[74]

William Mark and his travelling companion, John Emmerson, each described similar experiences, after being attracted to the Cariboo in 1862 by the glowing accounts of Donald Frazer, the Victoria correspondent of the *London Times*. Mark condemned Frazer for exciting "the attention of thousands of men in the British Isles, and on the European, American, and Australian continents" by describing the Cariboo gold fields "as surpassing the richness all [*sic*] other mines hitherto discovered; also representing the colony as possessing large tracts of rich land suitable for agricultural purposes, with a first-rate climate and abounding wild game of all description."[75] Having finally reached the Cariboo country with his two sons, after Emmerson had turned back at Williams Lake, Mark described how, from the snow-capped summit of "the great mountain, called Snow Shoes ... the whole range of Rocky Mountains lay stretched out in thousands before us, as far as the eye could reach; a vast number of them had their snow-crowned heads amid the clouds." So impressed was he by this view, Mark wrote, that it seemed "worth all the troubles and hardships we had passed through, and at the moment I felt that I could have forgiven Frazer for what he had done, but again, when I thought how many hundreds, nay thousands through his false statements, had been brought to ruin and starvation, my feelings were changed."[76] Finding no gold for all his efforts, Mark returned to England in the late fall when the "Cariboo was buried deep in snow, and report said that seventeen hundred pack animals had perished in the storm, and a vast number of men were missing. A fine specimen this of a great agricultural country, possessing a first-rate climate."[77]

The accounts of disappointed British gold seekers such as Mark were obviously not consciously aimed at promoting British colonial expansion, but their descriptions of the landscape were nevertheless a form of aesthetic colonialism. And, despite experiencing similar hardships and disappointments, the young London-born Harry Guillod, who had served an apprenticeship as a chemist, painted a more positive picture (also in 1862) of the mountainous environment. Guillod found "nothing pretty" about Port Douglas, at the beginning of the road built to avoid the dangerous Fraser Canyon, since it was "merely a row of log huts in a small clearing surrounded by the forest." For the next five days, however, the route was

> through deep valleys with snowcapped mountains towering above the trees in the distance; every mile or two we came to a swift running stream of deliciously cold water from the mountains, dashing and spraying over the stones; or we crossed a rough bridge of pine-trees over a cascade which bounded over the rocks far below; then would come to a level road through pine forests for a few miles; again we went up hill round the side of a mountain, only to descend again far down the valley, shut in by large trees and cool even in the heat of the day, but never out of the sight of huge mountains, principally covered with fir. George [Guillod's brother] said it put him in mind of the Highland scenery, but altogether on a larger and grander scale.[78]

When they emerged onto "a large undulating plain" three days later, Guillod described the countryside as "thoroughly English looking … with here and there a clump of trees or range of bushes and the whole covered with good green grass." He admitted that, for the most part, the grass that covered the hill in this arid region was "yellow, dry and coarse," but he preferred to focus on the aesthetically pleasing by describing a "beautiful spot" where there was "a stream winding along the side of our path, hidden among the long grass and rushes and a literal bed of roses and other flowers." Guillod claimed that he had never seen "such a quantity of roses of all shades; they were growing on low bushes, and after the shower everything looked so fresh and smelt so sweet that it was quite a treat and afforded me as much pleasure as any garden I ever saw in England."[79]

Unlike the explorers who climbed mountains to depict the unfolding scenery beneath them as detailed landscape panoramas, the eyes of Guillod and his fellow gold seekers tended to be drawn to the mountains themselves, and not simply as obstacles in their path. Despite losing their pack horse, running out of flour, and being plagued by health problems, Guillod was inspired to produce a painterly description of the Cascade Mountains in which any sense of fear and awe produced by the towering cliffs is dispelled by the colour of the covering vegetation: "The general appearance of the mountains at this season is beautiful in colouring as they are covered here and there with shrubs and small trees exhibiting every shade of colour from red through orange to pale yellow; which contrasted with the deep unfading green of the pines adds greatly to the beauty of the steep and majestic piles of frowning rocks."[80]

Guillod's journal then becomes largely devoted to accounts of the difficulties he and his partners faced reaching Van Winkle near Barkerville in the Cariboo region, working the useless claim they had invested $500 in, and walking back to Victoria "in the remnants of my clothes and without a cent in my pocket."[81] The somewhat desperate Guillod spent the ensuing winter breaking stones, the only job available to a "non-mechanic" like himself. In short, Guillod's journal – like that of Champness – becomes an example of sentimental travel writing that focused largely on personal experience and adventure. "Things happen" to the sentimental protagonist, Pratt states, "but he endures and survives" and, by doing so, he contributes to the civilizing mission (the anti-conquest) that is distinctively European, male, and middle class in nature.[82] Why such passive behaviour should be coded as distinctively male is somewhat puzzling, since Victorian female travellers also expressed pride in their stoic endurance, but in the following section we will examine this "civilizing mission" from a different perspective, focusing on the views these men recorded of the First Nations inhabitants they encountered.

"Fallen from Nature": The Human Landscape

In his distinctively pompous style, the imperial adventurer, Kinahan Cornwallis, observed of his situation as a gold miner in the Fraser Valley:

> I am egotist enough to believe that I had sufficient magnanimity of mind and character to know and to feel that I stood up in the, till now, almost primeval territory of aboriginal dominion an usurper, and was, together with the motley crew by which I was surrounded, but too painfully emblematic, in my own mind, of the coming misery and eventual, yea, rapid extermination of the race of the Red Man – the valiant children of the riant wilderness.

The ever-romantic Cornwallis waxed indignant against "ignorant conventional old women, and domesticated men" who "pray for the conversion of the heathen, and look down upon them as degraded beings, lost in the darkness of sin and iniquity; when the fact is, that they themselves are the sinful and iniquitous, compared with which the rover of the woods is very often a personification of magnanimity and virtue," that is, until they meet "the blasting, withering power of a perverted and vicious civilization."[83]

Inextricably linked to this Noble Savage stereotype was the assumption that First Nations society was doomed to extinction, an assumption bolstered on the Northwest coast by the fact that smallpox had had a devastating impact on the Coast Salish as early as 1782, even before Vancouver and Galiano sailed into the Strait of Juan de Fuca.[84] Furthermore, Cornwallis's sympathetic attitude towards the Aboriginal peoples was not shared by most of the other English newcomers, for the gold rush took place at a time when the Indian Mutiny, the scientific theory of evolution, and British disillusionment with the results of slavery emancipation in the West Indies had resulted in harsher notions of fixed racial differences.[85] As early as 1852 the dyspeptic Colquohoun Grant wrote that "No pigstye could present a more filthy aspect than that afforded by the exterior of an Indian village," with its "pile of cockle-shells, oyster-shells, fish-bones, pieces of putrid meat, old mats, pieces of rag, and dirt and filth of every description, the accumulation of generations."[86] Similar comments were currently being made about the London poor,[87] but Grant also asked – after describing how a slave had been tortured to death – "can it then be wondered at that the civilized nations with whom they have been brought into contact have preferred their extirpation to any amalgamation with such truculent villains."[88]

The other explorer of inland Vancouver Island, Robert Brown, was less judgmental. He described the "green maples and alder shading the houses" of the first village encountered on the Cowichan River, "giving it a pleasant look." Canoes dashed "hither and thither with the eager fishermen," but, while "Indian life – in the heyday of summer and plenty – looked pleasant enough," Brown complained about the stench of the decaying salmon and the demands that he supply "a plug of tobacco or a pipeful of paint" in return for "some service to somebody or other – date and circumstance not very clear." Brown did recount the "tales of war, and of love, and of the forest glade" narrated by Kakalatza, the old chief who guided his expedition to the West coast of the island, but he expressed amusement that some of these myths were now "smoked and theorised over by dreamy German *savans*, who, I fear, make much more of them than either the teller or the recorder ever did."[89]

Though he was a gunboat commander, Lieutenant Verney generally advocated a lenient policy towards the First Nations.[90] He declared in his first letter from Esquimalt, however, that the local Natives were "hideously ugly and atrociously dirty: their customs are beastly, manners they have none." From Fort Rupert the following year he wrote: "the natives are very quiet, dirty, tame and uninteresting," and, still further north, he described the Bella Coola people as "a very degraded set; they speak a harsh dialect most grating to the ear; we saw them herding together like animals, some quite destitute of clothing." Verney was more impressed with the physical features of the interior Natives north of Lillooet, describing them as "not so flat in the face, and much more intelligent looking." He added a few days later that "I have within the last few days seen finer specimens of the Indian than I ever saw before; many of the men with eagle eyes and aquiline noses and a few of the women fairly entitled to be called beautiful." Like Cornwallis, Verney was clearly drawn to the image of the Noble Savage, an image based largely on the buffalo-hunting Plains peoples. But Verney could not resist expressing disappointment in even the Lillooet group as horsemen, writing that "I had pictured to myself that they would have among them some sort of rude chivalry. But no! Their horses were miserably wretched and poor because they begin to work them as colts and consequently they die at an early age and are never allowed to reach their full size and strength."[91]

The yachtsman Barrett-Lennard also claimed to be disillusioned, having arrived with Fennimore Copper's romantic image "of the wild denizen of the vast unexplored regions of the west," only to find that the Aboriginals "appear insensible to anything like chivalry or generous feeling, killing and slaying with remorseless cruelty, undeterred by any sentiment or compunction." This did not prevent him from describing First Nations customs, habitations, and economy at some length, and admitting to finding some of the younger women attractive, but he then added that "their charms, if any discoverable, are very short-lived."[92]

Similarly, while the naturalist John Keast Lord's lengthy memoir describes in fascinating detail the ingenious techniques used by the First Nations to harvest a wide variety of fish and other sea life, his attitude towards these "crafty savages" is condescending when not contemptuous. Thus, he states that the Natives of the colony's interior would die "a miserable death, starved alike of cold and hunger," were it not for the salmon provided by providence.[93] Likewise, myriads of oolichans, "in obedience to a wondrous instinct, annually visit the northern seas containing within themselves all the elements necessary for supplying light, heat and life to the poor savage who, but for this, must perish in the bitter cold of the long, dreary winter."[94]

Robert Burnaby's descriptions were no more positive. While prospecting for coal on Burrard Inlet, for example, he painted a dehumanizing picture of Aboriginal domestic life:

> there is a group of the 'Siwash' as they call the natives, round the door of the tent, an old man munching some clams (a species of escallop) which he has just cooked at our fire on a stick like 'Kabobs,' his mate a dirty wrinkled old hag, smoking a pipe and five small 'Klootchmen' or girls squatted about, they have great strings of glass and brass beads round their necks, are exceedingly dirty, a dab or two of red paint on their cheeks and just down the parting of the hair, old shawls and print dresses that might have lain by in a rag shop for years without getting their present musty appearance. Two of them are busily engaged, one actively the other passively, in an entomological hunt of a peculiar nature and evidently with great success securing I am sure a fine bag of game.[95]

Even though this family was literally at his door-step, Burnaby adopted the stance of the outside observer called for by the ethnographic manners and customs discourse favoured by European travel writers of the time.[96]

Pratt argues that such portraits are complementary to the construction of colonial space as landscapes because both represent abstractions, and both are ultimately aimed at capitalist exploitation of their subjects, but – even though his business depended on trade with the First Nations – Burnaby saw no place for them in the colony's future.[97] A more obvious link between the physical and human landscapes, as far as he and his fellow Englishmen are concerned, was that the natural abundance of the Northwest coast made it too easy for the indigenous peoples to survive with minimal effort by fishing for salmon and gathering berries and other "wild" produce. Burnaby complained that "None of them seem to have any idea of any improvement or advancement, in their trails thro' the woods they will not remove a twig or bough they can pass under or step over, their houses are miserable huts, just a few boards and sticks laid together with a slanting roof, fire on the floor and all the place full of smoke, dirty and wretched." He was particularly appalled that the men would gamble all their possessions away, or give them away in potlatches, though he considered the latter events to be exotic enough to describe them in detail.[98]

The only positive comments Burnaby made about British Columbia's indigenous peoples were reserved for those who visited from far up the coast and the Queen Charlotte Islands: "These tribes, 'the Stickeens, Hyders, Bella Bella's' etc. are more hardy and warlike than the Indians round these parts, muscular and tall, and all being more industrious, skilful in carving and metal work and shewing greater capabilities for self government and civilization." Burnaby regretted, however, that "their contact with white folks has taught them all the vices and positively none of the virtues of the superior race." Exactly how superior that race considered itself to be was illustrated in Burnaby's next letter to his mother when he wrote that two of the northern chiefs, when imprisoned for drunkenness, "drew their knives and slashed about right and left, till they were both shot dead which was very soon, they luckily did no damage of any moment to the officers."[99]

Just as he failed to eroticize the landscape in the manner said to be characteristic of colonializing males, so Burnaby expressed little sexual interest in Aboriginal women despite the lack of White females in the colony. Describing the young mixed-blood women (identified derogatively as Sitcums) who attended the balls in Victoria, Burnaby noted that, their vivacity aside, "you can detect in their black eyes, high cheek bones, and flattened head whence they came." Burnaby felt free, however, to express his attraction to a man he identified as "a Canadian

Indian from far away up the country now staying in our rooms." He wrote to his brother that "he is a fine fellow with raven black hair and such eyes, speaks broken French, and tells marvels about quartz and gold in the upper country, I should like to keep him as a servant and bring him to England with me one of these days."[100]

Perhaps not surprisingly, Burnaby never married,[101] but, whatever his sexual proclivities were, not all the men he admired were young and handsome. He also described the old voyageur Presse as "one of a singular class of men who have lived all their lives in this rough camp fashion, seems as if an iron constitution were united with a mind full of resources. Sallow complexion, dark piercing eyes, hook nose, long raven hair, a care worn expression in his face, spare of body, very quiet and always doing something."[102] Robert Brown's account of his Vancouver Island expedition included a similar figure, the slightly sinister one-armed Tomo, son of an Iroquois voyageur from Canada and a Chinook woman from the Columbia River, and "famous among hunters and trappers from Vancouver Island to Rupert's Land."[103] These old men were held in some awe because of their survival skills, and because of the part they had played in advancing the fur trade frontier westward. They may have symbolized the past, but by working as guides they could be romanticized as agents of imperial progress, while no language was too pejorative for the more independent Aboriginals. Their economic activities, based on traditional practices that did not alter the environment in easily discernable ways, were perceived to be of only temporary importance. Their presence was, therefore, little more than a blight on the landscape to most of the English observers, including those who joined the gold rush. W. Champness, for example, wrote that "The native races of British Columbia exist in a condition of even greater degradation and squalor than the other aboriginal tribes of the Far West. Many of them inhabit holes and caves; others move about and erect temporary tents or huts of bark ... They are exceedingly filthy in their mode of life, swarm with vermin, are very licentious, superstitious, and cruel."[104]

Harry Guillod's initial impression of the First Nations was much the same. He confided in his diary:

> A journey out here soon destroys all romantic illusions with regard to the Indians; instead of anything noble they are dirty, immoral and fond of tawdry finery ... The favorite dress of the men seems to be a common cap with a band of tinsel paper round it[,] a rusty black coat, cast off trousers

> of any colour and boots. When they want to be swellish, they streak their faces with vermillion and put on one of the wonderful large necklaces, the cloth coat with these additions making a 'tout ensemble' difficult to imagine. The women are mostly in old gowns or dirty blankets; the more fortunate with an ornamentation of red paint and some even wear crinoline for I have seen them here and farther up with that adornment.[105]

But Guillod's own standards of hygiene and dress necessarily became more relaxed during his wilderness sojourn, and he gained some respect for the ability of the Natives to survive in this harsh environment after he came to depend upon them for food when he was hungry, and for directions when he was hopelessly lost. Unlike most of his fellow Englishmen, Guillod did not moralize about Aboriginal "idleness," remarking at one point that "An Indian indeed will pack a hundredweight, and make money at the work but I found that I could not get along comfortably with more than thirty pounds, and that was quite enough to destroy all the pleasure of walking on a trail of this sort."[106] Guillod was the only writer to describe prolonged personal interaction with First Nations, aside from the occasional hired guide, so perhaps it is not surprising that he became a catechist in several of the Church of England's Native missions, as well as an "Indian" agent.[107]

As one would expect of a missionary, Bishop Hills never allowed himself to use the pejorative terms about the First Nations that are to be found in the letters, journals and memoirs of his fellow English newcomers.[108] For example, after visiting one Songhee lodge in Victoria where he found a woman weaving a mat from rushes and grasses, and a man making a paddle, Hills observed that "I was struck by the industrious character of these poor people." He also described how Natives netted salmon from their canoes, and reported that they played a key role in transporting goods and people to and from the mining camps. Ascending the Fraser, Hills remarked how "The Indians seemed to love danger & the sight of a breaking, foaming, roaring cascade, up which our frail bark was to ascend, inspired them with ardour." He admired, as well, one group speeding down the river wearing shirts of red, orange, and various other colours "which with their black flowing hair & handsome painted canoe with rising prow formed a romantic & pleasing sight." Hills noted approvingly that the women in this canoe paddled with as much strength as the men. He also observed, without the moralization that characterized most British observers of indigenous societies, that women carried the heavier loads along trails in the Fraser Canyon where the footing in places was not more than half an inch.[109]

Rather than being entirely fatalistic about the future of the First Nations, Hills assumed that it was his church's role to improve their lives and save their souls by educating and converting them. While he admired the Aboriginals as people, he felt they were living in a primitive – indeed fallen – state. Towards the end of his first year in the colony, Hills speculated as follows:

> You enter an Indian abode. You are struck with fine manly form, the bright & intelligent countenance, the majestic gait, the eloquent attitudes of the Indian. In the women too, there is a grace, a softness of voice, a truly feminine submission, and sometimes even a beauty. But all else is utterly out of place. These noble forms are crouched upon the damp & filthy ground. Fish & decayed flesh render unbearable the atmosphere, they are eaten up by vermin & dirt. They paint their faces, sometimes all of the brightest red, or striped, or black. They scrape their faces at times until the skin is torn, they make cuts in the lip to make it protrude in the most forbidding manner, of clothing they have little or none. Yet the cold winds & frosts & rain mercilessly enter & spread death around. Infants are subjected to the torture of flattening the skull, til the head is squeezed into all sorts of shapes.

Hills concluded that none of these conditions reflected "the true native character which belongs to those beautiful specimens of the Creator's work. No they are fallen from Nature." Only "Christian civilization" could bring them back to "true nature" and "teach them to live for the true object of human existence."[110] This theme of degradation from a once-noble past was common to most of the colonial observers we have examined. The main difference in Bishop Hills' case was that he believed that the First Nations' full human "nature" could be restored through Christianization and assimilation, while the other newcomers – Guillod aside – adopted a more Darwinian perspective.

Conclusion

Questioning the value of focusing on explorer/settler perceptions, Cole Harris has argued that more concrete forms of power should be privileged in historical studies of British Columbia because the colonial project there was essentially about displacing Natives to make way for White settlers.[111] To this standard critique of postcolonial history,

Kathleen Wilson has responded that "the maintenance of European national identities and ties were [*sic*] as crucial as settlement to the legitimization of claims of legal and political 'dominium,' or territorial possession and rights to govern."[112] Travel narratives played a vital role in this process, for Margaret Hunt claims that they "helped change racism from a rather unsystematic, if nonetheless widely held, medley of popular beliefs into an elaborately worked out taxonomy that embraced the entire globe; made claims to be scientific; and situated Europeans, and especially the English, at the pinnacle of the racial hierarchy."[113] The confinement of British Columbia's Indigenous peoples to small economically unviable reserves was probably due less to the threat they represented to the "colonial project" than to the hardening racial attitudes of the colonial era.[114]

Perhaps the most striking feature of the narratives produced by the middle-class Englishmen who visited Britain's northern Pacific colonies is the sharp contrast between the almost idyllic images of the rugged physical landscape and the often jarringly pejorative descriptions of the Native peoples. One might ascribe these polarities to a subconscious attempt to compensate for appearing too feminine on the one hand, and too lacking in sensitivity on the other, although genteel British women could be equally contemptuous in their descriptions of the social "inferiors" they met in the colonies.[115] Certainly, the disjuncture between the descriptions of the physical environment and the Natives who inhabited it had not been typical of the earlier colonizing eye, for the Jesuits of New France, like the Puritans of New England and the Protestant missionaries in the Prairie West, depicted the wilderness as a desert or wasteland in order to convey metaphorically the spiritual condition of the indigenous peoples.[116] Indeed, eighteenth-century science posited a direct link between human bodies and their natural environments, making it possible – Alan Bewell claims – "for writers to draw parallels between the 'geography of places' and the 'geography of peoples.'"[117] Elizabeth Vibert notes, for example, that when the fur traders of the Columbia Plateau "were among people they considered hostile, the landscape too took a hostile turn."[118]

Perceptions had obviously changed by the gold rush era, even in inland areas of British Columbia where the biblical identification of wilderness with desert made nearly as much sense as in the Prairies. One possible reason, aside from the emergence of scientific racism by 1858, is that imbedded in the eighteenth-century link between the physical environment and the people who inhabited it, according to Bewell, was the notion that "the ideal environment for human development ... was one that encouraged human beings to improve it."[119] This, British Columbia, with its abundant salmon and other fish, wild game, and edible plants, apparently did not do.[120] Indeed, the First Nations of the more environmentally challenging interior were considered to be superior in every respect to those on the coast, and those on the North coast superior to those further south, just as those who hunted buffalo in the Plateau region of northwestern North America were considered by British fur traders to be superior to those in the same region who relied largely on fishing.[121]

As for the role of gender, Sara Suleri argues that it was the distinctive colonializing role of British women in India to produce visual and verbal representations that temporarily converted all subcontinental threats into watercolours,[122] but much the same role was assumed by middle-class British men in British Columbia, as it undoubtedly was in other colonial environments. The picturesque views of the landscape – like the distancing images of the indigenous inhabitants and the close-up idyllic descriptions of the natural environment – would also serve to dispel any fears that the newcomers were experiencing a cultural regression on this remote and challenging frontier of civilization.[123] In short, the picturesque landscape perspective was quite compatible with the rule of a male-dominated colonial elite, for – as a form of anti-conquest – it reflected a confident sense of refined superiority that, in their view, made their mission a truly civilizing one.

NOTES

1 Kinahan Cornwallis, *The New El Dorado; or British Columbia* (London: Thomas Cautley Newby, 1858), xiii–xiv. (Canadian Institute for Historical Microreproductions [hereafter CIHM] 33342).

2 Paul Phillips, "Confederation and the Economy of British Columbia," in W. George Shelton, ed., *British Columbia and Confederation* (Victoria: University of Victoria, 1967), 46; Sharon Meen, "Colonial Society and Economy," in Hugh J.M. Johnston, ed., *The Pacific Province: A History of British Columbia* (Vancouver: Douglas and McIntyre, 1996), 112–13; Cole Harris, *The Resettlement of British Columbia: Essays on Colonialism and Geographical Change* (Vancouver: UBC Press, 1998), 30, 146, 281n12.

3 Harris, *Resettlement*, 68. On the economic development of this era, see Harris, *Resettlement*, chapter 3; and Mean, "Colonial Society," 99–112.

4 Derek Gregory, "(Post)Colonialism and the Production of Nature," in Noel Castree and Bruce Braun, eds, *Social Nature: Theory, Practice and Politics* (Malden, MA: Blackwell, 2001), 85.
5 Daniel Clayton, *Islands of Truth: The Imperial Fashioning of Vancouver Island*, (Vancouver: UBC Press, 2000).
6 Elizabeth Vibert, *Traders' Tales: Narratives of Cultural Encounters in the Columbia Plateau, 1807–1846* (Norman, OK: University of Oklahoma Press, 1997), chapter 3; Noel Elizabeth Currie, *Constructing Colonial Discourse: Captain Cook at Nootka Sound* (Montreal and Kingston: McGill-Queen's University Press, 2005). A study of photography, which was first introduced to British Columbia in 1859, pays little attention to the wilderness landscape, stating that the main preoccupations in the colonial era were "the orderly march of Euro-American settlements and [...] the acculturation of indigenous inhabitants." Carol J. Williams, *Framing the West: Race, Gender, and the Photographic Frontier in the Pacific Northwest* (Oxford: Oxford University Press, 2003), 7.
7 Margaret Hunt, "Racism, Imperialism, and the Traveler's Gaze in Eighteenth-Century England," *Journal of British Studies* 32 (1993): 338.
8 See, for example, Alexander Rattray, *Vancouver Island and British Columbia, where they are; and what they may become* (London: Smith, Elder and Co., 1862) [CIHM 39818]; and William Carew Hazlett, *The Great Gold Fields of Cariboo* (1862, reprinted [Victoria]: Klanak Press, 1974). Robert Brown wrote to a friend in 1872 that there had been so many books published on travel in British Columbia and Vancouver Island, that those by Mayne, Whymper, and others were commercial failures. Berenice Gilmore, *Artists Overland: A Visual Record of British Columbia, 1793–1886* (Burnaby: Burnaby Art Gallery, 1980), 58.
9 On the significance of the editing process, see I.S. MacLaren, "Exploration/Travel Literature and the Evolution of the Author," *International Journal of Canadian Studies* 5 (1992): 39–68; and Currie, *Constructing*.
10 For one female perspective, focused on the Victoria area and published many years after the author had returned to England, see Eleanor Smyth, *An Octogenarian's Reminiscences* (Letchworth, Eng.: s.n, 1916).
11 Mary Louise Pratt, *Imperial Eyes: Travel Writing and Transculturation* (London: Routledge, 1992), 213.
12 Susan Morgan, *Place Matters: Gendered Geography in Victorian Women's Travel Books About Southeast Asia* (New Brunswick, NJ: Rutgers University Press, 1996), 15.
13 Cheryl McEwan, *Gender, Geography and Empire: Victorian Women Travellers in West Africa* (Aldershot, UK: Ashgate, 2000), 65–6; Anne McClintock, *Imperial Leather: Race, Gender and Sexuality in the Colonial Contest* (New York: Routledge, 1995), 23.

14 Annette Kolodny, *The Land Before Her: Fantasy and Experience of the American Frontiers, 1630–1860* (Chapel Hill: University of North Carolina Press, 1984), 12. For a critical commentary on Kolodny's thesis, see Karen Dubinsky, "'The pleasure is exquisite but violent': The Imaginary Geography of Niagara Falls in the Nineteenth Century," *Journal of Canadian Studies* 29 (1994): 80–1.

15 Simon Ryan applies the same Freudian-type analysis to early nineteenth-century Australian explorers, even while demonstrating that they resorted to the picturesque convention. Simon Ryan, *The Cartographic Eye: How Explorers Saw Australia* (Cambridge: Cambridge University Press, 1996), chapters 3 and 7.

16 Currie (*Constructing*, 45) writes that Burke's definition of the beautiful "rested on notions of male power over women," while the sublime "made the male viewer feel like a woman, smaller and weaker than the object viewed, perhaps the cause of psychic terror." The picturesque is obviously more androgynous, for Linda Revie identifies it as male, while Elizabeth McKinsey argues that it was female. Linda L. Revie, *The Niagara Companion: Explorers, Artists, and Writers at the Falls, from Discovery through the Twentieth Century* (Waterloo, ON: Wilfrid Laurier University Press, 2002), 8, 116; Elizabeth McKinsey, *Niagara Falls: Icon of the American Sublime* (Cambridge, MA: Harvard University Press, 1985), 170–1.

17 Keith Thomas, *Man and the Natural World: Changing Attitudes in England, 1500–1800* (London: Allen Lane, 1983), 264, 267.

18 Currie, *Constructing*, 46. See also Ryan, *Cartographic Eye*, 58; and I.S. MacLaren, "Retaining Captaincy of the Soul: Response to Nature in the First Franklin Expedition," *Essays on Canadian Writing* 28 (Spring 1984): 59–60.

19 Hugh Honour, *The New Golden Land: European Images of America from the Discoveries to the Present Time* (New York: Pantheon Books, 1975), 197–8; Terry Abraham, *Mountains So Sublime: Nineteenth-Century British Travellers and the Lure of the Rocky Mountain West* (Calgary: University of Calgary Press, 2006), 74–5.

20 Christopher Mulvey, "Ecriture and Landscape: British Writing on Post-Revolutionary America," in Mick Gidley and Robert Lawson-Peebles, *Views of American Landscapes* (Cambridge and New York: Cambridge University Press, 1989), 103–4.

21 Maria Tippett and Douglas Cole, *From Desolation, From Desolation to Splendour: Changing Perceptions of the British Columbia Landscape* (Toronto: Clarke, Irwin, 1977), 16, 26–7.

22 W. Colquhoun Grant, "Description of Vancouver Island," *Journal of the Royal Geographical Society* 26 (1852): 269, 272 [CIHM 18767]; Tippett and Cole, *From Desolation*, 30.

23 Grant, "Description," 282.

24 Gilmore, *Artists Overland*, 17–18. British poets and artists had long depicted the Alps almost exclusively in terms of the awe-inspiring sublime, but Burke's sublime had been tempered by this time to evoke spirituality rather than tumult, vastness, and obscurity, and, much to the chagrin of John Ruskin, mountaineering clubs and tourism had diminished the mystique of the Alps. See Marjorie Hope Nicholson, *Mountain Gloom and Mountain Glory: The Development of the Aesthetic of the Infinite* (New York: W.W. Norton, 1963); Simon Schama, *Landscape and Memory* (Toronto: Random House, 1995), 490–513; and Currie, *Constructing*, 47.

25 The British surveyors, Palliser and Hind, depicted the Prairie grasslands in terms of the sublime, and the parklands (which they felt were much more suitable for colonization) as picturesque. I.S. MacLaren, "Aesthetic Mappings of the West by the Palliser and Hind Survey Expeditions, 1857–1859," *Studies in Canadian Literature* 10, nos 1–2 (1985), 24–52. See also Greg Gillespie, "'I Was Well Pleased with Our Sport among the Buffalo': Big-Game Hunters, Travel Writing, and Cultural Imperialism in the British North American West, 1847–72," *Canadian Historical Review* 83, no. 4 (2002): 555–84.

26 Tippet and Cole, *From Desolation*, 29–30.

27 Anne Burnaby McLeod and Pixie McGeachie, eds, *Land of Promise: Robert Burnaby's Letters from Colonial British Columbia, 1858–1863* (Burnaby, BC: City of Burnaby, 2002), 58, 62–3.

28 John Keast Lord, *The Naturalist in Vancouver Island and British Columbia* (London: R. Bentley, 1866), 36.

29 Roberta L. Bagshaw, *No Better Land: The 1860 Diaries of the Anglican Colonial Bishop George Hills* (Victoria, BC: Sono Nis Press, 1996), 249, 252. Only the first year of Bishop Hills' thirty-three-year diary has been published. It is this volume that will be referred to in this essay.

30 MacLaren, "Aesthetic Mappings," 30; Ryan, *Cartographic Eye*, 62. Arnold states that "invoking comparisons and seeing resemblances was thought to aid critical observation and facilitate subsequent reflectionist recall." Arnold, *The Tropics*, 98.

31 Peters, *Painting*, 16. Brown was accompanied by the artist and writer, Frederick Whymper, who took part in the colony's two other major expeditions during the 1860s, and whose scenes, with a couple of interesting exceptions, are distinctly picturesque. Gilmore, *Artists Overland*, 49–51, 92–7; and Tippett and Cole, *From Desolation*, 40–4.

32 Robert Brown, "The First Journey of Exploration across Vancouver Island," in H.W. Bates, ed., *Illustrated Travels: A Record of Discovery,*

Geography, and Adventure (London: Cassell, Petter, and Galpin [n.d]), 254–5 [CIHM 15273].

33 Brown, "First Journey," 304.

34 Felix Driver and Luciana Martins, "Views and Visions of the Tropical World," in Felix Driver and Luciana Martins, eds, *Tropical Visions in an Age of Empire* (Chicago: University of Chicago Press, 2005), 6–7.

35 Pratt, *Imperial Eyes*, 27–8, 33. Onno Oerlemans states that thick description (in his words, "nature as material essence") was typical of both male and female Victorian travel literature. Onno Oerlemans, *Romanticism and the Materiality of Nature* (Toronto: University of Toronto Press, 2004), chapter 5, especially 180–1. But Pratt (*Imperial Eyes*, 50) contradicts this statement, as well as herself, by stating that "no world is more androcentric than that of natural history." On botanical science and colonization, see Richard Drayton, *Nature's Government: Science, Imperial Britain and the 'Improvement' of the World* (New Haven: Yale University Press, 2000); and Arnold, *The Tropics*, chapter 6.

36 Brown, "First Journey," 350.

37 Jonathan Raban, *Passage to Juneau: A Sea and Its Meanings* (New York: Vintage Books, 1999), 160.

38 Allan Pritchard, ed., *Vancouver Island Letters of Edmund Hope Verney, 1862–65* (Vancouver: UBC Press, 1996), 94.

39 Pritchard, *Vancouver Island Letters*, 169–72.

40 Ryan, *Cartographic Eye*, 90–100.

41 Dwight Smith, ed., *A Tour of Duty in the Pacific Northwest: E.A. Porcher and H.M.S. 'Sparrowhawk,' 1865–1868* (Fairbanks: University of Alaska Press, 2000), 92.

42 Lord, *The Naturalist*, 157.

43 Lord, *The Naturalist*, 162.

44 Reprinted in Willard Ireland, ed., "First Impressions: Letter of Colonel Richard Clement Moody, R.E., to Arthur Blackwood, 1 February 1859," *British Columbia Historical Quarterly* 15 (1951): 92. See also Governor Douglas's picturesque imagery of the lower Fraser Valley as quoted in Commander R.C. Mayne, *Four Years in British Columbia and Vancouver Island* (London: John Murray, 1862), 391–2 [CIHM 36542].

45 McLeod and McGeachie, *Land of Promise*, 69.

46 McLeod and McGeachie, *Land of Promise*, 95.

47 Pratt, *Imperial Eyes*, 204–5.

48 McEwan, *Geography, Gender, and Empire*, 76.

49 McLeod and McGeachie, *Land of Promise*, 78. In a later letter (*Land of Promise*, 96), Burnaby wrote that "the ferns and wildflowers and fruits are

abundant everywhere, roses, lupins, guelder roses, syringas, maidenhead fern, and variety on variety, salmonberry like monster raspberries with the flavor of blackberries, blue berries and whortle berries and now forming the brambleberry and cranberry." McLeod and McGeachie, *Land of Promise*, 96. On the popularity of the flower garden in England, see Thomas, *Man and the Natural World*, 223–41.

50 McEwan, *Geography, Gender and Empire*, 80; Kolodny, *Land Before Her*, xiii, 7–12.

51 McLeod and McGeachie, *Land of Promise*, 74.

52 Pratt, *Imperial Eyes*, 56–7.

53 McLeod and McGeachie, *Land of Promise*, 74.

54 McEwan, *Gender, Geography, and Empire*, 76–9. Further support for my argument can be found in Kate Teltscher, "Writing Home and Crossing Cultures: George Bogle in Bengal and Tibet, 1770–1775," in Kathleen Wilson, ed., *A New Imperial History: Culture, Identity, and Modernity in Britain and the Empire* (Cambridge: Cambridge University Press, 2004).

55 McLeod and McGeachie, *Land of Promise*, 75–6.

56 McLeod and McGeachie, *Land of Promise*, 79, 98, 111.

57 Lord, *The Naturalist*, 347–8.

58 Tippett and Cole, *From Desolation*, 25–6.

59 Vibert, *Traders' Tales*, 84–104; James R. Gibson, *Farming the Frontier: The Agricultural Opening of the Oregon Country, 1786–1846* (Vancouver: UBC Press, 1985), 194.

60 Tippett and Cole, *From Desolation*, 32. Similarly, Terry Abraham (*Mountains So Sublime*) states that the nineteenth century British traveler generally saw the Rockies as sublime, yet – aside from the examples in his chapter 5 – most of the excerpts he selected from their writings either conform to the picturesque convention or are a somewhat confused combination of the two.

61 Mayne, *Four Years*, 105; Tippett and Cole, *From Desolation*, 35. Interestingly enough, Tippett and Cole point out that while the descriptions of the Rocky Mountains in Lieutenant Henry J. Warre's published narrative are "clichéd and conventional," in his private journal they "are kept in reserved perspective and are genuine and convincing." *From Desolation*, 34.

62 Mayne, *Four Years*, 95. Mayne commanded the survey ship, *Plumper*, but was also sent on a lengthy inland reconnaissance tour in 1859. Gilmore, *Artists Overland*, 39.

63 Tippett and Cole, *From Desolation*, 35; Capt. C.E. Barrett-Lennard, *Travels in British Columbia* (London: Hurst and Blackett, 1862), 142–4 [CIHM 27936].

64 Gilmore, *Artists Overland*, 40.
65 Mayne, *Four Years*, 112, 115, 132.
66 See the discussion of this expedition in Harris, *Resettlement*, 114–18.
67 Bagshaw, *No Better Land*, 119, 125, 127.
68 Bagshaw, *No Better Land*, 160, 169, 180.
69 Cornwallis, *New El Dorado*, 208.
70 Cornwallis, *New El Dorado*, 212–13.
71 Cornwallis, *New El Dorado*, xvi–xvii.
72 D. Graham Burnett, *Masters of All They Surveyed: Exploration, Geography, and a British El Dorado* (Chicago: University of Chicago Press, 2000), 11. For a contemporary description of the young English gold seekers of 1862, see Eleanor Smyth, *An Octogenarian's Reminiscences* (Letchworth, Eng.: s.n., 1916), chapter 10.
73 W. Champness, "To Cariboo and Back: An Emigrant's Journey to the Gold Fields of British Columbia" (from the "Leisure Hour," 1862), 260 [CIHM 16722].
74 Champness, "To Cariboo," 246–8.
75 William Mark, *Cariboo: A True and Correct Narrative* (Stockton: William Wright, 1863), 3, 18–19. CIHM no. 17146. Emmerson complained that Frazer had written glowing reports of the Cariboo while neglecting to report the considerable funds required to reach the mines as well as exploit them. John Emmerson, *British Columbia and Vancouver Island: Voyages, Travels and Adventures* (Durham, UK: s.n., 1865), 92–6 [CIHM 64030].
76 Mark, *Cariboo*, 31.
77 Mark, *Cariboo*, 34.
78 "Harry Guillod's Journal of a Trip to Cariboo, 1862," *British Columbia Historical Quarterly* 19 (1955): 199, 203.
79 "Harry Guillod's Journal," 205.
80 "Harry Guillod's Journal," 209, 229.
81 "Harry Guillod's Journal," 195.
82 Pratt, *Imperial Eyes*, 77–8, 85. Another gold rush narrative of this type is R. Byron Johnson, *Very Far West Indeed: A Few Rough Experiences on the North-West Pacific Coast* (London: Sampson Low, Marston, Low, and Searle, 1872).
83 Cornwallis, *The New El Dorado*, 240–2.
84 Harris, *The Resettlement*, chapter 1.
85 See Catherine Hall, *Civilising Subjects: Metropole and Colony in the English Imagination, 1830–1867* (London: Polity Press, 2002), especially chapter 4.
86 Grant, "Description," 300–1.

87 Françoise Barret-Ducrocq, *Love in the Time of Victoria: Sexuality, Class, and Gender in Nineteenth-Century London* (London and New York: Verso, 1991).
88 Grant, "Description," 305.
89 Brown, "First Journey," 274, 276.
90 On the role of the naval gunboats on colonial British Columbia's coast, see Barry M. Gough, *Gunboat Frontier: British Maritime Authority and Northwest Coast Indians, 1846–1890* (Vancouver: UBC Press, 1984).
91 Pritchard, *Vancouver Island Letters*, 38–43, 62, 151, 157, 167, 171. Commander Mayne's explanation for the superiority of the "inland tribes" over the "Fish-eating Indians" was that "the athletic pursuits and sports" of the former were much more conducive to "healthy physical development than the life of the Coast Indian passed, as it is, almost entirely in his canoe, in which he sits curled up like a Turk." Mayne, *Four Years*, 242. See also Grant, *Description*, 296–7; and Elizabeth Vibert, "Real Men Hunt Buffalo: Masculinity, Race, and Class in British Fur Trappers' Narratives," in Joy Parr and Mark Rosenfeld, eds, *Gender and History in Canada* (Mississauga, ON: Copp Clark, 1996).
92 Although he played down the physical differences between coastal and interior Natives, Barrett-Lennard wrote that "the physical attributes" of the tribes from the north "are superior to those of the dwellers in the south." Barrett-Lennard, *Travels in British Columbia*, 41, 44–6.
93 Lord, *The Naturalist*, 64–5.
94 Lord, *The Naturalist*, 94.
95 McLeod and McGeachie, *Land of Promise*, 97, 107.
96 Pratt, *Imperial Eyes*, 120–1; Ryan, *Cartographic Eye*, 132–4.
97 Pratt, *Imperial Eyes*, 64–5; McLeod and McGeachie, *Land of Promise*, 126, 140, 149. Burnaby became a Victoria merchant in 1859.
98 McLeod and McGeachie, *Land of Promise*, 111, 144, 151–2. On the invention of the concept of idleness, see McClintock, *Imperial Leather*, 252–3; William Cronon, *Changes in the Land: Indians, Colonists, and the Ecology of New England* (New York: Hill and Wang, 1989), 35, 53, 56, 79; and Vibert, *Traders' Tales*, 120–7. On gambling as a method of exchange, see Vibert, *Traders' Tales*, 140–4.
99 McLeod and McGeachie, *Land of Promise*, 143, 147.
100 McLeod and McGeachie, *Land of Promise*, 59, 65, 67, 131.
101 On homosocial culture in colonial British Columbia, see Adele Perry, *On the Edge of Empire: Gender, Race, and the Making of British Columbia, 1849–1871* (Toronto: University of Toronto Press, 2001).
102 McLeod and McGeachie, *Land of Promise*, 76.
103 Brown, "First Journey," 275.

104 Champness, *To Cariboo*, 23. See also Emmerson, *British Columbia*, 50–2; and Mark, *Cariboo*, 20, 23.
105 "Harry Guillod's Journal," 200.
106 "Harry Guillod's Journal," 211. On the responses of the First Nations of the Fraser Valley to the gold rush, see Harris, *Resettlement*, chapter 4.
107 "Harry Guillod's Journal," 191–3.
108 Kim Greenwell states, on the other hand, that the missionaries' pictorial images of unassimilated Natives were entirely degrading. "Picturing 'Civilization': Missionary Narratives and the Margins of Mimicry," *BC Studies* no. 135 (2002): 3–45.
109 Bagshaw, *No Better Land*, 56, 75, 114–16, 127, 143, 152, 155, 252–3, 258. John Emmerson's critical view concerning the First Nations' gendered division of labour (Emmerson, *British Columbia*, 49–50) was much more typical, for European Enlightenment thinkers had weighed the relative advancement of a society by the degree to which its women no longer served as "beasts of burden." Alan Bewell, "Constructed Places, Constructed Peoples: Charting the Improvement of the Female Body in the Pacific," *Eighteenth-Century Life* 18 (1994): 48–52. See also Gail Bederman, *Manliness and Civilization: A Cultural History of Gender and Race in the United States, 1880–1917* (Chicago: University of Chicago Press, 1995) 25, 27–8; and Vibert, *Traders' Tales*, 127–31.
110 Bagshaw, *No Better Land*, 270–1.
111 Cole Harris, "How Did Colonialism Dispossess? Comments from an Edge of Empire," *Annals of the Association of American Geographers* 94 (2004): 165–82.
112 Wilson, "Introduction," 4. On the imperial "vision" or "gaze" see Arnold, *The Tropics*, 6, 28–9; and on the materiality of discourse see Beth Tobin, *Colonizing Nature: The Tropics in British Arts and Letters, 1760–1820* (Philadelphia: University of Pennsylvania Press, 2005), 14. Also, John Sandlos makes a direct link between the European and Canadian aesthetic vision of the North and the displacement of Aboriginal caribou hunters. See his "From the Outside Looking In: Aesthetics, Politics, and Wildlife Conservation in the Canadian North," *Environmental History* 6, no. 1 (2001): 6–31.
113 Hunt, "Racism, Imperialism," 346.
114 Harris examines these attitudes in *Making Colonial Space: Colonialism, Resistance, and Reserves in British Columbia* (Vancouver: UBC Press, 2002), 50–6.
115 See, for example, Lucy Peel's many pejorative descriptions of her American neighbours in J.I. Little, ed., *Love Strong as Death: Lucy Peel's*

Canadian Journal, 1833–1836 (Waterloo, ON: Wilfrid Laurier University Press, 2001).

116 Carole Blackburn, *Harvest of Souls: The Jesuit Missions and Colonialism in North America, 1632–1650* (Montreal and Kingston: McGill-Queen's University Press, 2000), 48–9; Roderick Nash, *Wilderness and the American Mind* (New Haven: Yale University Press, third edition, 1982), 34–7; Doug Owram, *Promise of Eden: The Canadian Expansionist Movement and the Idea of the West, 1856–1900* (Toronto: University of Toronto Press, 1980), 24; A.A. Den Otter, "'The wilderness will rejoice and blossom like the crocus': Bishop David Anderson's Perceptions of Wilderness and Civilization in Rupert's Land," *Historical Papers 2001: Canadian Society of Church History*, 94.

117 Bewell, "Constructed Places," 38. On this theme, see also chapter 6 in this volume.

118 Vibert, *Traders' Tales*, 104.

119 Bewell, "Constructed Places," 46. See also Hall, *Civilising Subjects*, 217, 250.

120 Only recently have researchers discovered that Northwest coast Natives depended upon estuarine gardens for a substantial proportion of their diet. See Douglas Duer and Nancy Turner, eds, *Keeping It Living: Traditions of Plant Use and Cultivation on the Northwest Coast of North America* (Seattle: University of Washington Press; Vancouver: UBC Press, 2005).

121 See Vibert, "Real Men Hunt Buffalo," 4–21.

122 Sara Suleri, *The Rhetoric of English India* (Chicago: University of Chicago Press, 1992), 75–6. For a useful discussion of this theme from a Canadian perspective, see Suzanne James, "Gathering Up the Threads: Generic and Discursive Patterns in Catharine Parr Traill's *The Backwoods of Canada*" (PhD dissertation, Simon Fraser University, 2003), chapter 5.

123 On the fear of cultural regression, see John Darwin, "Civility and Empire," in Peter Burke, Brian Harrison, and Paul Slack, eds, *Civil Histories: Essays Presented to Sir Keith Thomas* (New York: Oxford University Press, 2000); and Ana Laura Stoler and Frederick Cooper, "Between Metropole and Colony – Rethinking a Research Agenda," in Frederick Cooper and Ana Laura Stoler, eds, *Tensions of Empire: Colonial Cultures in a Bourgeois World* (Berkeley: University of California Press, 1997), 2–3.

4 Scenic Tourism on a Canadian-American Borderland: Lake Memphremagog's Steamboat Excursions and Resort Hotels, 1850–1900

In 1926 the Newport, Vermont printer, William Bryant Bullock, described the "bewitching scene" on Lake Memphremagog as he imagined it would have unfolded for the lake's first settler, Nicholas Austin, a Loyalist from New Hampshire.[1] Setting out by canoe in 1791 from the lake's southern tip, Austin would have viewed "emerald islands scattered in profusion upon the cerulean expanse of the lake; the jutting points and promontories; the sylvan bays lined with pebbled beaches; the receding vistas of headlands, shores and mountains, bathed in the soft glow of the summer sunshine." Further north, having crossed into the British colony of Quebec, he would have been awed by "the rugged grandeur of Owl's Head, the towering highlands of Magoon's Ridge and the uneven heights of Sugarloaf Mt."[2] Austin and the American settlers who followed in his footsteps likely had more pressing preoccupations than the scenery, but Bullock was drawing on imagery that had long been used to promote local tourism. Following the norms defined in late eighteenth-century England by Edmund Burke, William Gilpin, and others, local newspapers and railway guidebooks described the view from the deck of a steamboat as it crossed the forty-fifth parallel and sailed northward into the "wilderness" of Canada as transforming from the beautiful, to the picturesque, to the sublime.[3]

Historians have tended to associate the passenger experience aboard steamboats with that on trains which, cultural historian Wolfgang Schivelbusch notes, restricted the view and superimposed modern, metropolitan concepts of time and space over traditional, local ones.[4] But Lake Memphremagog's steamers zig-zagged between small settlements, resort hotels, and even the docks of the wealthy estate owners as they made their way up the lake (see figure 4.1).[5] During the 1880s

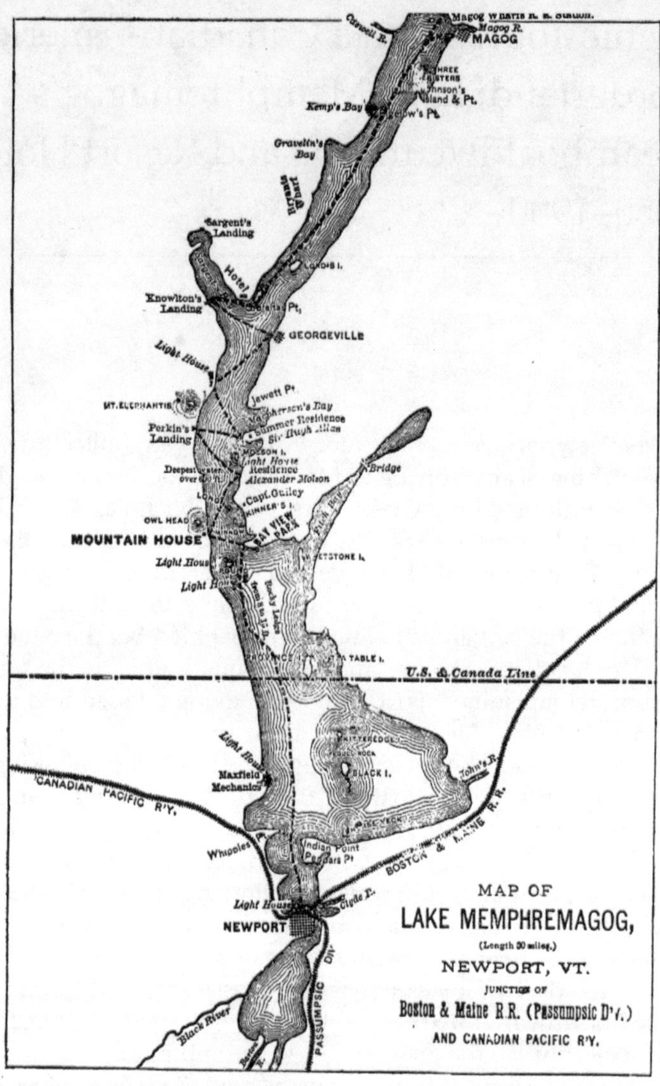

4.1 *Map of Lake Memphremagog* by Geo. C. Merrill. *Beautiful Memphremagog*. This map of the lake in the 1880s provides a good illustration of the rail and steamboat transportation network that focused on Newport and extended into Quebec during the latter half of the nineteenth century. Only after crossing into Quebec did steamers start to zigzag between resort hotels, summer estates, and small communities.

American historian Theodore Clarke Smith, who spent many summers at a local lakeside camp, recalled that the *Lady of the Lake* "was usually behind time." On one occasion, as the steamer approached Newport, the captain "glanced at his watch and observed 'Late is our watchword.'"[6] Reflecting the narrowness and great length of the lake, the view was described in the promotional literature as a slowly unfolding panorama, just as it was to steamboat tourists further south on the Connecticut and Hudson Rivers.[7]

The northern Appalachians generally become less elevated on the northern side of the border before ending at the St Lawrence Valley, and, as we saw in chapter 2, it was the picturesque pastoral nature of the Canadian region known as the Eastern Townships that was promoted in the 1830s by settlement brochures published by the British American Land Company. But the western shore of Lake Memphremagog is an exception in that it is more mountainous to the north, with the result that it became the focus of tourist brochures and landscape paintings after mid-century when railways finally made the region readily accessible.[8] Paradoxically, the fact that scenic tourism relied upon and encouraged a romantic, anti-modern sensibility did not prevent it from stimulating consumerism and capitalist expansion.[9] Although many studies of tourism have claimed that local economic development was sacrificed on the altar of a nostalgic rural myth that cast resident populations as passive victims of the "tourist gaze" (to use sociologist John Urry's term), the inhabitants of the Lake Memphremagog area attracted little interest as rustic relics of the past.[10] In fact, tourism provided a market for the area's farmers and labourers, and local entrepreneurs took part in the construction and operation of the steamboats and resort hotels. Furthermore, frequent descriptions of the scenic landscape in local newspapers encouraged inhabitants of this borderland region to join paddle-wheel excursions and to emulate the aesthetic sensitivity, well-regulated sociability, and consumption of leisure that characterized the urban middle-class tourist.[11]

Tourism developed relatively slowly in Vermont and the Eastern Townships not only because the region was not readily accessible by water but because it lacked the mineral springs that attracted vacationing upper-middle class individuals further south.[12] Mountain scenery was challenging mineral spas in popularity by the time railways began penetrating northern Vermont, but the state's Green Mountains and their Canadian counterparts were overshadowed by the more elevated White Mountains of New Hampshire and the Adirondacks of New

York.[13] The pastoral landscape of Vermont finally became popular in the last quarter of the nineteenth century with middle-class families eager to find a summer retreat from the pressures and temptations of big city life.[14] Farm vacations and abandoned farms were offered to urbanites seeking rural refuge and drawn to Vermont by its association with their country's rural, Jeffersonian heritage. On the Canadian side of the border, however, English-speaking farmers moving West simply sold their properties to French Canadians who were migrating into the region in increasing numbers.[15]

The main attraction for tourists in the Eastern Townships was its lakes. They were described in romantic terms by one promotional publication in 1860 as "its great glory," for "by them the glens, the mountains, and the woods are illumined, and its 'rivers made to sing for joy.'"[16] The largest and most accessible body of water in the region for American tourists is the scenic Lake Memphremagog, a little more than a quarter of which lies in Vermont.[17] The 43.5 kilometre-long lake, with depths to 208 metres, has several mountains on its western shore, the highest of which are Owl's Head (750 metres) and neighbouring Sugarloaf (later known as Mount Elephantis).[18] These mountains were rugged enough to warrant characterization of the area as the Switzerland or Geneva of Canada (or even America) by its more enthusiastic promoters, and to evoke the sublime in watercolours produced by well known itinerant English artist William Henry Bartlett when he visited the lake in 1838.[19] Just as late eighteenth-century English tourists viewed the Lake District as if it were a series of paintings by Claude Lorrain,[20] Bartlett's oft-imitated paintings provided an object lesson in how sensitive and knowledgeable individuals were supposed to view the scenic borderland landscape (see figure 4.2).

Lake Memphremagog's role as a trade route between Vermont and Lower Canada declined with the arrival of railways in the second half of the nineteenth century, but those railways did bring the promise of a lucrative tourist trade in search of scenic views as well as healthful air. Indeed, local entrepreneurs on both sides of the border were as quick as any in North America to capitalize on the growing middle-class desire to escape from the rapidly expanding cities for at least a short time during the summer. With the aid of outside capital, they built steamboats and resort hotels (see figure 4.3), relying upon guidebooks and newspaper correspondents to present an image of the lake as an unspoiled picturesque and even sublime wilderness at a time when "fashionable" resorts such as Saratoga Springs were increasingly criticized as places of artifice and immorality.[21]

4.2 *View over Lake Memphremagog (from the Sugar Loaf)*, ca 1838, by William Henry Bartlett. N.P. Willis and W.H. Bartlett, *Canadian Scenery* (1842). This view from Mount Elephantis, previously known as the Sugar Loaf, creates a vast sense of space, exaggerating the elevation and the distance from the village of Georgeville, across the lake in the middle ground. Bartlett's engraved sepia-washed drawings of this and other scenes on Lake Memphremagog would greatly influence artistic interpretations throughout the remainder of the century.

There had long been inns in the small towns and villages of Lake Memphremagog, but only with the arrival of the railway were hotels built specifically for the tourist trade.[22] Among them, the Mountain House was completed at the base of Owl's Head around 1852, and replaced by a larger structure when it burned down in 1855. A local promoter enthused, "looming up amid the trees and wild, dissevered rocks" the new hotel "looks like an eastern temple embowered in its sacred grove."[23] The message was clearly that guests would be in an ideal position to meditate upon sublime nature from a safe and comfortable site. One satisfied customer wrote in 1860 that the once-again

4.3 *The Connection at Newport, Lake Memphremagog, Vermont, 1867*, by William Notman. McCord Museum, N-0000.94.42. This Notman photograph illustrates the symbiotic relationship between Newport's Memphremagog House, the Connecticut and Passumpsic Railroad, and the steam passenger vessels on Lake Memphremagog.

4.4 *Mountain House Hotel*, n.d. Eastern Townships Resource Centre (Bishop's University), P020–77–9a. This photograph illustrates the wilderness setting and impressive size of the Mountain House Hotel at the base of Owl's Head. Like many resort hotels of this era, its design as a large house reflected the domestic values tourism brought to wilderness settings. A billiard room was added onto the rear right corner in 1892, after this photograph was taken.

enlarged hotel boasted "a reading room," "ample dining-room," "airy bed-chambers, spotless linen, and most attentive servants," plus "a charming Chinese summer-house, looking from a rock, covered with fern and foliage, close by the landing" (see figure 4.4).[24]

Vital to the resort hotels on the Canadian side of the border were the paddle-wheel steamers that offered a comfortable passage between Newport, Vermont, and Magog, Lower Canada (Quebec after 1867). In fact, a steamboat excursion was an intrinsic part of the tourist experience even for those who chose a hotel in Newport. The lake's first steamer, the 105-foot *Mountain Maid*, was launched by the appropriately named George Washington Fogg at the small Canadian customs port of Georgeville in 1850 (see figure 4.5).[25] The *Mountain Maid*'s timbers were hand-sawn from a variety of local tree species, but the engine and boiler were

4.5 *Captain Fogg and Steamer Mountain Maid, Georgeville, QC, about 1860.* By William Notman. McCord Museum, N-0000.193.44.1. This photograph of the first steamer on Lake Memphremagog was the first of many to be taken on the lake by the skilled photographer, William Notman. Captain Fogg is presumably standing at the bow beneath the Stars and Stripes while the Red Ensign hangs at the stern.

built in Montreal, from whence it took twenty-five yoke of oxen and twenty-four days to transport them to the lake. Fogg mounted a public subscription drive in northern Vermont and the Eastern Townships to raise the $3,500 required to complete the *Mountain Maid,* though his main financial backer was Colonel Ephraim Cross of New Hampshire who began the construction of Mountain House that same year.[26] The Canadian *Stanstead Journal,* like the American *Newport Express and Standard,* was a consistently strong promoter of the steamboat enterprise, referring to the *Mountain Maid* in 1855 as "a tight, natty little craft, well adapted to the business for which she was intended," and to Captain Fogg as "a gentleman who wins 'golden opinions from all sorts of people.'"[27]

The *Journal* also carried laudatory accounts by passengers and hotel guests, some of whom were clearly local boosters. A passenger on the *Mountain Maid* in the fall of 1850 found "the scenery, from one end of the Lake to the other ... a grand panorama, reminiscent of the Highlands seen from the Hudson River." At Owl's Head in particular, he wrote, "the eye loves to linger, attracted by its magnificent height, its rugged top and its broad base dipping in the calm waters below." Noting that a hotel (the future Mountain House) was planned for this spot, the correspondent declared that "to scale the mountain, fish in the Lake, or enjoy the shady coolness of the woods around, would be quite enough to lure travelers from the noise and bustle of the cities, the hurry and confusion of the railroads and the artificial amusements of the fashionable watering places."[28] Excursionists attempted to outdo each other with poetic imagery, such as the following in July 1851: "The pure, unruffled waters of the Lake, studded with islets, and cradled in the embrace of giant mountains – the impressive solitude of the scene, disturbed only by the monotonous dash of the steamer's wheels, or the mournful cry of the frightened water-fowl – the primitive wildness of Nature, luxurious in all her unfettered strength – form not the least charms of a picture worthy the artist's pencil."[29]

Mountain hiking was becoming popular in the neighbouring New England states by mid-century, and those in search of a more expansive view from the top of Owl's Head could disembark at the base of the mountain and be picked up on the steamer's return journey in the afternoon.[30] Hikes to the top reportedly took an hour and a half, though "parties with ladies [might] take three hours."[31] According to a mid-century Maine newspaper the view from Owl's Head combined the grand and the beautiful with sweeping vistas and "a few gem-like islands 'well set' and luxuriantly covered."[32] Little attention was paid to the cultivated landscape on the eastern shore of the lake (although the fields of the Connecticut Valley were integral to descriptions of the view from Mount Holyoke),[33] clearly reflecting American disinterest in signs of civilization north of the border.

Despite such publicity, summer tourism still developed slowly as the railway tracks inched their way northward to Newport. Judging from the local newspaper coverage, Captain Fogg depended heavily during the 1850s on excursions by people from the surrounding communities, which suggests that the consumption of leisure and appreciation of the view were not confined to the metropolitan centers or even the middle class.[34] A round-trip passage between Newport and Magog cost a dollar and took a leisurely eleven hours in 1855. There were also "cheap excursions" via the *Mountain Maid* and the Grand Trunk Railway's Sherbrooke station (fifteen miles from Magog) to Montreal or Quebec City at a return fare of five dollars.[35] The entrepreneurial Captain Fogg also capitalized on holidays, scheduling two runs from Newport to Mountain House on American Independence Day in 1856, as well as hiring an orchestra and setting off fireworks from the boat in the evening.[36]

The *Stanstead Journal* had already advised local residents that they were "under some obligation to aid in maintaining a Steamboat on our beautiful Lake."[37] Again in 1857 the editor assured his readers that "during the warm weather, when even the busy inhabitants of the "rural districts" may be excused for taking an occasional holiday, there is not a more pleasant excursion than to our own beautiful Memphremagog" where the *Mountain Maid* "affords the means of cheap and comfortable transportation to the Mountain, or any other part of the beautiful shores of the Lake."[38] After 1858 the Stanstead chapter of the Masonic Lodge held an annual meeting near the top of Owl's Head, thus giving guidebooks the opportunity to arouse popular curiosity by mentioning the cabalistic signs inscribed on the rock face of the "natural" lodge room.[39]

The lake tour, nevertheless, lacked the romantic historical associations created for the Hudson Valley by James Fenimore Cooper's *The Pioneers*, or Washington Irving's *Sketch Book*, with its adaptations of German folk tales in the form of "Rip Van Winkle" and "The Legend of Sleepy Hollow."[40] In 1882 George Monro Grant's *Picturesque Canada*, whose Eastern Townships illustrations were largely restricted to Lake Memphremagog and area, made a gesture in this direction by evoking the Abenaki raids on the New England frontier during the French Regime, as well as the expedition of Roger's Rangers in 1759: "From the heights we look out on the scenes of many a wild expedition, romantic or tragic ... Many the lawless adventure of love and war in the old days of Partizan and Ranger, who often helped out the glamour of romance by picturesque finery or Indian costume"[41] (see figure 4.6). But

LAKE MEMPHREMAGOG, FROM OWL'S HEAD.

4.6 *Lake Memphremagog, From Owl's Head*, ca. 1882, by F.B. Schell. Engraver W.H. Redding. George Monro Grant, ed., *Picturesque Canada*, vol. 2, 685. This was the scene that guests at the Mountain House Hotel, shown in the middle ground, and others would purportedly see from the top of Owl's Head. Emphasis by the American artist is placed on the rugged nature of what was actually a rather tame landscape, though the two steamboats serve as a reminder of the mountain's accessibility to tourists.

there were no physical traces of these expeditions, which consequently received little mention in the tourist guidebooks, and no reminders of the Abenaki occupation of the lake aside from its name and a few stock legends. Furthermore, neither Owl's Head, supposedly named after an Abenaki chief, nor Mount Elephantis, said to resemble a sleeping elephant, achieved the iconic status of the profile known as the Old Man of the Mountain in Franconia Notch, New Hampshire.[42]

Among the main points of interest on the lake, aside from Owl's Head, were the east-shore estates of several Montreal magnates such as Hugh Allan and Alexander Molson, but they failed to attract the kind of attention lavished on their grander counterparts in the Hudson Valley (see figure 4.7).[43] The guidebook authors were more interested in Balance Rock and Skinner's Cave.[44] The former was an example of the Victorian interest in natural anomalies, and the latter – said to have once been inhabited by a local smuggler – evoked the hermits' caves that were a standard element in the gardens of the English gentry (see figure 4.8). But Samuel June Barrows, Boston newspaper editor and annual summer camper on the lake, was dismissive of both, writing that "Memphremagog must rather depend upon the general charm of mountain, forest, island, and water, than upon any eccentric curiosities."[45] To help make up for the lack of other interesting features, half-joking reference was occasionally made to the lake's "serpent," marketed in today's tourism literature as "Memphre."[46]

Considerable outside attention was attracted when the visiting governor-general, Sir Edmund Walker Head, embarked on a well-publicized lake cruise in the fall of 1855. Lake Memphremagog was also mentioned briefly the following year in the railway guidebook, *The Canadian Tourist*.[47] Finally, well-known Quebec City artist Cornelius Krieghoff produced a dramatic painting of a volcanic-looking Owl's Head in 1859 (see figure 4.9).[48] It would be some time, however, before Canadian tourists materialized in significant numbers. The *Stanstead Journal* had noted in 1852 that "our Provincials are not much in the habit of pleasure-seeking abroad,"[49] but in truth the tourist attractions of the upper and lower St Lawrence were simply more accessible.

Furthermore, the *Mountain Maid*'s schedule favoured American tourist traffic. The steamer departed early each morning from Newport, a village of only 127 inhabitants in 1858 when the Connecticut and Passumpsic railhead was still fifteen miles away by stage coach.[50] That year, a journalist from the Boston periodical, *Ballou's Drawing Room Pictorial*, arrived "in Search of the Picturesque." Claiming that he had "grown

4.7 *Owl's Head from Fern Hill, Lake Memphremagog, QC, 1867*, by William Notman. McCord Museum, I-29054.1. After leaving the base of Owl's Head, the Lady of the Lake steamed northward and across the lake to the picturesque summer estate of wealthy Montreal entrepreneur, Alexander Molson. As this photograph illustrates, Molson's house overlooked an expansive garden as well as the lake and mountains on the opposite shore.

weary of the fashionable summer resorts," he found the Memphremagog area delightful: "the shores of the lake are indented with lovely bays, and bold headlands stretch out grandly. No better place for the union of music and moonlight could possibly be imagined."[51] In a similar vein, the editor of the *Stanstead Journal* made a direct appeal to the "denizens of Sun-scorched, feverish cities," to "fly to this cool retreat of the North." In this "fairy land" of "distant blue peaks," "waving forests," "delightful water," and "gravelly beaches," the *Mountain Maid*

4.8 *Looking out of Skinner's Cave, Lake Memphremagog, QC, 1867*, by William Notman. McCord Museum, I-29066.1. In an island across the lake from Owl's Head, the much-photographed Skinner's Cave was mentioned in nearly all the tourist guidebooks as being the former hiding place of a local smuggler. The story was embellished by adding that he died there after evading capture by customs agents.

4.9 *Owl's Head, Memphremagog, 1859,* by Cornelius Krieghoff. National Gallery of Canada. This painting by the first well known artist to visit Lake Memphremagog after Bartlett is somewhat unique in that it portrays a storm-tossed lake and dark brooding Owl's Head, unlike the picturesque images that subsequent artists would produce. It is also rather unique insofar as Krieghoff's landscape paintings are generally characterized by their colourful portrayals of *habitant* life. Note the inclusion of the opening to Skinner's Cave on the lower left.

was "the crowning jewel of the picture, wending her way across, and up and down, with her gay freight, and sounds of enjoyment (without overmuch care) and her jolly captain walking the planks as if he felt himself in the place he was made for."[52]

W.S. Hunter of Stanstead also aimed to "enlighten the public at home and abroad upon the merits of this part of the Province" with his publication in 1860 of a volume depicting local scenery. It included five engravings of Lake Memphremagog which he referred to as "the principal feature among the scenic beauties of the Eastern Townships" (see figure 4.10).[53] More widely circulated were the Currier and Ives prints

4.10 *View from Sugar Loaf Looking North Lake Memphremagog*. From W.S. Hunter, Jr., *Eastern Townships Scenery*, 1860. DeVolpi and Scowen, *Eastern Townships, A Pictorial Record*, plate 44. The local, self-taught artist and engraver, W.S. Hunter, copied somewhat artlessly from Bartlett's Lake Memphremagog engravings. The perspective, when compared to figure 4.2. is flattened and a conscious effort made to domesticate the scene. Note, for example, the female hikers in the corner miniatures (and the fact that the man hanging precariously on the cliff edge in the Bartlett etching now stands safely on top of it). Also, as a local booster, Hunter could not resist illustrating his community's progress by including a more detailed view of the village and the fields behind it, as well as two plumes of smoke that presumably represent industry in the town of Magog and beyond. Note as well that the two sailboats in Bartlett's engraving have been replaced by a steamboat.

which, like those of Hunter, closely plagiarized Bartlett's views of Lake Memphremagog.[54] Descriptions of the lake and how to get there also began to appear in distant newspapers such as the *New York Observer and Chronicle* and *New York Times*.[55] The publicity bore fruit, for the *Mountain Maid* added Mondays to its sailing schedule, and the *Stanstead Journal* now noted excursions by groups such as the students of Mrs Sherman's Family Boarding School in Hanover, New Hampshire.[56] Guests of Mountain House in 1859 included "a number of distinguished New Yorkers" as well as the mayors of Sherbrooke and Montreal.[57]

But the most famous visitor was undoubtedly English novelist Anthony Trollope who stayed at Mountain House with his wife in the fall of 1861. Trollope, who clearly felt that he was experiencing the true North American wilderness, noted that he had "seldom been in a house that seemed so remote from the world, and so little within reach of doctors, parsons, or butchers." Yet the hotel was "well kept," and he concluded that "on the whole we were more comfortable there than at any other inn in Lower Canada." Having discovered that the only "active enterprise" available to the traveller, "unless fishing be considered an active enterprise," was the ascent of Owl's Head, Trollope decided to climb the mountain in the afternoon as the view was said to be better in the evening light. After being informed that she would likely be unable to make the climb, though "young women" sometimes did it, Trollope's wife also "resolved she would see the top of the Owl's Head, or die in the attempt." They were not disappointed, for Trollope reported that "the view down upon the lakes and the forests around, and on the wooded hills below, is wonderfully lovely. I never was on a mountain which gave me a more perfect command of all the country round."[58] Despite his use of the masculine word "command," Trollope was not resorting to the imperialist rhetoric that marked many of his British counterparts descriptions of the view from Quebec City's Cape Diamond, as we saw in chapter 1.

The Civil War killed the American tourist trade for a time,[59] but prospects improved in 1864 when the Connecticut and Passumpsic Railroad finally reached Newport. The company acquired the town's main hotel, Memphremagog House, and leased the *Mountain Maid* for tourist excursions.[60] Also hoping to benefit from a resurgence in the tourist traffic, summer resident Alexander Molson launched a small steamer to make four return trips between Newport and Mountain House each day.[61] And helping to ensure that the interest of American tourists was rekindled, John Ross Dix's *A Hand Book for Lake Memphremagog* – "to be had at all railway depots" – was published in Boston the same year. The first page noted that "travellers to White and Franconia Mountains can leave the Mountains in the morning and reach Newport and Lake Magog at noon." Furthermore, no change of cars was required between Boston and Newport where passengers could step directly into the railroad depot in the basement of Memphremagog Hotel, "thus avoiding the importunities of coach drivers and the inconvenience of looking after baggage." Dix promised summer tourists for whom "Mount Washington, Niagara, Newport, Cape May, the Mammoth Cave, and many other 'Lions' of travel, have all been 'done'" that Lake Memphremagog represented "something new!" Particularly targeted was anyone with a taste for the outdoors: "artist, hunter after the picturesque, seeker after health, gunner in search of game, angler for trout, pickerel or longe [sic], bold mountain climber, strong-armed boatman, lady wanderer who loves to saunter in verdurous groves and winding mossy ways – you will, each and all of you, exclaim after a sojourn on the banks of this lovely lake – EUREKA!"[62]

Americans clearly found the prospect of such a vacation appealing.[63] To accommodate the increase in tourist traffic a new hotel was built in Newport in 1866, and the following year a new steamer was launched by the Lake Memphremagog Navigation Company whose chief shareholder and president was the shipping and railway magnate (as well as summer resident), Sir Hugh Allan. Described as a "first class pleasure boat," with an iron hull designed and built in Glasgow and a dining room large enough for fifty people, the 155-foot long *Lady of the Lake* could travel from one end of Lake Memphremagog to the other in less than three hours, stops included, making two round trips a day possible (see figure 4.11).[64]

Hotels continued to enjoy a brisk trade, with Newport's Memphremagog House registering 240 guests, not including family members, during one week in mid-July 1868, and 373 the following week.[65] The through-traffic business on Lake Memphremagog did suffer, however, with the completion of the railway link from Newport to the Grand Trunk station in Lennoxville, Quebec in July 1870. This connection, with its direct link to Quebec City and the "therapeutic" salt-water beaches of the lower St Lawrence, also drew away tourists from Boston and other American cities.[66] There was a fear in 1872 that the *Lady of the Lake* would be removed to "more propitious waters," but hotel accommodation in Newport was expanded the following year with the completion of a direct rail link to Montreal, following which Canadian tourists finally began to visit the lake in large numbers.[67]

4.11 *Lady of the Lake at the Mountain House Wharf*, n.d. Eastern Townships Resource Centre, P020-77-6a. Note the large crowd on deck, while still more passengers appear to be boarding the vessel.

Montrealers had become more aware of Lake Memphremagog's attractions due to publications such as *The Canadian Handbook and Tourist's Guide*,[68] as well as the works of a number of the city's most accomplished artists. Among these were Robert S. Duncanson and Alfred Fitch Bellows, American members of the Hudson River School who lived in Montreal for relatively brief periods, and who painted the lake and Owl's Head in the early 1860s.[69] More fully identified as Canadian artists, John A. Fraser, Allan Edson, C.J. Way, and Henry Sandham also focused on the mountainous landscape of the lake's northwestern shore. Some of their works, appearing in publications such as the *Canadian Illustrated News* (see figure 4.12),[70] reached beyond the city's elite, as did, presumably, some of the photographic images produced by the renowned William Notman of Montreal. His range of subjects was broadened beyond Owl's Head and other mountains to include groups of people as well as the lake's steamboats and hotels (see figures 4.3, 4.5, and 4.7).[71] Still more available and affordable were the

4.12 *Owl's Head, Lake Memphremagog*, 1874, by Henry Sandham, published in the *Canadian Illustrated News*, vol. 10, no. 13, 204 Library and Archives Canada, record 1592. While the setting is very similar, there is a striking contrast in mood between Krieghoff's painting (figure 4.9) and this picturesque scene produced fifteen years later for a mass circulation newspaper. Like Notman, whose Montreal studio he worked in, Sandham was effectively advertising Lake Memphremagog for the tourist market.

stereographic cards produced by American photographers beginning in the late 1860s.[72]

Interest in Lake Memphremagog had spread to the French-speaking population by the early 1870s when a French-Canadian company based in Montreal began construction of the sixty-five-room "Gibraltar Castle" and a "village of cottages" directly across the lake from Georgeville, at an estimated cost of $300,000 (see figure 4.13).[73] A little further south, the Chateau Dasilva, built and managed by Georgeville's Nathan Beach for a Dr Codère of Montreal, was also opened in 1875. The goal was clearly to attract French-speaking tourists,[74] but both ventures fell victim to the economic recession that had started in 1873. The interior of the Gibraltar Hotel was never completed and the Chateau Dasilva (acquired principally by Hugh Allan in 1880) was not rebuilt after it burned to the ground in 1882.[75] The recession also forced the Mountain

4.13 *Hotel Gibraltar, Lake Memphremagog, QC, about 1870,* by anonymous. McCord Museum, MP-1991.12.9. This drawing illustrates the ambitious nature of the project launched by French-speaking entrepreneurs from Montreal to build a rather urban-styled 65-room hotel on Gibraltar Point, across the lake from Georgeville. The interior was never completed.

House hotel to close in 1876,[76] and the *Lady of the Lake* began to make fewer stops between the railway stations at Newport and Magog.

As railways opened up the far west, the northern Appalachians were eclipsed by the Rocky Mountains for American tourists in search of the wilderness sublime.[77] To offset declining revenues from distant urban tourists, the Connecticut and Passumpsic Railroad advertised a "cheap excursion plan" that offered group fares from thirty-three small communities in the Eastern Townships and northern Vermont. The excursion included dinner at the newly renovated Memphremagog House in Newport (where an orchestra greeted the trains), a cruise aboard the *Lady of the Lake*, a picnic at Owl's Head, and a stop at the new (indeed, unfinished) hotel on Gibraltar Point "for rest and refreshment."[78] In one mid-July week in 1876, two excursions from St Johnsbury and neighbouring communities in northern Vermont together attracted 2,400 people, intensifying concerns about public safety.[79] Theodore Clarke Smith later recalled that when a crowd of young passengers "got up dances in the saloon, to the music of a veteran piano it was a lively place."[80] Certainly, the *Mountain Maid* must have been a lively vessel on July 1, 1867 when – to celebrate the Confederation of Canada – the Magog militia embarked on a drunken voyage to Georgeville where they proceeded to march through the village firing their rifles in wild abandon.[81] Other essentially plebeian groups organizing lake excursions included the Stanstead (Quebec) and Derby Line (Vermont) firemen and various Odd Fellows' lodges from both sides of the border (see figure 4.14).[82]

There were also outings by more middle-class associations such as the Vermont Medical Society, the Vermont newspapermen, and the St Francis (Quebec) District Bar, and traffic from distant places began growing rapidly again by the early 1880s. In September 1882 the Georgeville correspondent for the *Stanstead Journal* reported that "there have been more visitors here this summer than ever before, and many were unable to find accommodations."[83] Most probably preferred not to linger at Newport's Memphremagog House, notorious – according to Theodore Clarke Smith – for its "extraordinarily bad food, hard beds and a railroad yard close at hand where freights were switched all night."[84] But in 1882 Mountain House at the foot of Owl's Head was reported to be again "open and kept in a first class way,"[85] and even in industrial Magog, at the head of the lake, the hotels and some private homes were reported to be full. With the demand for accommodation in Georgeville still greater than the supply in 1883, the owner of the picturesque old Camperdown raised $25,000 through the sale of public stocks to construct a new three-storey structure, with a tower and "observatory." He also installed telephones in all hundred rooms and built a proper sewage system.[86] Two years later, in 1885, the New Camperdown was reportedly filled with guests, many of whom were from Montreal, and the newly refurbished *Lady of the Lake* was booked for excursions almost every day in mid-August.[87] But the Camperdown Company had overreached itself,[88] for it went bankrupt the following year. Stripped of its expensive furnishings, the hotel continued to operate under lease, but it remained closed during the 1888 season.[89]

4.14 *Knights Templar Clam Bake, Owl's Head Landing*. Photo postcard by E.L. Chaplin, Newport, VT, 1909. Matthew Farfan, *Les Cantons de l'Est / The Eastern Townships* (2006), 162. This photograph indicates that local societies were still organizing lakeshore picnics after resort hotels such as the Mountain House, whose dilapidated wharf is shown here, had burned to the ground.

The *Stanstead Journal* insisted that tourists were attracted more than ever by the area's "delightful drives, woodland and mountain scenery, pure spring water; freedom from extreme heat, malarial diseases and mosquitoes … proximity to Lake Memphremagog and the general healthfulness of … [the] climate."[90] But in 1886 the newspaper also carried its first printed complaint that the natural beauty of Lake Memphremagog was being trampled and destroyed by development:

> Those who remember their trips on the old 'Mountain Maid' will recollect that a large portion of its banks, especially on the Western shore, were lined with the primeval forest, with here and there a break, a green oasis in the forest. But the lumberman has largely spoiled the beauty of the scene by uncovering the ragged, rocky shore and neighbouring hills. The lover of nature in its natural state regrets this desecration while the utilitarian

counts the result in dollars to the hardy woodsmen who will soon rob it of all the available 'lumber' about its borders, not sparing even Owl's Head, Elephantis and other less noticeable peaks. The lake is a beautiful sheet of water, but saw mills and logs by the million detract much from its original charm.[91]

The rarity of such observations is telling, for Newport's thriving sawmill industry, which was producing fifty carloads of lumber a week in the summer of 1875, depended heavily on logs from the Canadian side of the lake. Softwood log booms were sometimes as large as seven acres in size, and hardwood logs were transported on barges with as much as 200,000 board feet per tow.[92]

Loggers were not the only ones to alter the appearance of the shoreline, for the *Stanstead Journal* predicted in 1886 "that all desirable locations on the lake shore and on the islands will, before many years, be improved and occupied. Even now, land which could have been bought a year and a half ago for $20 per acre, is held at $400 to $600."[93] It was no longer only a handful of the wealthiest who owned recreational properties on the lake, though the first major real estate development, Lake Park, was clearly marketed to relatively affluent investors. Lying just south of the border where it was easily accessible by rail line,[94] Lake Park's promotional efforts included having its own newspaper correspondent who in 1888 touted the aesthetic improvements that the project was making on nature:

To anyone who visited Lake Park three years ago and today, the contrast would seem remarkable. The scenery was then no less grand, but the soberness and stillness of the various wooded points, the want of life upon the water and the absence of anything showing the hand of man, gave a lonely, a far-away feeling, especially as the shades of evening gave to the mountains a 'beary' look, not to be enjoyed except by the hereditary hermit. Now, however, while the hand of nature is predominant, changes have been wrought, that add not only to the comfort, but to the beauty of the scene.[95]

From this perspective, the attraction of Lake Memphremagog was not the romantic view of islands and mountains in their natural state so much as the possibility of owning and "improving" a piece of that shoreline.

Visual images in tourist brochures and promotional articles now focused more on foreground activities, such as fishing and sailing, and on close views of lakeside cottages. The brochures' authors emphasized not only tourist amenities such as campgrounds and boarding houses, but also local industries. As historian Blake Harrison has observed of Vermont tourist promotion during this era, industry and tourism were linked by "a common language and common pursuit of progressive economic growth."[96] A brochure published in 1895 by the Boston and Maine Railroad (successor to the Connecticut and Passumpsic) boasted, for example, that within seventy-five years the site of Newport had been transformed from "a forest of murmuring pines and hemlocks" to "a flourishing community of twenty-five hundred people, with handsome public buildings, attractive stores, well-kept and illuminated streets, and about as enterprising and as wideawake a class of citizens as one could meet on either side of the 'border.'" The claim that "Tales of smuggling seem to share with the Indian tradition in the romance of the Memphremagog region, and unconsciously give an added picturesqueness to the scenery itself," was followed directly by the statement that Newport had "a splendid court house," a "successful national bank and trust company," "great mills of modern construction," and a "progressive board of trade."[97]

Romantic conventions were still used to promote tourism, as well as the sale of lakeside lots, as illustrated by the travel guide disguised as a romantic potboiler published by the Connecticut and Passumpsic Railroad in 1885. Titled *My Canadian Sweetheart*, it featured villainous French-Canadian smugglers on Lake Memphremagog, as well as a Canadian damsel in distress and her heroic American rescuer who, naturally, fell in love with her.[98] But the emphasis was increasingly on recreation rather than romance. Thus, the Boston and Maine Railroad brochure of 1895 proclaimed that "the places that are now sleepy hamlets will blossom forth into 'resorts,' the cathedral woods along the shores of the now secluded lakes will resound with songs and merry laughter of the ubiquitous 'summer boarder,' and greatly will the easy-going 'native' on either side of the imaginary border line marvel at the transformation that has taken place in his quiet and peaceful realm."[99]

Tourism historian Orvar Löfgren has noted that, in purchasing summer properties, the middle class civil servants, academics, and office clerks "were eager to distance themselves from what they saw as the artificial and overceremonious traditions of the summer pioneers."

Rather than dressing in white suits to sip brandy and admire the sunset from the hotel verandah, the new middle class pursued comfort, informality, and playfulness.[100] Leisure time was now perceived as compensation for an increasingly intense and driven work schedule. In the words of American historian David Macleod, "leisure had to be *spent*; mere absence from work was insufficient."[101] It is not surprising, then, that one of the properties at Lake Park was purchased by the St Johnsbury Boat Club whose members owned sailboats, canoes, and other vessels.[102] As elsewhere in this broader borderland region, people were now more inclined to rent cabins or pitch tents in a campground than to stay in resort hotels.[103]

Aside from the rise of a more privatized and activity-oriented holiday culture, one that was less inclined to privilege appreciation of the view as a mark of respectable status, the resort hotels may have suffered from the very popularity of the scenic cruises, which would have undermined their value as signifiers of class distinction. Mountain House was reported in 1890 to have "had an unusually good run of custom ... being filled with a good paying class of boarders,"[104] but this did not prevent it from being "deserted and allowed to partially fall to pieces" by 1892. It then gained a new lease on life when purchased by Charles D. Watkins of New York. Watkins ensured that his paying guests would not have to rub shoulders with local steamboat passengers by acquiring a launch exclusively for his hotel. He also expanded the garden and added a bowling alley and billiard room to appeal to the new more active tourist.[105] By mid-August, the fifty-four room hotel was reportedly full with one hundred guests, "which is about double the number it has ever had before at one time,"[106] but it would burn to the ground in 1899, never to be rebuilt.

Meanwhile, even though Georgeville's New Camperdown remained closed, local contractor Nathan Beach opened the ungainly Hotel Elephantis by joining the first Methodist Church to part of the first Camperdown Hotel in 1894, after he had threatened to sue the municipality for refusing to grant him a liquor license (see figure 4.15).[107] Beach was clearly targeting local customers more than urban tourists, but his hotel was not rebuilt after it and the New Camperdown were destroyed by a fire in 1898.[108] By 1905 a local writer could observe that "no lake has been more sadly neglected, or contains more old-time ruins of summer hotels, cottages, and decaying wharves, than this beautiful and picturesque sheet of water ensconced among the hills."[109]

4.15 *Hotel Elephantis – Georgeville, between 1894 and 1898.* Eastern Townships Resource Centre, P020-77-1-11. As can be seen in this photograph, the Hotel Elephantis – constructed by a local entrepreneur in 1894 – was a rather ungainly union of part of the old Camperdown Hotel with the former Methodist Church that had been moved from beside the small red school house shown in the left background. To the right sits St George's Anglican Church, built in 1866 after the Methodist minister defected to the Church of England in order to serve the wealthy summer residents from Montreal, including the families of Judge Charles Dewey Day, Alexander Molson, and Henry Chapman. Although Sir Hugh Allan was a Presbyterian, he and his family attended the local Anglican services.

Conclusion

Tourism did not affect the Eastern Townships, taken as a whole, to the same degree that it did the region on the other side of the border during the later nineteenth century. In New England, states historian Dona

Brown, tourism "helped to forge a new landscape" out of the looming economic and social crisis.[110] But it did play an important role on the Quebec shores of scenic Lake Memphremagog where tourism promoters emphasized the picturesque (and sublime) views as a means of convincing potential customers that they would not simply be consumers engaging in a leisure activity but "sensitive lovers of scenery."[111]

In addition to the convivial atmosphere aboard its steamers and in its resort hotels, selling features for Lake Memphremagog were its fresh air, clear cool water, and relative freedom from black flies and mosquitoes. Furthermore, even though the people of the Eastern Townships had become – broadly speaking – more culturally conservative than their New England neighbours, American tourists were given the impression that the lake was essentially an extension of the United States, with the border referred to in the tourist guides as the "imaginary line."[112] American writers, nevertheless, tended to refer to the Canadian settlements as wilder and more socially backward than those on the American side of the border. The author of the Lake Memphremagog entry in *Picturesque America*, for example, noted that "the houses in the Canadian territory are slovenly and uncared for, without the evidences of prosperity and thrift that appear in those situated on our own soil."[113] As late as 1885 an article in the American *Frank Leslie's Popular Monthly* proclaimed of the Eastern Townships that "the entire region is still wild and uncultivated."[114] As we shall see in chapters 5, 6, and 7, this is what American travel writers tended to look for in Canada. The irony was that while the railway, followed by the protective tariff policy of 1879, was stimulating the industrialization and urbanization of Quebec's border townships, northern New England was stagnating economically, its white pastoral towns increasingly romanticized as "the last true bastion of the Yankee spirit."[115]

Lake Memphremagog's entrepreneurs, tradesmen, and farmers who supplied labour as well as wood to the steamers and produce to the hotels had clearly been dependent on tourism, as were the many who operated summer boarding houses, but not at the cost of industrialization, witness the expansion of Newport's lumber mills and Magog's emergence as an important textile manufacturing centre in the 1880s.[116] Rather, the tourism industry had injected welcome capital into the area. According to the *Eastern Townships Business and Farmers Directory* for 1888–1889, the village of Georgeville – with a population of 150 – included three stores, a saw mill, a lime kiln, a boat builder, a blacksmith, a contractor and builder, a carpenter, a mason and plasterer, a

4.16 *Georgeville from the Hill, looking across the Lake to Gibraltar Point and Bolton Cliffs on the West Side*, 1880, by Eugene Haberer, published in *Canadian Illustrated News*, vol. 22, no. 3, 36. Library and Archives Canada, record 96. In this illustration, identified as taken from sketches by W.S. Hunter, the *Lady of the Lake* is heading towards Newport from Georgeville. Across the lake from the bucolic-looking village the eye is drawn to the ill-fated Gibraltar Hotel, seemingly perched precariously atop the Bolton Cliffs.

painter, a mechanic, a pilot, a tailor, a dressmaker, a doctor, a teacher, a minister, a constable, a customs officer, as well as various services such as a post office and telegraph office, two stage coach operations, and an insurance agency (see figure 4.16).[117] Many of these businesses and individuals would have relied upon the summer tourist trade, either directly or indirectly. Furthermore, the *Mountain Maid* towed log booms to lakeside sawmills when it was not hauling sightseers, and the engine of one lake steamer even powered a sawmill during the winter months.

Historians of tourism have generally paid little attention to the response of the local residents, depicting them as passive or sometimes resentful objects of the tourist gaze,[118] but the fact that the *Stanstead Journal* and *Newport Advertiser* echoed much the same landscape litany as the tourist brochures indicates that the promotional appeal to an aesthetic sensibility was not aimed solely at the distant urban market. How local passengers on the steamboat excursions reacted to – or were influenced by – their experience is impossible to know for certain, but it is reasonable to assume that their outlook and behaviour were affected by their participation in a leisure activity clearly designed to demonstrate middle-class respectability. If the appeal of the view had been largely insignificant, it is unlikely that local promoters would have stressed it as much as they did. While the carefree social atmosphere was obviously a major attraction, particularly for the young, it is worth noting that the *Lady of the Lake* became a temperance boat in 1887.[119]

It might seem to be stretching the term to define local excursionists as tourists, but the lake cruise does conform to Urry's definition of tourism (the quintessential modernist experience) as "a limited breaking with established routines and practices of everyday life ... allowing one's senses to engage with a set of stimuli that contrast with the everyday and the mundane."[120] Tourism had a cultural impact even on individuals such as Morris Wilcox, the son of a poor Canadian lakeside farmer and carpenter, who had little opportunity to join in the lake's leisure activities. Later in life, as a retired Vermont state senator, Wilcox recalled that the Boston summer families for whom his father and mother worked, and to whom they sold goods, "put good hard American money into circulation regardless of a wet spring and early frost. At the same time they stirred us from our self-centered existence and sprinkled a little refinement and culture around Stanstead County."[121]

The passing tourists must have made a similar impact on the local people with whom they mingled on the decks of the paddlewheelers and in some of the lakeside hotels. If, as Harrison suggests, the popularization of the picturesque and sublime views represented the naturalizing of bourgeois social and cultural values over the subordinate classes,[122] the summer cottage era would bring a more material manifestation of social power relations as control of the lakeshore passed into the hands of the urban bourgeoisie. There were forty-five farmers in the Georgeville census district in 1901, but the heads of household also included eight tenant farmers and eleven farm labourers. And, while there were now two house builders and eight carpenters recorded as heads of household (as compared to only one of each listed in the 1889–1890 directory), the twelve domestic servants, six housekeepers, and three washerwomen suggest that taking in summer boarders was being replaced by wage labour as a means for women to contribute to the family income.[123]

While steam power had introduced the era of the railway, the paddle-wheel excursion, and the resort hotel to Lake Memphremagog, that era was coming to a close even before the turn of the century when the internal combustion engine gave rise to outboard motor boats and automobiles that would provide ready access to the entire lakeshore.[124] Scenic tourism had been upstaged to a considerable extent by a more active and family-centred outdoor recreation culture by the time Bullock penned the evocative description of Lake Memphremagog that opened this chapter. Not only were the sociability of the lake excursions and the incomes generated by the tourists diminished as the private sphere grew at the expense of the public, but villages such as Georgeville went into decline even as the process known in French as *villégiature* saw the size of the lake's population grow during the summer.[125] Rather ironically, it would be former residents of the region, drawn "home" in part by their nostalgic memories of the picturesque landscape, who would constitute the bulk of the summer visitors as the twentieth century progressed.[126]

NOTES

1 See Harry B. Shufelt, *Nicholas Austin the Quaker and the Township of Bolton* (Knowlton, QC: Brome County Historical Society, 1971).

2 William Bryant Bullock, *Beautiful Waters, Devoted to the Memphremagog Region* (Newport, VT: Memphremagog Press, 1926), 18–19.

3 The beautiful was defined as "pastoral, orderly, smiling, and serene," the picturesque as "rocky, irregular, alternating light and shadow," and the sublime as "inspiring awe, reverence, and humility." See Susan Glickman, *The Picturesque and the Sublime: A Poetics of the Canadian Landscape* (Montreal and Kingston: McGill-Queen's University Press, 1998), 9–12. For more details on the link between the picturesque and the sublime, on the one hand, and tourism on the other, see Orvar Löfgren, *On Holiday: A History of Vacationing* (Berkeley: University of California Press, 1999), chapter 1.

4 Wolfgang Schivelbusch, *The Railway Journey: Trains and Travel in the 19th Century* (Oxford, Basil Blackwell, 1979), 4. Löfgren's discussion of water cruises and railway journeys fails to note the distinction in the passenger experiences (*On Holiday*, 41–8), and Dona Brown also emphasizes the

speed of the steamboats. See her *Inventing New England: Regional Tourism in the Nineteenth Century* (Washington: Smithsonian Institution Press, 1995), 25. See also Leo Marx, *The Machine in the Garden: Technology and the Pastoral Ideal in America* (London, Oxford University Press, 1964, reprint 1972), 242–54.

5 John Urry, *The Tourist Gaze: Leisure and Travel in Contemporary Societies* (London: Sage Publications, 1990), 4, 10.

6 Theodore Clarke Smith, "Camp by the Cliff," chapter 1 (1884–1889), (unpublished typescript kindly made available by John Scott), 17.

7 John F. Sears, *Sacred Places: American Tourist Attractions in the Nineteenth Century* (Oxford: Oxford University Press, 1989), 49–52, 57–9.

8 Mountains and other wild landscapes had begun to be popularized in the United States during the period of rapid economic expansion that followed the War of 1812. Kenneth Myers, *The Catskills: Painters, Writers, and Tourists in the Mountains, 1820–1895* (Hanover and London: Hudson River Museum, 1987), 20, 31–2.

9 On the link between romance and consumerism in general, see Colin Campbell, *The Romantic Ethic and the Spirit of Consumerism* (Oxford and New York: B. Blackwell, 1987).

10 Urry, *The Tourist Gaze*. For a Canadian example, see Ian McKay, *The Quest of the Folk: Antimodernism and Cultural Selection in Twentieth Century Nova Scotia* (Montreal and Kingston: McGill-Queen's University Press, 1994).

11 In Bourdieu's terms, appreciation of the landscape provided the middle class with a cultural code of distinction, an opportunity – Dona Brown states – "to use the not-so-secret language of romantic scenery to demonstrate their education, their gentility, and their social status." Pierre Bourdieu, *Distinction: A Social Critique of the Judgement of Taste*, translated by Richard Nice (London: Routledge and Kegan Paul, 1984), 1–7; Brown, *Inventing New England*, 40. Brown expands on this theme on pp. 41–8, 52–9. Colin Campbell goes still further by suggesting that appreciation of the picturesque had come to serve as a measure of ethical sensibility and moral standing. Campbell, *Romantic Ethic*, 152–3.

12 See Cindy S. Aron, *Working at Play: A History of Vacations in the United States* (New York: Oxford University Press, 1999), chapter 1; Louise B. Roomet, "Vermont as a Resort Area in the Nineteenth Century," *Vermont History* 44 (1976): 1–5.

13 Mountains had begun to evoke a benign spirituality rather than tumult, vastness, and obscurity. Simon Schama, *Landscape and Memory* (Toronto: Random House, 1995), 490–8. On the physical geography of the Eastern Townships region, see *Les Cantons de l'Est: Aspects géographiques, politiques,*

socio-économiques et culturel (Sherbrooke, Université de Sherbrooke, 1989), part 1. On the White Mountains as a tourist attraction, see Brown, *Inventing New England*, chapter 2. On Vermont's handicap in this respect, see Roomet, "Vermont," 10–12; Andrea Rebek, "The Selling of Vermont: From Agriculture to Tourism, 1860–1910," *Vermont History* 44 (1976): 19; William C. Lipke, "Changing Images of Vermont Landscape," in William C. Lipke and Philip N. Grime, eds, *Vermont Landscape Images 1776–1976* (Burlington, VT: University Press of New England, 1976), 37–9; and Blake Harrison, *The View from Vermont: Tourism and the Making of an American Rural Landscape* (Burlington, VT: University of Vermont Press, 2006), 20–2.

14 Rebek, "Selling of Vermont," 22–6; Harrison, *The View*, 22–9, and chapter 2.

15 On the state's role in Vermont, see Brown, *Inventing New England*, 143–5; and Harrison, *The View*, 51–5. In Quebec the Catholic Church distributed lists of properties for sale in the Eastern Townships to potential French-Canadian parishioners. J.I. Little, "Watching the Frontier Disappear: English-Speaking Reaction to French-Canadian Colonization in the Eastern Townships, 1844–1890," *Journal of Canadian Studies* 14, no. 4 (1980–1981): 106–7.

16 W.S. Hunter, Jr., *Hunter's Eastern Townships Scenery, Canada East* (Montreal: John Lovell, 1860), 33.

17 One can only assume that the main reason tourists did not "discover" nearby Lake Massawippi until the 1880s was that it lay entirely north of the border. Philip James Handrick, "Institutions, Ideology, and Power: Social Change in the Eastern Townships of Quebec" (PhD dissertation, Michigan State University, 1981), 116–20.

18 Henry M. Burt, *The Wonders and Beauties of Lake Memphremagog: The Great Summer Resort of New England: How to Go There and What is to be Seen* (Springfield: New England Publishing Company 1872), 31; Bullock, *Beautiful Waters*, 17–25, 46–7, 56–62; Bea Aldrich Nelson and Barbara Kaiser Malloy, *Around Lake Memphremagog* (Portsmouth, NH: Arcadia, 2003), 29, 49, 63, 83.

19 See, for example, *The Canadian Tourist* (Montreal and Toronto: Hew Ramsay, 1856), 146; Hunter, *Hunter's Eastern Townships*, 34; *Owl's Head Mountain House Lake Memphremagog* (s.n., 1892), 5 [CIHM no. 54930]; and *Beautiful Memphremagog* (Newport, VT, 1907, reprint Ayer's Cliff, QC: Pigwidgeon Press, 1987), preface (no pagination). Bartlett's watercolours were published as engravings in W.H. Bartlett and N.P. Willis, *Canadian Scenery Illustrated*, 2 volumes (London: George Virtue, 1842). For a written example of the sublime convention, see the detailed description of Owl's Head in the *Newport Express and Standard*, 21 July 1868.

20 Peter Burke, *Eyewitnessing: The Uses of Images as Historical Evidence* (London: Reaktion, 2001), 43.
21 On the increased leisure time available to the growing middle class, as well as the relationship between railways and summer hotels, see Aron, *Working at Play*, chapter 2. On the moralistic critique of fashionable resorts, see Aron, *Working at Play*, chapter 3. On the proliferation of tourist guidebooks in New England, as well as their function, see Brown, *Inventing New England*, 28–33, 60–2.
22 On the distinction between inns and hotels, see Brown, *Inventing New England*, 25–7; and on the resort hotel in Vermont, see Roomet, "Vermont as a Resort Area," 6–9. On the early inns in Georgeville, see Davidson, *Copp's Ferry*, 5–6.
23 *Stanstead Journal*, 12 July 1855.
24 *Stanstead Journal*, 16 August 1860. The Mountain House had been enlarged by a new proprietor in 1858. *Stanstead Journal*, 1 July 1858.
25 The Canadian-born Fogg had previously operated a horse-propelled ferry from Georgeville across the lake to Knowlton's Landing as a link in the main stage coach road from Montreal to Boston. For a biography of Fogg, see the *Georgeville Enterprise*, 11, no. 1 (2002), 1–3.
26 Much of this information is based on the reminiscences of George C. Merrill, who was for many years purser on the Mountain Maid, and whose *Contribution to the History of Navigation on Lake Memphremagog* was published in 1887–1889 and partially reprinted in Emily M. Nelson, *Frontier Crossroads: The Evolution of Newport, Vermont* (Canaan, NH, Phoenix Publishing, 1977), 69–73. See also *Stanstead Journal*, 4 July 1850, 10 October 1850; "Iraneus Letters from the Lakes and the Hills," *New York Observer and Chronicle*, 17 August 1876; Eastern Townships Resource Centre [hereafter ETRC], P016, Dossiers Coupures de presse, unidentified newsclipping, 28 February 1942, by Pemberton Smith; and Bullock, *Beautiful Waters*, 26.
27 *Stanstead Journal*, 31 May 1855.
28 *Stanstead Journal*, 10 October 1850.
29 *Stanstead Journal*, 17 July 1851.
30 Myers, *The Catskills*, 72–5; *Stanstead Journal*, 10 October 1850.
31 *Stanstead Journal*, 16 August 1860. The *Stanstead Journal* claimed a year later (15 August 1851) that ladies found the ascent "quite easy compared with their expectations, and it gives them an excellent opportunity for a display of toilet unusual 'on the street.'" But ladies were advised by a guidebook published in 1864 that "The worse your attire, the better you will feel. Wear stout shoes or boots; if damp weather, rubbers; and should you have a Bloomer Costume, put it on by all means, for in some parts

of the ascent, you will 'bless your stars, and think it luxury' – at least you'll find it amazingly convenient." John R. Dix, *A Hand Book for Lake Memphremagog* (Boston: Evans and Co. [1864] [CIHM no. 33524], 35–44.

32 *Stanstead Journal*, 15 September 1853.

33 Sears, *Sacred Places*, 54–5.

34 Freight also made a substantial contribution to Fogg's livelihood. His ad in the *Stanstead Journal* for 31 May 1855 includes a detailed price list for the transportation of lumber and livestock. In 1857 Fogg and his partner advertised arrangements with railway companies to ship freight from Boston to anywhere on the lake at thirteen dollars per ton, and from Portland at eleven dollars per ton. *Stanstead Journal*, 2 July 1857.

35 *Stanstead Journal*, 13 September 1855, 21 August 1856, 14 July 1859.

36 *Stanstead Journal*, 26 June 1856.

37 *Stanstead Journal*, 29 May 1856.

38 *Stanstead Journal*, 16 July 1857. Local and working-class people, as well as farmers, also constituted a significant proportion of the "tourists" in the White Mountains. Brown, *Inventing New England*, 60.

39 Elisha Gustin, *History of Golden Rule Lodge, No. 4, Q.R., A.F. and A.M., Stanstead, P.Q., Canada* (s.n., n.d.), 33. For one example of the notice given to this ritual, see William Cullen Bryant, ed., *Picturesque America; or, The Land We Live In*, vol. 2 (New York: D. Appleton and Company, 1874), 456.

40 Sears, *Sacred Places*, 61–3; Myers, *The Catskills*, 33–6.

41 J. Howard Hunter, "South-Eastern Quebec," in George Monro Grant, ed., *Picturesque Canada*, vol. 2 (Toronto: Belden [1882]), 692.

42 Nelson and Malloy, *Around Lake Memphremagog*, 98. On the use of "Indian legends" in the White Mountains, and on the Old Man of the Mountain, see Brown, *Inventing New England*, 66–70.

43 Sears, *Sacred Places*, 64–6.

44 See Bullock, *Beautiful Waters*, 68–72, which recounts a suspiciously romantic "Abenaki legend" related to the rock. Included as well in *Beautiful Waters* (pp. 76–82) are poems about Uriah Skinner, the smuggler, and the sea serpent. For earlier references, see "Iraneus Letters," 17 August 1876; and Dix, *A Hand Book*, 27–32. For one description of the Allan and Molson estates, see Samuel J. Barrows and Isabel C. Barrows, *The Shaybacks in Camp: Ten Summers Under Canvas* (Boston and New York: Houghton, Mifflin and Company, 1888), 62–3. For another, see Marchioness of Dufferin and Ava, *My Canadian Journal, 1872–78* (New York, D. Appleton and Company, 1891), 445.

45 Löfgren, *On Holiday*, 24–5; Barrows and Barrows, *Shaybacks in Camp*, 64. Occasional reference was also made to a cave on Magoon's Point where

"marauders" had hidden a treasure chest stolen from a Roman Catholic cathedral. See, for example, Bryant, *Picturesque America*, vol. 2, 454.

46 See, for example, *Stanstead Journal*, 4 August 1853, 16 July 1868, 20 August 1868; Dix, *A Hand Book*, 48; and Nelson and Malloy, *Around Lake Memphremagog*, 110–12. In 1892 the *Stanstead Journal* reported that the caretaker of the Owl's Head Hotel had seen a monster of about 25 to 30 feet, with a head about three feet above the water. It commented: "This was no doubt the veritable 'Jewett's alligator,' which veteran fisherman, Uriah Jewett, so often asserted he had seen upon the lake 30 or 40 years ago. It was our pleasure to listen on many occasions to the old gentleman's stories of the 'sea serpent,' as he called it, and although no one believed his 'yarns,' they were quite interesting and we have no doubt but that he did see something of the sort." *Stanstead Journal*, 2 June 1892.

47 *Stanstead Journal*, 20 September 1855; *Canadian Tourist*, 146–7. Head returned with his family for a brief holiday in 1861, and the Mountain House would be on the itinerary for Governor-General Monk's tour of the region in 1864. *Stanstead Journal*, 26 September 1861, 7 July 1864.

48 See *L'art des Cantons de l'est / 1800–1950* (Sherbrooke: Univeristé de Sherbrooke, 1980), 16–18, 45–7; and Russell J. Harper, *Krieghoff* (Toronto: University of Toronto Press, 1979), 110–11, 185n47.

49 *Stanstead Journal*, 5 August 1852.

50 Nelson, *Frontier Crossroads*, 20.

51 Quoted in *Georgeville Enterprise* 11, no. 1 (Summer 2002), 3.

52 *Stanstead Journal*, 1 July 1858.

53 *Stanstead Journal*, 12 May 1859, 1 December 1859, 24 May 1860; Hunter, *Hunter's Eastern Townships*, 33–4.

54 See the Currier and Ives image closely replicating that of Hunter in Charles P. DeVolpi and P.H. Scowen, *Eastern Townships, A Pictorial Record: Historical Prints and Illustrations of the Eastern Townships of the Province of Quebec, Canada* (Montreal: Dev-Sco Publications, 1962), plate 31.

55 See "Profile Sketches of Lake Memphremagog by Wm. G. Prior," in *New York Observer and Chronicle*, 13 September 1860; and "The White Mountains and Lake Memphremagog," *New York Times*, 14 June 1866.

56 *Stanstead Journal*, 22 July 1858.

57 *Stanstead Journal*, 21 July 1859.

58 Anthony Trollope, *North America* (New York: Alfred A. Knopf, 1951), 58–9.

59 *Stanstead Journal*, 15 August 1861, 17 September 1863.

60 Nelson, *Frontier Crossroads*, 22, 97, 111–13.

61 *Stanstead Journal*, 1 September 1864.

62 Dix, *A Hand Book*, 1–4. Dix's detailed observations were based on his visit in the spring of 1859 (see p. 21).

63 *Stanstead Journal*, 29 June 1865, 20 July 1865.

64 *Stanstead Journal*, 23 August 1866, 6 June 1867, 29 August 1867, 12 September 1867, 3 October 1867, 24 October 1867, 25 June 1868; Burt, *Wonders and Beauties*, 16–17; J. Howard Hunter, "South-Eastern Quebec," in Grant, *Picturesque Canada*, vol. 2, 694; ETRC, P016, "1867 saw Magog"; J. Derek Booth, *Les Cantons de la Saint-François / Townships of the St. Francis* (Montreal: McCord Museum, 1984), 43–4. The second major investor in the *Lady of the Lake* was Lucius Robinson of Newport, and one of the directors was William Murray of Montreal's Beaver Line who also had a large acreage on Lake Memphremagog, but Allan eventually became the sole owner. *Stanstead Journal*, 16 July 1868, 29 April 1869.

65 *Newport Express and Standard*, 14 July 1868; 21 July 1868.

66 Burt, *Wonders and Beauties*, 26–9; J. Derek Booth, *Railways of Southern Quebec*, vol. 1 (Toronto: Railfare, 1982), 28–9. French-Canadian families had begun to spend summers in Kamouraska even before the steamboat era, and steamers had begun to carry American tourists to the north shore Charlevoix villages and the Saguenay by mid-century. Roger Brière, "Les grands traits de l'évolution du tourisme au Québec," *Bulletin de l'association des géographes de l'Amérique française* 11 (September 1967), 86–92; Dubé, *Charlevoix*, 46–52.

67 *Stanstead Journal*, 18 April 1872; *Newport Express and Standard*, 13 May 1873, 3 June 1873, 24 June 1873, 15 July 1873. For the week ending 19 August 1873, 465 guests were registered at Memphremagog House, which was expanded to 250 rooms in 1875. By this time the town's Bellevue Hotel, also newly expanded, and Memphremagog House were reporting as many as 500 and 700 guests, respectively. *Newport Express and Standard*, 19 May 1874, 30 June 1874, 25 May 1875, 20 July 1875, 13 June 1876; Nelson, *Frontier Crossroads*, 106–7.

68 H.B. Small, compiler, *The Canadian Handbook and Tourist's Guide: Being a Description of Canadian Lake and River Scenery* (Montreal: M. Longmoore, 1866), 54 [CIHM 32449]. This publication also promoted British settlement in the region. Also of a more broadly promotional nature, though aimed at an American audience, was the Quebec Central Railway's *Car Window Glimpses en Route to Quebec by Daylight* (New York: Leve and Aldent's Publication, 1887).

69 Monique Nadeau-Saumier, "Les Peintres et le Paysage des Cantons de l'Est," *Journal of Eastern Townships Studies* 20 (Spring 2002): 83–5; Dennis Reid, *'Our Own Country Canada': Being an Account of the National*

Aspirations of the Principal Landscape Artists in Montreal and Toronto, 1860–1890 (Ottawa: National Gallery of Canada, 1979), 44.

70 Reid, *Our Own Country*, 47, 96–8, 112–13, 121–6, 132–3, 135–7, 362–3.

71 See Stanley G. Triggs, *William Notman's Studio: The Canadian Picture* ([Montreal]: McCord Museum, 1992), 25, 37; Reid, *Our Own Country Canada*, 53–6. Another skilled Canadian photographer, Alexander Henderson, included a photograph of the *Mountain Maid* at Georgeville and a view of the wooded lakeshore in his *Photographic Views and Studies of Canadian Scenery* published in Montreal in 1865.

72 For examples, see figure 19; Matthew Farfan, *The Eastern Townships: In Town and Village* (Quebec: Les Éditions GID, 2006), 83, 100, 103, 126; and Matthew Farfan, *The Eastern Townships: On Lake and River* (Quebec: Les Éditions GID, 2008), 23, 43, 45, 49, 116–17, 120, 134–5, 141, 146, 159–62, 173, 185–6, 196–7. See also Lipke, "Changing Images," 40.

73 *Stanstead Journal*, 31 July 1873, 16 July 1874, 6 August 1874, 13 August 1874, 24 September 1874, 13 May 1875, 27 May 1875, 5 August 1875, 19 August 1875. The village of forty-eight houses and cottages also included a sawmill, furniture factory, three stores, and row of flats. See *Stanstead Journal*, 3 August 1876, 29 May 1890; and ETRC, P016, Dossiers Coupures de presse, unidentified 1938 newsclipping, George McAuley, Cap Gibraltar; *Beautiful Memphremagog*, n.p.; Smith, "Camp by the Cliff," chapter 1, p. 21.

74 French Canadians from the Quebec City area were targeted as well with the publication of *Grande excursion d'été de Québec au Lac Memphremagog, Boston et New York, revenant par Montréal: une excursion de neuf jours toutes dépenses comprises, pour cinquante piastres seulement* [s.n.], 1881 [CIHM 42071].

75 The Dasilva owner's name was spelled Codiere in the *Stanstead Journal*, 5 August 1875. See also Bullock, *Beautiful Waters*, 173. The Dasilva Hotel changed its name to the Revere House when Allan became the principal owner, but Beach continued to be the manager as well as part owner. *Stanstead Journal*, 3 June 1880, 27 April 1882. The cottages were said to be in ruins by 1895. Boston and Maine Railroad, *Lake Memphremagog and About There* (Boston: 1895), 25.

76 "Iraneus Letters," 17 August 1876; *Newport Express and Standard*, 7 August 1877.

77 Lipke, "Changing Images," 39.

78 *Stanstead Journal*, 10 August 1876.

79 *Stanstead Journal*, 27 July 1876, 3 August 1876. See also the group excursions noted in *Newport Express and Standard*, 11 July 1876.

80 Smith, "Camp by the Cliff," chapter 1, p. 17.

81 Lorne C. Macpherson, "Magog and District: 1867," Stanstead County Historical Society, *Centennial Journal* 2 (1967): 9–10. Clearly eager not to jeopardize the middle-class tourist trade, the unfailingly supportive *Stanstead Journal* very rarely mentioned such rowdy behaviour aboard the paddle wheelers. This was in sharp contrast to its bitter criticism of the drunkenness at the more plebeian Christian Adventist camp meetings in the neighbouring village of Beebe. See J.I. Little, "Railways, Revivals, and Rowdyism: The Beebe Adventist Camp Meeting, 1875–1900,'" in J.I. Little, ed., *The Other Quebec: Microhistorical Essays on Nineteenth-Century Religion and Society* (Toronto: University of Toronto Press, 2006), 197–221.

82 *Newport Express and Standard*, 16 June 1874, 21 August 1888; *Stanstead Journal*, 24 August 1882, 5 July 1883, 12 July 1883, 19 July 1883, 21 August 1884, 28 August 1884.

83 *Stanstead Journal*, 21 September 1882; *Newport Express and Standard*, 21 August 1888.

84 *Stanstead Journal*, 19 July 1883, 26 July 1883. The quote is from Smith, "Camp by the Cliff," chapter 1, p. 2. Smith states again on p. 16 that the Newport hotels were "unendurable." For a different impression, see *Snow's Hand-Book. Northern Pleasure Travel* (Boston: Noyes, Snow and Company, 1878); and Nelson, *Frontier Crossroads*, 113–15.

85 *Newport Express and Standard*, 1 August 1882.

86 *Stanstead Journal*, 28 July 1881, 9 August 1883, 23 August 1883, 22 November 1883, 1 May 1884, 17 July 1884, 24 July 1884, 21 August 1884. See the description of the old Camperdown in Barrows and Barrows, *Shaybacks in Camp*, 60–1.

87 *Stanstead Journal*, 3 July 1884, 16 July 1885, 13 August 1885, 20 August 1885, 27 August 1885, 3 September 1885.

88 An unidentified newsclipping blames "the falling off in trade brought about by the building of the railway through Magog," but Magog had been connected to Montreal by rail in 1878, six years before the new hotel was built. ETRC, P016, Fonds famille Davidson, Série: Georgeville, Dossier: Photographies (1888– [1977?]), "Georgeville – then and now" by Redherring.

89 *Stanstead Journal*, 17 June 1886, 24 June 1886, 5 August 1886, 26 May 1887, 28 July 1887, 12 July 1888.

90 *Stanstead Journal*, 28 July 1887.

91 *Stanstead Journal*, 2 September 1886.

92 *Newport Express and Standard*, 27 July 1875; C.F. Ranney, "Newport and Lake Memphremagog," *The Vermonter*, 3, no. 2 (September 1897), 27.

The Prouty and Miller Company owned 40,000 acres, mostly near the Canadian shore of the lake and along its tributaries. Bill Gove, "The Forest Industries of Lake Memphremagog," *Northern Logger and Timber Processor* 23 (1975): 18–19, 31–2, 34.

93 *Stanstead Journal*, 30 September 1886. On the parallel phenomenon in the Thousand Islands and Montreal regions, respectively, see Patricia Jasen, *Wild Things: Nature, Culture, and Tourism in Ontario, 1790–1914* (Toronto: University of Toronto Press, 1995), 76–9; and Michèle Dagenais, "Fuir la ville: villégiature et villégiateurs dans la region de Montréal, 1890–1940," *Revue d'histoire de l'Amérique française* 58, no. 3 (2005): 315–45.

94 *Stanstead Journal*, 19 May 1887, 16 June 1887, 28 September 1887, 16 August 1888. The plan to build a large wharf for the community was stymied by the American law that prohibited foreign boats from carrying freight or passengers between two American ports. *Stanstead Journal*, 13 October 1887.

95 *Stanstead Journal*, 5 July 1888. A more modest development was launched at Cedarville, on the Canadian side of the border and further removed from the rail line. The Lake Park correspondent reported somewhat condescendingly in 1889, that despite "the cheap sounding name, it is a very pretty place." Indeed, it "should be rated second only to Lake Park in attractiveness." *Stanstead Journal*, 2 May 1889, 18 July 1889. See also Ranney, "Newport," 30.

96 Harrison, *The View*, 18. See also 29–42.

97 *Lake Memphremagog and About There*, 11–12. See also the Quebec Central Railway's *Tourists' Guide Between Quebec and New England via Quebec Central Railway and Lake Memphremagog* (Sherbrooke, 1885) [CIHM 12264]; Frederic G. Mather, "A Summer at 'Magog' Lake," *The Continent: an Illustrated Weekly Magazine* 3, no. 21 (23 May 1883) [no page numbers]; and *Owl's Head Mountain House*.

98 *My Canadian Sweetheart; or, Aunt Tabby's Summer Boarders, A Story of Lake Memphremagog* (New York: Connecticut Valley and Passumpsic Railroads, 1885) [CIHM 45650].

99 *Lake Memphremagog and About There*, 30.

100 Löfgren, *On Holiday*, 123–4. Löfgren associates the origins of the summer cottage phenomenon with the 1920s and 30s, but his references are largely to Scandinavia.

101 David I. Macleod, *Building Character in the American Boy: The Boy Scouts, YMCA, and Their Forerunners* (Madison, WI: University of Wisconsin Press, 1983), 18.

102 *Stanstead Journal*, 15 August 1889. The Memphremagog Yacht Club acquired a large section of Newport's waterfront in 1908. Nelson, *Frontier Crossroads*, 80-3.

103 Roomet, "Vermont as a Resort Area," 10. A group of prominent social reformers from Boston began camping on Lake Memphremagog in the late 1870s, squatting on a local farmer's property before buying land and building cottages. See J.I. Little, "Life without Conventionality: Social Reformers as Summer Campers on Lake Memphremagog, 1878–1905," *Journal of the Gilded Age and Progressive Era* 9, no. 3 (July 2010): 281–311. By the mid-1890s Bacon's Bay on nearby Lake Massawippi had become known as the Old Orchard of the Eastern Townships. *Stanstead Journal*, 16 August 1894, 24 June 1897.

104 *Stanstead Journal*, 21 August 1890.

105 The name was also changed to Owl's Head Hotel. *Stanstead Journal*, 2 June 1892, 11 August 1892. On bowling and billiards, see Aron, *Working at Play*, 73–5, 86, 88.

106 *Stanstead Journal*, 18 August 1892; *Owl's Head Mountain House*, 25; Nelson and Malloy, *Around Lake Memphremagog*, 101. A plan of the hotel is printed as an appendix to *Owl's Head Mountain House*. It reportedly had a "very successful season" again in 1894. *Stanstead Journal*, 27 September 1894.

107 *Stanstead Journal*, 14 June 1894; Davidson, *Copp's Ferry*, 6–7. The Elephantis was leased to the owner of Newport's Memphremagog House in 1896. *Stanstead Journal*, 11 June 1896.

108 *Stanstead Journal*, 21 July 1898.

109 *Beautiful Memphremagog*, preface. The *Lady of the Lake* remained in operation until 1917. The propeller-driven *Anthemis* was built by E. Goff Penny in 1909, apparently in a fit of pique because the *Lady of the Lake* did not stop at his dock. At a cost of $10,000, and only 100 feet long, it was a much less impressive boat than the *Lady of the Lake*, but it did survive until 1951. ETRC, P016, Dossiers Coupures de presse, unidentified newsclipping by Judith Kellock-Heward; Booth, *Les Cantons*, 44.

110 Brown, *Inventing New England*, 8. For a more negative assessment, see Harrison, *The View*, 10–12. On the Eastern Townships, see Jean-Pierre Kesteman, Peter Southam, and Diane Saint-Pierre, *Histoire des Cantons de l'Est* (Sainte-Fo.y, QC: Les Presses de l'IQRC, 1998), 469–73.

111 See Margaret Hunt, "Racism, Imperialism, and the Traveler's Gaze in Eighteenth-Century England," *Journal of British Studies* 32 (1993) 333–57; Brown, *Inventing New England*, 6; Myers, *The Catskills*, 40, 49.

112 See, for example, Nelson and Malloy, *Around Lake Memphremagog*, 39; Bullock, *Beautiful Waters*, preface; Barrows and Barrows, *Shaybacks in Camp*, 77. On the growing sense of an English-Canadian identity in the Eastern Townships during the first half of the nineteenth century, see J.I.

Little, *Borderland Religion: The Emergence of an English-Canadian Identity, 1792–1852* (Toronto: University of Toronto Press, 2004).

113 Bryant, *Picturesque America*, vol. 2, 454. According to Burt (*Wonders and Beauties*, 7), "the boundary line is easily distinguished – south of it there being more thrift and enterprise than is seen just north over the line in Canada." See also, "Iraneus Letters from the Lakes and the Hills," 17 August 1876.

114 James B. Townsend, "Our Northern Lakes and Mountains," *Frank Leslie's Popular Monthly* 20, no. 1 (July 1885). While the local inhabitants generally did not attract much attention in the tourist publications, condescendingly humorous descriptions can be found in Frederick G. Mather, "On the Boundary Line," *Harper's New Monthly Magazine* no. 291 (August 1874): 335–50; and Mather, "A Summer at Magog Lake."

115 Stephen Nisenbaum, "New England as Region and Nation," in Edward L. Ayers, *et al.*, eds, *All Over the Map: Rethinking American Regions* (Baltimore: Johns Hopkins University Press, 1996), 39. See also Brown, *Inventing New England*, chapter 5; and Joseph A. Conforti, *Imagining New England: Explorations of Regional Identity from the Pilgrims to the Mid-Twentieth Century* (Chapel Hill: University of North Carolina Press, 2001), chapter 5.

116 *Newport Express and Standard*, 9 June 1868; Smith, "Camp by the Cliff," chapter 1, p. 18; Nelson, *Frontier Crossroads*, 116–21; Kesteman *et al.*, *Histoire des Cantons*, 368. Brown (*Inventing New England*, 3) argues that New England's tourist businesses "have often been at the cutting edge of capitalist development."

117 The list includes only one hotel, the Camperdown, but two boarding houses. In 1866 the compiler of the *The Canadian Handbook and Tourist Guide* wrote (p. 56) that the Camperdown was the principal hotel in Georgeville, "but if accommodation can be procured (and it generally may be had) at a farm house, by all means give it the preference; for however good an hotel may be, and however attentive the host, there is a restraint and a certain feeling of uneasiness, which at once vanishes in a quiet, country homestead."

118 For Quebec examples, see Lynda Villeneuve, *Paysage, mythe et territorialité: Charlevoix au XIXe siècle* (Sainte-Foy, QC: Les Presses de l'Université Laval, 1999), chapters 5–6; and James Murton, "La 'Normandie du Nouveau Monde': la société Canada Steamship Lines, l'antimodernisme et la promotion du Québec ancien," *Revue d'histoire de l'Amérique française* 55, no. 1 (2001): 3–44.

119 *Stanstead Journal*, 8 September 1887.

120 Urry, *Tourist Gaze*, 2, 11. Stephen Leacock's satirical story, "The Marine Excursions of the Knights of Pythias," nicely captures how eventful such an experience could be in the life of a small Canadian town. Stephen Leacock, *Sunshine Sketches of a Little Town*, Carl Spadoni, ed. (Peterborough, ON: Broadview Press, 2002), 43–60.

121 Morris R. Wilcox, *Keep Your Mind Off the Puddin': An Autobiography* (self-published, 1975) 44. (My thanks to John Scott for providing me with a copy of this memoir).

122 Harrison, *The View*, 7.

123 There were only two boarding-house keepers listed in the 1901 census, one a woman and one the man who owned the local hotel. Unfortunately, Georgeville is not isolated as a census sub-district in the 1891 manuscript census, so it is impossible to prove that the number of female labourers was increasing, but it was certainly abnormally high for a rural population. As for the number of carpenters, the Georgeville census sub-district had wider boundaries than the village, but nearly all the tradesmen who were household heads would presumably have lived in the village. There was also a considerable number of carpenters listed as unmarried sons in the 1901 census. Library and Archives of Canada, 1901 manuscript census reports on microfilm, reel T-6546.

124 One of the lake's first gas-powered boats was built in Georgeville in 1904. J.A. Davidson, *Copp's Ferry, Georgeville, 1797–1977* (s.l., n.d.), 16. Theodore Clarke Smith later recalled that "the days of the opening twentieth century were those of the motor boat," with "great numbers of dwellers on the lakeshore including farmers' operating them." Smith, "Camp by the Cliff," chapter 4, p. 9.

125 There is still a small inn in Georgeville, but, until recently, there had been no shop of any kind in the town for many years. For a study of how the "summer people" prevented economic development in nearby Lake Massawippi's North Hatley by exercising influence within municipal politics, see Handrick, "Institutions, Ideology, and Power," 95, 131–2, 149, 161–77. On the growing conflict between local and summer residents outside Montreal, see Dagenais, "Fuir la ville," 327–36.

126 This phenomenon grew quickly in the automobile era, but the *Stanstead Journal*'s social notes indicate that it was already well developed in the later nineteenth century. On 2 August 1883, for example, it reported that "There are a great many people from abroad visiting their 'country cousins' about this time."

5 Seeing Elemental Nature: An American Transcendentalist On and Off the Coast of Labrador, 1864–1865

Famously described by Jacques Cartier as the land that God gave to Cain, the rugged and isolated north Atlantic coast has never been a major attraction for scenery-loving travellers or tourists. It played an important role in the New England fishery, however, and during the later nineteenth century Labrador and Newfoundland became what literary historian Patrick O'Flaherty refers to as "an imaginative outpost of the eastern United States," recreated by American authors as "an image of their own vanishing frontier."[1] Lacking the usual nationalist rallying points, such as a royal family, a national church, and memorialized sites of important events, Americans had turned to the landscape as the source of their national character. Furthermore, it was the sublime – characterized by qualities of wildness, grandeur, and overwhelming power – that most distinguished their country from the more domesticated Europe.[2] Even though Labrador did not lie within the United States, then, it is not surprising that American adventurers were drawn to its rugged inhospitable landscape.

What attracted two well-known artists during the Civil War era, however, were the icebergs carried southward by the Labrador Current during the spring and summer, for the massive blocks of floating ice held a natural appeal to Americans who were accustomed to viewing the mountains, waterfalls, and canyons of their own country as icons of its greatness.[3] With their fantastical shapes, icebergs were mobile and ephemeral counterparts, in many respects, to the unusual rock formations that served as natural substitutes for architectural ruins in nationalistic publications such as *Picturesque America*.[4] They also combined Emmanuel Kant's geometrical sublime with his dynamic sublime, yet their most important feature for the landscape painters of that era was neither their awe-inspiring size nor their shifting shapes, but the opportunity they provided to capture light in nature, an opportunity that presented not only an aesthetic challenge but a spiritual one as well.[5]

Americans were not the first or only observers to be enthralled by the shapes and colours of icebergs. As early as 1819 the Scottish explorer John Ross described the first iceberg his ship encountered in search of the Northwest Passage as being shaped like "a white lion and horse rampant, which the quick fancy of the sailors, in their harmless fondness for omens, naturally enough shaped into the lion and unicorn of the King's arms, and they were delighted accordingly with the good luck it seemed to augur." Ross also wrote, "It is hardly possible to imagine any thing more exquisite than the variety of tints which these icebergs display: by night as well as day they glitter with a vividness of colour beyond the power of art to represent."[6] It was, however, American explorer Elisha Kent Kane's well-publicized search for the lost Franklin expedition that drew the widely travelled landscape artist Frederic Edwin Church to the northern Labrador coast in the summer of 1859.[7] As explained by Thomas Cole, founder of the Hudson River school and Church's instructor, the "scenes of solitude" to be found in sublime landscapes inspired contemplation of "eternal things" because they were the undefiled handiwork of the divine creator.[8] In keeping with the scale of Labrador's coastal landscape, Church focused on producing a single "great picture," the ten-by-six-foot *The Icebergs*, which has helped to solidify his reputation as the finest American landscape painter of the nineteenth century.[9] While explorers such as Kane published their own journals as well as embarking on promotional speaking tours to raise funds, Church instead invited Louis Legrand Noble – Episcopalian minister and author of Cole's biography[10] – to provide the publicity for his painting. It was not coincidental, then, that the unveiling of *The Icebergs* in 1861 was quickly followed by the publication of Noble's *After Icebergs With a Painter: Summer Voyage to Labrador and Around Newfoundland* (see figure 5.1).[11]

Less well known today is the series of articles titled "Icebergs and Esquimaux" written by Transcendentalist clergyman David Atwood Wasson.[12] This series appeared in the prestigious *Atlantic Monthly* in 1864 and 1865, and therefore reached an influential national and international audience.[13] Not only do these articles illustrate the impact of Darwinism and the Civil War on the second generation of Transcendentalists, as well as on the perception of Aboriginal peoples, they also

5.1 *The Icebergs* by Frederic Edwin Church (1861). Oil on canvas, 64.5 × 112.5 inches. Dallas Museum of Art, gift of Norma and Lamar Hunt, acc. 1979.28

reveal how Americans' nationalistic fascination with the sublime landscape could become an aesthetically colonializing force.

Like Noble, Wasson had been invited to become what Simon Schama refers to as a painter in prose by joining an iceberg-painting expedition to the coast of Labrador.[14] In this case the artist in charge was William Bradford, a less successful member than Church of the Hudson River school. Bradford was quite likely motivated by the celebrity of Church's painting even though the Civil War had, by this time, broken the nation's Arctic fever.[15] As its title suggests, Bradford's *Sealers Crushed by Icebergs* (see figure 5.2) would depict a hostile northern environment and owe as much to German painter Caspar David Friedrich's bleak *The Sea of Ice* (*Das Eismeer*), also called *The Wreck of Hope* (1824), as it did to Church's luminescent *The Icebergs*, with its broken cruciform mast in the foreground as the only reminder of life's fragility in the North.[16] Like Church and Noble, Bradford and Wasson would both focus on the colours imbedded in the icebergs, but the pessimistic view of nature that emerged from Bradford's "great picture" and Wasson's articles would reflect, as well, the experience and knowledge they gained about the

5.2 *Sealers Crushed by Icebergs* by William Bradford, 1866. Oil on canvas, 72.5 × 120.5 inches. New Bedford Whaling Museum, acc. 1972.33

dangers posed by shifting ice floes, not to mention the growing awareness during this Civil War era of the Darwinian struggle for existence in a hostile environment. That pessimistic perspective would also inform Wasson's depictions of the Inuit whom he described as representing an evolutionary dead end, and as therefore lacking the innate capacity for spiritual enlightenment that Transcendentalists believed was a basic trait of humanity.

Referred to by the famous Harvard psychologist and philosopher William James as "one of the great instructors of mankind," David Atwood Wasson wrote chiefly about socio-political and religio-philosophic matters, and "Icebergs and Esquimaux" is his only published travel narrative.[17] As a Transcendentalist, Wasson was one of an influential group of intellectuals who had moved beyond Unitarianism's rejection of New England's original Calvinism to embrace a new religious expression derived from Germany's philosophical idealism.[18] The two pioneer figures, Ralph Waldo Emerson and Henry David Thoreau, taught that because God was "immanent and active" within the human soul, mankind had the potential to transcend the material condition and attain a reality higher than the physical. Furthermore, a close connection with nature offered a heightened opportunity to tap into one's inner divinity.[19]

The fact remains, however, that neither Emerson nor Thoreau had the remote wilderness in mind,[20] and there is little in Wasson's travel narrative that evokes a more mystical connection to nature than one would find in the increasingly domesticated sublime convention of his era, including the romantic descriptions by Frederic Edmund Church's religiously conservative travelling companion, Louis Noble.[21] Wasson, in fact, held a more traditional view of nature than did the first generation of Transcendentalists. He ridiculed the assumption that nature was benevolent, arguing instead that it was either cruel or indifferent because it dictated that any species unable to survive would be inexorably swept from the earth. As for the idea that "natural man" was inherently good, Wasson argued instead that man was only potentially divine, though, as we shall see, he would not go even that far in describing the Inuit he met on the coast of Labrador.[22]

To Wasson the far North was nature at its most elemental, wilderness in the true sense of the term, and the Labrador coast represented "that period in Nature when her powers were all Titanic, untamed, – playing their wild game, with hills for toss-coppers and seas for soap-bubbles."[23] This was a sharp contrast, he added, to "The Wild" Thoreau claimed to have discovered at Walden Pond. In his journal entry of 30 August 1856, Thoreau had written: "It is in vain to dream of a wildness distant from ourselves. There is none such. It is the bog in our brains and bowels, the primitive vigor of nature in us, that inspires that dream. I shall never find in the wilds of Labrador any greater wildness than in some recess of Concord, i.e. than I import into it."[24] Wasson was not convinced. "Talk of finding it in a ten-acre swamp!" he scoffed, "Why, man, you are just from a cornfield, the echoes of your sister's piano are still in your ears, and you called at a post-office for a letter as you came! Verdure and mild heaven are above; *clunking* frogs and plants that keep company with man are beneath. But in the North nature herself is wild." Wasson added that the desert and the sea were untameable, but the North was still more so because "Commerce is but a surf on its shores." Its wildness, therefore, "goes to the very heart of things, immeasurable, immitigable, infinite; deaf and blind to all but itself and its own, it prevails, it is, and it is all."[25]

In short, where Thoreau studied morning frosts and frozen ponds seeking analogues in ice crystals to "reticulated leaves, feathered wings, [and] the harmonies of the universe,"[26] Wasson would look at ice on a much grander scale, and not only ice but the inhabitants of the northern coastline as well. Wasson's romantic descriptions of the icebergs were as much an exercise in aesthetic colonialism as were the paintings of Church and Bradford, but the writer's racialist descriptions of the indigenous northern inhabitants were a more concrete expression of the colonializing gaze. That gaze was shared at the time by students of anthropology who viewed Labrador as "a kind of Pompeii of the New World" with its indigenous inhabitants living – in the words of a later American explorer – "in a state far more primitive than in any other part of the continent of North America."[27]

To help fund his expedition, which he claimed cost him $4,000, Bradford invited paying passengers to join him.[28] The charge was $250, at least in one case,[29] so it is not surprising that the twelve who signed up were a rather genteel group, entirely male in composition, and nearly all from Massachusetts. No doubt they would have considered themselves to be travellers rather than tourists, for according to Wasson they included a lawyer, a judge, a retired navy surgeon, an Episcopal clergyman, a teacher of geology and natural history, an ornithologist, a retired army lieutenant who had been a Greenland voyager, a "Greek and Latin scholar who was rich as Croesus," and a photographer who was in Bradford's employ.[30] This unnamed photographer was William H. Pierce, who produced many images of arctic ice as well as what may be the earliest surviving photographs of Labrador (see figure 5.3).[31] Reflecting the fact that scientists were then considered indispensable to Arctic exploratory expeditions, the only member of the group named by Wasson was the young geologist Alpheus Spring Packard, whose *The Labrador Coast* would later describe the same cruise as it progressed northward during what was reportedly the coldest summer in forty years.[32]

The professional activities of Pierce and Packard aside, the main diversion of the passengers, once on land, was fishing, hunting, and gathering wild birds' eggs. The names of these other passengers are known only due to the relatively recent discovery of an unpublished journal written by a thirty-year-old fellow passenger named Algernon Willis, who spent more time assisting Pierce with his photographs than he did fishing or hunting.[33] Willis is not on Wasson's list, probably because his profession of travelling shoe salesman was not considered

5.3 *Labrador Fishing Station*, albumen print by William H. Pierce, 1864. In album *Photographs of Arctic Ice*. Library of Congress, Prints and Photographs Division, LC-USZ62-10281.

sufficiently prestigious to mention in the *Atlantic Monthly* articles, but his daily journal entries provide a more intimate account than does Wasson of life aboard the cramped sailing vessel during the seemingly endless days that it was boxed in by sea ice or stranded by lack of wind. Not mentioned in Wasson's articles, for example, are the scandalous behaviour of the Episcopal clergyman while on his frequent drunken sprees, the unappetizing meals served by the highly unhygienic "great greasy Scotchman" who had been employed as cook, or the increasingly vociferous demands of a number of passengers to return home before Bradford had the opportunity to fulfill the purpose of his expedition.[34]

The first Labrador landfall of the chartered 136-foot schooner *Benjamin S. Wright* was on June 14 at Sleupe Harbour. Willis's only comment was "There are deep snow banks lying among the rocks within stones [*sic*] throw of our vessel,"[35] but Wasson described the scene as "bleak, bare, and hard," with "not a tree, not a shrub, not a grass-blade" to be seen.[36] He added that the sloping shoreline of "gray, unbroken rock" dipping under the sea "like a shore of sand" was more "completely 'master of the situation'" than even "the mightiest cliff," "Grand, enduring, and awful" as it might be. The scars on a cliff's face, and the fragments at its feet, provided evidence "of what it endures," but "this scarless grey rock, thrusting its hand in a matter-of-course way under the sea, and seeming to hold it as in a cup, suggested a quality so comfortably immitigable that one's eyes grew cold in looking at it."[37] Resorting repeatedly to the word "grey" to describe the sky, the sea, the surrounding islands, and the remaining snow, Wasson wrote that one felt "as if all the ruddy and verdurous juices had died in the veins of the world … that Existence was dead, and that we stood looking on its corpse, which even in death could never decay."[38]

If this description challenged Thoreau's sense of the material world as sacred, Wasson's next instalment went still further by echoing Melville's critique of idyllic naturalism in his novel *Moby Dick* (1851).[39] Described in gory detail, as recounted to Wasson by the ship's captain, is the vicious attack on a huge right-whale by a large pod of "killer" cetaceans – presumably orcas – "hungry as famine, fierce as plague, dainty as a Roman epicure, yet omnivorous as time." The "epicure" reference refers to the attackers' focus on their victim's giant tongue, which Wasson was told weighed a ton and a half:

> They fly with inconceivable fury at their victim, aiming chiefly at the lip, tearing great mouthfuls away, which they instantly reject while darting for another. The bleeding and bellowing monster goes down like a boulder from a cliff, shoots up like a shell from a mortar, beats the sea about him all into crimson spray with his tail; but plunge, leap, foam as he may, the finny pirates flesh their teeth in him still, still are fresh in pursuit, until at length, to end one torment by submitting to another, the helpless giant opens his mouth, and permits these sea-devils to devour the quivering morsel they covet.[40]

A similar Darwinian perspective is reflected in Sir Edwin Landseer's popular painting, *Man Proposes, God Disposes*, first exhibited the same year as the Bradford cruise, for it alluded to the tragic fate of the Franklin expedition by focusing on two polar bears chewing on the ribs of dead men in an arctic shipwreck.[41] Bradford's *Sealers Crushed by Icebergs* also depicts a hostile nature, as already noted, but, like Church, he is said to have captured on canvas "a sensitive perception of the unique light, strange forms, and surprising colours of the Arctic regions."[42] This oscillation between the dark and tragic sublime and the colourful picturesque can also be found in Wasson's writing, for – in contrast to his description of the bleak shoreline – he described the moon's reflection on the water as being of "intensest gold verging upon orange, edged with an exquisite, delicate tint of scarlet." He also alluded to the "brilliant" phosphorescence below the water's surface, as well as the colours of the "blushing" dawn.[43]

As the ship came upon a massive ice field in the sunshine, Wasson wrote, the effect was "unlike anything known in more southern climates," for the day "warmed like summer and braced like winter." Rather than the flat cakes that he had expected, there were simulated "cliffs, basaltic columns, frozen down, arabesques, fretted traceries, sculptured urns, arches supporting broad tables or sloping roofs, lifted pinnacles, boulders, honey-combs, slanting strata of rock, gigantic birds, mastodons, maned lions, couching or rampant – a fantasy of forms, and, between all, the shining, shining sea." While these imaginative associations may have evoked the sublime insofar as they inspired a sense of awe,[44] the colours suggest the picturesque for they include "glistening white flecked with stars," "aërial purple," and "emerald intensity of green."[45]

Impressive as the twenty miles of shore ice was, Wasson claimed that it was dwarfed by the almost unbroken floe-ice which, during that unusually cold summer, was calculated to be more than a thousand miles in length and about a hundred miles in breadth.[46] This much-anticipated floe having finally been reached on the twenty-first day of the voyage, Wasson rhapsodized about the intensity of the blue, claiming: "This incomparable hue appears wherever deep shadow is interposed between the eye and any intense, shining white." Beyond the "cerulean and sapphire glory" shining from the two caves excavated by the sea were "the deep blue waters of York Bay," and further still "rose the purple gneiss hills" of the headland, "flecked with party [*sic*]-colored moss." Rowing the next day to the mouth of one of the ice-caverns, Wasson and Bradford found that the blue grew "deeper, intenser, more luminous, more awful in beauty, the farther inward, till in the depths it became not only a shrine to worship at, but a presence to bow and be silent before!" There is no hint, here, of a cold indifferent nature; instead, it is one of the rare moments when Wasson steers towards the transcendent, adding: "It is said that angels sing and move in joy before the Eternal; but there I learned that silence is their only voice, and stillness their ecstatic motion!"[47]

The main goal of the 800-kilometre Labrador cruise, however, was to view icebergs, which the ship first approached on June 30. Needless to say, Wasson spared no adjective in describing the "noble berg," including colours such as "infinitely delicate luminous green," and a blue "looking like lapis-lazuli." His focus was principally on texture and shape, however, referring to a surface like "the finest statuary marble," as well as like porcelain that would be "the despair of China." The "sculpturesque and architectural design" with "an intensely polished surface" was "surmounted by an elaborate level cornice, and above this the marble lace again."[48] In short, this was not Thoreau's mystical nature, but nature civilized as a classical Greek or Roman ruin.[49] Furthermore, the constant references to colour once again conform more closely to the picturesque than to the sublime. Paradoxically, the description of the same iceberg by the more prosaic Algernon Willis strikes a stronger religious chord: "I never gazed upon anything in nature with such wonder and admiration. I was awe struck. Its immense towering bulk glistening in a purity I never conceived of in this bright light, certainly inspired my religious nature more than I can tell."[50]

Boxed into a small harbour by floe-ice during the following two weeks (see figure 5.4), the passengers aboard the *Benjamin Wright* met a crew of fishermen who told stories about the summer of 1862 when more than thirty sealing vessels had to be abandoned in the pack ice of Green Bay. Further inspiring Bradford's "great picture," with its image of flames and thick black smoke rising skyward from an icebound vessel, many of these ships had been set ablaze in order to prevent them from drifting into the navigation lanes or being salvaged by others (thereby cancelling the insurance claims) once the ice had relaxed its grip.[51] In the meantime, the restless and bored American tourists were entertained by the July 4 celebration, with its 48-gun salute, oration by one of the passengers, sermon by Wasson, and banquet with champagne, blackberry wine, and whiskey punch. In addition, the firing of rockets and roman candles, as well as the burning of Bengal lights on the ice cakes, moved Willis to observe that "the effect was wonderful reminding one of fairy scenes."[52] Wasson, on the other hand, focused on the ice floes, writing: "Yard-wide spaces of emerald, amethyst, sapphire, yellow-green beryl, and rose-tinted crystal, grew as familiar to the eye as paving-blocks to the dwellers in cities."[53]

5.4 *The Schooner Trapped Two Weeks in Ice, Square Island Harbor*, albumen print by William H. Pierce, 1864. In album *Photographs of Arctic Ice*. Library of Congress, Prints and Photographs Division, LC-USZ62-4441.

When the second iceberg of the voyage came into view, Wasson's gaze shifted back to what he referred to as the "Northern architectural," describing it as "two immense Gothic churches ... each with a tower in front."[54] Despite warnings about the dangers of disintegrating or over-turning icebergs, Wasson was determined to have a closer look from his small skiff. Urged by the alcoholic Episcopal clergyman who had joined him at the last minute, and braving a heavy swell, Wasson even pushed into a small opening in the ice, "gazing upward and upward at the towering awfulness and magnificence of edifice, myself frozen in admiration."[55] This description is one of only two in Wasson's travel journal that might be said to sacralise the Labrador landscape, or rather ice-scape, but the experience of being frozen in admiration apparently did not lead to any deeper transcendental sensation.[56] In fact, Louis Noble's lengthy *After Icebergs* had effectively exhausted the descriptive vocabulary of the sublime with images such as domed mosque, Parthenon of the sea, gothic cathedral, huge man of war, marble mausoleum, and moving Alps of ice.[57] Religious conformist though he was, Noble's response to the icebergs was for the most part a more spiritual one than that of Wasson, though spiritual in the conventional Christian sense of viewing the natural world as evidence of design by a beneficent creator rather than as inherently sacred.[58]

If ice represented elemental nature, as far as Wasson was concerned, so too did the indigenous inhabitants of the Labrador coast. Indeed, he argued that they were "original and pre-Adamite man," adding that he meant it "not as a piece of rhetorical smartness, but in gravest characterization."[59] The idea that human beings had inhabited the earth prior to Adam was not a new one, for it had originated with tenth-century Islam and begun to appear in Christianity in the fourteenth century.[60] The "heresy" was strengthened by the "discovery" of new cultures in America, compelling Pope Julius II to decree in 1512 that American Indians were descended from Adam.[61] Attempts were made in subsequent centuries to reconcile pre-adamism with Christianity, but by the 1840s American ethnologists were rejecting the monogenetic theory that racial difference was the result of adaptation to different environments.[62] Wasson claimed that to him it was an open question as to whether the Inuit had become "children of the icy North" by slow modification, or – as the famous biologist and geologist Louis Agassiz claimed – they had originated "just as they are."[63] He was certain, nonetheless, that they had stopped evolving "at the point where human history begins." In short, "They belong not to spiritual or human, but to outward and physical nature."[64]

Rather ironically – given Wasson's militant abolitionism[65] – the polygenesis theory was used to defend slavery. In fact, one of the leading members of the American School of Ethnology, Samuel George Morton, had promoted polygenesis by postulating a racial hierarchy based on cranial measurements with Caucasians at the top, Native Americans in the middle, and Africans at the bottom.[66] As for the Inuit, whom Morton saw as a separate race from the other North American Natives, his *Crania Americana* (1839) pronounced that they were "crafty, sensual, ungrateful, obstinate and unfeeling, and much of their affection for their children can be traced to purely selfish motives ... Their mental facilities from infancy to old age, present a continued childhood ... In gluttony, selfishness and ingratitude, they are perhaps unequalled by any other nation of people."[67] In addition, explorer Dr John Rae's 1853 report that the Inuit had informed him of the doomed Franklin expedition's cannibalism had led to a strong backlash against the people who had been "England's favourite natives." Charles Dickens had led the attack against what he referred to as a "gross handful of uncivilised people," arguing that their story was a malevolent projection onto the explorers of habits natural to themselves.[68]

Having no sense of nationalist identification with the controversy over Franklin's fate, Wasson was free to profess a degree of admiration for the "Esquimaux," whom he described as primeval man. Cut off from civilization as well as from "the chief bounties of Nature," Wasson wrote, "He has done all for himself: he has developed his own arts, adjusted himself by his own wit to the nature which surrounds him. Heir to no Rome, Greece, Persia, India, he stands there in the sole strength of his native resources, rich only in the traditionary accomplishments of his own race."[69] There is a strong echo, here, of the Noble Savage myth embraced by Thoreau, who was fascinated by Native Americans.[70] As already noted, Transcendentalists professed that all persons share in a common nature, that grace is the birthright of all.[71] Wasson, however, dehumanized the Inuit. "Inseparable from the extreme North, the sea-shore and the seal," the "Esquimaux," according to Wasson's rather shocking description, was himself "a seal come to feet and hands, and preying upon his more primitive kindred. The cetacean of the land, he is localized, like animals, – not universal, like civilized man. He is no inhabitant of the globe as a whole, but is contained within special poles."[72]

The chief distinction between pre-adamite and adamite man, Wasson argued, was that the former simply responded to "outward Nature, to physical necessities," but the latter had begun – presumably with Adam or his near descendants – "to create necessities and supplies out of his own spirit, – to build architectures on foundations and out of materials that exist only in virtue of his own spiritual activity, – to live by bread which grows, not out of the soil, but out of the soul." Echoing the Victorian fascination with what was assumed to be the early beginnings of the human species (and the Inuit were the people most studied to this end),[73] Wasson claimed that a journey to the North was not only a journey across space, but also "over ages, epochs, unknown periods of time ... into the obscure existence that antedates history." Once one had arrived there, "Palestine and Greece, Moses and Homer" were "but a wild dream! Expel the impossible fancy from your mind! Go, spear a seal, and be a reasonable being!"[74] To Wasson, then, the Inuit effectively represented a dead end as far as evolution was concerned.

The Inuit Wasson encountered were living at the German-speaking Moravian mission of Hopedale, where Bradford's Labrador expedition ended because of the delays it had experienced.[75] Wasson conceded that these Inuit were outwardly beginning to borrow from civilization, but, being "unable radically to change," they were growing "inwardly poorer and weaker" due to those influences. Because civilization was forcing upon the Inuit "a rivalry to which he is unequal," Wasson concluded, "it wrests the seal from his grasp, thins it out of his waters; and he and his correlative die away together."[76] There was no need for Wasson to have read *Origin of Species*, which had been published in 1859, in order to express this view, for it had become commonplace in the United States by the 1840s.[77] Describing the scene in rather nightmarish terms, Wasson wrote that the Inuit's "squat and squalid huts ... with their grovelling toward the earth ... seemed rather dens than houses." The surrounding ground was "all trodden into mud," and nearby "a dead dog lies rotting; children lounge listlessly, and babies toddle through the slutch about it. Here and there a full-grown Esquimaux, in greasy and uncouth garb, loiters, doing nothing, *looking* nothing."[78] (In Pierce's staged photographs, on the other hand, the women and children are well dressed and the physical surroundings are quite tidy, see, for example, figures 5.5 and 5.6). Some of the girls, Wasson admitted, "are really pretty," but "always in a lumpish, domestic-animal style." Their hands and feet were "singularly small," and their fingers "nicely-tapered," but "Take hold of the hand, and you are struck with

5.5 *Esquimaux at the Moravian Mission, Hopedale, Labrador*, albumen print by William H. Pierce, 1864. In album *Photographs of Labrador*. Courtesy and copyright of Katamik Press.

5.6 *Skin Tent and Sod-Roof Houses at Hopedale*, albumen print by William H. Pierce, 1864. In album *Photographs of Labrador*. Courtesy and copyright of Katamik Press.

its *cetacean* feel. It is not flabby, but has a peculiar blubber-like, elastic compressibility, and seems not quite of human warmth."[79]

Only in relation to the kayak did Wasson describe the Inuit as evolved in any way, for this ingenious vessel was "a seal-skin Oxford or Cambridge, wherein he takes his degree as master of the primeval arts. Here he acquires not only physical strength and quickness, but self-possession also, mental agility, the instant use of his wits, – here becomes, in fine, a *cultivated* man."[80] Wasson also claimed admiringly that there was probably "no race of men on earth whose ordinary avocations present so constantly the alternative of rarest skill on the one hand, or instant destruction on the other." That skill simply reflected the Inuit's close link to nature, however, for kayak and rower appeared as "one creature," its "motion graceful as a flying bird."[81]

Far from criticizing the Inuit sense of morality, like Dickens, Wasson was impressed by their honesty. While Noble claimed that the Anglican Inuit of Fox Harbour "compare well with Christians anywhere,"[82] however, Wasson concluded that the religion of the Hopedale convert was essentially "a matter of personal relation between him and the missionaries. He goes to church as a dog follows his master, – expecting a bone and hoping for a pat in return." Wasson also wrote that pre-adamite man could not be truly religious because "religion implies ideas, in the blood at least, if not in the brain, as imagination, if not as thought; and ideas are to him wanting, are impossible." Furthermore, because of their docility, there was no chance that the Inuit would become post-adamite: "Had they been happy, had they been unhappy, I had hoped for them. They were neither; they were contented. A half-animal, African exuberance, token of a spirit obscure indeed, but rich and effervescent, would open for them a future. One sign of dim inward struggle and pain, as if the spirit resented his imprisonment, would do the same. Both were wanting. They ruminate; life is the cud they chew." In short, as pre-adamite man, the Inuit belonged "not to spiritual or human, but to outward and physical Nature," and, because civilization affected them only by "mechanical modification" and not "by vital refreshment and renewal," they had no future.[83] For evidence, Wasson pointed to the large number of local Inuit deaths – twenty-four out of approximately two hundred inhabitants in March alone. The cause, he suggested, was in part "The long winter of suffocation in their wooden dens, which lack the ventilation of the igloo that their untaught wit had devised." More fundamentally, however, "the hands of the great horologe of time have hunted around the dial, till they have found the hour of doom for this primeval race."[84]

Conclusion

The Reverend David Wasson's journalistic mission was aimed at attracting the attention of middle-class American readers who wished to turn their minds from their country's war and bloodshed to a cultured appreciation of the natural world.[85] He admitted that – unlike explorers such as Kane, Parry, and Franklin, who looked on "the very face" of the "Arctic Czar" – he and his fellow passengers wished only "to see the skirts of his robe, blown southward by summer-seeking winds."[86] But the weather proved to be unseasonably cold, and Wasson did not view Labrador as a sacred space, to use Mircea Eliade's term, but rather one in which people struggled against nature for basic survival.[87] The same essential message was reflected in the single iceberg painting of his patron, William Bradford, despite its inspiration by the transcendental painting of Edwin Church.

Although he was fascinated by the Inuits' survival capabilities, Wasson argued that such a society was ultimately doomed. As a firm believer in the Manifest Destiny of the United States, he had claimed in one of his earliest essays that in wresting the land from the Aboriginals who were merely "robbers in the domain of nature," Americans had become "God's curators for a mighty continent." Indeed, they represented "a new man, – not merely a migrated European" but a Teutonic blend that had produced the "Anglo-American."[88] In making this statement, Wasson was clearly inspired by Emerson's adamic myth which envisioned the virgin continent as the setting for the second beginning of history.[89] From this perspective, it was logical to conclude that what predated the Pilgrim settlers in North America was pre-history, and that, figuratively at least, the Aboriginals were pre-adamite peoples.[90]

A recent study claims that Wasson "cultivated a mystical sense of unity everywhere revealed in the universe that links him to the young Emerson,"[91] but he clearly had a restrictive view concerning what it meant to be religious. In fact, Wasson argued, the closer one was tied to nature the less one was capable of introspective contemplation, and, therefore, of spirituality.[92] Wasson's assessment of the Inuit was not particularly unique or controversial.[93] Elisha Kent Kane, for example, had expressed much the same attitude towards those who had saved the lives of himself and his crew, for he claimed that they were so close to humanity's natural state that they could not be judged by the standards of adult behaviour.[94] Even though Kane's fellow American explorer, Charles Hall, argued that the Inuit were reliable informants, he failed to challenge the prevailing view that they "represented a last bastion of savagery as yet untouched by the forces of civilization."[95] Americans were not alone in this view, for it was echoed by Scottish geologist John Francis Campbell who encountered Labrador Inuit the same year that Wasson did. In Campbell's pseudo-scientific view, "Lapps and Esquimaux who feed on fish, are some-what fish-like; and the last grow up within natural fat great coats like seals of the glacial period in which they live."[96]

Wasson's fellow passenger, the scientist A.S. Packard, was an exception in this respect, for he did not claim that the Inuit were incapable of adapting to the modern world. The education of those at Hopedale may not have been "so thorough-going as not to leave external traces at least of their savage antecedents," Packard wrote, but he also posed the rhetorical question, "may this not be said of all of us?" After all, "only a few generations ago our ancestors were in a state of semi-barbarism, and the Anglo-Saxon race can date back to the Neolithic Celts and bronze-using Aryan barbarians." The Inuit of the Labrador coast had, in fact, made rapid progress, according to Packard, for they were "a well-bred, kindly, intelligent, scrupulously honest folk, whereas their ancestors before the establishment of the Moravian missionaries on this coast were treacherous, crafty, and murderous."[97]

Furthermore, to a disinterested and relatively uneducated lay observer such as Algernon Willis, the Inuit were simply fellow humans, albeit culturally backward ones. Willis's first impressions of the families at Hopedale were that they were "all very fat many quite good looking. All smell strong of fish and oil. All the houses very dirty. The Women are dressed many of them like men with seal skin pants with a waddling gait, some of them with long hair, carry their babies on their backs are lively, jolly and friendly."[98] Willis further observed that "The Esquimaux are honest in every respect, yet they are shrewd and know how to trade." Bradford forbade the trading of rum, but Willis and the other passengers exchanged hard tack, tobacco, and old items of clothing for seal skins, fur-lined boots, bear skulls, leather bags, duck eggs, and carved objects such as miniature kayaks. They also acquired several dogs that frequently fought among themselves on the return journey.[99]

Willis's unpublished journal shines a revealing light back on Wasson, who endured constant pain because of an old injury. For example,

Willis recorded that one night, because Wasson alone was unable to sleep through the row among the dogs, he became "determined we all should suffer with him and he would not allow any of us to sleep as he screamed and jumped out of his berth and rang the dinner bell as loud as he could." The more cool-headed Willis could only conclude: "He seems to be nearly worn out and prostrated so that he shows a very irritable and unchristian disposition for a man in his position. I think this voyage will show to a disadvantage when he gives its story in the Atlantic Monthly."[100] As it turned out, Wasson's articles did not mention the quarrelsome dogs, and he was more generous to his mostly unnamed fellow travellers than some of them might have expected or deserved. His was clearly a colonializing gaze, however, insofar as it domesticated the icebergs, focusing on their shapes and colours while ignoring the danger they represented to sailors, and relegated the Inuit to an inferior branch of humanity. Iceberg tourism was slow to develop along the fog-bound north Atlantic coastline,[101] but even though Wasson's pre-adamite fantasy may not have gained much purchase in a literal sense, a century later the Inuit were still being referred to as a Stone Age people.[102]

NOTES

1 Patrick O'Flaherty, *The Rock Observed: Studies in the Literature of Newfoundland* (Toronto: University of Toronto Press, 1979), 83–5. On the New England fishery off the coast of Labrador, see Bill Rompkey, *The Story of Labrador* (Montreal and Kingston: McGill-Queen's University Press, 2003), 27–8.

2 David E. Nye, *American Technological Sublime* (Cambridge, MA: The MIT Press, 1994), 1, 24.

3 Nye, *American Technological Sublime*, 24–5, 32, 43.

4 *Picturesque America* was published as two volumes in 1872 and 1874. See Sue Rainey, *Creating Picturesque America: Monument to the Natural and Cultural Landscape* (Nashville and London: Vanderbilt University Press, 1994), 93–4, 113–15, 229, 232–8, 247. For the link between wilderness and nineteenth-century American nationalism more generally, see Nash, *Wilderness*, chapter 4.

5 Russell A. Potter, *Arctic Spectacles: The Frozen North in Visual Culture, 1818–1875* (Seattle: University of Washington Press, 2007), 180; Barry Lopez, *Arctic Dreams: Imagination and Desire in a Northern Landscape* (Toronto: Bantam Books, 1987), 219–20. On Kant's two basic manifestations of the sublime, see Nye, *American Technological Sublime*, 7–8.

6 John Ross, *A Voyage of Discovery, Made Under the Orders of the Admiralty* (London: John Murray, 1819), vol. 1, 30 (Internet Archives); "Ross, Sir John," *Dictionary of Canadian Biography online*. See also the descriptions by the Scottish amateur scientist and folklorist John Francis Campbell who likened an iceberg he encountered in Hamilton Inlet in 1864 to "a giant bust of the Duke of Wellington, 50 feet high." J.F. Campbell, *A Short American Tramp in the Fall of 1864* (Edinburgh: Edmonston and Douglas, 1865), 90 (Internet Archives); "John Francis Campbell, F.G.S., etc. (Iain Ileach), of Islay," *The Geological Magazine*, 1885, 191–2. https://www.cambridge.org/core/services/aop-cambridge-core/content/view/S0016756800151891. Viewed 23 May 2017.

7 Kane is said to have been the most famous man in the United States by the time he died as a young man in 1857. Potter, *Arctic Spectacles*, 4, chapter 5; Gerald L. Carr, *In Search of the Promised Land: Paintings by Frederic Edwin Church* (New York: Berry-Hill Galleries, n.d.), 36, 80.

8 Quoted in John Gatta, *Making Nature Sacred: Literature, Religion, and Environment in America from the Puritans to the Present* (New York: Oxford University Press, 2004), 4.

9 Gerald L. Carr, *Frederic Edwin Church: Romantic Landscapes and Seascapes* (New York: Adelson Galleries, 2007), 11; Theodore Stebbens, Jr, *Close Observation: Selected Oil Sketches by Frederic E. Church* (Washington, D.C.: Smithsonian Institution Press, 1978), 3. *The Icebergs* was purchased after its 1863 London showing by railway entrepreneur Sir Edward Watkin and subsequently vanished from public sight until it was donated to the Dallas Museum of Art in 1979. Carr, *In Search*, 80–3; Lopez, *Arctic Dreams*, 221. On the critical response at the time, see David Carew Huntington, "Frederic Edwin Church, 1826–1900: Painter of the Adamic New World Myth" (PhD dissertation, Yale University, 1960), 129–35.

10 "Virtual American Biographies," http://famousamericans.net/louislegrandnoble/. Viewed 30 June 2014.

11 Louis L. Noble, *After Icebergs With a Painter: A Summer Voyage to Labrador and Around Newfoundland* (New York: D. Appleton and Company, 1861).

12 Wasson had been installed as minister of the Congregationalist Church and Society in Groveland, Massachusetts, in 1851, but then broke away to form an independent religious society in the same town. He assumed charge of another independent congregation in Worcester, Massachusetts in 1856, moving to the old Thoreau house in Concord several years later, then on to Medford in 1860, and to Worcester in 1861. Wasson was invited to serve the Boston congregation of the very popular and influential Theodore Parker after the latter died in 1865. Charles H.

Foster, ed., *Beyond Concord: Selected Writings of David Atwood Wasson* (Bloomington: Indiana University Press, 1965), 9–16; W. Creighton Peden, *An Intellectual Biography of David Atwood Wasson (1828–1887): An American Transcendentalist Thinker* (Lewiston, ME: Edwin Mellen Press, 2008), 23–32, 49; Philip F. Gura, *American Transcendentalism: A History* (New York: Hill and Wang, 2007), 280–3.

13 On the *Atlantic Monthly*, see Gura, *American Transcendentalism*, 267–8.

14 Simon Schama, *Landscape and Memory* (Toronto: Random House, 1995), 7.

15 Michael F. Robinson, *The Coldest Crucible: Arctic Exploration and American Culture* (Chicago: University of Chicago Press, 2006), 63; John J. Wilmerding, "The Many Views of Frederic Edwin Church," in *Treasures from Olana: Landscapes by Frederic Edwin Church* (Ithaca, NY: Cornell University Press, 2005), 16. Noble's *After Icebergs* was on board Bradford's ship in 1864. Bradford visited the coast of Labrador every year but one between 1861 and 1867. He extended his range to Greenland in 1869, subsequently publishing *The Arctic Regions, Illustrated With Photographs Taken on an Art Expedition to Greenland* (republished in 2013 by David R. Godine, Boston, in association with the New Bedford Whaling Museum). See Richard C. Kugler, *William Bradford: Sailing Ships and Arctic Seas* (New Bedford Whaling Museum in association with University of Washington Press, Seattle, 2003), 14, 16, 21–8; Constance Martin, "Bradford, William," *Dictionary of Canadian Biography online*; and Potter, *Arctic Spectacles*, chapter 10.

16 Bradford worked on his *Sealers Crushed by Icebergs* from 1864 to 1866. It established his career by selling for $12,000 several months after it was first exhibited to the fee-paying public in Boston and New York, and after 300 chromolithographs were sold at $50 each. It failed, however, to come close to the fame of Church's "great picture." Linda Shanahan, "William Bradford's Sealers Crushed by Icebergs and the Green Bay Spring," *Newfoundland Quarterly* 107, no. 2 (Fall 2014): 25–7. The chromolithograph of Church's *The Icebergs* is reproduced in Carr, *In Search of the Promised Land*, 159. Bradford's *Sealers Crushed by Icebergs* is reproduced in Kugler, *William Bradford*, 121.

17 Quoted in Gura, *American Transcendentalism*, 283. In addition, Wasson was a literary critic and a minor poet. See the introduction to Foster, ed., *Beyond Concord*. Mott refers to Wasson as "one of the ablest essayists" of the 1860s (*A History*, 302), but Austin claims that he was "a minor writer" for the *Atlantic Monthly*, "except in quantity." Frank Luther Mott, *A History of American Magazines, vol. 3: 1865–1885* (Cambridge, MA: Harvard University Press, 1938), 302; James C. Austin, *Fields of the Atlantic*

Monthly: Letters to an Editor, 1861–1870 (San Marino, CA: The Huntington Library, 1953), 251, 258. For a bibliography of Wasson's publications, see Foster, *Beyond Concord*, 314–29.

18 Perry Miller, ed., *The American Transcendentalists: Their Prose and Poetry* (Garden City, NY: Doubleday, 1957), ix.

19 On what he refers to as the "correspondence" between the natural and the spiritual in Thoreau's writing, see Lawrence Buell, *The Environmental Imagination: Thoreau, Nature Writing, and the Formation of American Culture* (Cambridge, MA: Harvard University Press, 1995), 128–9, 263–4.

20 Emerson claimed that one's sacred connection to Nature could take place anywhere, including a village green, and Thoreau's experience of the "savage and dreary" wilderness of northern Maine in the late 1840s led him to prefer a middle ground. Gatta, *Making Nature Sacred*, 92–3; Nash, *Wilderness*, 85–6, 90–5; Leo Marx, *The Machine in the Garden: Technology and the Pastoral Ideal in America* (New York: Oxford University Press, 1964, reprint 1972), 246.

21 According to Potter (*Arctic Spectacles*, 184), Noble was "one of the first to trace in ice the apocalyptic overtones of these icy masses of shattered creation." In Noble's own words, however, icebergs were "crystalline vessels" that "like all the larger structures of nature … are freighted with God's power and glory, and must be reverently and thoughtfully studied, to 'see into the life of them.'" Noble, *After Icebergs*, 110.

22 Robert Spence, "D.A. Wasson, Forgotten Transcendentalist," *American Literature* 27, no. 1 (March 1955): 33–4.

23 D.A. Wasson, "Ice and Esquimaux," *The Atlantic Monthly*, vol. 15, issue 91 (May 1865), 566.

24 Quoted in Schama, *Landscape and Memory*, vii.

25 Wasson, "Ice and Esquimaux," vol. 14, issue 86 (December 1864): 728.

26 See Eric G. Wilson, *The Spiritual History of Ice: Romanticism, Science, and the Imagination* (New York: Palgrave Macmillan, 2003), 5.

27 Henry G. Bryant, *A Journey to the Grand Falls of Labrador* (Philadelphia: Geographical Club, 1892), 42. Quoted in O'Flaherty, *The Rock Observed*, 103.

28 Bradford also stated that he needed to acquire skeletons – presumably of humans – to offset his costs. Centre for Newfoundland Studies, Memorial University Libraries, Nfld. FF1041 W55 2003, Journal of Algernon Willis, July 1 [*sic* - the journal begins on June 2] to September 5, 1864: A Voyage to Labrador, as transcribed by his great-grandaughter [*sic*], Penelope Pendleton Beye [hereafter, Journal of Algernon Willis], 16 August 1864; Potter, *Arctic Spectacles*, 191.

29 Journal of Algernon Willis, 3 June 1864.
30 Wasson, "Ice and Esquimaux" (December 1864): 730–1; Krugler, *William Bradford*, 15.
31 Kugler, *William Bradford*, 15; William Bradford, *Photographs of Arctic Ice*, photograph album held by the Library of Congress Prints and Photographs Division.
32 Robinson, *The Coldest Crucible*, 4–6. Packard had first visited Labrador as a Bowdoin College student who joined the Williams College expedition organized by Professor P.A. Chadbourne in the summer of 1860. See Alpheus Spring Packard, *The Labrador Coast: A Journal of Two Summer Cruises to the Region* (New York: N.D.C. Hodges, 1891), chapters 4 and 5. According to Silver in 1908 (*Farm-Cottage, Camp and Canoe*, 186), "parties of eager students" from Yale and Harvard were still chartering fishing schooners each summer to cruise along the Labrador coast "combining in agreeable proportions the pursuit of science, sport, and travel."
33 Willis recorded in his journal that he turned 31 on July 28. His first page identifies Benjamin P. Mann as the son of Horace Mann, the prominent politician and education reformer; and Copley Amory as nephew of the famous painter, John Singleton Copley.
34 The quote is from Journal of Algernon Willis, 23 June 1864.
35 Journal of Algernon Willis, 12 June 1864.
36 Settlements had begun to be established along the southern Labrador coastline in the latter half of the eighteenth century. See Sean T. Cadigan, *Newfoundland and Labrador: A History* (Toronto: University of Toronto Press, 2009), 66–7, 99, 135–6
37 Wasson, "Ice and Esquimaux" (December 1864): 733.
38 Wasson, "Ice and Esquimaux" (December 1864): 734.
39 See Gatta, *Making Nature Sacred*, 73, 116–25.
40 Wasson further describes the killer cetacean as "a blue-fish on a big scale," "about fifteen feet in length," with a blunt nose and a large fin "some five feet long on the back, and eight or ten feet in length," "sloping away to a point, like the jib of ship." "Ice and Esquimaux" (January 1865): 44. See also Packard, *The Labrador Coast*, 113.
41 Diana Donald, "The Arctic Fantasies of Edwin Landseer and Briton Riviere: Polar Bears, Wilderness and Notions of the Sublime," in Nigel Llewellyn and Christine Riding, eds, *The Art of the Sublime*, January 2013. http://www.tate.org.uk/art/research-publications/the-sublime/diana-donald-the-arctic-fantasies-of-edwin-landseer-and-briton-riviere-polar-bears-r1136829. Viewed 23 May 2017.
42 Martin, "Bradford."

43 Wasson, "Ice and Esquimaux," vol. 15, issue 87 (January 1865): 40–1.
44 I.S. MacLaren notes that "landscape enthusiasts" indulged in associationism because their sensitivity was demonstrated by the ability "to derive a plethora of sensations – emotional and intellectual – from the contemplation of a scene." MacLaren, "The Aesthetic Map of the North, 1845–1859," *Arctic* 38, no. 2 (June 1985): 93.
45 Wasson, "Ice and Esquimaux" (January 1865): 41–2. Willis, similarly, mentioned the "brilliant" colours and the many "shapes and forms resembling man's heads, animals, birds, vases, urns and everything." Journal of Algernon Willis, 20 June 1864.
46 Wasson, "Ice and Esquimaux" (January 1865): 42.
47 Wasson, "Ice and Esquimaux" (January 1865): 45.
48 Wasson, "Ice and Esquimaux" (January 1865): 46.
49 The same classical reference is evoked by the broken twin pillars of theosophist Lawren Harris's *Icebergs, Davis Strait* (1930). According to poet and critic Eli Mandel, these pillars "form a gigantic gateway to an undreamed of place," and "an arch that could, completed, once and for all unify all shattered things, restore peace to a shattered world." Eli Mandel, "The Inward, Northward Journey of Lawren Harris," *artscanada* (October/November 1978): 22, 24.
50 Journal of Algernon Willis, 1 July 1864.
51 Packard briefly recounted the story in his journal, and it also appeared in the broadside accompanying Bradford's painting during its exhibition in 1866. Both accounts mistakenly dated the event to 1863 rather than 1862. Nor did they mention the burning of ships, but there were detailed descriptions in the Newfoundland press at that time. Packard states that twenty to thirty ships were lost, but the press set the number at approximately thirty-eight, with twenty-four set on fire. See Shanahan, "William Bradford's Sealers," 22–3, 25.
52 Journal of Algernon Willis, 4 July 1864.
53 Wasson, "Ice and Esquimaux" (January 1865): 47.
54 Wasson, "Ice and Esquimaux" (January 1865): 48. In a contemporary vein, Barry Lopez describes the icebergs he encountered as "monolithic; their walls, towering and abrupt, suggested Potala Palace at Lhasa in Tibet, a mountainous architecture of ascetic contemplation." He also argues that travelers compared icebergs to cathedrals because they both represent a passion for light. Lopez, *Arctic Dreams*, 184, 222.
55 Wasson, "Ice and Esquimaux" (January 1865): 48–9; Journal of Algernon Willis, 15 July 1864.
56 On sacralisation of the landscape, see Gatta, *Making Nature Sacred*, 6, 10.

57 Noble, *After Icebergs*, 28, 57, 85, 86, 113, 171.
58 See, for example, Noble, *After Icebergs*, 110, 113, 127, and 177. See also, William Closson James, *Locations of the Sacred: Essays on Religion, Literature, and Canadian Culture* (Waterloo, ON: Wilfrid Laurier University Press, 1998), 61–2.
59 Wasson, "Ice and Esquimaux," vol. 15, issue 90 (April 1865): 438.
60 Michael Barkun, *Religion and the Racist Right: The Origins of the Christian Identity Movement* (Chapel Hill, NC: University of North Carolina Press, 1994), 152.
61 David N. Livingstone, *Adam's Ancestors: Race, Religion, and the Politics of Human Origins* (Baltimore: The Johns Hopkins University Press, 2008), 16–24.
62 Livingston, *Adam's Ancestors*, 173–5; Reginald Horsman, "Scientific Racism and the American Indian in the Mid-Nineteenth Century," *American Quarterly* 27, no. 2 (May 1975): 152–68; Robert E. Bieder, *Science Encounters the Indian, 1820–1880: The Early Years of American Ethnology* (Norman, OK: University of Oklahoma Press, 1986), 99–100. According to Michael Banton, it was only at the end of the eighteenth century that some writers began to use "race" as denoting "a class of creatures with common characteristics, making it synonymous with either species or subspecies in modern classifications." Banton, "Historical and Contemporary Modes or Racialization," in Karim Murji and John Solomos, eds, *Racialization: Studies in Theory and Practice* (Oxford: Oxford University Press, 2005), 53.
63 After Agassiz emigrated to the US in 1846, he provided race theory with the aura of scientific authority. See Horsman, "Scientific Racism," 159; and Bieder, *Science Encounters*, 91–2, 216. Franz Boas, who in 1883 and 1884 became the first scholar to engage in prolonged fieldwork with the Inuit, would reject the theory of cultural evolution, becoming associated instead with the school of thought known as historical particularism. John L. Steckley, *White Lies About the Inuit* (Peterborough, ON: Broadview Press, 2008), 32–4.
64 Wasson, "Ice and Esquimaux" (April 1865): 448.
65 Wasson associated closely with the supporters of John Brown. Foster, *Beyond Concord*, 14–15; Gura, *American Transcendentalism*, 258–63. Wasson's letter to William Lloyd Garrison in 1860 is summarized in Peden, *An Intellectual Biography*, 54–5.
66 Livingston, *Adam's Ancestors*, 173–5, 179–80; Barkun, *Religion*, 152–3; Horsman, "Scientific Racism," 155–8; Bieder, *Science Encounters*, 89–91. Horsman (160) states that although "it has been contended in the case

of the Negro that the arguments of the American School of ethnologists were rejected in both North and South, concerning Indians they achieved considerable acceptability." As pre-adamism disappeared from scientific discourse, it became associated with attempts to reconcile theology with science, and, increasingly, with anti-Semitism and other forms of racial bigotry. See Livingston, *Adam's Ancestors*, chapters 7 and 8; and Barkun, *Religion*, 154–72, and chapter 9.

67 Quoted in Livingston, *Adam's Ancestors*, 177–8. On the place of the Inuit in the classification of human skulls, see also Francis Spufford, *I May Be Some Time: Ice and the English Imagination* (New York: St. Martin's Press, 1997), 225–6. The 1842 edition of the *Encyclopedia Britannica* claimed that the domestic economy of the Greenland Inuit was "uniformly filthy, and disgusting in the extreme." Quoted in Spufford, *I May Be Some Time*, 200.

68 Spufford, *I May Be Some Time*, 123–6, 196–8.

69 Wasson, "Ice and Esquimaux" (April 1865): 437.

70 Robert F. Sayre states that Thoreau studied "'the Indian' as the ideal solitary figure that was the white Americans' symbol of the wilderness and history." Sayre, *Thoreau and the American Indian* (Princeton, NJ: Princeton University Press, 1977), x.

71 Peden, *An Intellectual Biography*, 71–3, 327; Gura, *American Transcendentalism*, 18.

72 Wasson, "Ice and Esquimaux" (April 1865): 438. On the use of animal metaphors to describe the Tlingits of Alaska, see Robert Campbell, *In Darkest Alaska: Travel and Empire Along the Inside Passage* (Philadelphia: University of Pennsylvania Press, 2007), 147–8. See also the dehumanizing descriptions of the Montagnais by American travel writer Charles H. Farnham, as discussed in chapter 6 in this volume.

73 Spufford, *I May Be Some Time*, 210–35.

74 Wasson, "Ice and Esquimaux" (April 1865): 438.

75 The original aim had been to sail as far as the opening of Hudson's Strait. Wasson, "Ice and Esquimaux" 15, issue 90 (April 1865): 439. The Moravians had established their first Labrador mission at Nain in 1771. Hopedale followed in 1782. See Cadigan, *Newfoundland and Labrador*, 67–9, 100; and www.historicplaces.ca/en/rep-reg/place-lieu.aspx?id=11597. Viewed 19 June 2014.

76 Wasson, "Ice and Esquimaux" (April 1865): 439.

77 Horsman, "Scientific Racism," 153–4.

78 Wasson, "Ice and Esquimaux" (April 1865): 441–2.

79 Wasson, "Ice and Esquimaux" (April 1865): 443.

80 Wasson, "Ice and Esquimaux" (April 1865): 445. Dr John Rae was the first British explorer to advocate the adoption of Inuit technology, and – in 1865 – to describe their inventions as products of "scientific skill," but in that respect he was considerably ahead of his time. Spufford, *I May Be Some Time*, 195.

81 Wasson, "Ice and Esquimaux" (April 1865): 445–6. Spufford suggests that the northern counterpart of Edward Said's *Orientalism* might be titled *Borealism*, "and it would have much to say about animal imagery." Spufford, *I May Be Some Time*, 229.

82 Noble, *After Icebergs*, 194. Bradford, similarly, praised the results of the Christian missionaries among the Inuit of Greenland. Bradford, *The Arctic Regions*, 149–50.

83 Wasson, "Ice and Esquimaux" (April 1865): 447.

84 Wasson, "Ice and Esquimaux" (April 1865): 448.

85 On the growing popularity of the fictive travel movement in the later nineteenth century United States, see Kristin L. Hoganson, *Consumers' Imperium: The Global Production of American Domesticity, 1865–1920* (Chapel Hill: University of North Carolina Press, 2007), chapter 4.

86 Wasson, "Ice and Esquimaux" (December 1864): 729–30.

87 On Eliade's classic formulation of sacred space, see Gatta, *Making Nature Sacred*, 129–30.

88 Quoted in Spence, "D.A. Wasson," 35–6. See also Peden, "An Intellectual Biography," 84. These new Americans, Wasson argued, were able to grasp simple universal truths more effectively than were members of other cultures because they did not imprison themselves within symbols, creeds, and customs that limited free speech and free thought. Peden, *An Intellectual Biography*, 42. In Horsman's words, "Manifest Destiny was not simply a question of land hunger or of ports on the Pacific; it involved a belief in the destiny of a superior Anglo-Saxon race." "Scientific Racism," 164.

89 See R.W.B. Lewis, *The American Adam: Innocence, Tragedy and Tradition in the Nineteenth Century* (Chicago: University of Chicago Press, 1955). In his biography of Frederic Church, David Huntington claims that the artist's landscapes reflect this myth, with its assumption that in America "man" would recover his primal innocence and be reconciled with nature and God. Huntington, "Frederic Edwin Church," iii, 274–5. For Huntington's analysis of Church's *The Icebergs*, see "Frederic Edwin Church," 323–5.

90 As Anne McClintock notes, this was a standard colonialist trope, for "colonized people … do not inhabit history proper but exist in a permanently anterior time within the geographic space of the modern

empire as anachronistic humans, atavistic, irrational, bereft of human agency." *Imperial Leather: Race, Gender and Sexuality in the Colonial Context* (New York and London: Routledge, 1995), 30.

91 Gura, *American Transcendentalism*, 280.

92 Thoreau, himself, described his Walden Pond neighbour, a French-Canadian woodchopper, as "animal-man" rather than "spiritual man." Wilson, *The Spiritual History*, 64–5.

93 Peden refers to him as a "public intellectual" rather than an original thinker. Peden, *An Intellectual Biography*, 327.

94 Robinson, *The Coldest Crucible*, 46–7.

95 Robinson, *The Coldest Crucible*, 68–75. On Mark Twain's derogatory story, "The Esquimau Maiden's Romance," published in 1870, see Helen L. Harris, "Mark Twain's Response to the Native American," *American Literature* 46, no. 4 (1975): 500–1.

96 Campbell, *A Short American Tramp*, 104.

97 Packard, *The Labrador Coast*, 199–200. Rather ironically, Packard also recounted how he had stolen two Inuit skeletons that he had happened across on one of his rambles at Hopedale. *The Labrador Coast*, 207–8.

98 Journal of Algernon Willis, 30 July 1864.

99 Journal of Algernon Willis, 1 August 1864, 3 August 1864, 14 August 1864. Bradford also acquired a porcupine that would die of starvation. 16 August 1864.

100 Journal of Algernon Willis, 12 August 1864.

101 See Ewart Young, "Icebergs are Money-Makers," *Atlantic Guardian* 1, no. 10 (November 1945), 48. http://collections.mun.ca/PDFs/guardian/AG_V01N10.pdf. Viewed 25 July 2014. (My thanks to my colleague Willeen Keough for this reference).

102 See Joan Sangster, "Constructing the 'Eskimo' Wife: White Women's Travel Writing, Colonialism, and the Canadian North, 1940–1960," in Joan Sangster, ed., *Through Feminist Eyes: Essays of Canadian Women's History* (Edmonton: AU Press, 2011), 336–7.

6 Travels in a Cold and Rugged Land: C.H. Farnham's Quebec Essays in *Harper's Magazine*, 1883–1889

There have been a number of studies on British colonialist views of French Canada, both before and after Confederation,[1] but relatively few about the perceptions of Americans even though the northern tourist circuit extended from New England to Quebec City as early as 1828. The small number of travellers from the United States who published their impressions tended not to be as impressed with Quebec's historic or symbolic significance as were the British, which is hardly surprising, but they did share much the same condescending sense of superiority towards the people, based largely on superficial observations while making day trips from Quebec to Montmorency Falls and the shrine of Ste Anne de Beaupré.[2] Thus, the 1849 travel narrative of the Virginian J.C. Myers described the *habitants* as "a contented, gay, harmless people, easy and courteous in their manners, but very ignorant, few of them being able to read and write, as education is much neglected."[3] The well-known Massachusetts naturalist, Henry David Thoreau, made much the same observation a year later, in 1850, when he wrote that the people of Montmorency were so "behind the age" that they "fairly represented their ancestors in Normandy a thousand years ago."[4] Thoreau did concede that what he perceived to be the economic self-sufficiency of the *habitants* had the virtue of making them independent by nature,[5] but Henry James may have been the first prominent American visitor to describe (albeit briefly) this "genuine peasantry" in essentially positive terms, at least from his romantic perspective. Writing in 1871, James enthused about "their simple, unsharpened faces … their narrow patois … their ignorance and naïveté, and their evident good terms with the tin-spired parish church, standing there as bright and clean with ungrudged paint and varnish as a Nürnberg toy."[6] James's article did not appear in an edited collection until 1883, the same year that another American travel writer, Charles Haight Farnham, was sufficiently intrigued by this rural society to make an extended visit to the province, and to focus his attention on its rural inhabitants. The result was that a series of seven articles devoted largely to the lower St Lawrence appeared in the prestigious and widely read *Harper's New Monthly Magazine*.[7] And this was at a time when, according to magazine historian Frank Luther Mott, travel was second only to fiction in terms of the attention it received.[8]

Given that Farnham deliberately went to one the oldest and most economically isolated regions of the province, just as he would do when he visited and wrote about the "folk" of Cape Breton Island for *Harper's* in 1886 (as we shall see in chapter 7), it should not be surprising that his depiction of the *habitants* adhered closely to the traditional stereotype. What had changed by the 1880s was middle-class American attitudes towards that stereotype, for the growing fascination with what was still assumed to be a backward but contented people reflected what T.J. Jackson Lears has identified as the rise of antimodernism in that decade.[9] Thus, Farnham's repeated use of the word "folk" to identify the *habitants* of Quebec, like the Highlanders of Nova Scotia, signified that traditional customs and practices were now considered to be admirable alternatives to the drive for efficient control of nature.[10] Farnham was not particularly interested in folklore itself, however, and in contrast to Henry James, he remained too much the American liberal Protestant not to echo earlier American disapproval of what he perceived to be the authoritarian role of the Catholic Church in perpetuating *habitant* ignorance.[11] In short, his opinions reflected the values of his own bourgeois society, and his articles can be viewed as examples of what Adam Paul Weisman refers to as "imaginative colonization," namely the result of one culture imagining another "not on that culture's own particular terms, but as a feature of its own historical understanding."[12] Farnham was, nevertheless, a sensitive and sympathetic observer whose two winters in the lower St Lawrence region provided ample opportunity to record interesting details of daily life in what Americans generally assumed to be a "cold, rugged, and desperate" land.[13]

Little is known about Charles Farnham, aside from the fact that he was the son of two trail-blazing pioneers. His father, Thomas, was a lawyer who published a popular memoir about his experiences in the Oregon territory and California during the early settlement era of the 1840s. But Thomas died when Charles was still a child, so he was raised by his unconventional mother, Eliza Wood Burhans Farnham, who wrote several volumes about her own pioneering experiences in Illinois and California, as well as on prison reform, spiritualism, and women's rights.[14] As the son of Quaker parents, Charles had been sent to France during the US Civil War in order to avoid conscription, as well as to study drawing and music, after which he taught singing for a short time in New York. Upon moving to Boston, Farnham's familiarity with the famous New France historian Francis Parkman – with whom he camped on the Batiscan River in the summer of 1886, and whose biography he published in 1909 – clearly aroused his interest in Quebec as well as influencing his view of French Canadians.[15]

It was obviously no accident that Farnham gravitated towards the relatively isolated and longer-settled eastern part of the province where old traditions were more prevalent. But the fact that in his forties this highly cultured individual would choose to paddle what he called a canoe, but what an illustration reveals to be a kayak with a small sail (see figure 6.1), along the rugged north shore of the St Lawrence also reflects the growing American fascination with wilderness at a time when their own frontier was coming to a close.[16] In short, as Lears notes, the apparently backward-looking impulses of antimodernism were overlapping "with the more up-to-date agenda of revitalization."[17] Middle-class urban Americans were beginning to embrace summer camping and related activities as a means of combating neurasthenia, defined by historian Patricia Jasen as "the catch-all phrase for a host of ailments thought to be brought on by an 'impoverishment of nervous force.'"[18] Given the well-known adventures of his parents, and that Farnham remained single in an era when unwed males lacked the respect and authority of married men,[19] he may also have had more personal reasons to demonstrate his manhood.

Well-heeled Americans would already have had some familiarity with the lower St Lawrence because of the Saguenay tourist cruises that had begun in the 1840s.[20] In fact, *Harper's* had published an essay on one such cruise by an anonymous writer in 1859.[21] Fourteen years later, well-known American author William Dean Howells, who would later be employed by *Harper's*, set his novel *A Chance Acquaintance* partly on a cruise to "the great desolate river of the terrible country of the North."[22] His sister Annie Fréchette Howells covered similar ground in her "Summer Resorts on the St. Lawrence," which appeared in *Harper's* in 1884.[23] By this time, visiting artists as well had made the lower St Lawrence what one study refers to as a "paysage mythique,"[24] but

6.1 *Almost Swamped, Harper's New Monthly Magazine* 71 (September 1885), 71.

Charles Farnham's vision was of a harsh, unforgiving land, gripped by snow and freezing temperatures for much of the year, and firmly controlled by what he considered to be an obscurantist religion.[25]

Baie-Saint-Paul

The first article in Farnham's series, titled "The Canadian Habitant," appeared in August 1883, but the first stage of his journey was described in the richly illustrated "The Lower St. Lawrence," which appeared five years later in November 1888.[26] Farnham had an inauspicious start on the Ile d'Orléans, near Quebec City, for the local *habitants* refused to answer his questions despite their initial friendliness. The reason, he was later informed, was that personal names had once been recorded for service in the military, and "many of them believe that any man who has their names or their portraits can command their persons through occult forces." As a result, "even the census officer is often much annoyed unless the *curé* tells his flock to give him information." In short, Farnham was quick to create the impression of a superstitious and unprogressive people. The land itself was imbued with Catholicism in his evocative image of the road along the South shore as resembling "the string of a rosary, with French Canadian farm-houses for beads, and a spire every six or eight miles bearing a cross." In contrast to this southern shore, "with its strip of fertility and its rosary civilization," the North shore was a "mountain wall" from the gates of Quebec to Labrador, with "clefts" only at Baie St. Paul, La Malbaie, and the entrance to the Saguenay. "These bits of cultivation," Farnham added, "are but spots of light and human life in the wilderness."[27]

Farnham was charmed, however, by the "little archipelago of wooded islands" that he visited after leaving Ile d'Orléans. And he went beyond landscape views to include descriptions of communal work, such as the process on the North shore of harvesting rushes or "salt hay" (see figure 6.2). After being cut at low tide, Farnham observed, the fodder was floated to shore on the rising tide, becoming "quite an island of floating verdure." With the receding of the tide, "groups may be seen all along the foot of the bluffs – women with broad hats and bare ankles, men bare-legged and muddy, little one-horse carts standing by mounds of grass; and all work fast, pitching the dripping rushes, raking, hauling loads up the bank, and spreading the grass in the fields to cure. It is to me one of the prettiest scenes in Canada."[28] Aside from admiring the scene's picturesque qualities, Farnham was

6.2 *On the Rush Meadows*, *Harper's New Monthly Magazine* 77 (November 1888), 818.

clearly fascinated by the cooperation and arduous labour required by an economic activity that had apparently remained unchanged for centuries. Not surprisingly, he failed to mention the improved system of dikes that began to be built after mid-century to increase the size of the arable in response to market forces.[29]

Tellingly enough, Farnham's articles on the lower St Lawrence ignore Murray Bay (La Malbaie), served by tourist steamers since 1842 and touted as the Newport of Canada because of its wealthy American summer residents, including the family of future American president William Howard Taft.[30] Rather, Farnham's first *Harper's* article opens with a description of his rather frightening paddle into Baie-Saint-Paul, which had only a rudimentary pier prior to 1885.[31] With the ebb tide rushing over the reefs against the wind, Farnham wrote, the eighteen-mile-wide St Lawrence "leaped, foamed, and raged like a sea along its mountain walls." Having escaped the treacherous tide-races, he then faced "the celebrated Gouffre, or whirlpool, at the foot of Cap aux Corbeaux," so-named by sailors who imagined that "these birds of prey" (i.e., crows) "lived there to await wrecks and devour the victims."[32]

Humans had left little imprint on this mountainous landscape, in Farnham's view, for he described how "the bold shores along the foot of the capes are diversified with little houses among trees and fish-weirs along the rocks," and how distant houses could be seen "far up the walls, where horses and carts crawling along the roads look like flies."[33] In contrast to the wild environment that surrounded it, however, Baie-Saint-Paul is depicted as "a drowsy, straggling village, where the chief activity seems to be at the church doors." In fact, having landed on the shore, Farnham switched from the sublime convention to the picturesque, claiming that "When the full-bowed schooners lean over on the beach at low tide, and mists floating in from the river seem to lift the mountain-peaks up to the sky, it reminds me of Turner's picture of the harbor on Honfleur." Then, in a scene reminiscent of a European genre painting, Farnham describes coming across "a picturesque group of peasants sitting on the steps and piazza." In his words, "The warm yet sombre gloaming was a kindly light for their sturdy homespun figures and sunburned faces. It seemed as if the peace and gentleness of the evening were within them as well as about them." Farnham's article also moves beyond what Mary Louise Pratt refers to as the ethnographic manners-and-customs discourse of the outside observer when it introduces the proprietor, an "old gentleman" named M. Tremblay, noting that he was "a compact, muscular man of dark complexion" who offered lodging "with a willingness that put me quite at ease."[34]

In fact, Farnham gave a voice to some of the local "folk" long before pioneer anthropologist Marius Barbeau began to record the folklore of the region in 1916.[35] Entering his host's house, Farnham noticed a card on the door with the words, "Christus, nobiscum state," only to be informed that the parish priest had distributed the cards after the earthquake of 1870 in order "to protect us against disasters." Tremblay added that "we shall never have any more earthquakes, and the winds can't touch a house with these words on it."[36] The elderly *habitant* and his wife lived with their son and daughter-in-law as well as their ten grandchildren, and at supper they sat around a small table, "almost spoon-fashion, getting only one shoulder and arm up to the table." As bread and milk followed the pea soup,[37] Farnham wrote, "It was an odd sight to see those nine arms so actively and irregularly converging at the pan, and then withdrawing from the skirmish to re-appear at once." Rather than scoffing, however, he added that "the eating was not ill-mannered or untidy." Another description of the family's crowded but harmonious living conditions follows, with the fourteen members sharing bedsteads, trundle-beds, a large chest, and the space beneath the hollow seat of a bench. A buffalo robe and some blankets were spread on the floor for Farnham, and he was informed that the next night a bedstead would be prepared for him in the adjacent room with the rest of the family, where "it won't be so lonesome."[38]

Rising with the family at 4:30, Farnham accompanied them to church where he found "a crowd of genuine peasants." The American writer's lens was evidently filtering out all evidence of the modern for he wrote that "They wear dark coarse homespun; even the young women have scarcely a ribbon on their hats."[39] The local curé Charles Trudelle had observed in 1857, however, that "On ne voit presque pas ici, comme dans la Côte de Beauport et autour de Québec, des hommes avec des bonnets de laine grise ou rouge, et des femmes portant le jupon de drogue et le mantelet d'indienne ... véritable costume de la femme canadienne à la champagne [*sic*]."[40] The women were clearly in charge of their families' spiritual well-being, for it was the mother who said the evening prayers, at least in the family with whom Farnham was staying. Furthermore, women entered the church to pray on Sunday mornings while the men waited for the bell to ring, talking of horse trades or exchanging "the gossip of their respective neighbourhoods."[41]

Farnham claimed to feel "the extraordinary unity of Canadian life in this external monotony of the people," adding that they "seem a very sober people, even sombre, until you see their contented and amiable faces." Even the parish churches in this era of ultramontane ascendancy and ornate ecclesiastical structures were described by Farnham as "exceptionally consistent with the doctrine and life of the people – simple, economical, and austere," but this did not mean that he had any sympathy for Catholicism. Referring to the sermon delivered on the day he attended church in Baie-Saint-Paul, Farnham wrote that it "happened to be an excellent illustration of the power of the Church and the attitude of the people." Because "Canada, with an arctic winter and the greater part of its soil almost sterile, seems designed by nature to be the Norway of America, a land of forests," the youth were naturally attracted by "our Protestant republic." But the Archbishop of Quebec had issued a mandate blaming the parents for spending money on "luxury and intemperance" rather than "preparing new lands for their children." Observing that "Such criticism of a civilization made up of homespun, deal chairs, pea soup, and hay carts seems very odd to one coming from the banks of the Hudson," Farnham added that the parish priest "talked to his people with the air and the words of an absolute ruler giving orders that are beyond dispute; and he emphasized very forcibly the assertion that damnation awaits the emigrant to the United States."[42]

Farnham expressed sympathy for the young people, "quite ashamed and subdued" after the church service, as their parents "were now triumphant in the strength of their opposition to emigration." Despite criticizing the stance of the parish priest, however, Farnham saw much to admire in what he considered to be an unchanging non-materialist culture. The homes might be bare, with gardens producing not fruit or flowers but only "a few cabbages, onions, and tobacco," yet Farnham felt that "this austere, plain civilization has a certain charm: you respect its homeliness without dilapidation or untidiness, and you like its antique simplicity and quaintness." He admired the fact that "everything is done by hand, slowly, carefully." Clothes were washed in the river, and from the river water was drawn to fill a barrel near the door for household purposes; floors were scrubbed "with a bunch of spruce boughs" and swept with "a cedar broom"; and cloth was produced in the shadowy garret where Farnham liked to sit "while the women spin or weave, and sing their quaint national songs, or the austere, plain chants of their worship."[43] Farnham also described how, on one of his walks, he had come across a group of bare-armed women under the trees swingling flax that had been spread on poles over an open fire to loosen the fibres (see figure 6.3). As he left the grove, "resplendent

6.3 *Swingling Flax, Harper's New Monthly Magazine* 67 (August 1883), 391.

with autumn colors and sunshine, it was musical with the merriment of those contented women." In short, having been raised since the age of seven exclusively by his industrious mother, Farnham was particularly drawn to the work of the women, stating that "their productions are at least as necessary as those of the men."[44]

As for agriculture, recent research shows that significant progress was being made by those farmers in the Charlevoix valley bottoms who were able to take advantage of the growing tourist market,[45] but Farnham wrote that the farming practices of the Baie Saint-Paul *habitants* were "as primitive as their domestic economy. They reap with sickles, some of their ploughs are home-made with straps of iron on wooden mould-boards, and their travelling vehicle is a cart with wooden springs."[46] Rather than adopting a critical stance, however, Farnham expressed approval of handicraft production well before the American "Arts and Crafts Movement" was launched after the turn of the century.[47] Claiming that such "crude objects of mere utility have an air of antiquity that saves them from suggesting a rough, coarse life," he added that "they all have the marks of the hand of a man or a woman, and so express personal experience and character." And, echoing the growing reaction against the dehumanizing effects of factory production, Farnham wrote approvingly that "This civilization rests on the labor of the hand alone, unaided by mechanical powers; and its narrow, slow, economical, but self-supporting life thus acquires something of the dignity of manhood." In contrast to the United States, "where man seems to retire behind his engines and improvements," here "your undivided sympathy goes straight to the spinners and reapers. Moreover, this civilization has the novelty of antiquity, for it is the life of the Middle Ages in the nineteenth century."[48] Or even the biblical era, for Farnham enthused that "Ruth would not have been a stranger gleaning with those homespun women in short skirts and broad-brimmed hats."[49]

Relying largely on visual observation, Farnham was not interested in the oral tradition as such, and he was highly critical of the illiteracy that folklorists valued so highly, but he did relate a supposedly first-hand story about how a spurned beggar's spell had spoiled a farmer's milk, and how a medal given by the local *curé* had removed the spell.[50] And he did claim to have witnessed a religious procession to eradicate potato bugs, a ritual condoned by Bishop Saint-Vallier's *Rituel du Diocèse de Québec* of 1703.[51] According to Farnham, "The chorus sang the litany of the saints as the procession passed down the road; the priest cast holy water here and there along the way, and, after a march of half a mile or more the procession returned and disbanded in the church." When Farnham pointed out to his host a few days later that there were still beetles on his potato plants, the answer was reportedly, "Yes, sir; but these are another lot the Lord has sent."[52]

Farnham claimed to "miss very sadly even a spark of intellectual light or a suggestion of the possibility of progress," but even as an anti-Catholic his antimodern sensibility was attracted to religious ritual and mysticism.[53] Thus, he romanticized how the French-Canadian peasant "surrounds his labors here with a poetic accompaniment of religious observances, legends, superstitions, and quaint customs," and how "his character is in harmony with his external existence – simple-minded, ignorant, virtuous, austere, and courteous." Farnham concluded that Canada might be "our twin brother in chronology and geography; and yet no other contiguous lands differ more widely."[54] He left no hint, then, that some farmers in the region he was writing about produced surpluses for the local market – which they did,[55] that Charlevoix was one of the poorest and most traditional counties in the province of Quebec, that Quebec was quite distinct from other provinces in Canada, or that such "folk cultures" were also to be found in his own country.

Rivière Ouelle

Farnham's second article, "A Winter in Canada," opens on All Saints' Day (November 1), when an auction is taking place for the souls in Purgatory. The image is of a poor people sacrificing what little they could to raise money to pay for masses for their departed family members. Goods such as a turnip, a pair of woollen socks, and an eel were piled high on a table, but undercutting Farnham's theme of a priest-dominated society is his description of Rabelaisian sociability. Thus, the "homespun peasants" engage in "good-humored talk," the auctioneer's lively patter competes with the loud cackling of the geese and turkeys, and some boys retire to the barn-yard to enjoy a cock-fight with the fowls they have purchased.[56]

Turning to the landscape of the south-shore parish of Rivière Ouelle, Farnham painted an evocative word picture:

> The receding lines of gables and chimneys down the roads, each with its stream of white smoke, the long low barns with great windmills striding through the air, the schooners and lumber lighters laid up on the bank, the hay cocks far off on the edge of the salt-meadows along the two bays, the

> long fences of dark wicker-work running out over the mud-flats to catch eels, the point of rocks and forests separating the bays, and far out in the St. Lawrence, a pound or yard made of stakes to capture white porpoises – all these details serve to interest and please the eye.[57]

But this was also a dangerous landscape, for "belated vessels caught in October or November gales are driven about in the treacherous currents or in the blinding snow till they ground on some reef or bar far out from land. The crew escape perhaps in boats, to reach a land where an arctic winter must be passed, perhaps, in starving and freezing on some barren island." During the winter, "hunters creep over the fields of ice along shore to shoot seals, until the wind or tide changes, and threatens to carry their dangerous float out to sea." In fact, Farnham claimed, "this arm of the northern sea is dreaded, whether it lies still with a sinister gleam under the clear sunshine, or hides its restless anger under the veil of a lightsome gale of snow."[58]

With the onset of cold weather, the villagers "collected everything into the barn and the house, put up double sashes and doors – in short, they went into their burrows to hibernate." While "grim winter looks down from a leaden sky, and the world becomes dumb in the gray pallor of death," Farnham wrote, "I gladly retreat from the outer world to give myself up to the warmth and cheer of social life." Comfortably lodged in the village inn, Farnham socialized with the local notables, observing that "In this parish today I still find virtually the classes and characters of two hundred years ago – seigniors, priests, gentlemen, peasants – and also a civilization that, in spirit at least, might take its place in a picture of the seventeenth century."[59] For an explanation, Farnham returned to the dominant position of the Catholic Church, claiming that the religious focus of the education offered by the convents and colleges meant that students "generally remain strangers to the modern discoveries in the arts, sciences, and even industries." Furthermore, the emphasis on memory meant that "they very seldom have any love of reading when turned loose in practical life." Girls were taught "orderly habits and good moral conduct," and boys were "moulded more or less on the pattern of the unpractical, conservative, polished gentlemen of old times." The result of this "high and unpractical education of the gentry, and entire neglect of the peasantry," was "sharp class distinctions" and "a state of society quite impossible in our democratic nation." Farnham added – rather absurdly – that there were "no studies to improve industries or agriculture, no public works to discuss, no reforms to agitate," and that the handful of newspapers available in the parish were "utterly worthless to an intelligent mind, for they are filled with trashy serial stories and politico-personal matters of incredible insignificance." The few books "in the best houses" were "safe old classics, or goody-goody weaklings of newer birth," and there were "no lectures, no radical talkers in private circles. The only instructor of this people is the priest, and you might as well dig their fields for diamonds as search their minds for gleaming ideas."[60]

Whether or not Farnham would have found the intellectual stimulation he was craving in the small villages of his own country, he did admit that "in spite of the narrowness of this existence, life here is full of a certain charm that you can seldom find, and only in small circles, in our republic."[61] While noting that the local elite formed "a circle that has been polished by this classical education and generations of good breeding," Farnham felt that "this national happiness comes chiefly from a near and homely source quite accessible to all peoples – the practice of politeness." In fact, he claimed to be "surprised to see how agreeable a commonplace existence is made simply by the arts of polite intercourse, without much dependence on literature, fine arts, sciences, and set amusements."[62] Farnham did acknowledge, however, that there were two men in the parish "whose reading carries them beyond this narrow field." One was Luc Letellier de Saint-Just, the province's former lieutenant-governor who "commanded my admiration by the liberality of his mind and the versatility of his information as well as by the dignity, simplicity, and courtesy of a typical Canadian gentleman." The other was Abbé Casgrain, "a radical priest and writer of unusual force" whose "fruitful explanations have given me a sympathy and understanding I could not otherwise have enjoyed in studying an antiquated, ultra-Catholic civilization so foreign to the spirit of our national life."[63]

But Farnham also interviewed one of the local *habitants* in order to gain insight into how he and his neighbours passed the time during the winter. The response made it clear that there was plenty of work to do even in that dead season. After feeding the livestock, "the two principal labors" were "hauling wood to keep the house warm, and threshing grain to eat." Only after evening chores was there time to visit a neighbour. As for the women, "their work is never done." They made the fire, cooked breakfast, and milked the cows before washing the children for school, then, the sweeping done, "they sit down to spin, weave, or knit all day." Unlike the men, they rarely left the farm except to go to church. The chief social events were weddings. The priest "then permits dancing among relatives, and allows unusual expenses to be incurred," but he had directed that courtships must be "short and circumspect." In fact, "engagements are made very much after the pecuniary interests followed in France."[64] There is evidence from a nearby parish to suggest that Farnham's observation about short engagements and unromantic marriages among the *habitants* – perhaps gleaned from Abbé Casgrain – was quite accurate.[65] Farnham to the contrary, however, the annual reports of Quebec's parish priests to their bishops made it clear that they had little power to prevent dancing among young people.[66]

Indeed, Farnham's own depiction of a wedding party suggests that dances were not a rare occurrence in Rivière Ouelle. Characterizing the fiddler as "a stamping machine with a fiddle attachment," Farnham described a jig performed by a "burly uncombed farmer sixty-eight years old" who "devoted himself seriously to the task in hand, thumping the floor, with enlivening regularity, with feet shod in moccasins." His dance partner was one of the young brides who, "holding her trim fine figure erect, took her mincing steps with delicate poise and restrained agility; she watched his steps with downcast eyes, now and then rejecting him with a haughty turn of the head as she pirouetted and chasseyed at the changes of the tune." Couple then succeeded couple until the exhausted fiddler "lost all sense of artistic contrast, and settled down to a monotonous hard pounding of the floor." Finally, "At midnight the old women began to yawn rather pitifully; a crusty old fellow lying on the floor behind the stove had fewer jokes to send up at the girls as they passed," and "the company went off like bundles of robes down the road."[67]

Also breaking the daily routine were the celebrations of Christmas and New Year, as well as the carnival season. On these occasions, cards and "simple round games" were played, songs occasionally sung, and a story teller "may relate some fanciful legend." Dismissive as he may have been about the oral tradition, Farnham was a keen observer of local customs. Thus, he wrote that New Year's day began with a blessing from the family patriarch, then "relatives called on one another and ate doughnouts and drank a glass of liquor," and everyone went to church where "Even those who had been unfriendly went about seeking one another, and meeting with at least frank and cordial faces, to begin the new year with fair intentions." Farnham was clearly impressed, for he wrote that "I have never seen elsewhere so public and general a demonstration of forgiveness and good-will."[68] As anthropologist Gerry Sider has observed of Christmas mumming in outport Newfoundland, such new-year rituals served a vital role in relaxing tensions that had inevitably built up in close-knit, isolated communities.[69]

The Saguenay

As a side excursion to his travels down the St Lawrence, Farnham boarded a steamer bound for the Saguenay river, then paddled his kayak from the head of navigation at Chicoutimi to Lac Saint-Jean, a colonization region whose isolation, in Farnham's words, made it "one of the best examples of the border civilization that the Canadian of to-day creates when left to himself and his Catholic leaders in a favourable locality."[70] Predictably, Farnham wrote that the "Canadian" (meaning French Canadian) "is an excellent pioneer up to a certain point; no one surpasses him in enduring hardships, labor, want; he lives and increases where others will not remain. But when he has cleared a few acres and won half of a living he feels satisfied, and generally fails to carry his civilization to the higher plane of comfort, cleanliness, and taste."[71] According to historian Gérard Bouchard, the region's farmers were actually increasing their dairy production during the 1880s to take advantage of the greater access to the extra-regional market, yet his analysis does suggest that Farnham was partially right because the money generated by the sale of butter and cheese was reinforcing the existing social order by enabling families to sustain a high birth rate and to expand the settlement zone.[72]

Farnham paid little attention to farming, however, instead writing a detailed description of a group of blueberry pickers he had met while scanning for a place to beach his kayak for the night. The small group welcomed him to their camp on a narrow ledge overlooking the river, a place "filled with social warmth" that "seemed like the sheltering hollow of a mighty hand stretched out in space." The berry crop was a poor one that year, and the nine girls, two or three "haggard old women," and a "sharp-featured, keen-eyed, gray little man" had picked only six or seven boxes a day, for which they were paid a mere sixteen cents for each box of four gallons. Similarly, a group of fourteen that Farnham met at the berry market in Grand Bay had received only $2.40 for the sixteen boxes they had picked after travelling more than eighty kilometres. Meagre as their sales were, the pickers claimed to have no other option because blueberries were their only source of cash, "and we'd starve to death on the farm alone."[73] Like any travel writer, Farnham may have focused his gaze on the marginal and the exotic, but the fact that the colonists of this region referred to blueberries as "la manne bleue" suggests that the fruit played an important role in their diet if not their economy.[74]

If one French-Canadian stereotype was the parish-bound *habitant*, the other was the adventuresome voyageur, a figure that would certainly have been familiar to any American who had read Parkman's monumental history of New France. Indeed, Farnham reported that his chief goal in ascending the Saguenay was to study the voyageur. As for the inconvenient fact that such a figure no longer existed, Farnham simply altered the meaning of the word to include men who worked in the woods, especially those who explored the timber limits, engaged in the dangerous task of driving logs down the swollen streams in the spring, "or at the lowest wield nothing inferior to the axe." Describing how crews of three would man boats or canoes to "land on the rocks and work at loosening the logs" that were jammed in mid-stream, Farnham added: "The voyageurs that I have known all possessed keen observation, a cool judgment, and a decisive turn of mind."[75]

Farnham paid less attention to labour, however, than to the leisure activities in the timber shanties (see figure 6.4). The cook, who was called "the mistress of the house" and had complete authority over the shanty, allowed the men to stay up late on Saturday nights when they were encouraged to engage in "games and pastimes" as a means of keeping them "from quarrelling and abandoning the hard labor of lumbering." Farnham was clearly fascinated by the somewhat homoerotic character of rough games such as "codfishing," "passing the rat," "the foxes," "selling sheep," and "bucking horse," and he noted that the youngest man "could scarcely appear on the floor and escape the embraces of one or another; they made sweet speeches to him, hugged him, and insisted that his hot resistance was due to the shyness and coquetry of a girl." Farnham insisted, however, that his main interest was in "the childishness of the men; even the gray-haired worked at entertainment with perspiring zest; the room rang with their boisterous laughter; the loud talking of all at once, the orders of half a dozen masters of ceremonies; and the leading spirits often jumped and danced about with uncontrollable excitement."[76] Forestry historians have tended to ignore what René Hardy and Normand Séguin refer to rather dismissively as "les divertissements, les rigodons et les jeux de force,"[77] but Farnham's lively description suggests that the timber shanty is fertile ground for historians of masculinity and homosociability.[78]

6.4 *Political Discussion in a Lumber Shanty, Harper's New Monthly Magazine* 76 (March 1888), 551.

The Montagnais

Approximately eighty miles down the St Lawrence from Tadoussac and the mouth of the Saguenay lies Betsiamites, which Farnham identified as "the chief mission of the Montagnais Indians" (see figure 6.5). He was fascinated by the Aboriginals' way of life, and claimed to feel awe in their presence, but the main reason was that he felt they represented an earlier stage of human evolution and were "absolutely a part of nature."[79] Resorting repeatedly to dehumanizing animal imagery as had David Atwood Wasson at Hopedale on the Labrador coast (see chapter 5), Farnham wrote that "the Indian's home, properly speaking, does not exist; he is not so domestic as the beaver, which builds a house and raises its family in a given locality. He owns land, yet moves about more than a bird which nests in a tree. Even the bear is a better

6.5 *Street Scene, Harper's New Monthly Magazine* 77 (August 1888), 379.

tenant, and the woodchuck is an older settler in his neighbourhood." Thus, the small whitewashed houses built for the Natives many years earlier were used only for storage while the families lived in wigwams, which Farnham described as having "a natural form, like the mound of a mole."[80]

Although he claimed that "In addressing an Indian I realize that I am talking to nature," Farnham did at least identify a man named Louis who provided a detailed account of his family's household economy. In response to the question, "What does it cost you to live in the woods?" Louis answered: "It costs you a good deal. Every year we buy about five barrels of flour, forty pounds of tea, eighty pounds of sugar, several pounds of lard, and eighty pounds of pork, that much for each family, four to six persons." Half was consumed in the village during the summer, and the other half en route to the winter hunting grounds, "for we take with us only enough provisions to last till we reach the woods, it is such hard work to make the portages." Louis added that "supplies, traps, clothes, etc., cost us about $250 or $300 per year," and that "We need about 3000 hares, 100 beavers, a great many fish" to pay the expenses and live. The best hunters harvested $400 worth of furs, but "most of us get from $100 to $200."[81]

Farnham failed to mention how such a "child of Nature" managed to be so familiar with the market economy, or the fact that the Montagnais had in recent years been forced to turn increasingly to trapping in the interior because they could no longer depend on the coastal seal or salmon fishery due to overexploitation of these resources by non-Natives.[82] As with the Saguenay blueberry pickers, however, we do at least hear the voice of a marginalized member of the North shore society. And Farnham once again demonstrated considerable interest in women's work, reporting that they "often throw a shawl or blanket over some poles, and compose a picturesque group in the shade, sewing, splitting spruce roots for canoe-making, and chatting away as glibly as if they knew English." Racist as this apparent attempt at humour may have been, Farnham clearly admired the Montagnais women's industriousness, reporting that they also cut and carried the firewood on their backs, set seines for fish, and butchered the seals, as well as preparing the meals.[83] But Farnham's most detailed attention, not surprisingly, was directed at the construction of the birch-bark canoe, which he described as "the Indian's chef d'oeuvre," and not only "a beautiful object" but "a suggestive emblem of his life." Resorting to poetic imagery, Farnham wrote that the Indian canoe "floats through mountain lakes with the beaver, and runs rapids with the otter; indeed, all of its companions are creatures of the forest; it is faithful to nature to the very last, when it retires to the shore of some lonely pond to mould under its mound of feathery moss."[84] Readers may have seen the parallel between the canoe and the First Nations, who were commonly assumed to be on the path to extinction.

Although he had been informed by Aboriginals themselves about the increasing difficulties of living off the land, and was well aware of the impact of infectious diseases, Farnham echoed the social Darwinism of his friend Parkman when he wrote that "The disappearance of the Indians must be due to some hidden psychological influence rather than to any adverse material conditions. Even here, under the best attainable relations with civilization and the least possible change of habits, they are diminishing about as fast as our abused tribes."[85] In Farnham's view, the modern Montagnais had "degenerated," and some of them "seem but half-formed lumps of flesh, bowlegged, in-toed, and as awkward as a goose on land," yet his own antimodern impulses meant that he envied their contentment which he claimed to find "at times almost supernatural."[86]

Life was rather idyllic during the summer at Betsiamites ("the Newport of the Indians"), where "the youths play ball, the maids frolic, the men smoke and chat in groups about the checker-board, the card-playing on the floor, or the canoe-making, and the women are not silent over their sewing, washing, and butchering." In addition, "their differences are always settled by a quiet conference, or by the judgment of the chief or the missionary, and their domestic life is peaceable and contented."[87] Lest his readers be left with the impression that the Montagnais were essentially a domesticated folk society, however, Farnham ended with a description of a dance he had witnessed as it reached its climax: "the music rose in the most frantic *crescendos* and savage discords; the actors, bounding about, bent over and tore the scalps from their prostrate victims, while yells and groans filled the air. It was the ancient war-dance, lacking only the lurid fire on the plumes and bloody tomahawks of the naked, painted savages."[88]

Labrador

Posing a much more tangible danger to the canoe or kayak paddler was the long coastline that stretched northeastward, and Farnham's two-part essay on Labrador begins with the words: "The shadow of death seemed to stretch before me for a thousand miles as I headed my canoe for Labrador." Reminding readers that Jacques Cartier had named that coastline "the land given to Cain," Farnham added that "It is a treeless waste of rock so sterile that even the most desirable places have barely soil enough to cover the dead." Furthermore, "with its treacherous currents, reefs, fogs, icebergs, and tempests, the sea here is a fitting companion of such a shore." Despite his foreboding, Farnham claimed to be attracted by "the purity of an untarnished world made of rock, sea, and air, the grandeur and simplicity of its pictures, the overpowering solitude of its arctic desert, and more than all else the human tenderness and heroism here and there contrasting so forcibly with the relentless character of the region."[89]

Noting that the inhabitants on the Canadian shore of Labrador were French Canadians, Farnham wrote that their houses "perch like anxious water-fowls on the bare rocks; they never impress me as homes, for they make for themselves no niche or place in the surface of the earth; you expect them to be washed or blown away at the next gale – as they sometimes are." He added that in "the best places," however, "there may be in a hollow a little sand, where a few turnips and cabbages manage to show themselves during a brief season." The people, themselves, were "courteous and kind, and they observe well their religious rites." One fisherman complained that there were schools in only three settlements, so that "our children are growing up as ignorant as we are – just like the dogs." Furthermore, the priest visited only once or twice a year, "and that's very inconvenient about dying, for pleurisy and consumption are very headstrong." With no doctors, or roots or herbs for medicine, the community relied on "pain-killers and salts that the traders sell."[90]

Farnham was clearly impressed by his fisherman informant's account of how he and his wife had cut all the timber for their buildings, sawed it in a pit, and rafted it downriver in the spring, yet he wrote that the "most astonishing traits" of the Labrador people "are laziness and improvidence here in sight of heart-rending hardship and want." Fishing, sealing, and trapping had once given "even the indolent a sure though a miserable living," enabling them "to idle away three-fourths of the year," but with fish, oil, and fur "no longer so abundant," the government was often obliged "to distribute flour and pork to prevent actual starvation." Although he had praised how the *habitants* and the Montagnais privileged the group over the individual, Farnham was too much the nineteenth-century liberal not to feel that self-reliance was a higher virtue, and he added disapprovingly: "The lazy depend upon the industrious, the provisions are shared, and if navigation is tardy, the first sail is watched for in the spring with eagerness."[91]

But at least Farnham did not dehumanize the Labrador fishermen, as he did the Montagnais, for he described without moralizing their various methods of killing seals, and noted of their harsh treatment of sled dogs: "with wolfish heads, bushy tails, and rough, ragged coats," the animals' ferocity "keeps your sympathy within bounds."[92] As if to reassure the reader that his sensitivities had not been dulled, however, Farnham ended the essay on an almost Transcendental note by describing the Labrador coast as possessing a beauty "more of heaven than of earth, more of light and color and mystery in the sky than of form and substance."[93] He also enthused that "I have never seen anything more rare and fascinating than icebergs," those "strange shy phantoms of the north," adding that "At night, when the aurora shines, they glow on the sea like a burning ship."[94] Farnham appears to have found life on the North Atlantic coast to be too elemental to foster a deep-rooted folk culture, but he clearly felt that his readers would be interested in how people managed to survive in such a harsh environment. In fact, as we shall see, even the cities north of the forty-fifth parallel could seem exotic if visited in the off-tourist season when they were buried in winter snow.

Quebec City

Quebec City's image as a medieval outpost in the New World meant that it appealed to American tourists in a way that none of their own more modern cities did.[95] Thus, the following romantic passage from Farnham's article on the provincial capital does little more than echo guidebooks that had begun to appear in the late 1820s, as we saw in chapter 1:

> Quebec is the mellowest nook of this raw continent, a cozy corner filled with materials for imagination to work over. It is verily a dusty, shadowy garret – where else can the poet lodge? – furnished with intellectual rubbish and bric-à-brac of the Middle Age [*sic*]; striking pictures of monk, nun, soldier, seigneur, savage; said to be actually haunted by the devil and his spirits, and defended by God and His angels; with miracles of daily occurrence; the air full of legends and superstition, as well as of religious zeal; peopled by quaint folk of medieval times; and the whole made misty with dust and cobwebs, comfortable with somnolence, and rich with the glow of social warmth.[96]

But rather than focusing on the city's historic sites, Farnham took the innovative step of describing the city in winter, after the tourist season had passed. Writing that "After a heavy snowfall Quebec seems to be a hoary city of the dead," Farnham claimed that in the suburbs "fences, hedges, even some roofs, are covered with snow-drifts; you can snowshoe anywhere, even up to some chimney-tops; all that breaks the white desert is a smoking chimney veiled by the exquisite tracery of bare trees against the blue sky."[97] While his rural essays generally depict winter in bleak terms, at least outdoors, Farnham now wrote that "the Canadian winter, excepting during a tempest, is a season full of comforts and enjoyments; for business sleeps, the Lower Town seems empty, and life turns either to frolicsome out-door sports – for which the good air provides abundant vigor – or to warm and intimate pleasures." Even though "the shipless port of Quebec" was now "a great valley of arctic snow," with "deserted wharves at low tide" rising up "like walls of icebergs," the frozen river had become "a park of amusement." Thus, "On a fine afternoon you may see the artillery wend its way from the citadel down the declivities of the town and out on the ice, lines of foot-passengers, city carioles and habitants, market sleds passing between Levis and Quebec; crowds of people standing about the race-track, the open-air skating rink, the slide built for coasting, the booths for the sale of cakes and liquor, and the gamblers with cards and wheels of fortune."[98]

Taking advantage of market day to maintain his focus on the *habitants*, Farnham complained that they were now less inclined than they once had been to wear homespun, but added that there were still "some quaint figures, and a general medieval tone interesting to a visitor." Due to a "pinched economy and industry of a very limited range," Farnham observed, "nobody brings a load of anything, everybody brings a little of everything – the superfluities from the house or the garden." Thus, in a single sled, one might see "a frozen carcass of mutton" looking like "a headless and footless wooden toy of my childhood; a pale calf's head in beatific repose; a blood-pudding; onions; a basket of milk frozen in round cakes; little balls of parsley and other herbs preserved all winter in brine; homespun cloth; crude paper flowers; socks; mittens; maple sugar; bunches of brightly colored grasses and mosses; wild birds in a cage; two or three button-hole bouquets of scarlet geraniums from the plants on the window sill."[99]

City life, itself, was folk-like in Farnham's narrative, for he ignored Quebec's many factories and other work places, aside from the manual loading of square timber onto aging Norwegian sailing vessels.[100] Instead, he focused on the annual Corpus Christi procession, describing the cloud of flags hovering over the streets, the evergreen arches, the booths "for the sale of beer and cakes," the miniature chapels hanging from house fronts, the strips of white muslin attached to hedges that "served as a background for hanging various objects that are supposed to arouse religious fervor – such as the motto, "Pas de rose sans épine," the portrait of Napoleon Bonaparte, photographs of esteemed members of the hanger's family, lithographs of the Holy Family, and marine views." To Farnham's amusement, one of the arches was even decorated with "a profusion of sporting articles and surmounted by the effigy of an Indian snow-shoer." As for the procession itself, Farnham described in some detail how it consisted of religious orders, civic societies, confraternities, charity boys and girls, college and university students, a brass band, firemen "in red, in blue, or in purple shirts," and, finally, "the Host, with the accompanying priests and attendants in fluttering white robes." After explaining the Catholic belief in transubstantiation, Farnham noted that as the Host passed "every one fell on his knees and bowed low; it seemed as if some magic spell swept along the street and mowed people down just where it found them – in the house, on the walk, or in the mud," though within minutes they had resumed their "social recreations." Farnham claimed to be "touched in seeing how this Catholic people mingle their religion with their daily duties and pleasures," for it gave him "a delicious sense of the picturesque," yet he could not resist concluding that "the subjects suffer – half unconsciously – in their ignorance of nature, science, art, and human life."[101]

Montreal

Farnham's *Harper's* series ends in Montreal, a city that was clearly too modern to be of much interest to him or, presumably, his readers. In contrast to the long-night darkness of the countryside in winter, Farnham's Montreal was a city of light. Thus, toboggans "flash upon your sight like a magic picture, from the dimness of night into the vividness of red light or a green, or the shadowy glow of a bonfire"; and the ice palace is "an opalescent castle intensely brilliant in the sunshine, with walls of translucent shadows edged with prismatic hues." Finally, there was the electrically lit indoor skating rink with its "continual kaleidoscopic interchange of colors and costumes."[102] Modern as these popular urban amusements were, in many respects, perhaps it was no accident that tobogganing and ice palaces, if not skating, also recalled the preindustrial past.[103]

The final impression Farnham left of Montreal, however, was a negative one (similar to that of Rupert Brooke, discussed in chapter 10), for he concluded disapprovingly that there were "the usual clubs for the reading of Shakespeare and Browning," but "no public general library, excepting the Frazer Institute, just struggling into existence," and the press "is very much hampered by the constant necessity of being politic in a sharply divided community." Furthermore, music (Farnham's passion) "is not an important part of social life," and the city was only beginning "to adorn itself with painting and sculpture."[104] But rather than pointing to the philistinism of Montreal's wealthy anglo-Protestant elite, Farnham once again blamed the Catholic Church for what he described as the lack of "social leaders, amusements of worth, intellectual, scientific, and artistic centres and activities" in what was the "largest and most wealthy of French Canadian communities."[105]

Conclusion

Even though only a small percentage of the adult population of the United States read *Harper's Magazine*, they were what one literary historian refers to as a "highly influential and socially prominent readership" during an era when there was no competition from radio, motion pictures, or television.[106] Like even the most informed and talented travel writers, however, Farnham could not stray far beyond cultural stereotypes if he wished to find an audience for his material.[107] Thus, at a time when Canadian nationalists were cultivating the myth that the northern climate was producing a hardy, self-reliant race (as we shall see in chapter 8), Farnham's colourful and evocative accounts of his sojourns in Quebec tended to reinforce the American perception of Canada as a cold and barren land, one that was inhabited by a poor and ignorant people on the very doorstep of their own progressive and democratic country. In a sense, as William A. Williams has noted of British travel narratives set in pre-famine Catholic Ireland, such accounts served to clarify and justify the values of the industrial capitalist culture that was remaking its own country.[108] British and American confidence in that culture was weakening somewhat by Farnham's time, however, with the result that he depicted the *habitants* as a people whose traditional values and sense of community were to be admired and even envied. As on Cape Breton Island, the goal Farnham set for himself was to discover and report on a "simple homespun folk," and not simply out of idle curiosity; the friendliness, generosity, and contentment that characterized the *habitants* as well as the Aboriginal people whom he met, were values that were rather alarmingly giving way in modern America to the unchecked growth of materialistic individualism. Farnham's anti-modernism was balanced, if not contradicted, by his liberalism, but as time passed and the pace of urbanization accelerated, folklorists and tourism promoters would depict the *habitants* in increasingly idealized and simplified terms.[109] In fact, that image would represent the "true" French Canadian until it was erased by the Quiet Revolution of the 1960s.[110]

NOTES

1 See, for example, R.G. Moyles and Doug Owram, *Imperial Dreams: British Views of Canada, 1880–1914* (Toronto: University of Toronto Press, 1988), chapter 4; and Alain Parent, *Entre empire et nation: les representations de la ville de Québec de ses environs, 1760–1833* (Quebec: Les Presses de l'Université Laval, 2005).

2 See J.I. Little, "In Search of the Plains of Abraham: Viewing a Symbolic Landscape, 1793–1913," in Phillip Buckner and John Reid, eds, *Remembering 1759: The Conquest of Canada in Historical Memory* (Toronto: University of Toronto Press, 2012), 92–4.

3 J.C. Myers, *Sketches on a Tour Through the Northern and Eastern States, the Canadas and Nova Scotia* (Harrisonburg, VA: J.H. Wartmann, 1849), 224 (CIHM 38369).

4 Henry D. Thoreau, *A Yankee in Canada* (1866) (Montreal: Harvest House, 1961), 83.

5 Thoreau, *A Yankee in Canada*, 88.

6 Henry James, *Portraits of Places* (Boston: Houghton, Mifflin and Company, 1883), 358–9.

7 In 1885 *Harper's New Monthly Magazine* had a circulation of 200,000 in America and 35,000 in Great Britain, giving it "the widest readership of any magazine of its kind." Eugene Exman, *The House of Harper: One Hundred and Fifty Years of Publishing* (New York: Harper and Row, 1967), 79.

8 Frank Luther Mott, *A History of American Magazines, Volume 3: 1865–1885* (Cambridge, MA: Harvard University Press, 1957), 258.

9 Lears makes a sharp distinction between the longstanding American agrarian concern about urban "effeminacy" and "luxury" and the more broad-sweeping dissatisfaction with "rationalization" that emerged in the 1880s. T.J. Jackson Lears, *No Place of Grace: Antimodernism and the Transformation of American Culture, 1880–1920* (New York: Pantheon Books, 1981), 5–7.

10 On the origins of the folk culture concept, see Ian McKay, *The Quest of the Folk: Antimodernism and Cultural Selection in Twentieth-Century Nova*

Scotia (Montreal and Kingston: McGill-Queen's University Press, 1994), 8–30. On its use by French-Canadian novelists, beginning in the middle of the nineteenth century, see Serge Gauthier, *Charlevoix ou la création d'une région folklorique: étude du discours de folkloristes Québécois (1916–1980)* (Lévis, QC: Les Presses de l'Université Laval, 2006), 42. On the rise of rural tourism in Vermont towards the end of the nineteenth century, see Blake Harrison, *The View From Vermont: Tourism and the Making of an American Rural Landscape* (Burlington, VT: University of Vermont Press, 2006), chapters 1 and 2.

11 Note the parallel with Prince Edward Island, where American travellers were "charmed by what they considered the Island's old world, rustic qualities, and yet took a patronizing view of Island 'backwardness.'" Alan Andrew MacEachern, "Discovering an Island: Travel Writers and Tourism on Prince Edward Island," *The Island Magazine* 29 (1991): 11. Lears notes (*No Place of Grace*, 6) that American antimodernism remained more liberal than its European counterpart.

12 Adam Paul Weisman, "Postcolonialism in North America: Imaginative Colonization in Henry David Thoreau's *A Yankee in Canada* and Jacques Poulin's *Volkswagen Blues*," *The Massachusetts Review* 36, no. 3 (Autumn 1995): 478.

13 Myers, *Sketches on a Tour*, 224. Myers wrote (p. 225) that there were very few settlements below the Montmorency River, "as the province becomes still more rugged, cold and sterile ... and of course becomes unfit for the abode of man."

14 See the bibliography in JoAnn Levy, *Unsettling the West: Eliza Farnham and Georgiana Bruce Kirby in Frontier California* (Berkeley, CA: Heyday Books, 2004), 320. Thomas Farnham died in California in 1848, when his son Charles was only seven. Eliza Wood Burhans Farnham died of tuberculosis in 1863, after nursing the wounded following the Battle of Gettysburg. W. David Lewis, "Farnham, Eliza Wood Burhans," in *Notable American Women, 1607–1950: A Biographical Dictionary*, vol. 1 (Cambridge, MA: The Belknap Press of Harvard University Press, 1971), 598–600; Levy, *Unsettling the West*, 5–6, 216–19, 232. C.H. Farnham provides a brief autobiography in his "Labrador, First Paper," *Harper's New Monthly Magazine* [hereafter *HNMM*] 71 (September 1885): 500.

15 Charles Haight Farnham, *A Life of Francis Parkman* (Toronto: George N. Morang and Company, 1909), ix, xi, 9, 37–8. Farnham cites Parkman at some length concerning the reasons for the contrast between the "mellow civilization" of French Canada and "the life of our enterprising, practical,

unfinished republic." Farnham, "A Winter in Canada," *HNMM* 68 (February 1884): 395–6.

16 See Roderick Nash, *Wilderness and the American Mind*, revised edition (New Haven: Yale University Press, 1973), chapter 9.

17 Lears, *No Place of Grace*, xii.

18 Patricia Jasen, *Wild Things: Nature, Culture, and Tourism in Ontario, 1790–1914* (Toronto: University of Toronto Press, 1995), 107. On neurasthenia, see also Lears, *No Place of Grace*, 46–58; and on early family camping, see J.I. Little, "Life without Conventionality: American Social Reformers as Summer Campers on Lake Memphremagog, Quebec, 1878–1905," *Journal of the Gilded Age and Progressive Era* 9, no. 3 (July 2010): 281–311.

19 Anthony Rotundo, *Manhood in America: Transformations in Manhood from the Revolution to Modern Era* (New York: Basic Books, 1993), chapter 3. Farnham died in Florida in 1929, having reportedly worked for many years on an unfinished encyclopedia of the arts. Levy, *Unsettling the West*, 213, 271, 317–18.

20 Prior to the middle of the twentieth century, the tourism literature generally referred to the "Kingdom of the Saguenay" rather than "Charlevoix." Gauthier, *Charlevoix*, 88, 97–8, 102.

21 Anonymous, "The Saguenay," *HNMM* 19 (June/November 1859): 158.

22 Quoted in Philippe Dubé, *Charlevoix: Two Centuries at Murray Bay*, translated by Tony Martin-Sprey (Montreal and Kingston: McGill-Queen's University Press, 1990), 55. According to James Doyle, Howells "insisted on seeing Canada not as a retarded contrast to the progressive republic, but as an inevitably flawed, yet legitimate and valuable social and political response to the conditions of the New World." James Doyle, ed., *Yankees in Canada: A Collection of Nineteenth-Century Travel Narratives* (Downsview, ON: ECW Press, 1980), 135. Howells signed an employment contract with *Harper's* in 1884. Exman, *The House of Harper*, 153–4.

23 Annie Fréchette Howells, "Summer Resorts on the St. Lawrence," *HNMM* 69 (June–November 1884): 197–209. For details on the career of Annie Fréchette Howells, see James Doyle, *Annie Howells and Achille Fréchette* (Toronto: University of Toronto Press, 1979). Another *Harper's* article on Canada, published in 1874, focused on the region southeast of Montreal. See Frederic Gregory Mather, "On the Boundary Line," *HNMM* 49 (August 1874): 335–50. Finally, there is a brief 1881 article on the popular shrine at Ste Anne de Beaupré, east of Quebec City. See Frank H. Taylor, "A Canadian Pilgrimage," *HNMM* 63 (March 1881): 502–5.

24 Lynda Villeneuve, *Paysage, mythe et territorialité: Charlevoix au XIXe siècle: pour une nouvelle approche du paysage* (Lévis: Les Presses de l'Université Laval, 1999), 1.
25 Ironically, as Villeneuve notes, the image of a homogenous and static rural society was also promoted by French-speaking ultramontane conservatives. *Paysage, mythe et territorialité*, 270–2.
26 Time is not entirely linear in that article, for it includes material from more than one visit, serving as a sort of addendum to the series.
27 C.H. Farnham, "The Lower St. Lawrence," *HNMM* 77 (November 1888): 814–15.
28 Farnham, "The Lower St. Lawrence," 819–24.
29 See Claude Boudreau, Serge Courville, and Normand Séguin, *Atlas historique du Québec: Le territoire* (Sainte-Foy, QC: Les Presses de l'Université Laval, 1997), 64–5.
30 Christian Harvey, "L'histoire des bateaux blancs dans Charlevoix: essor et déclin de la Ligne du Saguenay," *Revue d'histoire de Charlevoix* 68 (June 2011): 6. The Tafts were summer residents for four decades. Dubé, *Charlevoix*, 77, 99–101.
31 Harvey, "L'histoire des bateaux blancs," 11.
32 C.H. Farnham, "The Canadian Habitant," *HNMM* 67 (August 1883): 375–6.
33 According to Gauthier (*Charlevoix*, 112–13) this was the prevailing view of the Charlevoix landscape until the arrival of automobile tourists in the 1960s. See, for example, Creighton, "The Lower St. Lawrence," 704.
34 Farnham, "The Canadian Habitant," 376; Mary Louise Pratt, *Imperial Eyes: Travel Writing and Transculturation* (London: Routledge, 1992), 120–1. Folklorists also adopted the distanced perspective. Gauthier, *Charlevoix*, 59.
35 Barbeau attributed his discovery of Charlevoix folklore to a First Nations resident of the Lorette reserve near Quebec City. Gauthier, *Charlevoix*, 125–6. Villeneuve (*Paysage*, 272) notes that the detailed study of a single *habitant* family in St Irénée, published by French sociologist C.H.P. Gauldrée-Boilleau in 1862, gave them no voice. For analysis of this study, see Villeneuve, *Paysage*, 39–40, 264–72.
36 On the origins of the reputation of Charlevoix as an earthquake zone, see Gauthier, *Charlevoix*, 92–4.
37 On the local diet, see Normand Perron and Serge Gauthier, *Histoire de Charlevoix* (Sainte-Foy: Les Éditions de l'IQRC, 2000), 200–1.
38 Farnham, "The Canadian Habitant," 377–8, 385. According to Perron and Gauthier, the 1891 census reveals that one-fifth of the Charlevoix houses had only one or two rooms. *Histoire de Charlevoix*, 198.

39 Farnham, "The Canadian Habitant," 378–9.
40 Abbé Charles Trudelle, *Notes historiques sur Baie-Saint-Paul* (La Malbaie, QC: Éditions Charlevoix, 2010, first published in 1859), 68.
41 Though Farnham did not mention it, in at least some parishes men would also leave the church to continue their socializing during the sermon. See Ollivier Hubert, "Ritual Performance and Parish Sociability: French-Canadian Catholic Families at Mass from the Seventeenth to the Nineteenth Century," in Nancy Christie, ed., *Households of Faith: Family, Gender, and Community in Canada, 1760–1969* (Montreal and Kingston: McGill-Queen's University Press, 2002), 61–2.
42 Farnham, "The Canadian Habitant," 381–2. The research by Perron and Gauthier tends to support the dominant role of the priest and parish in Charlevoix society. *Histoire de Charlevoix*, 204–6.
43 Farnham, "The Canadian Habitant," 383–4.
44 Farnham, "The Canadian Habitant," 390. Charlevoix's domestic cloth production industry was well known throughout the province by the 1860s. Villeneuve, *Paysage*, 266.
45 See Villeneuve, *Paysage*, chapter 4.
46 Like Villeneuve, Perron and Gauthier stress the contrast between farms in the valleys and those in the hills to the rear, but they also state that in general "les instruments aratoires qu'il utilise sont de fabrication artisanale, comme la charrue tirée par un cheval ou un boeuf," and that the primary goal for most families was subsistence. *Histoire de Charlevoix*, 191–5.
47 See Lears, *No Place of Grace*, chapter 2.
48 Farnham, "The Canadian Habitant," 384. On what Lears refers to as "medieval mentalities," see *No Place of Grace*, chapter 4.
49 Farnham, "The Canadian Habitant," 389.
50 Farnham, "The Canadian Habitant," 386. On the assumed importance of illiteracy for the preservation of an oral tradition and therefore an authentic folk culture, see Gauthier, *Charlevoix*, 36–7.
51 The *Rituel* mentioned grasshoppers, caterpillars and other insects. Peter N. Moogk, *La Nouvelle France: The Making of French Canada – A Cultural Interpretation* (East Lansing, MI: University of Michigan Press, 2000), 244.
52 Farnham, "The Canadian Habitant," 388–9. On a religious procession to save the crops in nearby Ile aux Coudres and the subsequent elevation of *croix de chemins* throughout the island, see Perron and Gauthier, *Histoire de Charlevoix*, 205–6.
53 See Lears, *No Place of Grace*, chapter 5.
54 Farnham, "The Canadian Habitant," 385, 387.

55 Farnham claimed that with purchases essentially confined to a pound of tea, two pounds of chocolate, two gallons of syrup, "and fifty cents worth of raisins, almonds, etc.," the average annual expenditure of comfortable families was said to be no more than $150. "The Canadian Habitant," 391.
56 Farnham, "A Winter in Canada," 392–3.
57 Farnham, "A Winter in Canada," 393–4.
58 Farnham, "A Winter in Canada," 394.
59 Farnham, "A Winter in Canada," 395–6.
60 Farnham, "A Winter in Canada," 397. Two years later, Farnham wrote to the Protestant former-premier of Quebec, with whom he was on friendly terms, that the Quebec education system "is so bad in my opinion that it depresses me to treat the subject." Library and Archives Canada, Fonds Henri-Gustave Joly de Lotbinière, M786, 3562, C.H. Farnham to Henri-Gustave Joly, Boston, 20 December 1886.
61 Farnham, "A Winter in Canada," 397.
62 Farnham, "A Winter in Canada," 400.
63 Farnham, "A Winter in Canada," 400. The elderly Letellier de Saint-Just had actually retired to Quebec City in 1879, and died there in 1881, so it is rather unlikely that Farnham met him in Rivière Ouelle. Abbé Casgrain was no radical, but he was an ardent promoter of French-Canadian literature. A founder of *Les Soirées canadiennes*, a literary magazine that "encouraged writers to retell Canadian legends in prose and poetry," he was also author of *Légendes canadiennes* (1861), as well as a collection of poetry and a number of historical volumes and biographies, including one on Francis Parkman (1872). Robert Rumilly, "Letellier de Saint-Just, Luc," *Dictionary of Canadian Biography Online*; Jean-Paul Hudon, "Casgrain, Henri-Raymond," *Dictionary of Canadian Biography Online.*
64 Farnham, "A Winter in Canada," 401–2.
65 See Félix Albert, *Immigrant Odyssey: A French-Canadian Habitant in New England*, translated by Arthur L. Eno, Jr, from *Histoire d'un Enfant Pauvre* (Orono, ME: University of Maine Press, 1991), chapter 2.
66 See, for example, J.I. Little, *Crofters and Habitants: Settler Society, Economy, and Culture in a Quebec Township, 1848–1881* (Montreal and Kingston: McGill-Queen's University Press, 1991), 212–14; and Frank A. Abbott, *The Body or the Soul? Religion and Culture in a Quebec Parish, 1736–1901* (Montreal and Kingston: McGill-Queen's University Press, 2016), chapters 7–8.
67 Farnham, "A Winter in Canada," 405–6.
68 Farnham, "A Winter in Canada," 408.
69 Gerry Sider, "Christmas Mumming and the New Year in Outport Newfoundland," *Past and Present* 71 (May 1976): 102–25.

70 C.H. Farnham, "Canadian Voyageurs on the Saguenay," *HNMM* 76 (March 1888): 538.

71 Farnham, "Canadian Voyageurs," 541.

72 Gérard Bouchard, *Quelques arpents d'Amérique. Population, économie, famille au Saguenay, 1838–1871* (Montreal: Boréal, 1996), 98–9.

73 Farnham, "Canadian Voyageurs," 544–8.

74 Camil Girard and Normand Perron, *Histoire du Saguenay – Lac-Saint-Jean* (Quebec: Institut québécois de recherche sur la culture, 1989), 165.

75 Farnham, "Canadian Voyageurs," 538.

76 Farnham, "Canadian Voyageurs," 550–3.

77 René Hardy and Normand Séguin, *Forêt et société en Mauricie* (Montreal and Ottawa: Boréal Express and Musée nationale de l'Homme, 1984), 134. See, for example, Ian Radforth, *Bushworkers and Bosses: Logging in Northern Ontario, 1900–1980* (Toronto: University of Toronto, 1987).

78 On this theme, see Adele Perry, "Bachelors in the Backwoods: White Men and Homosocial Culture in Up-Country British Columbia, 1858–71," in Ruth Sandwell, ed., *Beyond the City Limits: Rural History in British Columbia* (Vancouver: UBC Press, 1998); and, from an anthropological perspective, Peter H. Harrison, "Life in a Logging Camp," in Richard Mackie and Graeme Wynn, eds, *Home Truths: Highlights from BC History* (Madeira Park, BC: Harbour Publishing, 2012), 338–59.

79 C.H. Farnham, "The Montagnais," *HNMM* 77 (August 1888): 379.

80 Farnham, "The Montagnais," 380.

81 Farnham, "The Montagnais," 382. See also 392–3.

82 In recognition of this loss of livelihood, the government in 1861 began providing $600 a year to the people of the newly created Betsiamites reserve. See Pierre Frenette *et al.*, *Histoire de la Côte-Nord* (Sainte-Foy: Les Éditions de l'IQRC, 1996), 337–41, 349–57.

83 Farnham, "The Montagnais," 380.

84 Farnham, "The Montagnais," 383. Construction details are on pp. 384–5.

85 Farnham, "The Montagnais," 384–7; Francis Jennings, "Francis Parkman: A Brahmin Among Untouchables," *William and Mary Quarterly*, third series, 42, no. 3 (July 1985): 305–28.

86 Farnham, "The Montagnais," 389.

87 Farnham, "The Montagnais," 389–90.

88 Farnham, "The Montagnais," 394.

89 Farnham, "Labrador, First Paper," 489. Farnham did not paddle his kayak the entire distance, for the last part of the excursion was aboard a fishing schooner.

90 C.H Farnham, "Labrador, Second Paper," *HNMM*, 71 (October 1885), 652.

91 Farnham, "Labrador, Second Paper," 653.
92 Farnham, "Labrador, Second Paper," 657.
93 Farnham, "Labrador, Second Paper," 661.
94 Farnham, "Labrador, Second Paper," 663–5.
95 See Catherine Cocks, *Doing the Town: The Rise of Urban Tourism in the United States, 1850–1915* (Berkeley: University of California Press, 2001), chapter 1.
96 C.H. Farnham, "Quebec," *HNMM* 76 (February 1888): 356.
97 Farnham, "Quebec," 358.
98 Farnham, "Quebec," 359.
99 Farnham, "Quebec," 362.
100 Farnham, "Quebec," 367–8. On Quebec City's industries, see Marc Vallières et al., *Histoire de Québec et de sa région, tome 2, 1792–1939* (Quebec: Les Presses de l'Université Laval, 2008), chapter 13.
101 Farnham, "Quebec," 368–72.
102 C.H. Farnham, "Montreal," *HNMM* 79 (June 1889): 83. Arc lights had been used to illuminate the Montreal ice palace at night in 1885. Sherry Olson, "'A Profusion of Light' in Nineteenth-Century Montreal," in Serge Courville and Normand Séguin, eds, *Espace et Culture / Space and Culture* (Sainte-Foy: Les Presses de l'Université Laval, 1995), 260.
103 Farnham also included a lengthy description of a snowshoe outing in his Quebec City article.
104 Farnham, "Montreal," 89.
105 Farnham, "Montreal," 91.
106 Janice A. Radway, "Learned and Literary Print Culture in an Age of Professionalization and Diversification," in Carl F. Kaestle and Janice A. Radway, eds, *A History of the Book in America, Volume 4: Print in Motion* (Chapel Hill, NC: University of North Carolina Press, 2009), 212.
107 On this theme, see Carl Thompson, *Travel Writing* (London and New York: Routledge, 2011), chapter 6.
108 William A. Williams, *Tourism, Landscape, and the Irish Character: British Travel Writers in Pre-Famine Ireland* (Madison, WI: University of Wisconsin Press, 2008), 198.
109 On the tourist guides, see Gauthier, *Charlevoix*, 154.
110 See Daniel Francis, *National Dreams: Myth, Memory, and Canadian History* (Vancouver: Arsenal Pulp Press, 1997), chapter 4.

7 "A fine, hardy, good-looking race of people": Travel Writers, Tourism Promoters, and the Highland Scots Identity on Cape Breton Island, 1829–1920

Referring to Scotland's influence on Canada, historian Edward J. Cowan has suggested that "there is perhaps no other example as graphic of one country being described in terms of another."[1] Cowan's examples are mostly from the pre-Confederation era, and Nova Scotia is the province that springs first to mind in thinking of Canada as a "new Scotland." Yet, according to historian Ian McKay, the province "became Scottish" only in the 1930s when Premier Angus L. Macdonald applied the state's cultural power to fuse "his own particularly romantic and essentialist reading of the Scottish tradition" with what he saw as "the redemptive power of tourism." Previously, McKay claims, writers had either "subordinated ethnicity to the story of material progress," or depicted the Scottish immigrants simply as "one rather uncivilized and undesirable group among many others in the province."[2]

The Scottishness referred to by McKay was that of the isolated Highlands and Islands. The demise of the traditional Gaelic culture in those areas following the clearances of the late eighteenth and early nineteenth centuries had paradoxically and ironically been followed by the invention of an ersatz Celtic identity for Scotland as a whole.[3] Historian T.M. Devine notes that this romantic clan-based identity was closely associated with the fiercely loyal Highland warrior. This was particularly so when the leading role played by the kilted regiments in the Seven Years' War and Napoleonic Wars "lent a new prestige and glamour to the wearing of tartan."[4] The Highland warrior image gained new life during the First World War when, McKay concedes, the kilts worn by the Cape Breton Highlanders would suggest that Nova Scotia tartanism "did not spring forth, fully kilted, from the forehead of Angus L. Macdonald."[5]

McKay's thesis, nevertheless, raises the question as to why the romanticization of the Highlanders that emerged in Britain shortly after the defeat of the Jacobite clans in 1746 would arrive so late to the shores of Nova Scotia.[6] It should be kept in mind, first, that even in Lowland Scotland and England the early romanticization process did not preclude the general view that the Highlands needed to be "improved."[7] Katherine Grenier's study on late nineteenth-century tourism on the Isle of Skye makes the important point that while the significance of the local crofters "lay in their perpetuation of values threatened by industrialization," their poverty "made them ambiguous figures." As a result, "the discourse on the people of Skye was liberally sprinkled with pejorative references to them as 'simple,' 'primitive' and naturally lazy, often within the same texts that honoured their goodness and simplicity."[8] Furthermore, it was easier to romanticize an Old World culture when it was in the process of being uprooted than after it had been transplanted to a New World settlement frontier where the focus was on adaptation and assimilation. But even though negative perceptions of Cape Breton's Scots persisted into the late nineteenth century, the rise of American antimodernism and the resurgence of British imperialism ensured that the Highland myth – including the romantic concept of a clan-based pre-industrial folk – did have a prominent place in travel narratives and tourism promotion long before Macdonald became premier in 1933.[9]

Originally inhabited by Mi'kmaq, Cape Breton was first colonized by Acadians, Loyalists, and Irish, in that order.[10] But the population balance shifted dramatically with the arrival of approximately 20,000 Scottish Highlanders and islanders from the Outer Hebrides between 1802 and the early 1840s. By 1871 approximately 50,000 of the 75,000 inhabitants of Cape Breton were of Scottish origin. As historical geographer Stephen Hornsby notes, it had become, in large part, a Scottish island.[11] Historical research has shown that rural Cape Breton society was much more stratified than the romantic myth of a tightly knit homogenous community would lead us to believe,[12] yet Hornsby argues that most of the island's population lived in rural communities that "were intensely local, even in the last decades of the century." In those communities, he adds, "Gaelic was still widely used, and much oral tradition, folk medicine, and music from the Highlands flourished."[13]

There was certainly little romance, however, in the descriptions of the rural Scots produced prior to the 1870s. For example, T.C. Haliburton, well known author of *The Clockmaker*, wrote in his *An Historical and*

Statistical Account of Nova Scotia, published in 1829, that "the great number" of the island's settlers "are indigent and ignorant Scotch islanders, every year receiving an increase of a thousand or two fresh emigrants, equally poor and illiterate, and almost all of the Roman Catholic persuasion."[14] Similarly, in his British-published travel narrative of 1832, John M'Gregor wrote:

> The Scotch Highlanders and Islanders, who form the majority of the population, are not mixed with settlers by whose example they might be stimulated to exertion, and from whom they might learn a better system of agriculture and domestic management. Contented to exist as their progenitors did, they seem careless about living in a more comfortable, cleanly, and respectable style.[15]

The message had become somewhat more mixed by the 1860s when the Cape Breton Scots were referred to as both industrious and unenterprising, sometimes in the same passages. Thus the Reverend Richard John Uniacke, Church of England minister in the coal town of Sydney, declared in his "Sketches of Cape Breton," originally published in London's *New Penny Magazine* between 1862 and 1865,[16] that "The chief settlers in this country at present are the poorer Scotch mostly from the Islands of Scotland. They are many of them industrious and frugal, and often succeed in making themselves tolerably comfortable upon a small piece of land: but they are not remarkably intelligent and do not bring with them a very extensive knowledge of farming, consequently in their hands agriculture makes slow progress."[17] In his travel article on Cape Breton, published in 1868, Nova Scotia native John Bourinot claimed similarly that "As a rule, the people are poor and unenterprising," but he then contradicted himself by writing that "The great majority of the people are Scotch, many of whom exhibit the thrift and industry of their race."[18]

The British travel writer John J. Rowan also focused on the social and economic characteristics of the Cape Breton Scots, but in a more uncompromisingly positive fashion. In *The Emigrant and Sportsman in Canada*, published in 1876, he observed that the local farmers "depend upon their cattle, for which the island is well adapted." Furthermore, "A stranger on seeing the rough and rugged nature of the pastures is astonished at the condition of the cattle, but the practical farmer knows the value of a large scope for his cattle, and the advantages of a variety of feed in keeping his stock in health." Nor were Cape Bretoners cut off from markets, Rowan observed, for they exported large quantities of beef and butter annually to Newfoundland "and other places."[19] Rowan criticized the Scots for being less willing to assimilate than the English or the Irish, but wrote that they were "a fine, hardy, good-looking race of people." His main concern was that their strength and health were being undermined by the new diet "of the finest American flour, badly cooked, and washed down with a black and bitter infusion called tea."[20] What Rowan failed to mention was that those who farmed the more fertile and accessible land were relatively prosperous, while the "backlanders" lived in considerable poverty.[21]

British travel writers generally passed the Maritimes by, however, particularly once the railway era began.[22] Instead, it was Americans who published the most widely read descriptions of Cape Breton, and, rather than being interested in the material conditions of the inhabitants, they were effectively scouting out picturesque destinations for other travellers or exotic material for their readers. But New Englanders and New Yorkers were not inclined to admire the role of the Highland regiments in the American War of Independence, or the part they played in the protection and expansion of the British Empire. In fact, many northerners associated Sir Walter Scott's novels with "misguided" southern chivalry, and the term "Highlander" with the backward and impoverished Appalachians.[23] Thus, in his humorously opinionated *Acadia; Or, A Month With the Blue Noses*, published in 1859, American yachtsman, marine artist, and travel writer Frederic S. Cozzens was being facetious when he professed his eagerness to meet in Cape Breton "the bold Highlandmen of romance; the McGregors, and McPhersons, the Camerons, Grahams, and McDonalds." Cozzens added that "as a century or so does not alter the old-country prejudices of the people in these settlements, we will no doubt find them in their pristine habiliments; in plaids and spleuchens; brogues and buckles; hose and bonnets; with claymore, dirk, and target; the white cockade and eagle feather, so beautiful in the Waverley novels."[24]

Had he been truly interested, Cozzens would have discovered a lively bagpiping culture in Cape Breton.[25] Yet, having arrived in Cape Breton, he reported that "the Celts in their wild settlements" were "without bagpipes or pistols, sporrans or philabegs; there was not even a solitary thistle to charm the eye; and, as for oats, there were at least two Scotchmen to one oat in this garden of exotics."[26] Continuing in this vein, Cozzens added: "I have a reasonable amount of respect for a Highlandman in full costume; but, for a carrot-headed, freckled, high-cheeked animal, in a round hat and breeches, that cannot utter a word of English, I have no sympathy." Finally, vaunting the superiority of the United States, as he did throughout his book, Cozzens criticized the colonial government for providing free land and setting low tariffs on foreign goods. The result, he claimed, was that "the colonist is only a parasite with all these advantages." Rather than being "a citizen, responsible for his franchise," he was "but a colonial Micmac, or Scotch-Mac; a mere sub-thoughted, irresponsible exotic."[27]

Beginning in the 1870s, however, more sympathetic descriptions of these "exotics" began to appear in American travel narratives about Cape Breton. No publication was more responsible for this shift than the prolific Charles Dudley Warner's oft-reprinted *Baddeck, and That Sort of Thing* which first appeared in 1874. Warner travelled by rail, stage, and ferry to reach the island, and much of his account chronicles the challenges faced on the journey.[28] There is no denying that – as with Cozzens before him – Warner's descriptions of islanders he encountered echo the satirical tone of contemporaries such as Mark Twain, with whom he had collaborated in writing *The Gilded Age* a year earlier.[29] Rather than providing detailed information for the prospective settler, investor, or tourist, *Baddeck and That Sort of Thing* was published largely for the entertainment of Warner's readers. According to McKay, Warner depicted the Cape Breton Scots as "peculiar, ignorant country folk, good-natured savages far removed from the modern age." Far from admiring their simplicity, McKay adds, Warner found them to be "a rich source of amusement."[30]

But, just as Dr Johnson's *Journey to the Western Islands of Scotland* (1773) could express scorn towards the Highlanders, yet convey a sentimental attachment to the old clan-based society,[31] so too in Warner's account one can detect a sense of nostalgia for what he viewed as the simpler, more innocent way of life in Cape Breton. Warner was clearly influenced by the initial stirrings of American antimodernism, which T.J. Jackson Lears has defined as "the recoil from an 'overcivilized' modern existence to more intense forms of physical or spiritual existence."[32] Thus, Warner observed of the McGregor family in Middle River that even though their house was "little better than a shanty," they refused to take payment for the pan of milk they offered and expressed "surprise that such a simple act of hospitality should have any commercial value." Warner also fretted that "travelers themselves destroy one of their chief pleasures," namely interaction with a generous and innocent folk, for he felt that by offering to pay for the milk he might have "planted the notion in the McGregor mind that the small kindnesses of life may be made profitable ... and probably the next travelers in that Eden will succeed in leaving some small change there, if they use a little tact."[33]

Warner also enthused about the beauty of Cape Breton's landscape. As a result, the island emerges in his book as a largely unspoiled refuge from the pressures of American city life. The "neat fishing village" of Whykokomagh, for example, is described as a "peaceful place," where "the lapsing waters of Bras d'Or made a summer music all along the quiet street; the bay lay smiling with its islands in front, and an amphitheater of hills rose behind. But for the line of telegraph poles one might have fancied he could have security and repose here."[34] Recalling his departure from Baddeck on a Bras d'Or Lake steamer, Warner exclaimed that "The most electric American, heir of all the nervous diseases of all the ages, could not but find peace in this scene of tranquil beauty, and sail on into a great and deepening contentment. Would the voyage could last for an age, with the same sparkling but tranquil sea, and the same environment of hills, near and remote!"[35] As foreshadowed by his comments about McGregor's milk and the Whykokomagh telegraph poles, Warner ended his travel narrative with a concern about the future:

> We received everywhere in the Provinces courtesy and kindness, which were not based upon any expectation that we would invest in mines or railways, for the people are honest, kindly, and hearty by nature. What they will become when the railways are completed that are to bind St. John to Quebec, and make Nova Scotia, Cape Breton, and Newfoundland only stepping-stones to Europe, we cannot say. Probably they will become like the rest of the world, and furnish no material for the kindly persiflage of the traveler.[36]

Only a year later, in 1875, the Boston-published tourist guide, *The Maritime Provinces: A Handbook for Travellers*, quoted some of Warner's more enthusiastic passages. It also claimed that the Scots Catholics of Judique "are famous throughout the island for their great stature, and are well known to the American fishermen on account of their pugnacity. Yankee crews landing on this coast are frequently assailed by these pugilistic Gaels, and the stalwart men of Judique usually come off victorious in the fistic encounters."[37] The American artist, diplomat and world traveller S.G.W. Benjamin was less impressed by such demonstrations of manliness, for he wrote in 1878 that the people of Grand Narrows "are a pretty rough set, with a decided talent for brawling and drinking."[38]

After a more extended visit five years later, however, Benjamin was more generous in his assessment. At Baddeck, on market day, he observed a "lassie" whose "flaxen elf-locks, bright blue-grey eyes, rosy cheeks, tall, shapely form, and elastic step were for all the world so thoroughly Scotch one might have sworn she was Burns's Highland Mary."[39] As Grenier observes of travellers writing about the Scottish Highlands, Benjamin's description of this young woman implied "a natural purity, healthiness, and modesty not to be found among the more sophisticated communities or among the urban working class."[40] Benjamin also wrote that most of the inhabitants of Cape Breton were "of Scotch descent, and a hale, hearty buxom race they are." While commenting on their unwillingness "to dare which is called enterprise," he added that "the yield of the mines and the fields and the large exportation of beef cattle are sufficient to keep the people comfortable, at least, if not wealthy." Furthermore, given that "They all own their own farms and homesteads, and every commodity is cheap," they had reason to feel contented. For those who felt otherwise, however, there was always emigration to the United States, and Benjamin felt they "should be welcomed, for they are of a nature to add real strength to the race now building up in this country out of various people flocking to our shores."[41] In short, the inherent racial characteristics of the Highlanders would make them impervious to the corrupting influences of modern American society.[42]

The first American writer to focus largely on the island's Highland customs and traditions, however, was Charles H. Farnham whose article, "Cape Breton Folk," appeared in the prestigious *Harper's New Monthly Magazine* in 1886.[43] Adopting much the same wryly humorous tone as Warner, Farnham challenged the myth of Highland hospitality by noting that "Cape Breton hospitality seems to be in strata." At a bay near Ingonish, for example, he and his travelling companion had "great difficulty getting shelter under any terms," being taken for "blacklegs" (strike breakers) by the local hotel keeper. At the next bay, fortunately, they ran into a "generous streak" and were even taken to a party "where reels and jigs helped to pass the night."[44] The article's main focus, however, is on Farnham's first-hand observations of the gathering of the clans, the local courtship custom, and the annual outdoor Communion service.

The "clan gathering" Farnham attended in the northeast Margaree valley was a privately sponsored event to raise funds to build a house. Farnham's rather sarcastic observation was that the "average" program featured "talking, swinging, and waiting to swing," interspersed by a "cold temperance lunch," though the event in question had the added attraction of a wrestling match.[45] Such a description tends to support McKay's observation that before the 1930s "we search high and low for the signs which today mark the Scot, and by extension the Nova Scotian: we look for the tartans, kilts, bagpipes, haggis and mods, and for the most part they are not to be found."[46] Farnham, however, was observing the adaptation of Old World customs to a New World environment, and he did report hearing bagpipe music, making the wry observation that "The pipes go well with the national emblem: they are a very thistle in your ear." Yet Farnham spent a day with one of the pipers whom he described as "a very tall, very dark, very shaggy man," and took notes on "some of the native airs of Cape Breton," one of which he included in his article. Having studied music in Paris, and taught singing in New York, Farnham was clearly interested in this folk tradition, for he also took the trouble to include the notes and words to a Gaelic song composed by another local musician, one that celebrated "the pastoral charms of the southwest Margaree."[47]

As for the local courtship custom, Farnham reported that, when a young man was ready to marry, he built a house and set out with a friend to act as his spokesman at the home of his prospective bride. In the case that Farnham described, the young woman withdrew from the sitting-room when the two men arrived, but agreed to marry after a brief discussion with the spokesman. The bride-to-be was then led to the middle of the floor where she took the hand of her intended husband, and "thus the 'contract' was accepted, under the usual penalty of forfeiting twenty dollars in case the engagement was broken." Unknown to Farnham, this was the old Hebridean custom of *rèiteach*, a Gaelic term meaning "clearing," for it cleared the way for a marriage. On the Isle of Lewis, it was in effect recognized as a popularly sanctioned marriage, with the "kirking" by the minister to take place at some future convenient time.[48] In the case Farnham described, however, the patriarchal tradition was subverted by the young woman who apparently had every intention of breaking the engagement because she was using it to prod into action another young man whom she preferred.[49]

If Farnham found the betrothal custom to be quaint and amusing, he was more moved by the traditional outdoor Communion service he attended at Englishtown on the north shore of St Ann's Bay where "the crowd was a gathering of austere and simple homespun folk." While noting that for the worldly minded it was an occasion for horse trading and other transactions, and that for the young it was a time of amusement, Farnham claimed that the over-all atmosphere was sombre. People "walked about greeting friends whom they had not seen perhaps for a year," but "the greeting was sober; sisters even did not kiss; many met at first in silence, with teeth set and eyes fixed, and shook hands vigorously for a long time with the motion of sawing wood."[50] Farnham was again particularly fascinated by the singing, noting that "The tunes have well-known names, such as 'Elgin,' 'St. Paul,' 'Bangor,' 'London,' 'Martyrs'; but the actual compositions and the rendering are unlike any other music on earth." He included the notes as sung by the precentor followed by those of the congregation, but added that "the effect of the singing can not be imagined from seeing the score, or from a rendering of it according to the usual musical expression." After observing that "so drawling is the execution that you just abandon all requirements of time, and accept the effects of intonation alone," Farnham concluded that "These Gaelic psalms often have an extraordinary effect; when the people at times happen to unite their plaintive voices on certain long notes and slurs, the multitude sends up a subdued wail that is wonderfully touching."[51]

Farnham was also impressed by the hospitality of the local host families upon whom the five-day event imposed a considerable burden. And he was just as moved by the congregation's "indifference to discomfort" as they listened to a sermon for hours in the rain and cold east wind, "the men's heads covered by handkerchiefs, the women's by black shawls." In short, "The occasion showed in a striking way the hardihood of this people, their indifference to discomfort, the force of tradition among them, and, in some cases, the absorbing sincerity of their piety."[52] Tellingly, Farnham's article was preceded by a sombre etching of black-clothed people in contemplation and prayer titled "The Open-Air Sacrament" (see figure 7.1).

The fact that Farnham paid more attention to the "folk" practices of the Cape Breton Highlanders than did his predecessors reflects the intensification of American antimodernism in the 1880s. According to Lears, traditional customs were now considered to be admirable alternatives to the drive for the efficient control of nature.[53] However, in his collection of essays titled *From Blomidon to Smoky*, published in 1894, the American nature writer Frank Bolles was rather critical of at

7.1 *The Open-Air Sacrament* by A.B. Frost. *Harper's New Monthly Magazine* (March 1886), 494.

least one local custom, namely the settlement of local conflicts without resorting to outside authorities.[54] Bolles, who was the secretary of Harvard University, described how a dispute over hay between "Rory This" and "Sandy That" resulted in the hay being burned "to quiet the trouble." This led Bolles to observe that he "could not reason out the process by which either Rory who had labored, or Sandy who had owned the grass, could find comfort in putting match to the hay."[55] Although Bolles had clearly missed the point of the exercise, which was to apply an extra-legal sanction against two members of the community who were disturbing its social harmony, he was not immune from the romanticization of the Cape Breton folk. He wrote, for example, that the Englishtown ferryman Torquil McLean had a face that held "many a suggestion of the Highland stock from which he is descended, and the wild north country in which he lives, and its counterpart in which his race was moulded."[56] Then, en route to Cape Smoky, Bolles and his wife spent a night at the home of fisherman Sandy McDonald where "Simple food, reading by McDonald from the Gaelic Bible, a long breath of ocean air, and the benediction of the stars fitted us for early and profound sleep."[57] The local folk had not entirely escaped outside influences, however, for some, according to Bolles' account, were eager to earn money from American tourists, and others were anxious to "try life under less picturesque but more profitable conditions."[58]

American travel writers appear to have lost interest in Cape Breton by the end of the century, just as Canadian-published promotional literature began to include tourism as a secondary strategy for economic development. Presumably because the image of a backward rural society would not be in keeping with this forward-looking economic goal, there was initially little effort to exploit the Highland myth. In 1884, *Picturesque Canada*'s Cape Breton chapter claimed that the island's scenery was "germane to Niagara and the St. Lawrence," that "the traditions of Louisbourg should kindle the imagination of the Canadian to as bright a heat as those which glorify Quebec," and that it possessed "riches in coal and minerals complementary to the bountiful harvests of the fertile West."[59] The only specific mention that the authors J. McLennan and R. Murray made of the Scots settlers was that they "still cherish their ancestral Gaelic, and cling to the ways of the Highlands and Islands."[60]

This pattern is repeated in *Cape Breton Hand-Book and Tourist's Guide,* which was published sometime after 1889. Aimed largely at promoting tourism as a means to attract outside investment, the guidebook consists largely of advertisements for local businesses.[61] For example, the "enterprise and integrity" of the MacDonald brothers, owners of the Glendyer Woolen Mills near Mabou, had reportedly "acquired for their products more than insular fame."[62] The town of Baddeck, much-loved by members of the American elite, was evidently the only one on the island not to have caught the entrepreneurial spirit. The guidebook's compiler Edwin Lockett wrote rather disapprovingly that it "can hardly be called a red hot enterprising town. The system is mostly long credit and long prices."[63] Tourists were promised, however, that at the town's Bras D'or House they would meet Maud, "whose tempting coffee warmed the heart of Dudley Warner."[64] Furthermore, in the "quaint village" of Little Bras d'Or were "many of those wierd [*sic*], tho interesting traditions, for want of a historian fast falling into the oblivion of the past."[65] Lockett also claimed that John McRae, known as John Bentinck, had "never for the last twenty years cut the full complete crop grown.

He fills his barn with perhaps two hundred tons; what more does he need, – the rest can go, he will get it all next year, and so the world moves on its axis."[66] In the *Cape Breton Hand-book*, however, such individuals are little more than objects of passing curiosity.

Another local publication that promoted tourism as a strategy for economic development was John M. Gow's encyclopaedic *Cape Breton Illustrated*, which appeared in 1893. To stem the exodus of the island's young men and women to the United States, Gow advocated more government investment and railway construction as a means of stimulating the coal mining, fishing, and tourism industries. After all, Gow claimed, "The scenery, the climate, the position, and the historic interest attaching to this part of the Dominion are unequalled."[67] Modernizing as this strategy was, there is a detectable shift from the earlier guidebooks insofar as Gow's descriptions of the Scots-descended inhabitants are distinctly romantic. He promised, for example, that "people will treat you with that old-fashioned courtesy and hospitality for which we have to seek in patriarchal times." There was also dignity: "If you want to see true dignity, either in man or woman, or if you want to meet with Nature's ladies and gentlemen, come to Cape Breton." Perhaps with the books by Cozzens and Warner in mind, Gow added: "Of course, there are antiquated ways and old customs and all that to laugh at, if you have the complaint distressingly bad; but then, perhaps, you have some new-fangled notions and ways that are just as laughable – at least as ridiculous and valueless as the old."[68]

Gow was not, however, uncritical of the local Scots. He claimed that in the western and northwestern parts of the island "there are men who have lost the staid respectability of the ancient Highlander" and become "the wildest and hardest in the world. They will yell and rave and drink and fight all day long, and go raving mad because there is no more fighting to do." On the positive side of this violent nature, Gow claimed, was loyalty, the "key-note" of the Highland character. Because they were "confined within a narrow glen or surf-beaten island," their loyalty admittedly "lost in breadth what it gained in intensity." With proper military leadership, however, that "deep and fervent spirit of loyalty" would "blaze upon the battle-field in historic splendour."[69] The clans had been broken up even before the migration to Cape Breton, but Gow clearly assumed that the Highlanders had an innate disposition towards obeying their chieftains for, as Grenier notes of Scotland, "Clans were widely understood to be military regiments and the chief was conceived as a commander."[70]

Ten years later, in 1903, C.W. Vernon's *Cape Breton at the Beginning of the Twentieth Century* struck a more pacifistic note, claiming that the island had "begun a new warfare," though "not to devastate and destroy, but to create and build up." Vernon believed that, with the discovery of readily accessible iron deposits on Newfoundland's Bell Island, Cape Breton – "so long untouched by the onward march of commercial progress" – was poised to become a major iron and steel producer.[71] Tourism would be an important part of this promising economic future because the island, "already famous for the beauty of its scenery of sea and mountain, lake and hill, deserves that the brightness of its skies, the invigorating properties of its pure air, the splendour of its crystal waters, and the loveliness of its landscapes should be still more widely known and appreciated."[72] Although he stressed the cosmopolitan composition of Cape Breton's population, Vernon quoted Charles Dudley Warner's "delightful classic" several times; he also included a chapter written in Gaelic by J.G. MacKinnon, editor of the Antigonish newspaper *Mac-Talla*. Furthermore, Vernon's own English-language chapter on the Highland settlements claims that Gaelic was still spoken in hundreds of homes as well as being used in rural Presbyterian services.[73] There was little place in Vernon's progressive vision, however, for rituals such as the open-air communion. The fact that it would "eventually become a thing of the past is indeed a pity," he wrote, "but the remorseless march of modern ideas, and that busier men live today, cannot but bring about this result."[74]

It was Vernon's publication that was out of step with the times, however, as far as tourism promotion and the images of the island were concerned. The Intercolonial Railway's *A Ramble and a Rest*, which appeared in 1895, promised that "The primitive simplicity which amused Charles Dudley Warner and other humorous writers is still to be found in many districts, but it is no longer a troublesome journey to reach even the mysterious Baddeck from any part of the continent."[75] The same statement was repeated in the company's travel guide, *Forest, Stream, and Seashore*, which circulated at the turn of the century.[76] The romantic image of the Cape Breton Highlander may have been fostered by American antimodernism, but it was also strengthened by the renewed growth of British imperialism and the militarism associated with the First World War. These developments help to explain why, in Henry Beckles Willson's *Nova Scotia: The Province That Has Been Passed By*, published in London in 1911, there is a renewed focus on Highland customs. The Montreal-born and London-based journalist and historian was a fervent imperialist. As might be expected from someone whose preface lamented the mass immigration of "alien peoples" to Canada,[77] Willson paid considerable attention to the "Gaelic folk." He claimed, for example, that on Cape Breton there were still many bards "who compose epic ballads as they did centuries ago in the land of Ossian. And the songs of the Highlands, the 'Fhir a Ohata,' the 'Tamhuil mòr, mac sheann Tamhuil,' still float out upon the air; while the traditions of old Highland feuds or the Jacobite risings of '15 or '45 still linger, eked out by such visible memorials as one may see, beside the rude chimney-piece – an ancient dirk or a rusty claymore that some long-vanished ancestor had flourished at Culloden or Falkirk."[78]

The militaristic tone was further amplified in Catherine Dunlop Mackenzie's "The Charm of Cape Breton Island" which appeared in *National Geographic* in 1920. Referring to the recent war, Mackenzie claimed that the strategic position "that once made her the mistress of the northern seas has given Cape Breton a new chapter in war history – a fascinating chapter, with its pageant of transport and convoy and patrol, and back of it the great war effort of her people."[79] This effort, Mackenzie made clear, was largely due to the martial ardour of the Highlanders, for "Here can be heard the old Celtic tongue that hurled defiance at Caesar from the shores of Britain two thousand years ago – a tongue that has sounded the slogan of the Highland clans on every battlefield of the Empire."[80] From the second battle of Ypres, to "the undying glory that was theirs at Vimy Ridge and Passchendaele, and the breaking of the Queant-Drocourt line," the Cape Breton companies had "stood a wall of fire around their much-loved isle."[81] In short, the trajectory of the Cape Breton Scot from backward peasant to noble warrior was now complete.

Conclusion

A travel narrative can reveal as much about its author and the author's own society as it does about the people and places it describes. For example, in the British travellers' accounts of Cape Breton Island can be detected a colonialist concern for social and economic development. And Frederick S. Cozzens' pejorative account of the Cape Breton Scots reflects not only a strong sense of upper-class American confidence and superiority but also a Yankee distaste for Highland romanticism in the pre-Civil War era. That tone changed considerably in 1874, with the publication of Charles Dudley Warner's *Baddeck and That Sort of Thing*, and especially with Charles Farnham's "Cape Breton Folk" a decade later. Just as British travellers in Scotland's Highlands had been searching for a culture whose closeness to nature and racial heritage contrasted, in Grenier's words, with their own "rational, mechanical, and progress-obsessed world," so the same could be said for the Americans who were attracted to Cape Breton in the later nineteenth century.[82] They may have valued the island primarily as a scenic retreat for yachting and fly fishing, but they were also fascinated by what they considered to be a traditional society that did not share the individualistic and materialistic values of the United States. Not surprisingly, then, Cape Breton's bitter coal mine strikes of the 1880s were simply ignored in the island's travel accounts.[83] The Canadian-published promotional materials adopted a more dispassionate tone, but the image of a clan-based, tradition-bound culture persisted and even regained strength with the rise of imperialism and militarism in the First World War era. The quest of the Nova Scotia folk would certainly become more intense and more sentimental after the onset of the Great Depression in the 1930s,[84] but Premier Angus L. Macdonald was building on a foundation that had already been well established by the travel and tourism literature that romanticized the Scots of Cape Breton Island.

NOTES

1 Edward J. (Ted) Cowan, "The Scots Imaging of Canada," in Peter E. Rider and Heather McNabb, eds, *A Kingdom of the Mind: How the Scots Helped Make Canada* (Montreal and Kingston: McGill-Queen's University Press, 2006), 4.
2 For example, travelers' accounts criticized the Presbyterians of Pictou for their religious factionalism and the Catholics of Cape Breton Island for their ignorance. Ian McKay, "Tartanism Triumphant: The Construction of Scottishness in Nova Scotia, 1933–1954," *Acadiensis*, 21, no. 2 (Spring 1992): 8–10.
3 See T.M. Devine, *Clanship to Crofters' War: The Social Transformation of the Scottish Highlands* (Manchester, UK: Manchester University Press, 1994), chapter 6; and John R. Gold and Margaret M. Gold, *Imagining Scotland: Tradition, Representation and Promotion in Scottish Tourism since 1750* (Aldershot, UK: Scolar Press, 1995), chapter 4.
4 Devine, *Clanship*, 87. See also, Peter Womack, *Improvement and Romance: Constructing the Myth of the Highlands* (Basingstoke, UK: Macmillan, 1989), chapter 3.

5 McKay, "Tartanism Triumphant," 15–16. See also, Ian McKay and Robin Bates, *In the Province of History: The Making of the Public Past in Twentieth-Century Nova Scotia* (Montreal and Kingston: McGill-Queen's University Press, 2010), 269. On the 185th Battalion, which became known as the Cape Breton Highlanders, see Barry W. Shears, *Dance to the Piper: The Highland Bagpipe in Nova Scotia* (Sydney, NS: Cape Breton University Press, 2008), 150–2; and Ken MacLeod, "Roots of 185th Cape Breton Highlanders Can Be Found in Broughton," *Cape Breton Post*, 5 September 2014. http://www.capebretonpost.com/living/2014/9/5/roots-of-185th-cape-breton-highlanders-c-3859512.html. Viewed 24 May 2017. On the popularity of Highland regiments in Canada, particularly after the First World War, see H.P. Klepak, "A Man's a Man because of That: The Scots in the Canadian Military Experience," in Rider and McNabb, *A Kingdom of the Mind*, 40–59.

6 Womack, *Improvement and Romance*, 2.

7 See, for example, J.I. Little, "Agricultural Improvement and Highland Clearance: The Isle of Arran, 1828–29," *Scottish Economic and Social History* 19, part 2 (1999): 132–54; and Krisztina Fenyo, *Contempt, Sympathy and Romance: Lowland Perceptions of the Highlands and the Clearances During the Famine Years, 1845–1855* (East Linton, Scotland: Tuckwell Press, 2000).

8 Katherine Haldane Grenier, "Tourism and the Idea of the Skye Crofter: Nature, Race, Gender and the Late Nineteenth-Century Highland Identity." *Victorians Institute Journal* 25 (1997): 113.

9 McKay dates the origins of Nova Scotia's folklorization to the late 1920s. Ian McKay, *The Quest of the Folk: Antimodernism and Cultural Selection in Twentieth-Century Nova Scotia* (Montreal and Kingston: McGill-Queen's University Press, 1994), 9. My main sources for identifying the travel literature discussed in this chapter were Elizabeth Waterston et al., eds, *The Travellers: Canada to 1900* (Guelph, ON: University of Guelph, 1989); Brian Tennyson, ed., *Impressions of Cape Breton* ([no city or publisher listed, 1986)]; and the online catalogue of the Nova Scotia Archives: http://novascotia.ca/archives/library/results.asp?Search=cape+breton. Viewed 24 May 2017.

10 On outside perceptions of the Mi'kmaq, see Tennyson, *Impressions of Cape Breton*, x–xiii, 81–6.

11 Stephen J. Hornsby, *Nineteenth-Century Cape Breton: A Historical Geography* (Montreal and Kingston: McGill-Queen's University Press, 1992), 31.

12 See, for example, Rusty Bittermann, Robert A. McKinnon, and Graeme Wynn, "Of Inequality and Interdependence in the Nova Scotia Countryside, 1850–70," *Canadian Historical Review* 74, no. 1 (1993): 1–43.

13 Hornsby, *Nineteenth-Century Cape Breton*, 123, 144. In addition to the rural settlements, Cape Breton's eastern coalfield employed approximately 2500 men and boys by 1890, many of them Scots from the island's thin-soiled backlands. Hornsby, *Nineteenth-Century Cape Breton*, 169–83.
14 Quoted in Tennyson, *Impressions of Cape Breton*, 101.
15 John M'Gregor, *British America*, vol. 1, 2nd edition (Edinburgh: William Blackwood; London: T. Caddell, 1833), 462.
16 The series was initially titled "Letters to a Friend," the friend in question being the Archbishop Whately of Dublin who died before it was completed. C. Bruce Fergusson, ed., *Uniacke's Sketches of Cape Breton and Other Papers Relating to Cape Breton* (Halifax, NS: Public Archives of Nova Scotia, 1958), 7–8, 36.
17 Fergusson, ed., *Uniacke's Sketches*, 64. Much the same assessments were made in the responses to the 1861 survey questionnaire distributed by R.G. Haliburton, Secretary of the Nova Scotia Commissioners for the International Exhibition. See *Uniacke's Sketches*, 33, 158–60, 170.
18 B.D. Tennyson, "Cape Breton in 1867," *Nova Scotia Historical Quarterly* 6, no. 2 (June 1976), 205. Bourinot also wrote (p. 204) that "the inhabitants are all Scots, and, as a rule, are a well-to-do class." The article was first published in *The New Dominion Monthly* in May 1868.
19 John J. Rowan, *The Emigrant and Sportsman in Canada. Some Experiences of an Old Country Settler* (London: Edward Stanford, 1876), 158–9, 163. On Cape Breton's Newfoundland market, see Hornsby, *Nineteenth-Century Cape Breton*, 59–61. According to Alan MacNeil, the poor reputation of Nova Scotia's Highland settlers as farmers was based on their focus on livestock as opposed to cereal crop production. Alan R. MacNeil, "Cultural Stereotypes and Highland Farming in Eastern Nova Scotia, 1827–1861," *Histoire sociale – Social History* 19, no. 37 (May 1986): 39–56. See also See D. Campbell and R.A. MacLean, *Beyond the Atlantic Roar: A Study of the Nova Scotia Scots* (Toronto: McClelland and Stewart, 1974), 56–7, 63–4, 86–91, 182–4.
20 Rowan, *The Emigrant*, 162.
21 See Hornsby, *Nineteenth-Century Cape Breton*, 131–43; and Rusty Bittermann, "The Hierarchy of the Soil: Land and Labour in a 19th Century Cape Breton Community," *Acadiensis* 18, 1 (Autumn 1988): 33–55.
22 Kevin Flynn, "Destination Nation: Nineteenth-Century Travels Aboard the Canadian Pacific Railway," *Essays on Canadian Writing* 67 (Spring 1999): 197–9.
23 See Michael Newton, *We're Indians Sure Enough: The Legacy of the Scottish Highlanders in the United States* (Auburn, NH: Windhaven Press, 2001), 255.

24 Frederick S. Cozzens, *Acadia: Or, A Month With the Blue Noses* (New York: Derby an Jackson, 1859), 198.
25 See Shears, *Dance to the Piper*.
26 Cozzens, *Acadia*, 199–200.
27 Cozzens, *Acadia*, 202–3.
28 Charles Dudley Warner, *Baddeck and That Sort of Thing*, 15th edition (Boston: Houghton, Mifflin and Company, 1892).
29 Tennyson, *Impressions of Cape Breton*, 163.
30 McKay, "Tartanism Triumphant," 11. Similarly, Womack (*Improvement and Romance*, 6) claims that the Highlander in Scotland was originally "textualized as the fool, as the rogue, and as the beggar."
31 Gold and Gold, *Imagining Scotland*, 45.
32 T.J. Jackson Lears, *No Place of Grace: Antimodernism and the Transformation of American Culture, 1880–1920* (New York: Pantheon Books, 1981), xv.
33 Warner, *Baddeck*, 149–50. Similarly, Grenier notes of travellers' perceptions of the Highlanders in Scotland that "having no access to the luxuries of life, they did not pine for them, thus their ignorance kept them at peace." Katherine Haldane Grenier, *Tourism and Identity in Scotland, 1770–1914* (Burlington, VT: Ashgate, 2005), 180.
34 Warner, *Baddeck*, 111–12.
35 Warner, *Baddeck*, 156.
36 Warner, *Baddeck*, 189–90.
37 M.F. Sweetser, *The Maritime Provinces: A Handbook for Travellers* (Boston: James R. Osgood and Company, 1875), iii–iv, 141–71. The quotation is from 169.
38 S.G.W. Benjamin, *The Atlantic Islands as Resorts of Health and Pleasure* (New York: Harper and Brothers, 1878), 226. Also in a similar vein, the British military officer and "sportsman" Richard Lewes Dashwood claimed that the Cape Breton Scots were "most kind and hospitable, but some of them very ignorant, and rather lawless." Richard Lewes Dashwood, *Chiploquorgan, Or, Life By the Camp Fire* (London: Simpkin, Marshall and Co., 1872), 75.
39 Tennyson, *Impressions of Cape Breton*, 187. Quoted from S.G.W. Benjamin, "Cruising around Cape Breton," *Century Magazine* (July 1884), 352–64. See also S.G.W. Benjamin, *The Cruise of the Alice May in the Gulf of St. Lawrence and Adjacent Waters* (New York: D. Appleton and Company, 1885). On Benjamin, see Alan Andrew MacEachern, "Discovering an Island: Travel Writers and Tourism on Prince Edward Island," *The Island Magazine* 29 (1991): 10.
40 Grenier, *Tourism and Identity*, 186–7.
41 Quoted in Tennyson, *Impressions of Cape Breton*, 185.

42 On this theme, see Grenier, "Tourism and the Idea of the Sky Crofter," 115–16.
43 *Harper's* at this time had a circulation of 200,000 in America and 35,000 in Great Britain, giving it "the widest readership of any magazine of its kind." Eugene Exman, *The House of Harper: One Hundred and Fifty Years of Publishing* (New York: Harper and Row, 1967), 79.
44 C.H. Farnham, "Cape Breton Folk," *Harper's New Monthly Magazine* 72 (December 1885): 610. This article was reprinted "with only minor omissions" and with a brief introduction by Stephen F. Spencer, in *Acadiensis* 8, no. 2 (Spring 1979): 90–106.
45 Farnham, "Cape Breton Folk," 617–18.
46 McKay, "Tartanism Triumphant," 14.
47 Farnham, "Cape Breton Folk," 618. Farnham provides a brief autobiography in his "Labrador, First Paper," *Harper's New Monthly Magazine* 71 (September 1885): 500.
48 The custom endured on Cape Breton into the 1920s, though by the late nineteenth century it was usually a predetermined event, with the couple having already come to a private agreement with the permission of the prospective bride's father. Peter Ward, *Courtship, Love, and Marriage in Nineteenth-Century English Canada* (Montreal and Kingston: McGill-Queen's University Press, 1990), 105–6. See also, J.I. Little, *Crofters and Habitants: Settler Society, Economy, and Culture in a Quebec Township, 1848–1881* (Montreal and Kingston: McGill-Queen's University Press, 1991), 199–200.
49 Farnham, "Cape Breton Folk," 615–16.
50 Farnham, "Cape Breton Folk," 620.
51 Farnham, "Cape Breton Folk," 622–3.
52 Farnham, "Cape Breton Folk," 624–5. For an excellent description, see Laurie Stanley-Blackwell, "'Tabernacles in the Wilderness': The Open-Air Communion Tradition in Nineteenth and Twentieth-Century Cape Breton," in Charles H.H. Scobie and G.A. Rawlyk, eds, *The Contribution of Presbyterianism to the Maritime Provinces* (Montreal and Kingston: McGill-Queen's University Press, 1997). For a reading of Farnham's article that stresses its romanticism, see Michael Vance, "Powerful Pathos: The Triumph of Scottishness in Nova Scotia," in Celeste Ray, ed., *Transatlantic Scots* (Tuscaloosa, AL: University of Alabama Press, 2005), 165–6.
53 Lears makes a sharp distinction between the longstanding American agrarian concern with urban "effeminacy" and "luxury" and the more broad-sweeping dissatisfaction with "rationalization" that he claims emerged in the 1880s. Lears, *No Place of Grace*, 5–7. On the perception of

Highlanders in Scotland as a folk community, see Grenier, *Tourism and Identity*, 176–94. On Farnham's use of the folk concept in his Quebec articles, see chapter 6 in this volume.

54 Tennyson, *Impressions of Cape Breton*, 217.

55 Frank Bolles, *From Blomidon to Smoky and Other Papers* (Boston: Riverside Press, 1894), 42.

56 Bolles, *From Blomidon to Smoky*, 23.

57 Bolles, *From Blomidon to Smoky*, 30.

58 Bolles, *From Blomidon to Smoky*, 19.

59 Rev. R. Murray and J. McLennan, "Cape Breton," in George Monro Grant, ed., *Picturesque Canada: The Country As It Was and Is* (Toronto: Belden [ca 1882], 841.

60 Murray and McLennan, "Cape Breton," 846–7. On *Picturesque Canada*, see chapter 8.

61 E. Lockett, *Cape Breton Hand-Book and Tourist's Guide, Containing in Addition Valuable Recipes, and Other Useful Information* (North Sydney and Sydney [no date]), 109.

62 Lockett, *Cape Breton Hand-Book*, 91, 201.

63 The only exceptions, apparently, were J.P. McLeod and J.E. Campbell who "seem to be pushing along and keep rather neat stocks." Lockett, *Cape Breton Hand-Book*, 95.

64 Lockett, *Cape Breton Hand-Book*, 19.

65 Lockett, *Cape Breton Hand-Book*, 57.

66 Lockett, *Cape Breton Hand-Book*, 21.

67 John M. Gow, *Cape Breton Illustrated: Historic, Picturesque and Descriptive* (Toronto: William Briggs, 1893), 406–9, 421–3. The quotation is from 408.

68 Gow, *Cape Breton Illustrated*, 366–7. Cape Breton writers were expressing resentment of Warner's book as late as 1930. See, for example, D.J. Rankin, *Our Ain Folk and Others* (Toronto: Macmillan, 1930), 162.

69 Gow, *Cape Breton Illustrated*, 358.

70 Grenier, *Tourism and Identity*, 186.

71 C.W. Vernon, *Cape Breton at the Beginning of the Twentieth Century: A Treatise of Natural Resources and Development* (Toronto: Nation Publishing, 1903), 3.

72 Vernon, *Cape Breton*, 4, 299, 302, 304. The last chapters in the book trace a number of travel routes, focusing on tourist attractions such as historic sites, picturesque views, and trout streams.

73 In the 1932 census 24,303 Nova Scotians are listed as having Gaelic as their mother tongue, making it the third most widely spoken language in the province, after English and French. McKay and Bates, *In the Province of History*, 260.

74 Vernon, *Cape Breton*, 61. Laurie Stanley-Blackwell claims that "By the first decade of the twentieth century the open-air communion had lost many of its communal and participatory aspects." Stanley-Blackwell, "'Tabernacles in the Wilderness,'" 116. On Vernon's publication, see McKay and Bates, *In the Province of History*, 263–4.
75 Intercolonial of Canada, *A Ramble and a Rest: Pure Air, Sea Bathing, Picturesque Scenery; Summer of 1895* (Ottawa, Government Printing Bureau, 1895), 27. CIHM no. 13056
76 Intercolonial Railway, *Forest, Stream, and Seashore* ([Springhill, NS: s.n., 1894?189- or 19-]), 115. Internet Archive.
77 [Henry] Beckles Willson, *Nova Scotia: The Province That Has Been Passed By* (London: Constable and Co., 1911), v, vi. The author's first name is not used in this publication, but he is identified as the author of books that were written by Henry Beckles Willson. For a brief biography, see Damien-Claude Bélanger, *Biographies of Prominent Quebec and Canadian Historical Figures*, http://faculty.marianopolis.edu/c.belanger/QuebecHistory/bios/hbwillson.htm.
78 Willson, *Nova Scotia*, 185–6.
79 Catherine Dunlop Mackenzie, "The Charm of Cape Breton Island. The Most Picturesque Portion of Canada's Maritime Provinces – A Land Rich in Historical Associations, Natural Resources, and Geographic Appeal," *National Geographic* 38, no. 1 (July 1920): 37.
80 Mackenzie, "Charm of Cape Breton," 39.
81 Mackenzie, "Charm of Cape Breton," 40, 42.
82 Grenier, *Tourism and Identity*, 176. Tourism did not become a major industry for the island, however, until the opening of the Canso Causeway in 1955. A recent study notes that the ceremony was marked by the cutting of a tartan ribbon by a ceremonial claymore, followed by the "March of the Hundred Pipers" playing "The Road to the Isles." The same study, though, claims that "interest in Scottish culture … was not apparent during the two decades following the opening of the causeway." See Meaghan Beaton and Del Muise, "The Canso Causeway: Tartan Tourism, Industrial Development, and the Promise of Progress for Cape Breton," *Acadiensis* 37, no. 2 (Summer/Autumn 2008): 68–9. On Nova Scotia tourist numbers, see McKay and Bates, *In the Province of History*, 63.
83 On these strikes, see Del Muise, "The Making of an Industrial Community: Cape Breton Coal Towns, 1867–1900," in Don Magillivray and Brian Tennyson, eds, *Cape Breton Historical Essays* (Sydney, NS: College of Cape Breton Press, 1980), 76–87; and David Frank, "Tradition and Culture in the Cape Breton Mining Community in the Early Twentieth Century," in

Kenneth Donovan, ed., *Cape Breton at 200* (Sydney, NS: University College of Cape Breton, 1985), 202–18. On the more complicated reaction to the Crofters' War of the same decade, see Grenier, "Tourism and the Idea of the Skye Crofter," 119–25.

84 See, for example, Rankin, *Our Ain Folk*; Neil S. MacNeil, *The Highland Heart in Nova Scotia* (New York: C. Scribner's, 1948); and Celia C. Dimock, *Children of the Sheiling* (Sydney, NS: Lynk Printing [n.d.]).

8 Picturing a National Landscape: Images of Nature in *Picturesque Canada*

Literary scholar Leon Surette claims that Canadian literature and culture became "topocentric" as a result of the common complaint that "we have had no revolution, no civil war, no Indian massacres, in short, no spilling of blood to stir the imagination and create a Canadian story or myth."[1] Prime Minister Mackenzie King complained, likewise, that Canada had too much geography and too little history, too much space and too little time.[2] But the Reverend George Monro Grant, Principal of Queen's University and prominent Canadian nationalist, would have disagreed. As editor of *Picturesque Canada: The Country as it Was and Is*, Grant ensured that the ambitious promotional guide, published in instalments between 1882 and 1884, included lengthy romantic descriptions of the heroic pioneer age, particularly that of the French Regime.[3] As its title suggests, however, *Picturesque Canada* also includes equally lengthy descriptions of the Canadian landscape, descriptions that complement the many illustrations that were distinctly picturesque in composition. In that fundamental sense, *Picturesque Canada* differs from its American model, for a more prominent aesthetic in *Picturesque America* is the sublime, characterized by qualities of wildness, grandeur, and overwhelming power.[4]

In exploring that contrast, this chapter will suggest that it reflects the desire to counter Canada's image as a northern wasteland, but also a fundamental difference between the political histories and ideologies of the two countries. The republican ideology of the United States, historian David Nye argues, assumed that politics would inspire rigorous political debate and continual self-examination. That ideology therefore

This chapter was presented to the Dominion of Nature: Environmental Histories of the Confederation Era workshop, University of Prince Edward Island, August 2014. My thanks go to the participants for their helpful comments.

also promoted popular identification with the American sublime as a means of overcoming disunity among the citizenry.[5] Similarly, Eric Kaufman argues that American geographic nationalism expressed itself as the naturalization of the nation, or what he refers to as identification with "the uncivilized, primeval quality of untamed nature" and a belief in its "regenerative effect upon civilization."[6] Kaufman suggests further that Canadian geographic nationalism, with its post-Confederation romanticization of the northern landscape, was similar to that of the United States and therefore distinct from the nationalization of nature in Europe where it played a passive role in a familiarized notion of landscape.[7] The fact is, however, that conservative English-Canadian nationalists such as George Grant were drawn to the rather tame picturesque imagery originally inspired by the English landscape.[8]

A number of illustrated Canadian tour guides – referred to by Patricia Jasen as booster travelogues – were published in the early post-Confederation era, but none were as ambitious in scope or as popular as *Picturesque Canada*.[9] Two years before the first instalment appeared, Grant had already produced a series of illustrated articles on the country for *Scribner's Monthly* of New York.[10] These articles, in turn, had been inspired by the success of *Ocean to Ocean*, the day journal Grant published as secretary to Sandford Fleming's survey expedition across western Canada in 1872.[11] In offering Grant the position of *Picturesque Canada* editor in December 1880, the publishers gave him complete control of the literary content. They also assured him of enthusiastic response by "the most influential men in Canada," and of "liberal patronage among the best circles in England."[12]

In the preface to *Picturesque Canada* Grant explained that his aim was to represent the "characteristic scenery" of the country as well as "the history and life of its people" in order not only "to make us better known to ourselves and to strangers," but to "stimulate national sentiment and contribute to the rightful development of the nation." Rather than beginning at the Atlantic coast and moving westward to the Pacific, the series starts in Quebec City "where our life began," and follows "the track of the fur-traders and coureurs de bois" up the St Lawrence and Ottawa Rivers to Lake Nipissing, Lake of the Woods, and "the thousand miles of alluvial beyond, where the Verendryes first built forts and made alliances with prairie chiefs, and where the foundations of mighty provinces are now being laid."[13] The historical foundation of the country having thus been laid, and the promise of its future in the Prairie West described, *Picturesque Canada* then returns to Ontario, heading eastward to Quebec's Eastern Townships and lower St Lawrence, and finally bookending itself with chapters on the Maritime region and British Columbia. Despite the fact that Chisholm's *All-Round Route Guide* had featured the work of noted Montreal photographer Alexander Henderson as early as 1869, and that photography could present a greater level of detail than paint, the publishers opted for landscape artists, presumably because of the liberties they could take with the viewpoint, composition, and lighting.[14]

Even though Grant had a nationalist agenda, *Picturesque Canada* was aimed in part at American tourists.[15] In fact, the publishers were two Americans, the Belden brothers, who modelled the project on the highly successful *Picturesque America* which had appeared in book form in 1872 and 1874.[16] Furthermore, despite the fact that the art director was Lucius Richard O'Brien, president of the Royal Canadian Academy, most of the illustrations were produced by American artists such as Frederic B. Schell, who had also contributed to *Picturesque America*.[17] As we shall see, however, the images in the Canadian publication were considerably tamer than those in the American one, reflecting a more colonial perception of the landscape. Furthermore, the first chapter of *Picturesque Canada*, written by Grant, made it clear that he had Canadian and British audiences primarily in mind, for he dismissed the possibility of annexation to the United States, declaring that "Their ways are not our ways; their thoughts, traditions, history, are not our thoughts, traditions, history." Nor was Grant's nationalism antithetical to support for continued ties with Great Britain, for he argued that "to break our national continuity in cold blood, to cut ourselves loose from the capital and centre of our strength" would only gain "A thousand possibilities of danger and not an ounce of strength."[18]

The Belden brothers, who had established themselves in Toronto as publishers of county atlases, clearly felt confident, then, that there were enough English Canadians with the means and the commitment to national unity to ensure their project's profitability. In fact, they informed Grant in 1880 that the subscription list was "much larger" than they had dared hope for, and over 20,000 customers subscribed to the monthly instalments.[19] When *The Globe* of Toronto described the new undertaking in May 1881, it concluded that "its progress will be watched with interest as a striking phase of national progress, and one that cannot fail to have far-reaching results in attracting attention to our material as well as our aesthetic advancement."[20] As historian Carl Berger has observed, however, late Victorian supporters of imperial federation such as the Reverend Grant might have sung the eulogies of progress and welcomed economic growth, but they also remained deeply suspicious of industrialization and urbanization.[21] Thus, even though *Picturesque Canada* featured as many images of towns and cities as of farms and wilderness, Montreal and Toronto are depicted as cities

8.1 *Collingwood Harbour* by F.B. Schell and Thomas Hogan. Engraver J. Hellawell. *Picturesque Canada*, vol. 2, 584. Note the dominance of sailing vessels and rowboats as well as the dark jumble of logs in the foreground contrasting with the straight geometrical lines of the white grain elevator in the background. The American artist F.B. Schell produced more than half the illustrations for *Picturesque Canada*, many in collaboration with Thomas Hogan.

of parks and leisure as well as centres of religion, education, and commerce – not of manufacturing.[22] This was not an entirely anti-modern stance, however, for – as Sue Rainey notes of *Picturesque America* – such urban scenes "created visions of order and stability that could build confidence in the future."[23]

If, in Rainey's words, *Picturesque America* is focused on "long-established industries rather than more recent and more disruptive large-scale factories,"[24] this is even more the case for *Picturesque Canada* with its distant smokestacks hinting at undifferentiated factories.[25] Grain elevators appear as prominent features on a number of skylines (see figure 8.1), but the only full view of a manufacturing

8.2 *Digging Mussel-Mud* by F.B. Schell and Thomas Hogan. Engraver J.E. Sharp. *Picturesque Canada*, vol. 2, 861. Mussel mud was used as fertilizer in Prince Edward Island.

industry, apart from a sawmill, is of the St Maurice Forges, an enterprise that dated to the French Regime.[26] The mills are nearly all water-driven, and featured prominently is muscle power provided by horses, oxen, and men labouring beside canals and in mines, forests, and fisheries, as well as on the land (see figure 8.2).[27] There are also stark images of extractive industries such as the relatively new oil-refineries in Petrolia, Ontario, the salt mines in the Goderich area, and the coal mines in Nova Scotia.[28] But the picturesque convention – with its emphasis on unspoiled and undomesticated nature – generally avoided evidence of the industrial revolution as characterized by the shift from an organic economy based on energy captured from water, wind, and plants to a mineral economy based on fossil fuels, notably coal.[29]

Aside from providing an important source of energy, water was the most important means of communication in Canada's pre-industrial era, so it is perhaps not surprising that it is the dominant physical feature in *Picturesque Canada*. Grant certainly enthused about the progress of the Canadian Pacific Railway across the western prairie, writing that "With congratulations and hope, we welcome the steel rails – harbingers of a new civilization and material pledge of the unity of the Dominion."[30] But the fact remains that there are only a dozen or so images of railways in *Picturesque Canada*, as compared with approximately forty in *Picturesque America* which appeared just as the American romance with railways was reaching its acme.[31] Furthermore, despite the fact that the construction of the Canadian Pacific Railway is commonly assumed to have unleashed an outburst of technological nationalism in Canada,[32] the railways depicted in *Picturesque Canada* are generally dwarfed by the surrounding landscape (see figure 8.3). Boats far outnumber trains, and waterways of various kinds appear in the great majority of the images, creating the impression that rivers and canals were still the main conduits for travel and commerce. Perhaps it was not coincidental that the Pacific Scandal of 1872 had, in the words of historian A.A. den Otter, "exposed the seamy flaw in technological nationalism and temporarily discredited the philosophy of railways."[33] Certainly, there is a distinct lack of enthusiasm for railways in the Niagara District chapter's declaration that even though they were displacing canal trade in the United States, "no means of communication is likely seriously to compete with the mode of transit [i.e., water] which is the distinctive feature of the trade of the Dominion."[34]

In keeping with the romantic associations of river travel,[35] as well as *Picturesque Canada*'s bias towards the organic economy, it is not surprising that steamboats share space with sailing ships, canoes, and rowboats in the illustrations. Furthermore, in the descriptive passages, rivers that have been tamed by industry remain picturesque. From the bridge across the Ottawa River, for example, "one looks at ease into the once mystic and awful, but now merely picturesque tumble and toss of living water, the famous Chaudière. Half a mile above, the long, graceful lines of a new and substantial iron railway bridge of eleven huge spans, give farther [*sic*] evidence of the mastery of man over this once wild spot."[36] But railway bridges were clearly not considered picturesque enough to be featured prominently.[37] In contrast to the many images of railway

8.3 *St John River, Near Newbury Junction* by F.B. Schell. Engraver J.W. Lauderbach. *Picturesque Canada*, vol. 2, 772.

bridges as striking examples of modernist engineering in Sandford Fleming's *The Intercolonial Railway. A Historical Sketch* (1876),[38] *Picturesque Canada's* description of the Grand Trunk Railway bridge at Ste Anne's is distinctly romantic. Thus, we read that its sixteen towers are as "massive as the keep of a fortress," and that they enhance the "magnificent" scenery of Lake St Louis (see also the bridge in figure 8.3).[39]

Even though the majority of the illustrations in *Picturesque Canada* were American-produced, they tend to be of tamer, less rugged landscapes than those depicted in *Picturesque America*. In fact, based on the assumption that the picturesque view was characterized by roughness, in contrast to the beautiful which was defined as pastoral, orderly, smiling, and serene, many of the Canadian illustrations were more beautiful than picturesque.[40] Furthermore, the literary imagery had the advantage of adding colour to bucolic scenes such as the one viewed from the path below Parliament Hill where "the silver river gleams, busy and beautiful, a hundred feet below; the white stems of the birch gracefully relieve the sombre gleam of hemlock and the fresher tints of maple." And there is also the sense of sound, for the same passage mentions the song of birds such as the oriole "with its uniform of black and orange," as well as "the faint buzz of the saw, and the noise of the 'Big Kettle' [the Chaudière Falls]."[41]

Bodies of water were, of course, not always serene, and Rainey notes that water in motion, "whether falling from a great height or roaring down a boulder-strewn cascade," was perceived "as evidence of nature's power and energy."[42] It is rather telling, therefore, that there are ninety-five views of waterfalls (in eleven per cent of the illustrations) in *Picturesque America*, but only forty-one (seven per cent) in *Picturesque Canada*, though it also depicts seventeen rapids.[43] The description of the Muskoka River's South Falls, with "the torrent, lashed into foam, hurling its mass of gleaming water down the ravine," captures the sense of energy referred to by Rainey. In fact, it conforms to the sublime convention with its emphasis on tumult and gloom,[44] though this does not hold the author's attention for long: "The vision while it delights also awes, and you are glad ere long to turn from it and get into the quiet beauty of still water, the sunshine glimmering softly down on the stream, or breaking in patches of light through the branches of the over-arching trees."[45] And much more numerous than the views of fast-flowing water are those of lakes, a few depicted as storm-tossed but most as placid and beautiful.

While *Picturesque America* responded to the charge that the coasts of the United States were low and dull by devoting considerable attention to waves and rocky coastlines,[46] there are only twelve scenes of wave-crested waters in *Picturesque Canada*. Six of these views are on the Great Lakes, three on the Atlantic, and none on the Pacific. And, even in describing a choppy Lake Superior, author George A. Mackenzie managed to evoke the picturesque: "What beauty there is in it all! though by sea-sick or half sea-sick passengers for the most part unregarded. The rainbow springing from the prow; the dark-green waves overlaid with glances and flashes of blue; the fantastic shapes, the mysterious shadings and colourings of the clouds – as restless as the waters below – proclaim that even in the midst of an uncomfortable gale, we are surrounded by infinite forms of divinist beauty."[47] To travellers who complained that the shoreline scenery consisted of an "endless skyline

8.4. *Thunder Cape* by L.R. O'Brien. Engraver R. Schelling. *Picturesque Canada,* vol. 1, 262.

of inhospitable cliffs," Mackenzie responded that "visited at leisure in a small boat – the bays and islands explored, the rivers followed up – reveal scenes of surpassing loveliness."[48]

In keeping with its emphasis on a wild nature, *Picturesque America* also depicts many geological features such as mountains, canyons, and caves. In fact, many of the chapters have titles such as "The White Mountains," "Cumberland Gap," and "The Mammoth Cave." *Picturesque Canada* does include an image of Lake Superior's Thunder Cape as a black monolith hovering over a paddle wheeler with whitecaps breaking against its bow, but it is an exception (see figure 8.4). There are only twenty-two illustrations (four per cent) focusing on Canadian geological features and the most famous one, "Cape Trinity," was modelled on O'Brien's romantic Turneresque painting, "Sunrise on the Saguenay."[49] Furthermore, while *Picturesque America* depicts at least one hundred unusual rock formations (in over eleven per cent of the illustrations) that serve as natural substitutes for architectural antiquities,[50] there are only eight such images in *Picturesque Canada*, four of which are from the long-settled Elora area, north of Toronto.[51] Paradoxically, the most vivid evocation of architectural romanticism is the view and description of Niagara Falls – generally considered to be the very essence of Kant's dynamic sublime – as a frozen fantasyland.[52] Thus, the reader is informed that after a few days of hard frost "No marvels wrought by genii and magicians in Eastern tales could surpass the wonderful creations that rise along the surrounding banks, and hang over the walls of the cataract. Glittering wreaths of icicles, like jewelled diadems, gleam on the brow of every projecting rock and jutting crag. Arches, pillars, and porticos, of shining splendour, are grouped beneath the overhanging cliffs, giving fanciful suggestions of fairy-palaces beyond."[53]

Admittedly, there is no Canadian equivalent to the Yellowstone Valley or the Grand Canyon where many of the rock features in *Picturesque America* are located.[54] It is rather surprising, however, that only one of the views in *Picturesque Canada* that focus on geological features is from West of Lake Superior. In fact, the contrast between the eastern and the western landscape is much less distinct in *Picturesque Canada* than in *Picturesque America*. In the eastern United States, according to Rainey, men fish in the streams and hunt in the forests – engaging in what she refers to as restorative "play" as well as quiet contemplation – but the western American wilderness is characterized by "sublime scenery as yet untouched by civilization." The message delivered by the artists who largely erased the presence of western railways, farms, mines, and mills, Rainey argues, was that "wilderness was still a special quality of the landscape of the United States," and "progress could be accommodated within the vast Western lands" without conflict between development and nature's sublimity.[55]

The message in *Picturesque Canada* is quite different; far from privileging the mountainous landscape, it relegates British Columbia to the end of the second volume.[56] As author of the chapter, Grant included a powerful description of the "cañons of the Homathico," where in a deep gorge beneath the towering rocks one could find "a mountain torrent, whirling, boiling, roaring, and huge boulders always in motion, muttering, groaning like troubled spirits." But this rather gothic image is countered somewhat by the observation that in every crevice there were "clumps of evergreen trees," and "wherever a handful of soil could rest it was sprinkled with wild flowers, amongst which bloomed

8.5. *Port Moody* by L.R. O'Brien. Engraver J.E. Sharp. *Picturesque Canada*, vol. 2, 874.

the sweet lily of the valley."[57] Furthermore, the illustrations generally place British Columbia's mountains in the distant background, making the scenes more picturesque than sublime.[58] And, to signal that the West coast province was about to be linked physically to eastern Canada, the illustration titled "Port Moody" is subtitled "Vessel containing first shipment of Canadian Pacific R.R. Iron"[59] (see figure 8.5).

Describing the potential of British Columbia's "exhaustless" fishery, Grant enthused that "An acre of water on the lower Fraser, or on one of the innumerable inlets that cut deep into island and mainland, will yield more than the richest prairie farm."[60] The fact remains, however, that *Picturesque Canada* reflects a strong sense of agrarian nationalism. The English picturesque had come, by this time, to favour the wild over the pastoral, and woodsmen over peasants,[61] but in Canada, art historian Marylin McKay argues, the depiction of farmland in art was "just as capable of evoking nationalistic sentiment" as was wilderness land.[62] Certainly, *Picturesque Canada* pays more attention to agriculture than does its American counterpart, which devotes only about thirty-five views (four per cent of the series total) to such features of the agricultural landscape as farming operations, hay wagons, or livestock.[63] The forty-four illustrations in *Picturesque Canada* that focus on farms or depict agriculture in some fashion represent more than three times the ratio (fourteen per cent) of those in *Picturesque America*. Furthermore, the written descriptions are highly idealized, with an emphasis on the picturesque. Dismissing Cobbett's characterization of Prince Edward Island as "a rascally heap of sand, rock, and swamp," for example, the Reverend R. Murray described how the province's red soil threw into relief "the tender green of meadow and lawn," and how in the autumn the rich fields "wave with golden grain."[64] Still more colourful is Louise Murray's description of the Niagara district's orchards:

> lovely in spring with the pink and white blossoms of peach and apple orchards, the delicate green of young leaves, and the deeper verdure of fields of wheat shooting into luxurious growth after their wintry sleep; and glorious in autumn with fields of red and golden maize, and yellow pumpkins, with apple orchards laden with ripe fruit, and with all the brilliant hues of dying forest leaves, every leaf burning in the flames of slow decay with its own tint and shade of beauteous light, and all blended together in a rainbow-like radiance of colour.[65]

Western agriculture clearly did not lend itself to such picturesque imagery, and Marylin McKay states that artists would not produce positive representations of western farmland until the twentieth century.[66] Yet, in contrast to *Picturesque America* – which includes no views of farms or farming from West of the Mississippi – there are eight such illustrations in *Picturesque Canada*'s West, including a composite one of a row of combines, a row of horse-drawn harrows, a steam-driven threshing machine, and a mechanical hay loader (see figure 8.6). There is also an engraving depicting the interior of a settler's cabin, and the Mennonites are favoured with their own short chapter, including two views that depict farming.[67] Grant, who wrote the Manitoba chapter, clearly favoured the labour-intensive methods of the Mennonites over the mammoth wheat farms with their steam-driven machines, writing that the latter were "no doubt useful as far as the best interests of the country are concerned, but, after all, poor affairs in comparison with the

8.6 *Modern Prairie Farming* by A.R. Waud. Engraver H. Baker. *Picturesque Canada*, vol. 1, 299.

log-house of the ordinary farmer; just as the deer-forest or grouse preserve in the Scottish Highlands is a miserable exchange for the wrecked shielings of the true-hearted clansmen, whose fathers died at Culloden for Prince Charles, and at Ticonderoga and Waterloo for us."[68] It is somewhat ironic, then, that Aboriginals are relegated to the margins of the activities depicted in this chapter's illustrations.[69] According to Grant's curt observation, they were "Bred and reared in poverty and dirt, and having generally the taint of hereditary disease, they are as a rule short-lived."[70]

There is one illustration of a Native "dog feast" in the chapter on the region between Manitoba and the Rockies, and another of a "half-breed camp,"[71] but otherwise Grant focused on the Northwest's economic potential. He wrote, for example, that "Towns and villages are springing up in every direction, and vast breadths of fertile land which had lain unoccupied for centuries are being broken in upon by the plough."[72] Grant claimed, further, that even the southern prairie, "formerly considered to be semi-desert," had been discovered by Dominion botanist John Macoun to have sufficient rainfall for the growth of cereals; in fact, settlers referred to it as "the garden of the Lord."[73] Much further north, the still undeveloped Athabasca region would, in Grant's boosterish words, become "the Banner Province of Canada," for the Peace River "offers fewer impediments to navigation than either the St. Lawrence or the Saskatchewan," and "The soil is as rich and the prairies are vaster than in Manitoba or Assiniboia."[74]

From an aesthetic perspective, Grant was not attracted to the treeless prairie landscape, for he wrote that the traveller "sees no living thing on the earth or in the air," causing his spirits to sink "as he rides deeper and deeper into this terrible silence, unless he has learned to commune with the Eternal."[75] Based on McKay's definitions, the prairie region in Grant's view was less an Arcadia in the sense of being "already perfect and readily available to the individual who seeks it out," than it was an Eden that "involves a quest on the part of a group for a site that, through hard work, will eventually provide a perfect homeland."[76] Given that the cause for the bald landscape was fires lit by the vanishing Aboriginals – Grant claimed – there was a remedy, namely "tree planting on an extensive scale."[77]

Grant was clearly influenced by the rapidly growing forest conservation movement, but, in contrast to the writers of *Picturesque America*, he was not particularly critical of the lumbering industry.[78] In fact, it is the one industry to have its own chapter in *Picturesque Canada*, one penned by Grant himself. Referring to the "practically boundless wealth of woodland" that stretched "from our frontier to the Pole, and almost the Atlantic to the Pacific," Grant wrote that the "regions of an all but Arctic winter are made endurable, if not a source of actual pleasure, because the youth of our country are enabled to engage in an industry manly, healthful and remunerative." This statement, coupled with the engraving "Exploring For New Limits" (see figure 8.7) represented a dramatic shift from the widely voiced concern that the logging industry exercised a corrupting influence on the rural population, and it foreshadowed the post-war embrace of Tom Thomson as the ideal of Canadian manhood and his paintings as symbols of the Canadian nation.[79] In Grant's words, the picturesque shanties, hardy exploring parties in birch-bark canoes, tangled log jams, and "navies of huge rafts towed or floating seawards" all had "a distinctive artistic interest." Canada was fortunate, then, that "Unlike the national industries of many other countries," lumbering blended with "instead of destroying, what is picturesque in Nature."[80] Grant did express concern, however, that wasteful logging practices and especially forest fires were a threat to the nation's future, and he advocated that government ensure the annual cut not exceed "the annual increment presented to us by Nature."[81]

The scenes of labouring woodsmen, as well as mussel-mud diggers, miners, harvest workers, and fishermen are clearly exceptions to geographer Brian Osborne's claim that – in contrast to late nineteenth-century Europe, the United States, and Australia – the didactic style of patriotic art, with its focus on heroic labour and the vernacular, did not develop in Canada.[82] Furthermore, even though winter scenes are said to have declined sharply in popularity in the artistic representations of post-Confederation Canada,[83] Grant's devotion of a chapter to the lumber industry provided him with an excellent opportunity to include a number of images set in that season (fifteen of the thirty-eight snow scenes are from this chapter), for snow was essential to the skidding of logs in the eastern Canadian woods. And, in contrast to *Picturesque America*, which confines snow almost entirely to the tops of distant mountains, in one *Picturesque Canada* scene it serves as an aesthetic camouflage for a clear-cut hillside.[84] Rather than ignoring Canada's winter as a deterrent to economic development, Grant embraced it by claiming somewhat fancifully in *Picturesque Canada*'s first chapter that "snow does much of our subsoil ploughing," and, as "the best possible mulch, shading and protecting the soil at no cost," it was known as "the poor man's manure." Furthermore, given that it

8.7 *Exploring for New Limits* by M.J. Burns. Engraver E.R. Tichenor. *Picturesque Canada*, vol. 1, p. 214.

8.8 *Arrival of Supply Train at Lumber Depôt* by F.B. Schell and Thomas Hogan. Engraver F. Geyer. *Picturesque Canada*, vol. 1, 226.

was essential "to almost all the amusements of the year – the sleighing, skating, snow-shoeing, ice-boating, tobogganing – that both sexes and all classes delight in," an excess of snow "can never be so bad as the pall that covers England and Scotland half the year and makes the people 'take their pleasures sadly.'"[85]

Even though nationalists such as Grant promoted the myth of Canadians as a hardy northern race,[86] however, he was careful to avoid creating an impression of Canada as a cold, inhospitable country. Commenting on one of the only two views in *Picturesque Canada* that depict winter storms (see figure 8.8), Grant observed that "it is a wild snow storm; the dark clouds are driven before fierce gusts of wind; thick snowdrifts shiver around the side of the depôt, but within all is warmth and good-cheer for the weary teamsters. Notwithstanding the wild weather, one of the depôt hands is driving a sleigh, with water-barrel, to the river, and the proprietor or superintendent, wrapped in fur coat and cap, has come over to take stock of the newly-arrived supplies."[87] The message, in short, was that snowstorms can neither intimidate hardy Canadians nor hinder economic activity. Furthermore, the close-up view early in volume 1 of a locomotive pushing a giant plough through a deep snow drift (a good but rare example of Nye's technological sublime) was surely a signal that modern technology was quite capable of overcoming such obstacles in the young northern nation.

Conclusion

Nye argues that Jacksonian America adopted the technological sublime because of the republican belief that mechanical triumphs such as the Erie Canal served to elevate the moral character of the people by promoting the industry and thrift necessary to safeguard democracy.[88] This would help to explain why, in Rainey's words, "the text of *Picturesque America* gave considerable attention to the development of natural resources, industry, and railroads." Rainey adds that the artists of this American publication were more ambivalent about such development than its writers,[89] but there is no such contrast between graphic imagery and descriptive text in *Picturesque Canada*. Carefully edited by Principal Grant,[90] its writers expressed as much ambivalence about industrialization as did its artists.

In writing about northern Ontario, for example, the Reverends Grant and A. Kemp complained that "We are at present, thanks to our constant struggle with nature, in that stage of existence in which tall chimneys are regarded as more beautiful objects than those which crowned the Acropolis. A mill is a vision of delight, proudly pointed out to the stranger, and the hum of machinery is sweeter than the music of the spheres."[91] The two authors did concede that when "Roughing it in the bush" meant "unremitting toil for a lifetime under the sternest conditions of living," one should not be surprised "that everything that looks in the direction of labour-saving machinery should come to be hailed as a blessing, or that factories should be regarded as the symbols of civilization."[92] Grant and the other writers of *Picturesque Canada* apparently felt, however, that mechanization and industrialization were necessary evils, at best. Thus, we read that "all that is distinctive and noteworthy in Grey, as in most of the counties of Canada, is to be found not in its towns, not at railway stations, but in the townships along the gravel roads and concession lines. There we meet the men and women who endured the rough welcome of the Genius in the wilderness; the men and women to whom we owe the smiling fields and orchards, and all the promise of the future."[93]

And just as Americans were much quicker to embrace the wilderness ethos than were Canadians,[94] so those smiling fields and orchards were a more characteristic feature of *Picturesque Canada* than of *Picturesque America*, which favoured views of rugged, untamed nature. This seems somewhat counterintuitive, given the less developed nature of Canada,[95] but it was nationalist pride that led Americans to focus not only on technology but on what made their country distinctive from Great Britain and Europe, with massive rock formations echoing and even trumping ancient ruins in stimulating a sense of awe. In Ramsay Cook's words, "In the United States, nature made man; in Canada, man civilized nature."[96]

Cook is misled, however, by the garrison thesis as formulated by Northrop Frye and Margaret Atwood, with their claim – based largely on literary fiction, poetry, and British immigrant journals – that nineteenth-century English Canadians viewed the natural environment as a hostile one.[97] This is not the image that emerges from *Picturesque Canada*, with its evocation of the picturesque aesthetic that had long been favoured by British landscape artists and travellers.[98] The colonialist legacy aside, perhaps the most important reason for the rather tame landscape depicted in *Picturesque Canada* was that Canada, again paradoxically, was still a young undeveloped country in the early 1880s. After all, by providing visible shape to the nation, as Stephen Daniels has pointed out, landscapes serve as exemplars of moral order and aesthetic harmony.[99] It was quite understandable, therefore, that Canadians would wish to reassure themselves as well as outsiders that the northern climate and vast stretches of unarable land were not an impediment to the nation's strength and progress. Thus, we read that the scenery of the upper Ottawa was "perhaps, the least known in Canada," yet "it is full of promise for the wealth and civilization of the future; unlimited wood-supply and water-power; land that bears the finest of cereals; marble that already decks the Chambers of our National Parliament; with hills and cliffs in whose womb lie, awaiting birth, the most useful of the economic metals."[100] The economic future for this region therefore lay in the exploitation of its natural resources, just as logging, mining, fishing, and especially farming would continue to eclipse urban manufacturing as the country's sources of wealth and identity.

NOTES

1 Leon Surette, "Here Is Us: The Topocentrism of Canadian Literary Criticism," *Canadian Poetry: Studies, Documents, Reviews* 10 (1982) [no pagination]. http://canadianpoetry.org/2011/06/06/volume-no-10-springsummer-1982/. Viewed 19 May 2014.
2 Brian Osborne, "Landscapes, Memory, Monuments, and Commemoration: Putting Identity in its Place," *Canadian Ethnic Studies* 33, no. 3 (2001): 40.
3 The book was published as two volumes in 1884, though the copyright is for 1882. George Monro Grant, ed., *Picturesque Canada: The Country as it Was and Is* (Toronto: Belden Brothers, 1882); Mary F. Williamson, "Illustrated Books, Periodicals, and Commercial Print," in Yvan Lamonde, Patricia Lockhart Fleming, and Fiona L. Black, eds. *History of the Book in Canada*, vol. 2, 1840–1918 (Toronto: University of Toronto Press, 2005), 393.
4 David E. Nye, *American Technological Sublime* (Cambridge, MA: The MIT Press, 1994), 1.
5 Nye, *American Technological Sublime*, 35. See also, John F. Sears, *Sacred Places: American Attractions in the Nineteenth Century* (New York: Oxford University Press, 1989).
6 Eric Kaufman, "'Naturalizing the Nation': The Rise of Naturalistic Nationalism in the United States and Canada," *Comparative Studies in Society and History* 40, no. 4 (1998): 667–8. In Ramsay Cook's words, "Americans wanted to 'Americanize' the west; Canadians were engaged in laying the basis for 'the Britain of the west.'" Ramsay Cook, "Imagining a North American Garden: Some Parallels and Differences in Canadian and American Culture," *Canadian Literature* 103 (Winter 1984): 12.
7 Kaufman distinguishes Switzerland and Scandinavia (Denmark excepted), in this respect, from England and France. See his "Naturalizing the Nation," 667–8, 681–4.
8 See David Lowenthal, "European and English Landscapes as National Symbols," in David Hooson, ed., *Geography and National Identity* (Oxford: Blackwell, 1994), 20–30; Keith Thomas, *Man and the Natural World: Changing Attitudes in England, 1500–1899* (London: Allen Lane, 1983), 260–9; and I.S. MacLaren, "The Limits of the Picturesque in British North America," *Journal of Garden History* 1, no. 5 (1985): 97–111. Grant was deeply influenced by Coleridge and Carlyle. Ramsay Cook, *The Regenerators: Social Criticism in Late Victorian English Canada* (Toronto: University of Toronto Press, 1985), 19.

9 Patricia Jasen, *Wild Things: Nature, Culture, and Tourism in Ontario, 1790–1914* (Toronto: University of Toronto Press, 1995), 76; D.M.R. Bentley, "Charles G.D. Roberts and William Wilfred Campbell as Canadian Tour Guides," *Journal of Canadian Studies* 32, no. 2 (Summer 1997): 79–99.

10 William Lawson Grant and Frederick Hamilton, *Principal Grant* (Toronto: Morang and Co., 1904), 245–7.

11 Dennis Reid, *Our Own Country Canada: Being an Account of the National Aspirations of the Principal Landscape Artists in Montreal and Toronto, 1860–1890* (Ottawa: National Gallery of Canada, 1979), 300; John S. Moir, "From Sectarian Rivalry to National Vision: The Contribution of Maritime Presbyterianism to Canada," in Charles H.H. Scobie and G.A. Rawlyk, eds, *The Contribution of Presbyterianism to the Maritime Provinces of Canada* (Montreal and Kingston: McGill-Queen's University Press, 1997), 166. A revised edition was published in 1879. See David Jackel, "Ocean to Ocean: G.M. Grant's 'round unvarnish'd tale,'" *Journal of Canadian Studies* 81 (Summer 1979): 17–18.

12 Grant was offered $1800, equivalent to $50 per section, plus a $200 retainer fee. Library and Archives Canada, George Monro Grant fonds, Series I, R3202–0-3-E (http://heritage.canadiana.ca/view/oocihm.lac_reel_c1871/1?r=0&s=1) (viewed 2 June 2014), H. Belden to G.M. Grant, Toronto, 8 December 1880, 1303–5. The publishers recommended that the authors receive only $60 to $70 a section, but one, at least, demanded $100. H. Belden to Grant, Toronto, 5 February 1881, 1322A; A.J. Bray to Grant, Montreal, 12 March 1881, 1335.

13 *Picturesque Canada*, iii.

14 Marylin J. McKay, *Picturing the Land: Narrating Territories in Canadian Landscape Art, 1500–1950* (Montreal and Kingston: McGill-Queen's University Press, 2011), 88; Joan M. Schwartz, "Photographic Archives and the Idea of Nation: Images, Imaginings, and Imagined Community," in Costanza Caraffa and Tiziana Serena, eds, *Photo Archives and the Idea of Nation* (Berlin: Walter de Gruyter, 2015), 17–40; Sue Rainey, *Creating Picturesque America: Monument to the Natural and Cultural Landscape* (Nashville and London: Vanderbilt University Press, 1994), 135.

15 Interest within the United States was sufficient to warrant republication of the two volumes in Chicago under the title *Picturesque Spots of the North.* Jasen, *Wild Things*, 121.

16 *Picturesque America* also included a chapter on the St Lawrence and the Saguenay, and another on Lake Memphremagog, most of which lies in Quebec. William Cullen Bryant, ed., *Picturesque America: or, The Land We*

Live In, vol. 2 (New York: D. Appleton and Company [1874]), 370–94, 451–6. Appleton of New York had also published *Picturesque Europe* and *Picturesque Palestine*, and some of the principals involved in *Picturesque Canada* would later publish *Picturesque Australasia*. Reid, *Our Own Country*, 298–9.

17 It appears that Canadian artists simply lacked the skills to make drawings suitable for conversion to wood engravings. On the bitter controversy resulting from the sidelining of Canadian artists, see Reid, *Our Own Country*, 308–16. On Schell, who produced more than half the illustrations, either alone or in collaboration, see Rainey, *Creating Picturesque America*, 280–1.

18 *Picturesque Canada*, 31. On Grant's support for closer ties with Great Britain, see Carl Berger, *The Sense of Power: Studies in the Ideas of Canadian Imperialism, 1867–1914* (Toronto: University of Toronto Press, 1971), 66, 121, 217–19.

19 Grant fonds, H. Belden to G.M. Grant, Toronto, 8 December 1880, 1303–5; McKay, *Picturing the Land*, 111.

20 Quoted in Reid, *Our Own Country*, 299.

21 Berger, *The Sense of Power*, 140. Lawrence S. Fallis, Jr notes that mid-Victorian Canadians were confident that Canada's social institutions, educational system, and attention to religion and morality "would insure her against an over-emphasis upon purely material development." Fallis, "The Idea of Progress in the Province of Canada: A Study in the History of Ideas," in W.L. Morton, ed., *The Shield of Achilles: Aspects of Canada in the Victorian Age* (Toronto: McClelland and Stewart, 1968), 172.

22 McKay, *Picturing the Land*, 111; *Picturesque Canada*, 104–41, 399–440. There is more focus on manufacturing in smaller centers such as Dundas and Galt. *Picturesque Canada*, 452, 464.

23 Rainey, *Creating Picturesque America*, 203.

24 Rainey, *Creating Picturesque America*, 199–202, 220–1. The quote is from p. 221.

25 *Picturesque Canada*, 519, 533, 584, 634.

26 *Picturesque Canada*, 97–9.

27 There are also several illustrations of windmills (*Picturesque Canada*, 147, 318, 320, 349). Swedish research shows that energy provided by moving wind and water during the nineteenth century was rather insignificant when compared to firewoood consumption or muscle energy. E.A. Wrigley, *Poverty, Progress, and Population* (Cambridge, UK: Cambridge University Press, 2004), 30n41.

28 *Picturesque Canada*, 537–40, 553, 839, 848.
29 Wrigley states that in an organic economy "the productivity of the land ultimately determined all else since the material artefacts useful to man were made from animal or vegetable raw materials." Wrigley, *Poverty*, 4, 46–52, 74–6, 220–2, 225–6.
30 *Picturesque Canada*, 342. In *Ocean to Ocean*, according to Jackel ("Ocean to Ocean," 14), Grant transformed the CPR "from a mere railroad into a moral agent."
31 Rainey, *Creating Picturesque America*, 219; Nye, *American Technological Sublime*, 72; A.A. den Otter, *The Philosophy of Railways: The Transcontinental Railway Idea in British North America* (Toronto: University of Toronto Press, 1997), 23–4. Reid claims, mistakenly, that in the Canadian cityscapes "the railway is much in evidence." Reid, *Our Own Country Canada*, 303.
32 See den Otter, *The Philosophy of Railways*, 4–9, 12.
33 den Otter, *The Philosophy of Railways*, 14.
34 *Picturesque Canada*, 387. The author of this chapter was Louise Murray. In his *Lament for a Nation* (1965), the nationalist philosopher George Grant – George Monro Grant's grandson – would complain that technology had unleashed continentalist forces that fused Canada into the American empire. See den Otter, *The Philosophy of Railways*, 10.
35 See Jasen, *Wild Things*, chapter 3.
36 *Picturesque Canada*, 174.
37 Rainey makes the same point for *Picturesque America*. See Rainey, *Creating Picturesque America*, 117.
38 Sandford Fleming, *The Intercolonial Railway. A Historical Sketch* (Montreal: Dawson Brothers, 1876).
39 *Picturesque Canada*, 149. On large steel bridges as examples of the "geometrical sublime," see Nye, *American Technological Sublime*, 77–87.
40 See Jasen, *Wild Things*, 9; Susan Glickman, *The Picturesque and the Sublime: A Poetics of the Canadian Landscape* (Montreal and Kingston: McGill-Queen's University Press, 1998), 10–11; and Ann Bermingham, *Landscape and Ideology: The English Rustic Tradition, 1740–1860* (Berkeley and Los Angeles: University of California Press, 1986), 66–7.
41 *Picturesque Canada*, 186.
42 Rainey, *Creating Picturesque America*, 206.
43 My count of 894 illustrations in *Picturesque America* and 583 in *Picturesque Canada* does not include the composite images.
44 Jasen, *Wild Things*, 8; Glickman, *The Picturesque and the Sublime*, 10.
45 *Picturesque Canada*, 612.
46 Rainey, *Creating Picturesque America*, 214–15.

47 *Picturesque Canada*, 250.
48 *Picturesque Canada*, 253.
49 *Picturesque Canada*, 716; Ellen Ramsay, "Picturing the Picturesque: Lucius O'Brien's *Sunrise on the Saguenay*," in Paul Simpson-Housley and Glen Norcliffe, eds, *A Few Acres of Snow: Literary and Artistic Images of Canada* (Toronto: Dundurn Press, 1992), 159, 163, 165–7, 170.
50 Rainey, *Creating Picturesque America*, 93–4, 113–15, 229, 232–8, 247.
51 *Picturesque Canada*, 262, 471, 475, 483, 484, 763. Examples of the geological theme can be found on pp. 571 and 676.
52 On Kant's division of the sublime into two forms, the mathematical and the dynamic, see Nye, *American Technological Sublime*, 7–8.
53 *Picturesque Canada*, 356.
54 Rainey, *Creating Picturesque America*, 209–11.
55 Rainey, *Creating Picturesque America*, 203–5. Rainey neglects to mention that there is, in fact, a considerable number of images of rock formations in the northern New England region.
56 One highly favourable British review noted that, due to space limitations, "one region, perhaps richer in promise than all, as blest with a more genial climate – British Columbia – has to be dismissed with some fourteen pages, and a hinted promise, which we hope to see fulfilled ere long, of a more adequate treatment hereafter." *The Spectator*, 21 November 1885, 18. http://archive.spectator.co.uk/article/21st-november-1885/18/picturesque-canada. Viewed 4 May 2014.
57 *Picturesque Canada*, 875–6.
58 According to Reid (*Our Own Country*, 302), the illustrations for British Columbia are half-tone photo-engravings, some of them after Notman photographs.
59 In addition, railway tracks share the foreground with the Fraser River in the engraving titled "Yale." *Picturesque Canada*, 879.
60 *Picturesque Canada*, 880. Approximately twenty-four scenes include fishermen, but only about half of these are of commercial fisheries.
61 Malcolm Andrews, *The Search for the Picturesque: Landscape Aesthetic and Tourism in Britain, 1760–1800* (Stanford, CA: Stanford University Press, 1989), 64.
62 McKay, *Picturing the Land*, 11.
63 Rainey claims that the ratio is 3 per cent, but she does not mention the total number of illustrations. *Creating Picturesque America*, 238–9.
64 *Picturesque Canada*, 854.
65 *Picturesque Canada*, 371.
66 McKay, *Picturing the Land*, 126.

67 *Picturesque Canada*, 318–24. For Quebec there are six views focusing on farms or depicting agriculture (63, 69, 76, 159, 696, 730), for Ontario twelve (206, 373, 378, 39–4, 441, 446, 495, 523, 578, 621, 626, 649), for New Brunswick none, for Nova Scotia five (823–5, 827, 845), and for Prince Edward Island two, including one of mussel mud being dug during the winter for fertilizer (861–2).

68 *Picturesque Canada*, 298. Jackel does not quite capture this sense of reservation when he notes of *Ocean to Ocean* that "The vastness of the land, and the urgency of the American threat, justify the use of technology in the opening of the west." Jackel, "Ocean to Ocean," 19–20.

69 See *Picturesque Canada*, 286, 289, 292.

70 *Picturesque Canada*, 301.

71 See the descriptions in *Picturesque Canada*, 332, 336. Natives figure more prominently in the chapter on Red River to Hudson's Bay.

72 *Picturesque Canada*, 330.

73 *Picturesque Canada*, 327–8. On Macoun's overly sanguine assessment of the area known as Palliser's triangle, see Doug Owram, *The Promise of Eden: The Canadian Expansionist Movement and the Idea of the West, 1856–1900* (Toronto: University of Toronto Press, 1980), chapter 7.

74 *Picturesque Canada*, 339.

75 *Picturesque Canada*, 340. Grant's perspective was similar to that of the Anglican Bishop of Rupert's Land, David Anderson. See A.A. denOtter, "'The Wilderness Will Rejoice and Blossom Like the Crocus': Bishop David Anderson's Perceptions of Wilderness and Civilization in Rupert's Land," Canadian Society of Church History, *Historical Papers* (2011), 81–100.

76 McKay, Picturing the Land, 6–7.

77 *Picturesque Canada*, 340. Other promoters made the same argument. See Owram, *Promise of Eden*, 110–11.

78 Rainey, *Creating Picturesque America*, 244.

79 See Graeme Wynn, "'Deplorably Dark and Demoralized Lumberers'? Rhetoric and Reality in Early Nineteenth-Century New Brunswick," *Journal of Forest History* 24, no. 4 (1980): 168–87; and Ross D. Cameron, "Tom Thomson, Antimodernism, and the Ideal of Manhood," *Journal of the CHA* 10 (1999): 185–208.

80 *Picturesque Canada*, 212. While citing *Picturesque Canada* as evidence of the conflict between logging and the picturesque, Ramsay's article ignores this chapter. Ramsay, "Picturing the Picturesque," 164.

81 *Picturesque Canada*, 234–8. The need for forest conservation is also stressed in the chapter on western Ontario, but largely for flood control and aesthetic purposes. *Picturesque Canada*, 487, 501.

82 Brian S. Osborne, "The Iconography of Nationhood in Canadian Art," in Denis Cosgrove and Stephen Daniels, eds, *The Iconography of Landscape* (Cambridge: Cambridge University Press, 1988), 167.

83 Osborne, "The Iconography of Nationhood," 166; Edward Cavell and Dennis Reid, *When Winter Was King: The Image of Winter in 19th Century Canada* (Banff: Whyte Museum of the Canadian Rockies, 1988), 71, 75. It was significant, however, that Notman's studio photograph of his young son on snowshoes in a fake snowstorm was produced in 1867 and titled "Young Canada." Schwartz, "Photographic Archives," 17–19.

84 *Picturesque Canada*, 235. Nearly all the illustrations in this chapter were produced by Schell with or without his frequent collaborator for *Harper's Weekly*, Thomas Hogan. Rainey, *Picturesque America*, 280.

85 *Picturesque Canada*, 4. The Ottawa chapter (see pp. 190–2) includes an illustration and a description of tobogganing on the slide at Government House. On winter sports in Montreal and Canadian nationalism, see Gillian Poulter, *Becoming Native in a Foreign Land: Sport, Visual Culture, and Identity in Montreal, 1840–85* (Vancouver: UBC Press, 2009), chapters 1 and 5.

86 See Carl Berger, "The True North Strong and Free," in Peter Russell, ed., *Nationalism in Canada* (Toronto: McGraw-Hill, 1966), 3–26; and McKay, *Picturing the Land*, 157–60.

87 *Picturesque Canada*, 225. The two descriptions of Prairie snow storms (284, 289–90) are more ominous, but elsewhere it is claimed that "on account of the dryness of the air the cold is not so much felt" as in eastern Canada (p. 300).

88 Nye, *American Technological Sublime*, 39.

89 Rainey, *Creating Picturesque America*, 246.

90 Grant and Hamilton, *Principal Grant*, 247–8.

91 *Picturesque Canada*, 564.

92 *Picturesque Canada*, 564.

93 *Picturesque Canada*, 574. On a similar note, Grant wrote that "Interesting, and after a fashion phenomenal as Winnipeg is, it must not be supposed that we can find the true North-West in its towns and cities." The "brood of barnacles and vultures" (namely the speculators) to be found there "are unbeautiful and uninteresting to the artist and to healthy human beings." *Picturesque Canada*, 293.

94 See Donald Worster, "Wild, Tame, and Free: Comparing Canadian and U.S. Views of Nature," in John M. Findlay and Ken S. Coates, eds, *Parallel Destinies: Canadian-American Relations West of the Rockies* (Montreal and Kingston: McGill-Queen's University Press, 2002).

95 Thus, painting in the late 1830s, the popular British artist William Henry Bartlett highlighted industrial progress in his American views but wild nature in those produced in Canada. See Brian and Ellen Harding, "Looking Forward; Looking Backward: American and Canadian Scenery in the 1830s," *British Journal of Canadian Studies* 8, no. 2 (1993): 163–79.
96 Cook, "Imagining a North American Garden," 12.
97 Cook, "Imagining a North American Garden," 13–14; Northrop Frye, *The Bush Garden: Essays on the Canadian Imagination* (Toronto: Anansi, 1971); Margaret Atwood, *Survival: A Thematic Guide to Canadian Literature* (Toronto: Anansi, 1972). This is also the argument of Marcia B. Kline, who states further that "as the century wore on and the Canadian artist became more mature and less provincial … the terror became more pronounced." *Beyond the Land Itself: Views of Nature in Canada and the United States* (Cambridge, MA: Harvard University Press, 1970), 46.
98 See, for example, Malcolm Andrews, *The Search for the Picturesque: Landscape Aesthetics and Tourism in Britain, 1760–1800* (Stanford, CA: Stanford University Press, 1989).
99 Stephen Daniels, *Fields of Vision: Landscape Imagery and National Identity in England and the United States* (Princeton, NJ: Princeton University Press, 1993), 5.
100 *Picturesque Canada*, 194.

9 Our Lady of the Snows: Rudyard Kipling's Imperialist Vision of Canada

Given that Rudyard Kipling never lived in Canada, it is perhaps not surprising that the country did little to inspire his poetry or fiction,[1] but the same cannot be said of his travel narratives. Said to have been the most popular writer in the English-speaking world, Kipling published accounts of his short visit to the Canadian West coast in 1889, and of his more extensive Canadian railway excursions in 1892 and 1907.[2] These travel narratives are far from being detailed and prosaic guidebooks; rather, they are essentially collections of Kipling's deeply opinionated and highly imaginative impressions during the era when, in the words of Helen Carr, travel writing was becoming "a more subjective form, more memoir than manual, and often an alternative form of writing for novelists."[3] But Kipling did have a political purpose in travelling across Canada, particularly with his excursion of 1907 when international tensions were growing. His goal was to strengthen what he considered to be the young country's crucial role in the British Empire by promoting English emigration to the Canadian West and stimulating Canadian pride as a junior partner in what was still the most powerful empire on earth.[4] Kipling's gaze was focused less on the landscape than on the people he observed both inside and outside his railway car as it rolled across the country, but he shared none of his fellow travel writers' fascination with the First Nations or the "folk," including the French-Canadian habitants. He aimed instead to depict Canada – and western Canada in particular – as a place with the potential to transform England's surplus population into a hardy northern race, a place that would thereby become the nursery of the British Empire. In short, Kipling's idealized Canada was what historian J.G.A. Pocock refers to as a neo-Britain, namely a settlement colony inhabited by a people defined by their "global Britishness."[5]

At the time of his first visit to Canada in 1889, the twenty-four-year-old Kipling was already a successful author, having written the popular *Departmental Ditties, Plain Tales from the Hills* as well as six slim volumes of stories in his native India. With the plan of moving to England in mind, he had joined a married couple in a seven-month tour from India across Southeast Asia, China, Japan, the United States, and the Atlantic. To pay for his expenses, Kipling contracted with his former Allahabad newspaper employer to write thirty-nine "letters of travel." Much to Kipling's annoyance, these letters were pirated in the United States as *American Notes*. A decade later, in 1899, he nevertheless had all but two of them revised and republished in the collection titled from *From Sea to Sea*.[6] Twenty of these letters were devoted to America, with the aforementioned side-trip to the British Columbia coast described in one of them.

Kipling's reason for travelling north from San Francisco to Vancouver was, in his words, to "Bask for a day under the shadow of the old Flag."[7] Three years after the town had been destroyed by fire, Kipling noted, its population had reached 14,000, many living in houses built of brick with dressed granite fronts. Kipling found Vancouver to be a welcome respite from the towns he had passed through in the United States, noting that "Men don't fly up and down the streets telling lies, and the spittoons in the delightfully comfortable hotels are unused." To an American who drew his notice to "the absence of bustle," Kipling replied: "Give me granite – hewn granite and peace, and keep your deal boards and bustle for yourselves."[8] Young as Vancouver was, Kipling wrote, "its streets are better than those in Western America. Moreover, the old flag waves over some of the buildings, and this is cheering to the soul. Also the place is full of English men who speak the English tongue correctly and with clearness, avoiding more blasphemy than is necessary, and taking a respectable length of time to getting through their drinks."[9]

Kipling's only criticism of Vancouver was that the terminus of the transcontinental railway – which would "throw actual fighting troops into the East when our hold of the Suez Canal is temporarily loosened" – was not properly fortified. All that was required was "a fat earthwork upon a hill – there are plenty of hills to choose from." Kipling added that the naval stations at Victoria and Esquimalt on Vancouver Island were nearby, but so was "a place called Vladivostok, and though Vancouver narrows are strait [*sic*], they allow room enough for a man-of-war." Kipling also mused that Vancouver would be a good place for an Anglo-Indian to retire. The cost of living was cheap, and "he can buy a boat and drift about the glossy Sound exploring a thousand islands, prospecting for gold if he likes" or, like the retired officer from a Highland regiment whom Kipling met, pretend to raise sheep at "perfectly ridiculous cost." As for "the memsahib, who follows her husband there is very pleasant English society, and it will presently grow."[10] Kipling was even persuaded by "a delightful English boy" to invest in a forested town lot, adding that he would not have bought it from an American who "would have overstated the case."[11] As it turned out, however, the speculation proved to be a loss, for when Kipling sold the land nearly forty years later, he received less than he had paid in property taxes.[12]

Before returning southward, Kipling also made a short visit to the provincial capital of Victoria where there was a sizeable community of Indian Army officer and Civil Service veterans.[13] Here, in contrast to Vancouver, Kipling was "consoled" by the distant sight of "three British men-of-war and a torpedo boat." Unlike most British travel writers, he expressed little interest in the coastal scenery, quoting with approval a discontented traveller's remark that "When you have seen a fine forest, a bluff, a river and a lake you have seen all the scenery of Western America." Kipling added, sardonically, "Men said if I went to Alaska I should see islands even more wooded, snow-peaks loftier and rivers more lovely than those around me. That decided me not to go to Alaska."[14]

Not quite three years later, in January 1892, Kipling embarked from London with his new American bride on a round-the-world excursion. To help defray the costs, he contracted with the London *Times* to submit travel articles that would be syndicated internationally.[15] The series was titled "From Tideway to Tideway 1892-5" and republished in his *Letters of Travel* in 1920.[16] Of the nine essays in this volume, two describe the Canadian section of the journey. Heading westward across North America, the young couple crossed into Canada at the Manitoba border where, Kipling wrote, he had the urge to shake hands with the young Mounted Police officer as he "swaggered" through the car "because he is clean and does not slouch nor spit, trims his hair, and walks as a man should."[17] This would not be the only occasion when Kipling depicted Canadian manhood as more respectable than its counterpart south of the border.

The prairie countryside in the early spring was less impressive to the newly-married Kipling who, on this trip, had other things on his mind besides the promotion of British emigration and imperialism. Anxious to revisit more exotic and warmer countries, he wrote: "For eight-and-twenty long hours did the bored locomotive trail us through a flat and hairy land, powdered, ribbed, and speckled with snow, small snow that drives like dust-shot in the wind – the land of Assiniboia. Now and again, for no obvious reason there was a town." One of these towns Kipling described memorably as "shut in among low, treeless, rolling ground" that featured a Mounted Police detachment with cemetery, and "a painfully formal public garden with pebble paths and foot-high fir trees." In addition there were Natives in red blankets selling buffalo horns, and two bears "standing up with extended arms in their pens and begging for food." After identifying the town as Medicine Hat, Kipling quipped that it was "the only possible name such a town could carry."[18]

Even the Rocky Mountains troubled Kipling for he described them in terms that are more gothic than sublime in nature. Reflecting the fact that the snow had not yet melted even in April, Kipling wrote, "The place is locked up – dead as a frozen corpse." Pine stumps were "capped and hooded with gigantic mushrooms of snow," and "dumb white lips curl up to the track cut in the side of the mountain, and grin there fanged with gigantic icicles." At a whistle stop "in a gigantic gorge walled in by the snows" a drunken man "reels from a tiny saloon into the middle of the track where half-a-dozen dogs are chasing a pig off the metals." A few miles down, "One of the hillsides moved a little in dreaming of the spring and caught a passing freight train."[19] In another place, a slide had hit the edge of a snow shed "and scooped it away as a knife scoops cheese."[20] Kipling clearly felt a strong sense of relief on reaching the lower Fraser Valley where "the pink blossoms of the wild currant were open, the budding alders stood misty green against the blue black of the pines, the brambles on the burnt stumps were in tenderest leaf, and every moss on every stone was this year's work, fresh from the hand of the Maker." Moved by "a breath of real spring," passengers sang, threw "squashy green marsh-flags" at the colts, and shouted with joy at a wild duck "that rose from a jewel-green lakelet."[21] Following this Arcadian description, Kipling simply ignored Vancouver, aside from noting that the city had "grown out of all knowledge" since he had visited it three years earlier.[22]

Auspicious to Kipling as the vessel name *Empress of India* may have been, when it reached Japan he discovered that the bank holding his funds had failed. As a result, he and his bride had no choice but to sail back to North America where they would settle in her native Vermont for four and a half of his most productive years. The Canadian Pacific Railway (CPR) provided free passage from Vancouver, perhaps hoping that Kipling would publish colourful descriptions of the scenery.[23] In contrast to his westward journey, however, Kipling's most evocative writing was of the sensation experienced inside the train. Romanticizing the technological, he observed that "A week on the wheels turns a man into a part of the machine ... The snort, the snap and whine of the air-brakes have a meaning for him, and he learns to distinguish between noises – between the rattle of a loose lamp and the ugly rattle of small stones on a scarped embankment – between the 'Hoot! Toot!' that scares wandering cows from the line, and the dry roar of the engine at the distance-signal." In England, Kipling added, the railway had arrived in a settled country where it remained "just a little outside daily life," but in Canada "it strolls along, with its hands in its pockets and a straw in its mouth, on the heels of the rough-hewn trail or log road – a platformless, regulationless necessity."[24] Kipling's admiration of the railway doubtless reflects an awareness of the close link between the technological advances in transportation and communication, on the one hand, and the imperial resurgence on the other. In the words of imperial historian Duncan Bell, oceangoing steamships and the submarine telegraph had transformed "the very perception of the political limits prescribed by nature."[25]

As for the countryside, Kipling adopted a more positive perspective than on his westward train trip, writing that "a great stretch" of the 3,000-mile distance "is as new as the day before yesterday, and strewn with townships in every stage of growth from the city of one round house, two log huts, and a Chinese camp somewhere in the foothills of the Selkirks, to Winnipeg with her league-long main street and her warring newspapers." Manitoba was then engaged in an election, and Kipling observed sardonically that "By reason of their closeness to the States, they have caught the contagion of foul-mouthedness, and accusations of bribery, corruption, and evil-living are many." He also mocked the scramble for each new town to have a railway connection, claiming that "For this it will sell its corrupted soul." Once "the glamour of the thing" had worn off, however, the local newspaper, "sliding down the pole of Pride with the hind legs of despair, says defiantly: 'At least, a veterinary surgeon and a drug store would meet with encouragement in our midst, and it is a fact that five new buildings have been erected in our midst since the spring.'"[26]

Unlike the poet Rupert Brooke, however (see chapter 10), Kipling did not dwell long upon the crude materialism of the Canadian West with its taint of American corruption, expressing, instead, his British pride in the rapid development of that imperial frontier.[27] Having satirized the small-town scramble for a railway connection, he changed his tone by observing that "From a distance nothing is easier than to smile at this sort of thing, but he must have a cool head who can keep his pulse level when just such a wildcat town – ten houses, two churches, and a line of rails – gets 'on the boom.' The reader at home says, 'Yes, but it's all a lie.' It may be, but – did men lie about Denver, Leadville, Ballarat, Broken Hill, Portland, or Winnipeg twenty years ago – or Adelaide when town lots went begging within the memory of middle-aged men?" Adopting a shamelessly boosterish tone, Kipling then proclaimed: "Anything is possible, especially among the Rockies where minerals lie over and above the mining towns," and where there were "literally scores upon scores of lakelets in the hills, buried in woods now, that before twenty years are run will be crowded summer resorts." Furthermore, "wheat will be grown for the English market four hundred miles north of the present fields on the west side; and British Columbia, perhaps the loveliest land in the world next to New Zealand, will have her own line of six thousand ton steamers to Australia, and the British investor will no longer throw away his money on hellcat South American republics, or give it a hostage to the States. He will keep it in the family as a wise man should." The problem was, Kipling concluded, that "it is hopeless to make people understand that actually and indeed, we *do* possess an Empire of which Canada is only one portion – an Empire which is not bounded by election-returns on the North and Eastbourne riots on the South – an Empire that has not yet been scratched."[28]

Kipling's enthusiasm for Canada only increased five years later, in 1897, when it became the first member of the Empire to support Joseph Chamberlain's tariff reform policy by granting preferential tariffs on English trade goods.[29] Kipling celebrated with a poem in *The Times* titled "Our Lady of the Snows," which issued a call for other former colonies to follow the Canadian example:

> They that are wise may follow
> Ere the world's war-trumpet blows,
> But I – I am first in battle,
> Said Our Lady of the Snows.[30]

9.1 "Au Revoir, Kipling!" *Canadian Courier*, 26 October 1907. From Angus Wilson, *The Strange Ride of Rudyard Kipling*, 274. In this cartoon satirizing Kipling's poem, "Our Lady of the Snows," he is shown to be suffering from Canada's hot weather during his cross-country speaking tour while a cool and manly mounted policeman shakes his hand and Lady Bountiful holds a basket of Canadian apples for him to eat on his way home to England.

Given his steadfast commitment to British emigration to Canada, Kipling was undoubtedly chagrined when Canadians denounced his poem as an impediment to tourism as well as immigration because it conjured up an endless winter. One Prairie pamphleteer even published a rejoinder titled "Lady Bountiful not the Lady of the Snows" (see figure 9.1).[31]

When Kipling made his third extended visit to Canada in the summer of 1907, he expressed none of the ambivalence about the countryside that he had in his previous two travel narratives. The trip had been initiated with the simple aim of having his wife visit her Vermont mother in Quebec City, for Kipling refused to return to the United States.[32] According to one of his letters, his travel plans had changed when, "Two hundred miles out at sea (may Allah confound Marconi) telegrams burst round us like shells and at Rimouski the strong hands of the Canadian Clubs took hold of us and literally and absolutely – a thing I did not know was possible – we had not one hour to ourselves unbroken till we were back in the steamer again."[33] Because Kipling had finally agreed to embark on a cross-country speaking tour at a time when support for British imperialism was approaching its peak in English Canada,[34] the CPR had placed at his disposal a luxurious passenger car, including the services of a "stately negro" who "received us with the airs of an archbishop."[35] Kipling made it clear to a friend that he was not particularly comfortable in this public role: "Altogether life is hellish swellish – or would be but for the fact that I have to make speeches at every town I stop at and see the bulk of the population in between times."[36]

This was somewhat of an exaggeration, however, for in the *Canadian Annual Review of Public Affairs* pro-imperialist editor J. Castell Hopkins complained that Kipling "did not meet the people at all; he addressed the Canadian Club at Toronto, Montreal, Ottawa, Winnipeg, Vancouver, and Victoria; his views were clearly enunciated, and far flung over the stretches of half a continent; but his personality did not touch the masses, who would have much liked to see and hear him."[37] If Vancouver was at all typical, though, the luncheon audiences consisted of many more than the club members. After being met by the mayor, presidents of the Board of Trade, and members of the provincial government, Kipling addressed an overflow audience of 500, including women who attended despite not being invited.[38] Perhaps Kipling had Hopkins' article in mind, then, when he warned Lord Milner in July 1908 that "You will have to face the impact of young, callous, curious and godlessly egotistic crowds who will take everything out of you and put nothing back. Their redeeming point is a certain crude material faith in the Empire, of which they naturally conceive themselves to be the belly-button." As for the Canadian press, Kipling suggested that Milner "Tell your bottle-holder to disconnect your bedroom telephone as soon as ever you get to an hotel. Otherwise you will continue to enjoy the horrors of publicity in your bath and in your bed."[39]

No such complaints were included in the published descriptions of the excursion to the West coast and back. Titled "Letters to the Family," the articles appeared in London's *Morning Post* before being published in pamphlet form shortly afterward, and finally in Kipling's *Letters of Travel* in 1920.[40] Kipling pointed to his political purpose at the outset by attacking Britain's Liberal government whose members had made it clear that "no possible advantage to the Empire outweighed the cruelty and injustice of charging the British working man twopence halfpenny a week on some of his provisions." Canada was not without its own drawbacks, however, for it "has to deal in the lump with most of the problems that afflict us others severally." To begin with, "she has the Double-Language, Double-Law, Double-Politics drawback in a worse form than South Africa, because, unlike our Dutch, her French cannot well marry outside their religion, and they take orders from Italy." Canada also had "something of Australia's labour fuss" exacerbated by "the influence of 'Labour' entrenched, with arms, and high explosives on neighbouring soil."[41] Kipling still believed that Canada had great promise, but he was concerned that the country's Liberal administration was resisting closer integration with the Empire. According to him, the explanation he was given for Prime Minister Laurier's alliance with Botha of South Africa in blocking "the onward rush" was England's aloofness, for Canada did not wish to be snubbed. Reasonable as this concern might be, Kipling added, the fact remained that "she was the Eldest Sister, and more was expected of her. She is a little too modest."[42]

Kipling claimed to have found among the Canadians on board the ship from London a "sometimes humorous, often bewildered, always polite contempt of the England of today," a contempt that was due to the sense that Canada's sacrifice in the Boer War had been for nothing, given England's current disinterest in the Empire.[43] Sailing up the St Lawrence, the Canadian passengers "identified point after point along their own beloved River – places where they played and fished and amused themselves in holiday time," leading the expatriate Kipling to observe wistfully: "It must be pleasant to have a country of one's very own to show off."[44]

Echoing the theory of the more strident English-Canadian nationalists that a hardy young Nordic race was being forged by the cold climate,[45] Kipling made the rather ridiculous claim that he had observed during the Boer War that "the Canadian, even when tired, slacked off less than the men from the hot countries, and while resting did not lie on his back or his belly, but rather on his side, a leg doubled under him, ready to rise in one surge." Likewise, at home, their footmarks "seem to throw an almost straight track, neither splayed nor in-toed," and while at ease "they did not drum with their fingers, fiddle with their feet, or feel the hair on their faces." Trivial as "these things" might seem, Kipling added, "when breeds are in the making everything is worth while."[46]

Such statements reflect what historian John Tosh describes as the highly masculinized nature of late nineteenth-century imperialism,[47] but Kipling made it clear that females also contributed to the "race." Thus, he fantasized about a tall young woman waiting for a tram whose portrait, he claimed, might hang in Ottawa's Parliament House as an ideal symbol of the country. She wore her "almost flaxen-gold hair waved, and parted low on the forehead, beneath a black astrakhan toque, with a red enamel maple-leaf hatpin" that served as "the one touch of colour except the flicker of a buckle on the shoe." There were "no trinkets or attachments" on her perfectly fitting "dark, tailor-made dress," and she carried "the weight of her superb body … evenly on both feet." But most striking, "next to the grave, tranquil eyes," Kipling wrote, was "her slow, unhurried breathing in the hurry about her." Even after she had disappeared from sight, "the power of the mouth, the wisdom of the brow, the human comprehension of the eyes, and the outstriking vitality of the creature remained."[48] Rather than being a sexualized image of a submissive woman, this description suggested that it was not only Canada's men but also its women who were self-collected and aloof, as well as strong and alert.

Self-consciously engaging in myth-making, Kipling further described Canadians as "driving the great world-plough which wins the world's bread up and up over the shoulder of the world – a spectacle, as it might be, out of some tremendous Norse legend. North of them lies Niflheim's enduring cold, with the flick and crackle of the Aurora for Bifrost Bridge that Odin and the Aesir visited." During the summer, Canadians had to "cram twelve months' work into six, because between such and such dates certain far rivers will shut, and, later, certain others, till, at last, even the Great Eastern Gate at Quebec locks, and men must go in and out by the side-doors at Halifax and St. John." Having ignored Canada's original all-season port of Portland, Maine, Kipling concluded that "These are conditions that make for extreme boldness, but not for extravagant boastings."[49]

Contributing to the myth of railway as nation-builder, Kipling exclaimed that "the railways – the wonderful railways – told the winter's tale most emphatically." Thirty-ton coal cars "thumped past statelily at midnight on their way to provident housekeepers of the prairie towns," while in the opposite direction "the bacon, the lard, the apples, the butter, and the cheese, in beautiful whitewood barrels, were rolling eastwards toward the steamers." Following behind was the lumber, "clean wood out of the mountains – logs, planks, clapboards, and laths, for which we pay such sinful prices in England – all seeking the sea." And yet to come was the western wheat, "the real staple which men for five hundred miles were threshing out in heaps as high as fifty-pound villas."[50]

This was a highly materialistic vision, yet, upon receiving an honorary doctorate at McGill University, Kipling delivered an address that one biographer claims was his "most direct and fierce attack upon materialism, a clear warning that the sterling quality of the students will be worth nothing if their sense of their duties is swallowed up by material prosperity."[51] Addressing the Canadian Club in Winnipeg, Kipling also proclaimed that without a strong sense of nationhood, "the biggest city the world has ever seen is merely a shack of organised enterprise," but with it "the meanest collection of packing-cases that was ever tack-hammered together on a prairie can uplift and dominate a continent."[52] The fact remains, however, that Kipling was no anti-materialist. Rather, as Andrew Hagiioannu has observed of his fiction, Kipling's goal was to infuse the softened urban consciousness that had emerged since the industrial revolution with the frontier spirit necessary for imperial expansion.[53] Thus, Kipling claimed in his *Letters of Travel* that no "eminent novelist, philosopher, dramatist, or divine of to-day has to exercise half the pure imagination, not to mention insight, endurance, and self-restraint, which is accepted without comment in what is called 'the materialist exploitation' of a new country." The drama and the "play of human virtues" in creating a new city, Kipling insisted, "would fill a book."[54] Furthermore, in addressing the Canadian Club in Toronto, Kipling encouraged the local businessmen to invest in other parts of the Empire, adding that "I can put my hand on the map and point to certain countries that I know, and I can show you how the natural resources of such and such areas must create vast and stable industries, rearing up power on a larger scale than the world has yet witnessed."[55]

Though he is often assumed to have been anti-urban as well as anti-materialist,[56] the cities Kipling travelled through in 1907 are described collectively in much the same terms as his idealized Canadians. Thus, "it was the dignity of the cities that impressed – an austere Northern dignity of outline, grouping, and perspective, aloof from the rush of traffic in the streets. Montreal, of the black-frocked priests and the French notices, had it; and Ottawa, of the grey stone palaces and the St Petersburg-like shining water-frontages; and Toronto, consumingly commercial, carried the same power in the same repose."[57] Kipling did admit, however, that the three cities had become somewhat contaminated by the "unstable, southern spirit" of "hustle," which "does not sit well on the national character any more than falsetto or fidgeting becomes grown men." The resulting "slapdasherie," Kipling complained, meant that the "assembly and dispersal of crowds, purchase of tickets, and a good deal of the small machinery of life is clogged and hampered."[58] This concern made it somewhat easier for Kipling to concede that the country's biculturalism had one advantage, for even though the French Canadians "are made to hang back in the work of development, their withdrawn and unconcerned cathedrals, schools, and convents, and one aspect of the spirit that breathes from them, make for good." After all, Kipling concluded, "it must be worth something to say your prayers in a dialect of the tongue that Virgil handled."[59]

If Americans were associated with "hustle" in Kipling's mind, English Canadians were associated with the more manly "drive," a quality he met with "up the Western Road where the new country is being made." Leaving behind the "Three Cities and the close-tilled farming and orchard districts" of central Canada, the train travelled northwestward through "a country of rushing streams, clear-eyed ponds, and boulders among berry-bushes; all crying 'Trout' and 'Bear.'" The names of the most remote rivers, Kipling claimed, were now "known in England, and men, otherwise sane, slip away from London into the birches, and come out again bearded and smoke-stained, when the ice is thick enough to cut a canoe."[60] In addition to sportsmen, prospectors "boarded the cars, and dropped off, and disappeared beyond thickets and hills precisely as the first widely spaced line of skirmishers fans out and vanishes along the front of the day's battle."[61]

Even though Kipling was able to romanticize the vast thin-soiled Canadian Shield, with its stunted conifers and boggy ground, Lake Superior troubled him, as it would Rupert Brooke six years later. In fact, Brooke's distinctively gothic imagery may well have been inspired by Kipling who wrote that "There is a quiet horror about the Great Lakes which grows as one revisits them. Fresh water has no right or call to dip over the horizon, pulling down and pushing up the hulls of big steamers; no right to tread the slow, deep-sea dance-step between wrinkled cliffs; nor to roar in on weed and sand beaches between vast headlands that run out for leagues into haze and sea-fog." Lake Superior "engulfs and wrecks and drives ashore, like a fully accredited ocean – a hideous thing to find in the heart of a continent." The lake had admittedly "produced a breed of sailors," but they "bear the same relation to the salt-water variety as a snake-charmer does to a lion-tamer."[62]

Perhaps Kipling's reaction, as well as that of Brooke, reflected their conservative mistrust of the unfamiliar, yet to Kipling the western prairies were "the High Veldt, plus Hope, Activity, and Reward." He enthused that Winnipeg was unrecognizable from his previous visit, adding that "Warehouses, railway-sidings, and such are only counters in the White Man's Game, which can be swept up and re-dealt as the play varies. It was the spirit in the thin dancing air – the new spirit of the new city – which rejoiced me. Winnipeg has Things in abundance, but has learned to put them beneath her feet, not on top of her mind, and so is older than many cities."[63] The imagery Kipling chose to describe the urban expansion was rather macabre, yet his aim was clearly to ennoble the process rather than condemn it. From the roof of a "monster building," he wrote, Winnipeg "seemed to overflow and fill with noises the whole vast cup of the horizon" as "all around its edges, jets of steam and the impatient cries of machinery showed it was eating out into the Prairie like a smothered fire."[64]

In contrast to his early cross-country journeys, Kipling had time in 1907 to explore the prairie countryside where, he claimed, the air became "different from any air that ever blew," and the space was "ampler than most spaces, because it runs back to the unhampered Pole."[65] The flat expanse challenged the British propensity for describing colonial landscapes as picturesque, but Stephen Daniels argues that it was often the very "otherness" of such places that made them compelling, "especially as a testing ground for imperial energy and imagination."[66] The difference between the Great Lakes and the Prairies, in this regard, was presumably that the latter could be colonized by British emigrants. In any case, Kipling assured his British readers that "When mere space and the stoop of the high sky begin to overwhelm, earth provides little ponds and lakes, lying in soft-flanked hollows, where people can step down out of the floods of air, and delight themselves with small and known distances."[67] And, rather than focusing exclusively on the landscape, Kipling again resorted to human images and myth-making, describing how at one halt "a woman drove straight down at us from the sky-line, along a golden path between black ploughed lands." Having arrived at the train, "she nodded mysteriously, and showed us a very small baby in the hollow of her arm." Although this new mother very likely felt a desperate need to connect with other humans, if ever so fleetingly, to Kipling she was "some exiled Queen flying North to found a dynasty and establish a country."[68] Once again, then, Kipling included a woman in his romantic vision of a hardy northern nation.

Resisting the cry of the "Afrites of the Railway" to head North to where "the Grand Trunk was laying down a suburban extension of a few thousand miles across the Continent," Kipling kept his gaze mostly on the prairie towns, noting that "The old, false-fronted, hollow-stomached Western hotels were gone; their places filled by five-storey brick or stone ones, with Post Offices to match."[69] After noting that "each town school carried the Union Jack on a flagstaff in its playground," Kipling drove home his political message with the added observation that "So far as one could understand, the scholars are taught neither to hate, nor despise, nor beg from, their own country."[70] Nor could he resist commenting that "if a tenth of that energy wasted on 'social reform' could be diverted to decently thought out and supervised emigration work ... we might do something worth talking about ... It makes one jealous and afraid to watch aliens taking, and taking honestly, so much of this treasure of good fortune and sane living."[71]

"Alien" immigration was the one blight that preoccupied Kipling in western Canada. "The Canadian," he wrote, "naturally purrs over an emigrant owing everything to the land which adopted him and set him on his feet." Kipling, on the other hand, could not "care much for those who have renounced their own country. They may have good reason, but they have broken the rules of the game, and ought to be penalised instead of adding to their score." Furthermore, "a few full meals and fine clothes" did not "obliterate all taint of alien instinct and reversion ... That was why the sight of the beady-eyed, muddy-skinned, aproned women, with handkerchiefs on their heads and Oriental bundles in their hands, always distressed one."[72] The women who captured Kipling's attention in this case, then, were a threat because they would enable the alien races to reproduce. The same hostile sentiment to non-British-origin immigrants was expressed in one of the poems that accompanied Kipling's Canadian articles in the *Morning Post*:

The Stranger within my gate,
He may be true or kind,
But he does not talk my talk –

I cannot feel his mind.
I see the face and the eyes and the mouth,
But not the soul behind.
...
The Stranger within my gates,
He may be evil or good,
But I cannot tell what powers control –
What reasons sway his mood;
Nor when the Gods of his far-off land
Shall repossess his blood.[73]

Heading into the Rocky Mountain foothills, Kipling observed that "The timber off their sides was ducking and pitch-poling down their swift streams, to be sawn into house-stuff for all the world." The Rockies, themselves, had been repeatedly described in terms of the sublime, but Kipling's imagery was, as in 1892, more gothic in tone, reflecting both his propensity to mythologize and his discomfort with a wild nature that resisted human settlement and development:

> There are many local gods on the road through the Rockies: old bald mountains that have parted with every shred of verdure and stand wrapped in sheets of wrinkled silver rock, over which the sight travels slowly as in delirium; mad, horned mountains, wreathed with dancing mists; low-browed and bent-shouldered faquirs of the way-side, sitting in meditation beneath a burden of glacier-ice that thickens every year; and mountains of fair aspect on one side, but on the other seamed with hollow sunless clefts, where last year's snow is blackened with this year's dirt and smoke of forest-fires. The drip from it seeps away through slopes of unstable gravel and dirt, till, at the appointed season, the whole half-mile of undermined talus slips and roars into the horrified valley.[74]

Kipling may have been somewhat obsessed by the possibility of a landslide, but he did reassure his readers that "From time to time the mountains lean apart, and nurse between them some golden valley of slow streams, fat pastures, and park-like uplands, with a little town, and cow bells tinkling among berry bushes; and children who have never seen the sun rise or set, shouting at the trains; and real gardens round the houses."[75]

Furthermore, the mountains were "only ten days from London, and people more and more use them for pleasure-grounds." Kipling encountered two women, for example, who were "black-haired, bareheaded, wearing beadwork squaw-jackets, and riding straddle" as "a string of pack-ponies trotted through the pines behind them." He assumed that they were "Indians on the move" until he noticed "the comprehending equal eyes of the civilised white woman which moved in that berry-brown face." To his further surprise, Kipling discovered in the hotel that evening that the eyes of the "slight woman in a very pretty evening frock ... were the eyes of the woman in the bead-work jacket who had quirted the piebald pack-pony past our buggy." The woman in question was Mary Schäffer of Philadelphia, who spent a number of summers organizing wilderness trips in the Canadian Rockies for daughters of affluent families. While, as we have seen, Kipling had mythologized two young fair-complexioned women who, he suggested, would give birth to a racially superior nation, he was less kind to Schäffer, perhaps because she was older and American, as well as only a seasonal visitor. Privately, he referred to her as a "flat-fronted old maid of a woman who looked as if she'd run from a mouse." In print he also minimized the challenge Schäffer and her friend posed to the gender divide by stressing the lack of danger they faced, writing that nowhere else could two women "go out for a three months" trek and shoot in perfect comfort and safety.'[76]

Upon arrival in British Columbia, Kipling noted that the province was blessed with "Lumber, coal, minerals, fit soil for fruit, dairy, and poultry farms," as well as a "superb climate." He then rhapsodized that "The natural beauty of earth and sky match these lavish gifts; to which are added thousands of miles of safe and sheltered waterways for coastal trade; deep harbours that need no dredge; the ground-works for immense and ice-free ports – all the title-deeds to half the trade in Asia." Obviously referring to Stanley Park, Kipling added that Vancouver, itself, boasted "one of the loveliest water-girt parks that we have outside the tropics." In the suburbs, sportsmen could find "salmon, trout, quail, and pheasant," and "Another town" (presumably Victoria), "is presented with a hundred islands, knolls, wooded coves, stretches of beach, and dingles, laid down as expressly for camp-life, picnics, and boating parties, beneath skies never too hot and rarely too cold. If they care to lift up their eyes from their almost subtropical gardens they can behold snowy peaks across blue bays, which must be good for the soul." Furthermore, though facing the sea, "out of which any portent may arise, they are not forced to protect or even to police its waters. They are as ignorant of drouth, murrain, pestilence[,] locusts, and blight, as they are of the true meaning of want and fear."[77]

In contrast to the Prairie provinces, however – where Kipling found the people to be infectiously enthusiastic – in British Columbia he "seemed to hear more about 'problems' and 'crises' and 'situations' ... than anywhere else." The problem was not economic stagnation, for the province was experiencing a protracted boom, but a shortage of "men and women to do the work in hand."[78] And that shortage was not only an economic problem, for it had resulted in Asian immigration, which in turn had resulted in anti-Asian riots and demands for Asiatic exclusion.[79] Somewhat surprisingly, however, Kipling had little sympathy for Asian exclusionists, declaring privately that "I do not understand how the Dominion proposes to control an enormous Oriental trade, and, at the same time, hold herself aloof from the Asiatic influx which is the natural concomitant of that trade."[80]

No one, Kipling was assured "objects to the biddable Chinaman. He takes work which no white man in a new country will handle, and when kicked by the mean white will not grossly retaliate." The only result of doubling the head-tax upon entry into the country, Kipling claimed, was that "the Chinaman now charges double for his services, and is scarce at that." The further result was that overworked White women now "die or go off their heads." To remedy that situation, "blocks of flats" were being built in order to "minimise the inconveniences of housekeeping without help," which would in turn cause the city's birth rate to decline.[81] According to Kipling's rather far-fetched reasoning, clearly inspired by current fears of "race suicide,"[82] a policy designed to keep British Columbia white would, therefore, have the opposite effect.

In addition to commenting on the Chinese, Kipling observed that "A fair sprinkling of Punjabis – ex-soldiers, Sikhs, Muzbis, and Jats – are coming in on the boats." They worked in the lumber mills, and, while "not understood ... they are not hated."[83] Kipling clearly felt a certain affinity for these natives of his birth country, for he described them in some detail. He also claimed that when the "little riot" had broken out in Vancouver that year, "these 'heathen' were invited by other Asiatics to join in defending themselves against the white man. They refused on the ground that they were subjects of the King."[84] The Japanese were a different story, Kipling noted, the objection to them being that "they are just a little too good, and when attacked defend themselves with asperity." Behind the demand to remove the Japanese, Kipling concluded, was the Labour movement which discouraged immigration,

White as well as Asian, and hindered business growth by demanding high wages.[85]

Having completed his cross-country observations, Kipling focused on his political message. In Canada, unlike the United States, he claimed, "The people, the schools, the churches, the Press in its degree, and, above all, the women, understand without manifestoes that their land must now always abide under the Law in deed and in word and thought. This is their caste-mark, the ark of their covenant, their reason for being what they are." But this did not mean that Canadians were a submissive people, for Kipling added that everywhere in the country, "as far as the white man can walk, the relentless spirit of the breed follows up, and oversees, and controls."[86] Kipling did complain, however, that – when it came to defence – Canadians found "refuge behind loose words and childish anticipation of miracles – quite in the best Imperial manner." He warned that "If she continues wealthy and remains weak she will surely be attacked under one pretext or another. Then she will go under, and her spirit will return to the dust with her flag as it slides down the halliards." For Canada could no longer rely on England for defence: "Canada's weakness is lack of men. England's weakness is an excess of voters who propose living at the expense of the State. These loudly resent that any money should be diverted from themselves; and since money is spent on fleets and armies to protect the Empire while it is consolidating, they argue that if the Empire ceased to exist armaments would cease too, and the money so saved could be spent on their creature comforts."[87]

It was therefore in the interest of the "nations of the Empire" to become "strong enough to endure a little battering unaided at the first outset – till such time, that is, as England were permitted to move to their help." Towards that end, "an influx of good men is needed more urgently every year during which peace holds – men loyal, clean, and experienced in citizenship, with women not ignorant of sacrifice."[88] And the supply of such men and women was at hand, for the English working class, "as yet undebauched by the temptation of State-aided idleness or State-guaranteed irresponsibility," was beginning to feel "that the future will be none too rosy for such as are working, or are in the habit of working." If they "could quietly be shown a way out of it all," many would collect their savings "and slip quietly away."[89]

When Kipling asked Canadians why they did not recruit English immigrants rather than the inferior "foreign" stock, however, the answer was invariably, "Because the English do not work. Because we are sick of Remittance-men and loafers sent out here. Because the English are rotten with Socialism. Because the English don't fit with our way of life. They kick at our way of doing things. They are always telling us how things are done in England." Kipling's response, "over three thousand miles of country," was that these justifiable criticisms were, in fact, "excellent reasons for bringing in the Englishman. It is true that in his country he is taught to shirk work, because kind, silly people fall over each other to help and debauch and amuse him," but in Canada "General January will stiffen him up." "You are always talking of the second generation of your Smyrniotes and Bessarabians," Kipling concluded, "Think what the second generation of the English are!"[90] By welcoming immigration from England (Kipling rarely referred to "Britain"), Canada would not only become strengthened militarily and more tied to the Empire emotionally, it would also rid the mother country of her surplus population, thereby strengthening her by undermining the enervating drive towards socialism.

Conclusion

Critiquing the rather exclusive focus of British imperial historians on what he refers to as "the binary coding of difference in relation to the exotic 'other,'" Duncan Bell argues in *The Idea of the British Empire* that the majority of the late Victorian theorists of empire were less concerned with the non-White colonies than with the projection and sustenance of a coherent sense of Britishness throughout the settler communities. He explains further that "While visions of Greater Britain were framed in relation to a putative global racial hierarchy, at the peak of which stood the Anglo-Saxons, they were also and equally focused on other factors, including the fear of increasing competition from other 'civilized' states, most notably France, Germany, and America, as well as anxiety about the dangers of socialism, the emergence of a degenerate 'underclass' and the perceived growth of a self-interested utilitarian liberalism among the British middle classes and governing elite."[91] In short, "the colonial empire was seen anew as a space for transformative moral and political action, for the shaping of a patriotic imperial citizenry, and for the salvation of the endangered 'mother country.'"[92]

Although Bell ignores Kipling, aside from referring to him rather dismissively as "the court poet of imperialism,"[93] the very popular British writer's Canadian travel narratives offer strong support for his thesis. Kipling may have described the country's non-British immigrants in distinctly racialist terms, but his idealized Canada was essentially a wide-open space, a frontier that was fashioning a new man as well as a new woman out of a British stock that was deteriorating in England under the influence of urbanization and social welfare. This neo-Briton conformed to the Turnerian frontier mould insofar as he/she was ruggedly independent, but Kipling made a sharp distinction for he repeatedly referred to American males as the antithesis to their polite, reserved, and honest English-Canadian counterparts.[94] The crucial undeclared difference was, of course, that the Americans had cast off their ties with the more civilized and nurturing mother country while the Canadians remained law-abiding and loyal subjects of the Crown. Furthermore, Kipling may have urged the United States to take up the "White Man's Burden" in his poem of that title in 1899,[95] but he clearly feared that Roosevelt's aggressive imperialism might pose a threat to Britain's sphere of influence.

Kipling returned to Canada for only one brief visit after his eventful 1907 journey,[96] but he maintained a considerable interest in the country throughout the remainder of his life. He became a friend of the Canadian-born Sir William Osler, who was Regius Professor of Medicine at Oxford University, and in 1910 he met and befriended the Canadian press baron Max Aitken, later Lord Beaverbrook, who advised him on Canadian financial investments.[97] Kipling also continued to be concerned about the Americanization of Canada, for he wrote to another friend in 1910 that "The Americans have been 'approaching' her with tariff proposals and whether they succeed or not I have enough faith in their methods to be well sure that they will leave a trail of green-backed corruption from Ottawa to either ocean; and it's bad for the young to be exposed to infection."[98]

The following year, when the *Montreal Star* asked for his views on the reciprocity agreement that the federal government was negotiating with the United States, Kipling's response was:

> I do not understand how nine million people can enter into such arrangements as are proposed with ninety million strangers on an open frontier of four thousand miles, and at the same time preserve their national integrity ... It is her own soul that Canada risks today. Once that soul is pawned, for any consideration, Canada must inevitably conform to the commercial, legal, financial, social and ethical standards which will be imposed upon her by the sheer admitted weight of the United States. She might, for example, be compelled later on to admit reciprocity in the

> murder-rate of the United States which at present, I believe, is something over one hundred and fifty million per annum.

Kipling added that Canada was a nation, and would "ere long, be among the great nations. Why then ... should she throw the enormous gifts of her inheritance and her future into the hands of a people, who by haste and waste have so dissipated their own resources that even before national middle life, they are driven to seek virgin fields for cheaper food and living?"[99] When the Laurier government lost the 1911 election, largely on the reciprocity issue, Kipling wrote to Lord Milner that he had been sitting in the sunshine at Sir Max Aitken's place while telegrams about the results "were handed to me on a lordly dish." Not only had the Laurier-Botha alliance been broken, Kipling exulted, but "French power" in Ottawa had been smashed "for good," and "the U.S. will now lose her temper and say rude things without reserve and that will stiffen Canada's national back."[100]

Pleased with Canada's rush to arms with the declaration of the First World War, Kipling visited the 33,000 Canadian soldiers quartered at Salisbury in 1915.[101] To the Canadian imperialist, Sir Andrew Macphail, he wrote that "I had a glorious time in the Canadian camp. They were *so* good and *so* damned young and conscientious and *so* full of their own small sins. Reminded me somehow of a revival meeting and the anxious seat."[102] Kipling's ideal Canadian, clearly, was not a glory-seeking warrior but an earnest young man ready to sacrifice his life for God, country, and Empire. Twelve years later, in 1927, Kipling was moved to write of Canada's diamond jubilee celebration held in Westminster Abbey that it was "a step on the threshold of a new life and self-knowledge for the Dominion and for the Empire – only the first step. Think what the next sixty years will bring of strength and achievement to grace such beginnings!"[103]

To Kipling, then, Canada was the anti-America. Apart from his repeated complaints about American bad manners, materialism, boastfulness, and dishonesty, he was also deeply unsympathetic to the democratic culture of the United States. Not only did that culture, in his view, make America an unreliable British ally in the struggle for Anglo-Saxon world domination,[104] it also threatened to contaminate and overwhelm what could well be England's best hope for the future, namely Canada. No longer a British colony, Canada was to Kipling a partner tied to the mother country by race, history, and tradition, as well as self-interest. "Daughter am I in my mother's house," Canada declares in the refrain to *Our Lady of the Snows*, "But mistress in my own." Kipling remained upbeat about Canada during the Great Depression, declaring to one of his correspondents two years before his death in 1936 that "Thinking things over, *the* greatest marvel, and proof of the working of Providence, is that Canada has been able to pursue her own destiny and 'find herself,' in spite of the relentless down-drag and moral disorder of the people south of the Border. It is a miracle."[105]

NOTES

Shorter versions of this chapter were presented to the Pacific Coast Conference on British Studies at the University of Nevada and to the Simon Fraser University Department of History Research Colloquium. I wish to express my thanks for the helpful suggestions I received on both occasions.

1 Marghanita Laski, *From Palm to Pine: Rudyard Kipling Abroad and at Home* (London: Sidgwick and Jackson, 1987), 109.
2 Andrew Rutherford, "General Preface" to Rudyard Kipling, *Plain Tales from the Hills* (Oxford: Oxford University Press, 1996), vii.
3 Helen Carr, "Modernism and Travel (1880–1940)," in Peter Hulme and Tim Youngs, eds, *The Cambridge Companion to Travel Writing* (Cambridge, UK: Cambridge University Press, 2002), 74.
4 According to Catherine Hall, approximately a third of the world was, at the turn of the twentieth century, dominated by Britain, "both economically and culturally." Hall, "Introduction: Thinking the Postcolonial, Thinking the Empire," in Catherine Hall, ed., *Cultures of Empire: Colonizers in Britain and the Empire in the Nineteenth and Twentieth Centuries* (Manchester, UK: Manchester University Press, 2000), 9.
5 Pocock's neo-Britains consist of the four dominions forming the "Commonwealth," namely Australia, New Zealand, South Africa, and Canada. J.G.A. Pocock, *The Discovery of Islands: Essays in British History* (Cambridge: Cambridge University Press, 2005), 20, 188, 190.
6 D.H. Stewart, ed., *Kipling's America: Travel Letters, 1889–1895* (Greensboro, NC: ELT Press, 2003), xiv–xv.
7 Stewart, *Kipling's America*, 48.
8 Stewart, *Kipling's America*, 78.
9 Stewart, *Kipling's America*, 79.
10 Stewart, *Kipling's America*, 80–1.
11 Stewart, *Kipling's America*, 79–80.

12 Kipling purchased a half interest in 1892, and the other half interest in 1897. He had also paid for a lot in North Vancouver that did not belong to the vendor. Thomas Pinney, ed., *The Letters of Rudyard Kipling, vol. 3, 1900–10* (London: Macmillan, 1996), 273, 276n4; "Rudyard Kipling in Vancouver," *The History of Metropolitan Vancouver*, www.vancouverhistory.ca/archives_kipling.htm. Viewed 25 November 2014.

13 John F. Bosher, "Vancouver Island and the Kiplings," *Kipling Journal* 83, no. 332 (June 2009): 10.

14 Stewart, *Kipling's America*, 81–2. On Kipling's account of his journey through the American West, see Landon Y. Jones, "Rudyard Kipling: At Large in the West," *Montana: The Magazine of Western History* 64, no. 3 (2014): 24–35.

15 Phillip Mallett, *Rudyard Kipling: A Literary Life* (Houndmills, Basingstoke, Hampshire, UK: Palgrave Macmillan, 2003), 72.

16 Stewart, *Kipling's America*, xxvii.

17 Rudyard Kipling, *Letters of Travel (1892–1913)* (London: Macmillan, 1920), 24.

18 Kipling, *Letters of Travel*, 25–6.

19 Kipling, *Letters of Travel*, 27.

20 Kipling, *Letters of Travel*, 31.

21 Kipling, *Letters of Travel*, 31–2.

22 Kipling, *Letters of Travel*, 32. Kipling not only refused to disembark from the train the evening it arrived in Vancouver, he also refused to grant an interview to a local reporter, adding that the ones published in Winnipeg had been "the product of the fertile imagination of Winnipeg newspapermen, and, as a humble worker in the field of fiction I have no doubt I shall read with interest in The World tomorrow of your interview with me tonight." Alan Twigg, "Famous Visitor," *BC BookWorld Archive*, 2006, www.abcbookworld.com. Viewed 25 November 2014.

23 Andrew Lycett, *Rudyard Kipling* (London: Weidenfeld and Nicolson, 1999), 251.

24 Kipling, *Letters of Travel*, 80–1.

25 Duncan Bell, *The Idea of a Greater Britain: Empire and the Future of World Order, 1860–1900* (Princeton: Princeton University Press, 2007), 29.

26 Kipling, *Letters of Travel*, 81–2.

27 A recent study claims, on the other hand, that "Kipling had been the principal lens through which in his [Brooke's] letters he had framed, defined and made sense of his experience of the Pacific." Henry Ricketts, "The Kiplingization of Rupert Brooke," unpublished essay delivered at the Kent Conference, 7 September 2007. www.kiplingsociety.co.uk/bookmart_fra.htm. Viewed 11 December 2014.

28 Kipling, *Letters of Travel*, 82–4.
29 Robert Craig Brown and Ramsay Cook, *Canada 1896–1921: A Nation Transformed* (Toronto: McClelland and Stewart, 1974), 20–1.
30 http://www.kiplingsociety.co.uk/poems_ladysnows.htm. Viewed 11 December 2014; Lycett, *Rudyard Kipling*, 296.
31 R. Douglas Francis, *Images of the West: Responses to the Canadian Prairies* (Saskatoon: Western Producer Prairie Books, 1989), 110; Angus Wilson, *The Strange Ride of Rudyard Kipling: His Life and Works* (London: Secker and Warburg, 1977), 253–4.
32 The Kiplings had moved from Vermont to London in 1896, and their six-year-old daughter had died of lung congestion during their visit to New York in 1899. Pinney, ed., *The Letters*, vol. 3, 308; Wilson, *The Strange Ride*, 195–7. Kipling claimed in print, however, that he had sailed to Canada in 1907 "mainly to escape the Blight, and also to see what our Eldest Sister [meaning Canada] was doing." Kipling, *Letters of Travel*, 121. See also Rudyard Kipling, *Something of Myself, For My Friends Known and Unknown* (Garden City, NY: Doubleday, Doran and Company, 1937), 212–15.
33 Pinney, ed., *The Letters*, vol. 3, 308. Kipling's claim about the telegrams was confirmed by a note in *The Times*. Pinney, ed., *The Letters*, vol. 3, 310n1.
34 See Carl Berger, *The Sense of Power: Studies in the Ideas of Canadian Imperialism, 1867–1914* (Toronto: University of Toronto Press, 1970), especially chapter 10.
35 Pinney, ed., *The Letters*, vol. 3, 267–8. Kipling wrote privately that he had at his disposal "negro King, hot and cold water, smoking room, private stateroom, cathedral aisle, etc. etc. etc. It hooks on behind any train that looks as if it would be amusing and when we are tired it is unhooked and lies off in queer sidings, on prairies or among mountains till we feel like going on again." Pinney, ed., *The Letters*, vol. 3, 274.
36 Pinney, ed., *The Letters*, vol. 3, 274–5.
37 Quoted in Wilson, *The Strange Ride*, 254.
38 Twigg, "Famous Visitor."
39 When Kipling referred to Canada as "a constipating land," he meant that such phone calls interfered with his bowel movements. Pinney, ed., *The Letters*, vol. 3, 330. Milner began a two-month tour of Canada in September. Pinney, ed., *The Letters*, vol. 3, 331n4.
40 Pinney, ed., *The Letters*, vol. 3, 330; 331n6; Lycett, *Rudyard Kipling*, 377–8.
41 Kipling, *Letters of Travel*, 119–21.
42 Kipling, *Letters of Travel*, 122. On Laurier and British imperialism, see H. Blair Neatby, *Laurier and a Liberal Quebec* (Toronto: McClelland and Stewart, 1973), chapter 7.

43 Kipling, *Letters of Travel*, 124–5.
44 Kipling, *Letters of Travel*, 126.
45 See chapter 9 and Carl Berger, "The True North Strong and Free," in Peter Russell, ed., *Nationalism in Canada* (Toronto: McGraw-Hill, 1966), 3–26.
46 Kipling, *Letters of Travel*, 131.
47 John Tosh, *Manliness and Masculinities in Nineteenth-Century Britain: Essays on Gender, Family and Empire* (Harlow, UK: Pearson Educational, 2005), chapter 9.
48 Kipling, *Letters of Travel*, 137.
49 Kipling, *Letters of Travel*, 131–2.
50 Kipling, *Letters of Travel*, 133.
51 Wilson, *The Strange Ride*, 255. The degree had been awarded in 1899, but Kipling had not been able to receive it at that time. Lycett, *Rudyard Kipling*, 374. Excerpts from the address were later published as "Values in Life," in Rudyard Kipling, *A Book of Words: Selections From Speeches an Addresses Delivered Between 1906 and 1927* (London: Macmillan, 1928), 15–21.
52 Kipling, *A Book of Words*, 36.
53 Andrew Hagiioannu, *The Man Who Would Be Kipling: The Colonial Fiction and the Frontiers of Exile* (Houndmills, Basingstoke, Hampshire, UK: Palgrave Macmillan, 2003), 76.
54 Kipling, *Letters of Travel*, 135.
55 Kipling, *A Book of Words*, 28. Stewart notes that even though Kipling viewed India as an almost feudal and pastoral alternative to the crowding, dirt, and class turmoil of industrial England, he also romanticized Britain's colonial programme of building railways, bridges, dams, and canals, and he sometimes glorified machinery. Stewart, *Kipling's America*, xvii.
56 See, for example, Hagiioannu, *The Man*, 72.
57 Kipling, *Letters of Travel*, 141.
58 Kipling, *Letters of Travel*, 144.
59 Kipling, *Letters of Travel*, 141–2. In a private letter to his son and daughter, however, Kipling infantilized the French Canadians by describing "the queer narrow French farms," each with "a little wooden house and a pilliwinky windmill." Pinney, ed., *The Letters*, vol. 3, 267.
60 Kipling, *Letters of Travel*, 144–5.
61 Kipling, *Letters of Travel*, 146.
62 Kipling, *Letters of Travel*, 148–9.
63 Kipling, *Letters of Travel*, 172–3. On the utopian image of the Prairies at this time, see Francis, *Images of the West*, chapter 4.
64 Kipling, *Letters of Travel*, 174–5.

65 Kipling, *Letters of Travel*, 175.
66 Stephen Daniels, *Fields of Vision: Landscape Imagery and National Identity in England and the United States* (Princeton, NJ: Princeton University Press, 1993), 5.
67 Kipling, *Letters of Travel*, 176. On other examples of how the picturesque was imposed upon the prairie, see Francis, *Images of the West*, 120.
68 Kipling, *Letters of Travel*, 176.
69 Kipling was somewhat unique, in this respect, for most promotional writers focused on the rural agricultural west. See Francis, *Images of the West*, 111, 122.
70 Kipling, *Letters of Travel*, 177.
71 Kipling, *Letters of Travel*, 179.
72 Kipling, *Letters of Travel*, 158–9.
73 http://www.poetryloverspage.com/poets/kipling/stranger.html. Viewed 29 December 2014; Lycett, *Rudyard Kipling*, 378–9.
74 Kipling, *Letters of Travel*, 185–6. Kipling's description in his letter to his son and daughter was more conventionally sublime, for he wrote, "In the night I looked out of my window and I could just make out the mountains all black against the stars and below me I could just see a roaring ribbon of ghostly grey and I knew we were still climbing round that terrible river." Pinney, ed., *The Letters*, vol. 3, 271.
75 Kipling, *Letters of Travel*, 187.
76 Kipling, *Letters of Travel*, 188–9; E.J. Hart, *A Hunter of Peace: Mary T.S. Schäffer's Old Indian Trails of the Canadian Rockies* (Banff, Alberta: The Whyte Foundation, 1980). In his letter to Holland, Kipling identified Schäffer as a "Mrs. Schaeffer of Montreal." Pinney, ed., *The Letters*, vol. 3, 274.
77 Kipling, *Letters of Travel*, 190. Were he "an intending immigrant," Kipling added, "I would risk a good deal of discomfort to get on the land in British Columbia; and were I rich, with no attachments outside England, I would swiftly buy me a farm or a house in that country for the mere joy of it." Kipling, *Letters of Travel*, 191.
78 Kipling, *Letters of Travel*, 189–90; Robert A.J. McDonald, "Victoria, Vancouver, and the Economic Development of British Columbia, 1886–1914," in W. Peter Ward and Robert A.J. McDonald, eds, *British Columbia: Historical Readings* (Vancouver: Douglas and McIntyre, 1981), 377–86.
79 To his son and daughter, Kipling wrote that Vancouver "is a queer city. The air is as soft and heavy as the air of England: people drag about instead of walking briskly and the streets are full of Chinamen, Japs, Hindus, Sikhs and such like." Pinney, ed., *The Letters*, vol. 3, 272.
80 Quoted in Wilson, *The Strange Ride*, 254–5.

81 Kipling, *Letters of Travel*, 162.
82 Bederman, *Manliness*, 200–6.
83 Kipling, *Letters of Travel*, 162–3.
84 Kipling, *Letters of Travel*, 194. Kipling also argued that the "Hindus" did not pose a threat to the province's future because they planned to return to their homeland. Wilson, *The Strange Ride*, 255. On the riot, see Peter Ward, *White Canada Forever: Popular Attitudes and Public Policy Toward Orientals in British Columbia* (Montreal and Kingston: McGill-Queen's University Press, 2002), chapter 4.
85 Kipling, *Letters of Travel*, 167–71.
86 Kipling, *Letters of Travel*, 199–200.
87 Kipling, *Letters of Travel*, 201.
88 Kipling, *Letters of Travel*, 202.
89 Kipling, *Letters of Travel*, 202–3. Kipling struck a similar note in his speech to Victoria's Canadian Club when he warned, "the time is coming when you will have to choose between the desired reinforcement of your own stock, and the undesired rush of races to whom you are strangers, whose speech you do not understand, and from whose instincts you are separated by thousands of years. That is your choice. Myself, I think that the time for making that choice is on you NOW." *Colonist* (Victoria), 10 October 1907. Quoted in Bosher, "Vancouver Island," 16.
90 Kipling, *Letters of Travel*, 159–60.
91 Bell, *The Idea*, 24.
92 Bell, *The Idea*, 9.
93 Bell, *The Idea*, 76.
94 According to historian Gail Bederman, the American middle-class ideal of a self-restrained, high-minded "manliness" was, by the turn of the twentieth century, giving way to a more aggressively physical "masculinity." Gail Bederman, *Manliness and Civilization: A Cultural History of Gender and Race in the United States, 1880–1917* (Chicago: University of Chicago Press, 1995), 11–20.
95 Bederman, *Manliness*, 187.
96 The Kiplings spent a few days in Montreal in 1930, when they were returning to England from Bermuda. Lord Birkenhead, *Rudyard Kipling* (London: Weidenfeld and Nicolson, 1978), 338–9.
97 Lycett, *Rudyard Kipling*, 375–6, 415; Wilson, *The Strange Ride*, 255–6.
98 Pinney, ed., *The Letters*, vol. 3, 417.
99 The letter appeared on September 7. Thomas Pinney, ed., *The Letters of Rudyard Kipling, vol. 4, 1911–19* (Iowa City: University of Iowa Press, 1999), 46–7, 48n2.

100 Pinney, ed., *The Letters*, vol. 4, 50.
101 Lycett, *Rudyard Kipling*, 451,
102 Pinney, ed., *The Letters*, vol. 4, 276.
103 Thomas Pinney, ed., *The Letters of Rudyard Kipling*, vol. 5, *1920–30* (Houndmills, Basingstoke, Hampshire, UK: Palgrave Macmillan, 2004), 376.
104 See Stewart, *Kipling's America*, xvii–xix; George Shepperson, "The World of Rudyard Kipling," in Andrew Rutherford, ed., *Kipling's Mind and Art: Selected Critical Essays* (Stanford, CA: Stanford University Press, 1964), 142–4; Hagiioannu, *The Man*, chapter 3; and Judith Plotz, "Kipling's Very Special Relationship: Kipling in America, America in Kipling," in Howard J. Booth, ed., *The Cambridge Companion to Rudyard Kipling* (Cambridge, UK: Cambridge University Press, 2011), 40–51. Plotz claims that Kipling regained his popularity in the United States at the turn of the twenty-first century because American spokesmen began to invoke his 1899 challenge to assume "the White Man's Burden." Judith Plotz, "How 'The White Man's Burden' Lost its Scare Quotes; or Kipling and the New American Empire," in Caroline Rooney and Kaori Nagai, eds, *Kipling and Beyond: Patriotism, Globalisation and Postcolonialism* (Houndmills, Basingstoke, Hampshire, UK: Palgrave Macmillan, 2010), 37–57.
105 Thomas Pinney, ed., *The Letters of Rudyard Kipling, vol. 6, 1931–36* (Iowa City: University of Iowa Press, 2004), 234.

10 A Country without a Soul: Rupert Brooke's Gothic Vision of Canada

If journeys are primarily either about the traveller or about the worlds the traveller encounters,[1] the North American travel journals Rupert Brooke published in 1913, at the age of twenty-five, are indisputably in the former category. Brooke did not follow the introspective approach of many of today's travel writers, adopting instead an ironic distancing tone, yet his haunting gothic images of the Canadian landscape do reflect his tortured psyche.[2] Unique as Brooke's imagination and literary skills may have been, however, his vision of Canada was neither completely idiosyncratic nor without influence among his contemporaries, particularly those of his privileged social class. Brooke's travel journals, written at a time when ties between former colony and mother country remained strong, therefore deserve more attention than they have hitherto received from either his biographers or Canadian literary scholars and historians.

Conflicted by sexuality as well as the dictates of domesticity, like many other upper-middle-class English men of his era,[3] Brooke was impelled to travel to North America by romantic entanglements that had resulted in a nervous collapse.[4] His hope was presumably that a continent with wide-open spaces might serve as the rest cure that his trips to European recreation sites such as the Swiss Alps and Cannes no longer provided. To cover his expenses, Brooke contracted to submit travel articles to the prestigious *Westminster Gazette*, which, according to historian Stephen Koss, preferred to write the masses off as customers rather than write down to them.[5] These articles reappeared posthumously in 1916 as *Letters from America* in a volume that included an introduction by the highly respected Henry James who had published his own impressions of Quebec City and Niagara Falls.[6]

Brooke's printed descriptions of the outdoor advertisements of New York City and of a baseball game at Harvard University leave the impression that he was fascinated by the energy of the United States.[7] Privately, however, he wrote that "This is *not* a land for a civilized man. There are three things worth some praise; the architecture, the children's clothes, and the jokes. All else is flatulence and despair and a living Death."[8] Although he reported being warned by Americans that Canada was "a country without a soul,"[9] in turning northward the sensitive young poet felt "heartened" that he was "in a sense, going home."[10] It would seem that, in a kind of reverse colonialism, he was hoping to find a younger and better Britain, but he was soon disappointed in that regard. English Canadians he found to be as materialistic as the Americans, but more repressed, making them exceedingly dull, though there was some solace to be found outside the major urban centres and particularly in the western provinces.

Brooke's challenge as a travel writer was to describe the tourist sites that were invariably associated with Canada – including Quebec City, Niagara Falls, and the Rocky Mountains – without tarnishing his reputation as a rising literary star by resorting to the clichéd images of his many predecessors. Because, in Brooke's opinion, Canada's landscapes had yet to be interpreted by a great artist or poet, they were not fully alive. His role as a travel writer was therefore to give birth to them, paradoxically, by conjuring up death-related images that humanized the physical environment in accordance with gothic conventions (sometimes referred to as Dark Romanticism).[11] This was an approach to the Canadian landscape that was much less original than Brooke perhaps realized, for literary scholar Cynthia Sugars writes that one feature of early Canadian literature posited the wilderness "as a Gothic landscape inhabited by savage creatures (animal and human) which posed a threat to the European adventurers."[12] Brooke's articles, nevertheless, offer little support for the thesis, associated most famously with Northrop Frye and Margaret Atwood, that writers in Canada felt a strong antipathy towards nature.[13] Brooke, in fact, took an enjoyable side-trip into the Canadian wilderness, as we shall see. His highly imaginative gothic images did at times reflect a genuine sense of unease, as we shall also see, but much of the time it was fear of an absence rather than of a genuine danger. In that sense, Brooke's journal exemplifies what Sugars refers to as the second feature of the gothic in Canada, namely a perception that the country was "a terrifying *terra nullius* that was devoid of Gothic effects or ghosts."[14] Aside from reflecting his troubled psyche,

Brooke's images suggest on a more self-conscious level that he felt he was bestowing upon the uncultured young country the "soul" that it so lamentably still lacked.

Brooke's first impression of Montreal was that it "consists of banks and churches." The Scots, who dominated the British part of the city with its "rather narrow, rather gloomy streets," "aggressively prosperous buildings," and "air of dour prosperity," spent their time in "laying up their riches in this world or the next."[15] One feature of the city that did interest the young English traveller was its cultural duality. He observed that even though "The French and British in Canada seem to have behaved with quite extraordinary generosity and kindliness towards each other ... it is not in human nature that two communities should live side by side, pretending they are one, without some irritation and mutual loss of strength."[16] In short, Brooke shared the romantic nationalist assumption that a strong nation had a "soul" based on a common ancestry. He was perhaps also thinking of his own internal sexual conflicts when he wrote that "Montreal and Eastern Canada suffer from that kind of ill-health which afflicts men who are cases of 'double personality' – debility and spiritual paralysis."[17]

Brooke had a relatively high opinion of the national capital, however, for in his words Ottawa could be praised without resorting to "statistics of wealth and the growth of population; and this can be said of no other city in Canada except Quebec." The fact that Ottawa was a city of civil servants and homely wooden houses, and that in the evening light the Parliament buildings "seem to have the majesty and calm of a natural crown of the river-headland," clearly appealed to Brooke's search for security and stability. But the face of commerce was still quite visible, even on Parliament Hill: "just to show that it is Canada, and not Utopia – the line of national buildings will always be broken by an expensive and superb hotel the Canadian Pacific Railway has been allowed to erect on the twin and neighbouring promontory to that of the Houses of Parliament."[18]

Brooke's personal correspondence reveals that his travel narrative is misleading in suggesting that he visited Ottawa before doubling back to Quebec City.[19] Ottawa appears in the same article as Montreal simply because neither city was considered interesting enough to warrant more detailed description. Quebec was quite a different story, however, for the old fortress city appealed to Brooke's strong antimodernist sensibility. To mark the contrast with Montreal, the chapter on the provincial capital begins with the traveller's departing view of the former city, a view that recalls Blake's dark satanic mills. Mount Royal, "crouched, black and sullen," overlooks a harbour that is "filled with volumes of smoke, purple and black, wreathing and sidling eastwards." Brooke added that this "inferno" and "mirk" suggested either that "diabolic invisible hands" were moulding the "pitchy and Tartarian gloom" into a city, or that the city was already "disintegrating into its proper fume and dusty chaos."[20] In short, the threat was not nature or the wilderness in this case, as literary scholars such as Coral Ann Howells and Faye Hammill have argued was characteristic of Canadian gothic imagery, but the urban and industrial.[21]

As his vessel approached Quebec the following morning, Brooke found, in sharp contrast, that "The air was full of gaiety and sunshine and the sense of singing birds, though actually, I think, there were only a few gulls crying." With "the individuality and the pride of a city where great things have happened, and over which many years have passed," Quebec was as "refreshing and as definite after the other cities of this continent as an immortal among a crowd of stockbrokers."[22] As an "aesthete's aesthete,"[23] Brooke idealized the innocence of youth and worshipped beauty. He, therefore, paid Quebec the ultimate compliment when he wrote that the city had "the radiance and repose of an immortal; but she wears her immortality youthfully."[24] Inspired by the Plains of Abraham, and reflecting his ongoing shift from Fabian pacifism to British imperialism, Brooke apparently saw no contradiction between his idealization of youthful innocence and his suggestion that if warfare were replaced by commerce, then patriotism would die and Quebec City would become "a forgotten ruin."[25]

As we saw in chapter 1, British travel writers were not only generally enthusiastic about Quebec City, they were by this time inclined to take a positive view of what their predecessors had once found so reprehensible, namely the French-speaking *habitants'* apparent resistance to agricultural improvement.[26] Given that he was the central figure in the group of Cambridge friends whom Virginia Woolf named the Neo-pagans by virtue of the fact that they went on hiking and camping expeditions and idealized the simple rural life,[27] it is not surprising that Brooke would describe the *habitants* as "a jolly sight." In his words, "They are like children in their noisy content. They are poor and happy, Roman Catholics; they laugh a great deal; and they continually sing. They do not progress at all." But his view of the priests was another matter. Reflecting his Protestant prejudices, Brooke resorted to gothic imagery when he wrote that those on board the boat descending the St Lawrence to the Saguenay "diffused an atmosphere of black, of unpleasant melancholy … Their eyes were small, shifty, and cruel, and would not meet the gaze."[28]

Arriving at the mouth of the Saguenay as darkness was falling, Brooke felt shut in by "walls rising sheer from the water to the height of two thousand feet, going down sheer beneath it … to many times that depth." As it ascended the "lifeless" river, whose waters were "inky and sinister" even in the daytime, the "homeless, irrelevant, tiny steamer seemed to hang between two abysms." Writing that "The whole scene seemed some Stygian imagination of Dante," Brooke added that "this region was the abode of devils."[29] One might assume that a gothic image depicting the landscape as distinctly alien reflected an anti-colonial sensibility, but Sugars argues that the gothic tradition had been imported by early Canadian writers to provide "legitimating substance to the settler-invader experience of occupation."[30] As a self-confessed imperialist, Brooke presumably felt, at least subconsciously, that his dark romantic images were bestowing the young country with a much-needed mythological soul, albeit one not likely to attract the average tourist. Only at the mouth of the river, in the historic village of Tadoussac and under a light blue, English-like sky, was Brooke able to shake off his sense of unease, at least temporarily. Plunging naked into the water, as he had done many times in England with his Neo-pagan friends, Brooke found that "Stray shreds of the St Lawrence were warm and cheerful." But the gothic was apparently inescapable, for he added that the black current of the Saguenay was "cold as death" and he retreated shivering to his hotel.[31]

Brooke claimed to feel more at ease in rural Ontario because its "weather-beaten farm-houses, rolling country, thickets of trees, little hills green and grey in the distance, decorous small fields, orchards, and, I swear, a hedge or two," reminded him of England. Particularly important was the fact that "this country has seen the generations pass, and won something of that repose and security which countries acquire from the sight."[32] Here, in short, Brooke found traces of the pastoral myth that he was strongly drawn to, and which Frye has defined as an idealization of childhood memory.[33] Unfortunately, the picturesque Thousand Islands had been largely spoiled, Brooke lamented, by the fact that each island, "if big enough, has been bought by a rich man – generally an American – who has built a castle on it. So the whole isn't much more beautiful than Golder's Green."[34]

Once his boat reached the Great Lakes, Brooke began to feel emotionally uneasy once again.[35] Like Kipling before him (see chapter 9), Brooke observed that there was "something ominous and unnatural" about those large bodies of water. In his imagination, "Rivers are human," and even though the cruel and treacherous sea "has no soul," it was still "all right" because mankind had engaged it in an "age-long feud." But "these monstrous lakes, which ape the ocean, are not proper to fresh water or salt. They have souls, perceptibly, and wicked ones." Lake Ontario "was a terrible dead-silver colour," with a surface that was "inexplicably sinister and dead, like the glint on glasses worn by a blind man." As on the Saguenay, and in language that evoked Joseph Conrad's *Heart of Darkness* (first published in 1899), the boat mysteriously "appeared to leave no wake." But it did leave a trail of black smoke "very close over the water, like an evil soul after death that cannot win dissolution."[36] Nature, in short, did not present a threat in the real sense, with crashing waves threatening to capsize the vessel, but in the highly imagined sense that again evoked the gothic.

This gothic sensibility shifted radically on reaching Toronto, "the soul of Canada," or what Brooke might have more consistently referred to as the "non-soul." Toronto, Brooke found to be simply boring: "a clean-shaven, pink-faced, respectably dressed, fairly energetic, unintellectual, passably sociable, well-to-do, public-school-and-'varsity sort of city."[37] In short, it was "all right," the depressing thing being "that it will always be what it is, only larger, and that no Canadian city can ever be anything better or different."[38] In a sense, then, Canada's true wilderness – as defined by a cultural and spiritual emptiness – was to be found in its larger cities.

Despite its commercialism, however, Brooke was deeply moved by Niagara Falls, writing privately: "I'm so impressed by Niagara. I hoped not to be. But I horribly am. The colour of the water, the strength of it, and the clouds of spray – I'm afraid I'm a Victorian at heart, after all. Please don't breathe a word of it: I want to keep such shreds of reputation as I have left."[39] Referring in particular to Niagara Falls, historian Elizabeth McKinsey claims that the American sublime had, indeed, become long passé by the turn of the century, but Brooke rose to the challenge of surpassing literary predecessors such as Charles Dickens and Anthony Trollope by resorting to gothic imagery.[40] After complaining that Niagara was "the central home and breeding-place for all the touts of the earth," but ignoring the fact that major hydroelectric projects had subdued much of Niagara's wild energy and come to epitomize humanity's victory over nature,[41] Brooke described the river above the falls in exceptionally animated terms, using words such as "chattering," "leaping," "laughing," "springing," and "weaving." But these words only heightened the sense of fatalistic tragedy as the waters, "borne impetuously forward like a crowd of triumphant feasters ... seem to fling themselves on with some foreknowledge of their fate, in an ever wilder frenzy." Finally, "On the edge of disaster the river seems to gather herself, to pause, to lift a head noble in ruin," before taking the plunge "into the eternal thunder and white chaos below."[42] Despite referring to the river as female, Brooke may have had his own recent psychological collapse in mind ... or a deep-seated fear that his female lovers were sapping his masculine strength. Thus, he described the rapids below the falls as masculine, for "Here the inhuman life and strength are spontaneous, active, almost resolute; masculine vigour compared with the passive gigantic power, female, helpless and overwhelming, of the Falls. A place of fear."[43] Succumbing to a pessimistic fatalism, or what might be viewed as a gothic sense of doom, Brooke added that "In such places, one is aware, with an almost insupportable and yet comforting certitude, that both men and nations are hurried onwards to their ruin or ending as inevitably as this dark flood."[44]

Uncompromising anti-modernist as he was, Brooke shunned the railway for the leg of his journey between Sarnia and Port Arthur (today's Thunder Bay), noting that by boarding a boat in the afternoon and waking up at Sault Ste Marie in the morning, "you have done with the rather colourless, unindividual expanses of Huron." Sailing along the shoreline of Lake Superior with its picnickers and campers, "The human race seemed a jolly bunch, and the world a fine, pleasant, open-air affair," but, once out of sight of land, Brooke's sense of unease returned. As the vessel slid through "a queer, pale mist," he wrote, "We seemed to be ploughing aimlessly through the phantasmal sand-dunes of another world, faintly and by an accident apprehended."[45]

Describing his trip on the night train from Port Arthur to Winnipeg, Brooke began with the romantic view from his lower berth of a "wild starlit landscape," but, according to Patricia Jasen, tourist interest in northern Ontario had faded after resource exploitation had left "an atmosphere of desolation and emptiness."[46] Not surprisingly, then, Brooke soon turned to gloomier images. Thus, he wrote, "For four hundred miles there is hardly a sign that humanity exists on the earth's face, only rocks and endless woods or scrubby pine, and the occasional strange gleam of water, and the night and the wind." Areas where forest fires had passed through lent themselves to particularly gothic imagery, for the grey pine trunks "appear stricken by calamity, intolerably bare and lonely, gaunt, perpetually protesting, amazed and tragic creatures."[47]

Although editors Sandra Martin and Roger Hall obviously overlooked these passages in suggesting that after Brooke left Montreal there was "a shift to a state of contentment that became obvious in his writings,"[48] he did become uncharacteristically cheerful once he reached Winnipeg. Sharing his contemporary British travellers' enthusiasm for the Canadian West,[49] Brooke noted that its people were "more friendly, more hearty" than those of the eastern provinces. The architecture might be even more hideous than that of Montreal or Toronto, but it was "cheerily and windily so." And even though one could find "poverty and destitution" in the Prairie city, at least it was "less dingy, less depressing" than Birmingham. Claiming to sense a community spirit in Winnipeg, perhaps a reflection of frontier optimism and energy, Brooke wrote that "one can't help finding a tiny hope" that it "may yet come to something," and "That cannot be said of Toronto."[50] Brooke's personal letters reveal that while in the West he was repeatedly asked about his political views, and this is reflected in much of his writing on Winnipeg and its surrounding area, with the discussion of tariffs, the naval bill, East European immigration, and the cooperative movement.[51]

But the highlight of Brooke's Manitoba sojourn was a side trip with "an old Rugbeian I found in Winnipeg" to the remote Lake George, eighty miles northeast of the city.[52] Here, he was finally inspired by the soul's "indefinite room to expand," writing that "no one else is *thinking* of the lakes and hills you see before you. They have no tradition, no names even; they are only pools of water and lumps of earth, some day, perhaps, to be clothed with loves and memories and the comings and goings of men, but now dumbly waiting their Wordsworth or their Acropolis to give them individuality, and a soul."[53] William Laskowski observes of such passages that "It is as if such things cannot exist until artists, with their nominative capacity, conjure them up with the power of time and its experience,"[54] but by participating in the longstanding tradition of configuring wilderness Canada as a *terra nullius* Brooke was erasing in a literary sense the First Nations' ties to the landscape.

Despite the fact that he packed Ben Jonson and Jane Austen "to keep me English" while in the Manitoba backwoods,[55] Brooke was drawn to what he felt was a virgin landscape where "The air is unbreathed, and the earth untrodden." He even slipped briefly into the clichéd picturesque convention that he generally avoided: "All things share this childlike loveliness, the grey whispering reeds, the pure blue of the sky, the birches and thin fir-trees that make up these forests, even the brisk touch of the water as you dive." In fact, it was the sensual experience of swimming in a Canadian lake, Brooke wrote – "and none of sight or hearing" – that impressed him most as a "token" of the country:

> It is not languorous, like bathing in a warm Southern sea; nor grateful, like a river in a hot climate; nor strange, as the ocean always is; nor startling, like very cold water. But it touches the body continually with freshness, and it seems to be charged with a subtle and unexhausted energy. It is colourless, faintly stinging, hard and grey, like the rocks around, full of vitality, and sweet. It has the tint and sensation of a pale dawn before the sun is up. Such is the wild of Canada.[56]

To Brooke, diving into a fresh clear body of water was a baptism of sorts, a washing away of the guilt associated with sex, and a reinvigoration to face the world anew.[57] As Peter Conrad points out, however, and as the Saguenay example noted above illustrates, such freedom was also a flirtation with destruction, for "the swimmer has only his stroking limbs to keep him buoyant."[58]

Ambiguity towards nature has been said to be "the mark of true Gothicism,"[59] but Brooke was more concerned about the despoliation of nature than about its destructive powers, for he predicted that in the future the timber would be "cut down and made into paper," the land "divided into town-lots and sold, and sub-divided and sold again, and boomed and resold," with the parts not suitable for development "given in exchange for great sums of money to old ladies in the quieter parts of England." In the towns would be built "churches, hotels, and a great many ugly sky-scrapers," as well as "hovels for the poor, houses for the rich, none beautiful."[60] Even where there was no sign of such development, then, Brooke's enjoyment of the natural environment was tainted by his forebodings of what he prophesized lay in store for it.

Abnormally wet weather spoiled Brooke's appreciation of the Prairie landscape en route to Calgary, for he observed that the "interminable, oblique, thin rain took the gold out of the wheat and the brown from the distant fields and bushes, and drabbed all the colours in the grass." Seeing no inhabitants on that "Sabbath morn," he observed sardonically that it was not clear whether they were at work, in church, "or had shot themselves from depression induced by the weather." Brooke clearly found it amusing that long-time residents "tell me they get very homesick if they go away for a time. Valleys and hills seem to them petty, fretful, unlovable. The magic of the plains has them in a thrall."[61]

Despite such condescending comments, however, Brooke genuinely admired the fact that in the Prairies, "among all the corruption, irresponsibility, and disastrous individualism," there were "some faint signs of the sense of community." As a literary person, he was particularly impressed by the public libraries, writing that they improved as one moved West from Montreal, "which is unable to support one," until in Calgary "you find a very neat and carefully kept building, stocked with an immense variety of periodicals, and an admirable store of books, ranging from the classics to the most utterly modern literature. Few large English towns could show anything as good."[62] Despite his sophisticated urbane manner, Brooke was clearly enthralled with the romantic myth of the Old West, writing that "For no great reward, but the love of the thing," the fearless members of the North-West Mounted Police had "imposed order and fairness upon half a continent." But "The tragedy of the West" was that the pioneer generation had now passed, and "what they lived and died to secure for their race is now the foundation for a gigantic national gambling of a most unprofitable and disastrous kind." Thus, "where good men worked or perished is now a row of little shops, all devoted to the sale of town-lots in some distant spot that must infallibly become a great city in the next two years, and in the door-way of each lounges a thin-chested, much-spitting youth, with a flabby face, shifty eyes, and an inhuman mouth, who invites you continually, with the most raucous of American accents, to 'step inside and ex-amine our Praposition.'"[63] In sharp contrast to Kipling, then, Brooke saw the Prairie Eden as being contaminated by the corrupting influence of capitalist greed, represented here not by a wealthy banker or developer but by a somewhat diabolical creature who might have emerged from an urban slum.

Boarding the train for the West coast, Brooke had to compete with American tourists for a perch in the open-sided observation car, but he was deeply impressed by the Rockies, reporting that they had a "kindlier" beauty than the Alps because their rock was "of a browner colour." The advantage of the Alps, however, was that "There, you are always in sight of a civilisation which has nestled for ages at the foot of those high places." The Rockies, in contrast, were "irrelevant to humanity. No recorded Hannibal has struggled across them; their shadow lies on no remembered literature."[64] The promotional material of the Canadian

Pacific Railway (CPR) depicted the company's rail line as a civilizing force in the Rocky Mountain wilderness,[65] but Brooke ultimately found that same wilderness to be disturbing because nature was "there alone, scarcely a unity in the heaped confusion of these crags, almost without grandeur among the chaos of the earth." Describing the moving landscape as a panorama, and humanizing it in a distinctively gothic vein, Brooke wrote of pines that "drooped and sobbed," rivers that "roared and plunged with aimless passion down the ravines," and clouds that "trailed along the valleys, a long procession of shrouded, melancholy figures, seeming to pause, as with an indeterminate, tragic, vain gesture, before passing out of sight up some ravine."[66] In short, then, Brooke was again transferring his own rather gloomy sensibility, and the animated sense of a soul, to a country that he apparently felt was sorely in need of one.

Nor was Brooke's mood always bleak, for at Lake Louise he found the picturesque scenery that every genteel English traveller longed for. It was not so much the glacier at the end of the lake, or the fact that the field of ice climbed to "one of the highest and loveliest peaks in the Rockies," that impressed Brooke. Rather, he rhapsodized over the view from his hotel window where the ever-changing lake "is Beauty herself, as nearly visible to mortal eyes as she may ever be." The water "beyond the flowers" was an ever-changing green, sometimes "shot with blue, of a peacock tint." When a breeze ruffled the surface, the lake became "milky emerald," and when the sun caught it, it became "the opal distillation of all the buds of all the spring." The image of the "shrouded, melancholy figures" viewed from the platform of the CPR caboose resurfaces, but now as "dark, processional pines, mounting to the sacred peaks, devout, kneeling, motionless, in an ecstasy of homely adoration, like the donors and their families in a Flemish picture."[67] Finally, if briefly, then, the jaded young traveller felt able to express a sense of contentment, though only by imagining the physical landscape as an antiquated European painting.

And, as his readers would by this point have anticipated, Brooke's mood shifted again as he climbed one of the nearby mountains at sunset. Rather than adopting the monarch-of-all-I-survey perspective famously identified with male imperialism by Mary Louise Pratt,[68] he contemplated the "strangeness" that he had observed throughout his North American travels, namely that to love what was "an empty land" was "like embracing a wraith."[69] England's soil was "heavy and fertile with the decaying stuff of past seasons and generations," but in the

Rocky Mountains "there is nothing lurking in the heart of the shadows, and no human mystery in the colours, and neither the same joy nor the kind of peace in dawn and sunset that older lands know."[70] Even where capitalist development was not a threat, as it was in Calgary, Brooke felt dissatisfied. The land might be "virginal," every lake "new-born," and the flowers "less conscious than English flowers," but, he lamented, "one misses the dead."[71]

Despite his ignorance concerning the presence, history, and culture of the First Nations in what he described as an "empty land," Brooke's romantic anti-modernism predisposed him towards the myth of the "Noble Savage," a myth that had long served those who were critical of European materialism, individualism, and corruption.[72] In contrast to those he labelled as the "French and Scotch half-breeds" who "frequent the borders of civilisation" further East,[73] Brooke depicted those Aboriginal peoples whom he imagined as relatively "unspoiled" by European contact as children of nature, though he did slip into the past tense when describing their virtues. Thus, he wrote, they might have a weakness for gambling and warfare, but they had once "enjoyed a 'Nature-Worship,' believed rather dimly in a presiding Power, and very definitely in certain ethical and moral rules." He also described them as loyal, brave, and stoical, and he claimed that they had also been monogamous, good parents to their children, and completely honest.[74] In short, the indigenous peoples had once embodied the very ideals that the young neo-Pagans had also aspired to.

As for physical appearance, the traveller known as England's "young Apollo"[75] wrote that the older men on the Stony reserve he visited in Alberta had "superb" physiques, "their features shaped and lined by weather and experience into a Roman nobility that demands respect."[76] But these men represented the past, for "Civilisation, disease, alcohol, and vice" had reduced the Stonys "to a few scattered communities and some stragglers, and a legend, the admiration of boyhood."[77] Even though he evidently had no knowledge of how the rich Aboriginal oral tradition forged a symbolic tie to the land he travelled across, Brooke criticized the government's assimilation efforts, posing the rhetorical question: "Shall we preserve these few bands of them, untouched, to succeed us, ultimately, when the grasp of our 'civilisation' weakens, and our transient anarchy in these wilder lands recedes once more before the older anarchy of Nature? Or will they be entirely swallowed by that ugliness of shops and trousers with which we enchain the earth, and become a memory and less than a memory?"[78] The colonialist implications of what Pratt refers to as the "anti-conquest" narrative, namely "strategies of representation whereby European bourgeois subjects seek to secure their innocence in the same moment as they assert European hegemony,"[79] becomes clear with Brooke's rather arrogant conclusion that "They are that already. The Indians have passed. They left no arts, no tradition, no buildings or roads or laws; only a story or two, and a few names, strange and beautiful."[80] As Owram and Moyles point out, this was a commonly shared view among British travel writers of the day.[81] The romantic young poet would have to cross the Pacific to the South Sea islands before discovering, at least in his own mind, the Rousseauesque paradise that he was searching for.

Brooke's *Westminster Gazette* articles ended before he reached this paradise, or even the West coast of Canada, but a letter to his mother reveals that he was quite impressed with Vancouver where he spent several days, for he wrote that "The country and harbour are rather beautiful with great violet mountains all around, snow-peaks in the distance."[82] And, in the clear ocean waters off Victoria, Brooke observed, "A few gigantic stalks of glossy brown seaweed seemed to be shouldering their way shoreward through the calm. The opal light caught them, and passed, and breathed over the waters. There was great peace and beauty in the mountains and the sea." Finally, as children played nearby on the beach, Brooke's conflicting thoughts turned to Canada: "I thought of her possibilities, and of her wealth and corruption and individualism and ugliness."[83]

Conclusion

Brooke was writing at a time of renewed imperialist interest in the former colonies, as reflected in the revival of British travel writing on Canada. Himself a recently converted imperialist, Brooke promoted Canada's contribution to the British navy and opposed East European immigration to the Prairies, yet his travel articles reflect a sense of alienation rather than the confident imperialism of Rudyard Kipling, among other British visitors of the pre-war era. By the time Brooke reached the West coast he had clearly had enough of the country without a "soul," and was eager to set sail for San Francisco. Although informed by the *Westminster Gazette* that they never published more than six articles in a series, Brooke reported to his friend and agent that he was continuing to keep a journal in the hope that that there might be a second series, or that the articles could be sold singly, but those on Vancouver and

Victoria have survived only in hand-written fragments.[84] Two years after leaving Canada, "the handsomest young man in England"[85] – whose famous war poems welcomed death as a purging of the sins of the flesh – would die in uniform from an infected mosquito bite and be buried on an obscure Greek island. Although he had not reached the war zone, the final irony was that Brooke was lionized as a sacrifice for the preservation of a pastoral England that was succumbing to forces unleashed by the same conflict he had enlisted to fight in.

Laskowski's optimistic interpretation of *Letters from America* is that it records Brooke's "internal odyssey to 'health' as much as it documents the reactions of a young Cambridge Apostle to America in the years immediately preceding World War I."[86] But this assessment misses the travel narrative's bleak sense of fatalism, and the reason why, as historian Modris Eksteins observes, the troubled young writer became "a symbol of the spiritual confusion and longing of his generation."[87] Peter Conrad is closer to the mark than Laskowski when he refers to Brooke's adventure as his "renunciatory journey, traveling through civilization to bid it farewell."[88] Brooke's aim was not to renounce civilization, however, as much as it was to escape it temporarily in order to restore his mental health and reassert his manliness. Thus, in a letter to the London actress who was one of his love interests, Brooke described in somewhat gothic terms how he had participated in the night-time butchering of a deer at Lake George: "the black water of the lake, muddy with trampling at the edge, and streaked with blood … the head gazing reproachfully at us from the ground, everybody using the most frightful language, and the rather ironical and very dispassionate stars above. Rather savage."[89] Brooke's reference to the onlooking stars suggests that he saw his own role essentially as theatrical performance. Reflective of his inner torments as the gothic convention may have been, it also enabled Brooke to endow what he perceived to be a young and unexotic country with the soul he felt it lacked, if only for the sake of making his articles more interesting. Rather than renouncing civilization, Brooke's travel narrative lamented what he perceived to be the cultural void, not only of the wilderness landscape but also within the principal cities of the New World, infected as they were by materialism and individualism. In short, the conservative young poet was ill at ease in the present and his journey across Canada offered little hope for the future; what he longed for was the irretrievable past with its comforting traditions, rituals, and hierarchies.[90] That said, his highly personal descriptions of the Canadian landscape, and his avoidance of the clichéd picturesque perspective, pointed towards the post-war artistic turn to modernism.

NOTES

1 Onno Oerlemans, *Romanticism and the Materiality of Nature* (Toronto: University of Toronto Press, 2002), 149.
2 On the obsession with death in Brooke's poetry, see Adrian Caesar, *Taking It Like a Man: Suffering, Sexuality and the War Poets* (Manchester: Manchester University Press, 1993), 17–18, 46–8. Catherine Spooner refers to "a modernist understanding of gothic as interior drama rather than dramatic spectacle." See her "Gothic in the Twentieth Century," in Catherine Spooner and Emma McEvoy, eds, *The Routledge Companion to Gothic* (London: Routledge, 2007), 39. For a more detailed discussion, see Margot Northey, *The Haunted Wilderness: The Gothic and Grotesque in Canadian Fiction* (Toronto: University of Toronto Press, 1976), 3–9.
3 John Tosh, *A Man's Place: Masculinity and the Middle-Class Home in Victorian England* (New Haven and London: Yale University Press, 1999), 189.
4 Caesar, *Taking It*, 37–40; Paul Delany, *The Neo-pagans: Rupert Brooke and the Ordeal of Youth* (New York: The Free Press, 1987), chapter 8.
5 Stephen Koss, *The Rise and Fall of the Political Press in Britain: The Twentieth Century*, vol. 2, (London: Hamish Hamilton, 1984), 10.
6 Originally written in 1871, James' two articles appeared in a volume of his travel essays in 1883. Henry James, *Portraits of Places* (Boston: Houghton, Mifflin, 1883).
7 Peter Conrad argues, however, that Brooke had a modernist sensibility, claiming that his travel journal "is the first modern imaginative appreciation of the country [United States] because it joyfully discerns in America not social accoutrement or complication of detail but irrelevance, irresponsibility, absence." Peter Conrad, *Imagining America* (London: Routledge and Kegan Paul, 1980), 89.
8 Brooke to Cathleen Nesbitt, Noo [*sic*] York, Sunday, 1 June 1913, in Geoffrey Keynes, ed., *The Letters of Rupert Brooke* (New York: Harcourt, Brace and World, 1968), 469.
9 Many British travellers had much the same impression. See R.G. Moyles and Doug Owram, *Imperial Dreams and Colonial Realities: British Views of Canada, 1880–1914* (Toronto: University of Toronto Press, 1988), 217–25.
10 Rupert Brooke, *Letters from America* (Toronto: McClelland, Goodchild, and Stewart, 1916), 49.
11 Emma McEvoy, "Gothic and the Romantics," in Spooner and McEvoy, eds, *Routledge Companion*, 20.
12 Cynthia Sugars, "Canadian Gothic" in David Punter, ed., *A New Companion to the Gothic* (Somerset: Blackwell, 2012), 410.

13 Northrop Frye, "Conclusion to a Literary History of Canada," in Branko Gorjup, ed., *Mythologizing Canada: Essays on the Canadian Literary Imagination* (New York: Legas, 1997); and Margaret Atwood, *Survival: A Thematic Guide to Canadian Literature* (Toronto: Anansi, 1972). For a persuasive critique of this thesis, see Susan Glickman, *The Picturesque and the Sublime: A Poetics of the Canadian Landscape* (Montreal and Kingston: McGill-Queen's University Press, 1998), 45–58.
14 Sugars, "Canadian Gothic," 410.
15 Brooke, *Letters*, 50–1.
16 Brooke, *Letters*, 52–3.
17 Brooke, *Letters*, 53. See Caesar, *Taking It*, 15, 34.
18 Brooke, *Letters*, 55–6.
19 Brooke wrote from the Chateau Frontenac on July 3, and Ottawa on July 9. Keynes, ed., *Letters*, 479–80.
20 Brooke, *Letters*, 61.
21 Coral Ann Howells, "Canadian Gothic" in Spooner and McEvoy, eds, *Routledge Companion*, 105–14; Faye Hammill, "'Death by Nature': Margaret Atwood and Wilderness Gothic," *Gothic Studies* 5, no. 2 (2003): 47–63. For contemporary comments made concerning the visual pollution caused by smoke in Montreal, with its impact on public health, see Nicolas Kenny, "Corporeal Understandings of the Industrial Environment," in Stéphane Castonguay and Michèle Dagenais, eds, *Metropolitan Natures: Environmental Histories of Montreal* (Pittsburgh: University of Pittsburgh Press, 2011), 62–5.
22 Brooke, *Letters*, 63–4.
23 Modris Eksteins, *Rites of Spring: The Great War and the Birth of the Modern Age* (Toronto: Lester and Orpen Dennys, 1989), 123.
24 Brooke, *Letters*, 64.
25 Brooke, *Letters*, 65–6.
26 See Moyles and Owram, *Imperial Dreams*, 92–3; and chapter 1 of this volume.
27 Delany, *The Neo-pagans*, xii.
28 Brooke, *Letters*, 6–8. Other British travellers shared this view of the Catholic Church. See Moyles and Owram, *Imperial Dreams*, 96–100.
29 Brooke, *Letters*, 68–9. Brooke wrote to Cathleen Nesbitt, "My dear, it's not a river: it's a part of Hell, got loose … It's like some ghastly dream of Dante's." Letter to Cathleen Nesbitt, Chateau Frontenac, Quebec, 3 July [1913], in Keynes, ed., *Letters*, 479–80.
30 Sugars, "Canadian Gothic," 410. According to William Hughes and Andrew Smith, however, "the Gothic is, and has always been, *post-*

colonial." See their "Introduction: Defining the Relationships between Gothic and the Postcolonial," *Gothic Studies* 5, no. 2 (2003): 1.

31 Brooke, *Letters*, 68–71.

32 Brooke, *Letters*, 75–6.

33 Frye, "Conclusion," 88.

34 Brooke, *Letters*, 76. Golders Green had developed rapidly as a London suburb after a tube station was opened there in 1910. "Golders Green." en.wikipedia.org. Viewed 5 March 2013.

35 Henry James, too, had complained that Lake Ontario offered "the blankness and vacancy of the sea," yet "without that vast essential swell which, amid the belting brine, so often saves the situation to the eye." James, *Portraits*, 364–5.

36 Brooke, *Letters*, 77–8.

37 Brooke, *Letters*, 79.

38 Brooke, *Letters*, 82, 84.

39 Letter to A.F. Scholfield, Toronto, July–August 1913, in Keynes, ed., *Letters*, 491.

40 Elizabeth McKinsey, *Niagara Falls: Icon of the American Sublime* (Cambridge: Cambridge University Press, 1985). McKinsey's sole quote from Brooke that "Niagara means nothing" (*Niagara Falls*, 274) is clearly misleading. On various literary responses to Niagara Falls, see Patricia Jasen, *Wild Things: Nature, Culture, and Tourism in Ontario, 1790–1914* (Toronto: University of Toronto Press, 1995), 31–5; and Linda L. Revie, *The Niagara Companion: Explorers, Artists, and Writers at the Falls, from the Discovery through the Twentieth Century* (Waterloo: Wilfrid Laurier University Press, 2003), chapter 2.

41 Brooke, *Letters*, 89; Patrick McGreevy, *Imagining Niagara: The Meaning and Making of Niagara Falls* (Amherst: University of Massachusetts Press, 1994), 7–8, 106.

42 Brooke, Letters, 90. The normally restrained Henry James resorted to even more animated imagery (see James, *Portraits*, 370, 374) though Revie (*Niagara Companion*, 108) claims that it was meant to be satirical.

43 Brooke, *Letters*, 94. Karen Dubinsky has noted the common identification of Niagara Falls as female. See her *The Second Greatest Disappointment: Honeymooning and Tourism at Niagara Falls* (Toronto: Between the Lines, 1999), 42–5. On Brooke's Victorian attitude towards female sexuality, see Caesar, *Taking It*, 29–30.

44 Brooke, *Letters*, 95–6. Privately, Brooke wrote: "I sit and stare at the thing and have the purest Nineteenth Century grandiose thoughts, about the Destiny of Man, the Irresistibility of Fate, the Doom of Nations, the fact

that Death awaits us all, and so forth. Wordsworth Redivivus. Oh dear! Oh dear!" Letter to Scholfield, in Keynes, ed., *Letters*, 491. McGreevy rather surprisingly ignores Brooke's journal, but writes that "The Niagara literature offers glimpses of nineteenth-century soul-searching and speculation that are symptomatic of a more general cultural turmoil." McGreevy, *Imagining Niagara*, 11.

45 Brooke, *Letters*, 99–101. To the English literary critic Edmund Gosse, Brooke wrote: "I have a perpetual feeling that a lake ought not to be this size. A river and a little lake and an ocean are natural; but not these creatures. They are too big, and too smooth, and too sunny; like an American business man." Letter to Gosse, Lake Superior, 27 July 1913, in Keynes, ed., *Letters*, 494.

46 Brooke, *Letters*, 101; Jasen, *Wild Things*, 103.

47 Brooke, *Letters*, 101–2.

48 Sandra Martin and Roger Hall, eds, *Rupert Brooke in Canada* (Toronto: PMA Books, 1978), 19.

49 Moyles and Owram, *Imperial Dreams*, 119–20.

50 Brooke, *Letters*, 103–5.

51 Brooke, *Letters*, 102–13.

52 Letter to A.F. Scholfield, Toronto, July–August 1913, in Keynes, ed., *Letters*, 491.

53 Brooke, *Letters*, 117–18.

54 Laskowski, *Rupert Brooke*, 89–90.

55 Brooke, *Letters*, 111.

56 Brooke, *Letters*, 118.

57 Delany, *The Neo-pagans*, 207.

58 Conrad, *Imagining America*, 87.

59 Northey, *Haunted Wilderness*, 22–3.

60 Brooke, *Letters*, 118–19.

61 Brooke, *Letters*, 123–5.

62 Brooke, *Letters*, 126.

63 Brooke, *Letters*, 129–31.

64 Brooke, *Letters*, 148.

65 Elsa Lam, "Rails, Trails, Roads, and Lodgings: Networks of Mobility and the Touristic Development of 'The Canadian Pacific Rockies,' 1885–1930," in Ben Bradley, Jay Young, and Colin Coates, eds, *Moving Natures: Mobility and the Environment in Canadian History* (Calgary: University of Calgary Press, 2016), 277–9.

66 Brooke, *Letters*, 149–50. Jonas Larsen argues that in contrast to the static "tourist gaze" with its focus on "*foregrounds*, details, particularities

and orderliness" travel by rail as well as automobile allows one to experience landscapes as "living wholes." Jonas Larsen, "Tourism Mobilities and the Travel Glance: Experiences of Being on the Move," *Scandinavian Journal of Hospitality and Tourism* 1, no. 2 (2001): 91–2. DOI: 10.1080/150222501317244010. Viewed 25 July 2015.

67 Brooke, *Letters*, 151–2.

68 Mary Louise Pratt, *Imperial Eyes: Travel Writing and Transculturation* (London: Routledge, 1992), 213.

69 Brooke, *Letters*, 153.

70 Brooke, *Letters*, 154–5.

71 Brooke, *Letters*, 156.

72 See Daniel Francis, *The Imaginary Indian: The Image of the Indian in Canadian Culture* (Vancouver: Arsenal Pulp Press, 1992).

73 Brooke, *Letters*, 136.

74 Brooke, *Letters*, 138–9.

75 Delany, *The Neo-pagans*, ix.

76 Brooke, *Letters*, 141.

77 Brooke, *Letters*, 139.

78 Brooke, *Letters*, 143.

79 Pratt, *Imperial Eyes*, 7.

80 Brooke, *Letters*, 143.

81 Moyles and Owram, *Imperial Dreams*, chapter 7.

82 Letter to mother, Vancouver Hotel and the boat to Victoria, 8 September 1913, in Keynes, ed., *Letters of Rupert Brooke*, 508.

83 Quoted in Martin and Hall, *Rupert Brooke*, 141–2.

84 Letter to Edward Marsh, San Francisco, 1 October [1913], in Keynes, ed., *Letters*, 513–14. The two fragments are published in Martin and Hall, eds, *Rupert Brooke*, 139–43.

85 Michael Hastings, *The Handsomest Young Man in England: Rupert Brooke* (London: Michael Joseph, 1967).

86 Laskowski, *Rupert Brooke*, 83.

87 Eksteins, *Rites of Spring*, 26.

88 Conrad, *Imaginary America*, 88.

89 Letter to Nesbitt, Lake George, 1 August [1913], in Keynes, ed., *Letters of Rupert Brooke*, 496. Two days later, however, he admitted to her that "I'm glad that I'm no 'sportsman.'" Letter to Nesbitt, Lake George, 3 August [1913], in Keynes, ed., *Letters of Rupert Brooke*, 497.

90 It is therefore difficult to include Brooke with the young men whom Eksteins claims welcomed the war "as a pathway to the future, to progress, to revolution, to change." Eksteins, *Rites of Spring*, 133.

Afterword: An Unknown Country?

The First World War may have resulted in the rejection of many Victorian and Edwardian pieties, as well as the emergence of bold new art forms, but the picturesque perspective remained well entrenched in Canada, as reflected in what was perhaps the most popular of the books describing the country in the twentieth century. Written by *Vancouver Sun* journalist Bruce Hutchison and published for an American audience in 1942, *The Unknown Country: Canada and Her People* was reprinted in Toronto the following year, when it won the Governor-General's Award for non-fiction.[1] Other editions followed, including one published by McClelland and Stewart in 1965, and another by Oxford University Press in 2010.[2] Also in 2010, sizeable chunks were included in geographer John Warkentin's edited collection on nineteenth and twentieth century descriptions of Canada. According to Warkentin, Hutchison's book remains "at the pinnacle of regional geographical writing on Canada."[3]

The automobile had by then liberated cross-country travellers from the narrow path of the railway track, not to mention the lateral vision from the passenger rail car and the inability to stop at points of interest. Rather fittingly, then, rather than being a narrative of a single coast-to-coast journey, *The Unknown Country* is a fragmented account that describes the experiences and impressions of several excursions in various parts of the country, some of them by bus.[4] Far from reflecting the rapid onset of modernity, however, Hutchison's picture of Canada would be familiar to anyone who had read the travel narratives and tourism literature of the pre-automobile era. Although the book is largely concerned with the country's history, politics, geography, economy, and society, it includes many lyrical descriptions of the landscape as well as of rustic and aged individuals who represent the heroic backbone of the country. The perspective is that of a westerner proud of his province's rapid development, but the tone is nostalgic and the message strongly anti-urban, offering readers during and after the war a sense of rootedness and stability in a rapidly changing era.

The Unknown Country begins rather boldly by claiming of Canada that "No guidebooks have pictured it, no historian has told its story, no poet has sung its song," yet it covers well-trodden ground, beginning in the first chapter with a *habitant* household on the Isle of Orleans. In the same vein as the nostalgic anti-modern scenes described by American reporter C.H. Farnham in the 1880s, Hutchison muses: "These are the things that distinguish the French Canadian from the rest of America – his grip on things, on the earth, on reality, where we have come to accept shadow for substance, radio jokes for the simple, profound humours of the day's work, desiccated breakfast powders for bread, and the synthetic celluloid fornication of the screen for life."[5] Once in Quebec City, however, Hutchison succumbed to his own fantasies, writing: "as I walk these quiet streets I feel that behind the walls is a life, strange, exotic, rich, that I shall never see or know. Probably there are only ordinary people on the other side of these shutters, sitting down to a roast of beef and an apple pie, but I will never believe it. Still, somewhere there, if you could only peer through the keyhole, are candlelight, hooped skirts, swords, shoe buckles, fans, flirtations, and splendid adulteries."[6] Like Farnham again, Hutchison describes Montreal as the modern antithesis to Quebec City, yet with a sense of style, "a certain glittering sinfulness and sophistication, which makes us simple western Canadians feel very young, innocent, and gauche."[7]

Although a native of Ontario, Hutchison could not resist making repeated references to how Toronto and its surrounding manufacturing centres were prospering at the expense of the West due to Canada's protective tariffs. Hutchison states that Ontario is the heart of the country, yet his chapter on that province is titled "The Wedge," suggesting a divisive influence. The following passage is reminiscent of Rupert Brooke's dark, animated descriptions: "Here beats the great industrial heart, with the steady beat of forges, factories, and arsenals. Here breathes steadily the lung, sucking commerce through river and canal. Here also is the stomach, absorbing nourishment from the rest of the country with ravenous appetite. Here is the chief nerve ganglion of electric power. At the top of the wedge is the nation's brain in Ottawa."[8]

As for Toronto, Hutchison echoes the stereotypical image of the city as "a gentleman in a top hat walking to church on Sunday with a Bible under his arm, and frowning at the neighbour who is cutting the grass. Few cut grass in Toronto on Sunday."[9]

Even the description of Niagara Falls echoes Brooke's romantic anti-modernist sensibility: "They are being ruined. Their water supply is protected against the demands of industry, but the skyline of New York state, the grimy factories and hideous hotel tower, the Neon signs and small skyscrapers must spoil the whole picture as surely as a single garbage can would ruin the design of the largest and finest room."[10] In one of the book's few passages to describe the passing scene from the automobile, Hutchison creates a nightmarish image of "the suppurating sores of modern industry, the slums growing like rank water weeds beside the canal, the horrid factory towns that mean wealth for the nation and poverty for the inhabitants. All of them were heralded … by a rash of billboards, those painted whores of the written word that should be kept where they belong, in restricted areas."[11]

Not far from the "reach of industry" on the Niagara River, however, were "clusters of apple and peach trees and long fields of grapes; old brick farmhouses under immemorial elms; fat barns reeling drunkenly homeward over the hills; cool lanes and rambling country roads." Hutchison even makes explicit the link with the English picturesque by adding, "Why, you could stand a mile away, anywhere in this little pocket of cultivation and, looking across at spire and old house, at stone bridge and gnarled tree, swear that you were in the Cotswolds." He reminds the reader, however, that the garden-like Niagara peninsula is "less than a postage-stamp size" on the Canadian map, and that "A few miles away stretches forever and forever the solemn wilderness, or the raw lands which men have tortured, raped, and butchered."[12] There "glooms the dark, somber shore of Lake Superior, the pinched cold towns at its ragged edge, the steel mills of the Soo, and those ghastly, eyeless monuments of concrete, the round grain elevators of Fort William, where the prairie wheat is loaded on the lake boats."[13] In contrast to the stories referred to in Atwood's *Survival*, it is not the wilderness that has killed those who ventured into it, but rather the reverse.

Before moving on to the Prairies, *The Unknown Country* doubles back to the East coast, claiming that poverty had followed the passing of the age of wood, wind, and water, yet Nova Scotia had not "sunk down, hopeless and apathetic, like the slums of cities and the sad ruins of farming towns out West. The shore accepts poverty as a natural state and has learned to live with it, decently and unashamed. It keeps its clothes patched, its shoes shined, its plain, square houses painted, and every face glistens with soap and water."[14] There is no hint of an industrial economy, for in Digby, with its "perfection of white houses scattered like dice on the hillside," Hutchison observes "the busy wharves, the cargoes of dried cod ready for shipment, the well-scrubbed people, the clean little town, the scallop boats starting out for Fundy, the tangle of rigging and masts by the shore, the swoop and dart of the white gulls everywhere and sea vigor in the air – making you feel all at once a pleasure in living – making you forget what sort of world lies beyond the Gut, where the big ships are loading in St. John for the Battle of the Atlantic."[15]

The war receives another fleeting mention in the chapter on Halifax where Hutchison describes "little Canadian destroyers" herding merchantmen, "barking at them like sheep dogs."[16] Returning to the noble poverty theme, we are informed that "Some parts of Halifax are run-down and dingy, after years of genteel poverty, but the gentility does remain. None of the blaring crudity of our western cities is there, none of the push and salesmanship, but a kind of sober, trim, cheerful life which, though it is essentially North American out of New England, makes you think of life in a faded mansion on the coast of England."[17] New Brunswick's capital city of Fredericton, on the other hand, is described as "still the kind of North American town that Emerson lived in." Somehow missed by time, it is – in Hutchison's nostalgic imagination – "the last surviving Home Town of America, uncorrupted and innocent as your grandmother, rocking on her porch chair."[18] With its "neat, orderly squares," its "leafy graveyard in the center," and its "old rambling wooden houses, obese and expansive, with vests unbuttoned for comfort, basking in the shade," the old Loyalist city was a throwback to towns where "America used to swing on the porch hammock and kiss its girl in the darkness, where dinner was at noon, with hot roast, and father stoked the furnace and split the wood, and a house was a home, not a camp on the route of march."[19]

The Prairies could offer no such comforting escapism, or even the optimism of Kipling, for the flat landscape clearly did not inspire Hutchison who focused instead on politics, settlers, and the hardships of the depression-era drought and wartime wheat glut.[20] The reader turns with some relief to Hutchison's beloved British Columbia where "the size of everything … the bulk of the mountains, the space of the valleys, the far glimpses of land and sea, the lakes and rivers, all cast in gigantic mold ... make a man feel bigger, more free, as if he had come out of a crowded room."[21] Avoiding the expansive views from the wilderness mountaintops, however, Hutchison describes a garden-like landscape where the Fraser Canyon "widens suddenly and there are the fields of the Pacific coast, deep green, rank, overgrown, and succulent, each with its own mountain in the corner." Reminiscent of Robert Burnaby, Robert Brown, and other writers of the colonial era, Hutchison describes "the wild current blossoms dripping red and smelling of all the Aprils of the ages, the fierce growth of bracken, the white plumes of elderberry, and everywhere the hungry forest, marching back, with scouts of fern and alder, with shock troops of fir and hemlock, upon the settler's clearing."[22] Despite Hutchison's anti-urban bias, he depicts the rapidly growing city of Vancouver as a lush paradise where "every man can have a garden, can bask on a beach or sail a boat," and where people can leave their "gardens in bloom and swarm up the North Shore mountains to ski."[23]

Still, the pastoral landscape of southern Vancouver Island – referred to by Hutchison as the land of the lotus eaters – was clearly more to his taste: sailing "down the Gulf of Georgia, flecked with its little green islands, and along the Straits of Juan de Fuca, glistening before the blue line of the Olympic Mountains on the Washington shore ... Victoria suddenly appears, like an arrangement of toy houses, an architect's dream of the perfect human habitation, rising tier on tier from the sea upon a green hillside. It looks like the south coast of England. It looks like an artist's picture from which every disagreeable feature has been carefully removed. It looks like the ancient island of the Blest."[24] One of Victoria's chief attractions, in Hutchison's view, was its English character. Thus, a few miles up the coast, on the Saanich Peninsula where he lived, "you should easily find Keats's female Autumn, her hair soft-lifted by the winnowing wind, for it is with us a season of mists and mellow fruitfulness so like England that I fancy the poet would hardly know, if set down here now, that he had left home."[25]

Hutchison clearly felt most at home in what Leo Marx refers to as the middle landscape between "corrupt" city and "raw" wilderness,[26] but he admitted that the "essential" British Columbia was not to be found in the Saanich Peninsula or the Lower Mainland. Rather it was up the northern coast with its "little pulp mill towns and fish canneries,"[27] and in the arid interior where Cariboo rancher Michael O'Shea "had learned the satisfaction of land and space and had never known, in this stillness, the loneliness of cities."[28] Neither the North coast nor the Cariboo could easily be described as a middle landscape, yet they are places inhabited and domesticated to a certain extent by hardy, independent British Columbians whom Kipling would have strongly approved of. Similarly, *The Unknown Country* celebrates the loggers who cut down the giant trees of the old-growth coastal forest for, in Hutchison's view, that resource was limitless: "For miles and miles out to the horizon the forest land is flattened and blackened as man harvests this crop. But see, among the old black logs, some green is sprouting – bold sprouts of willow, alder, maple, and nameless brush; at last the squat thrust of fir and hemlock seedlings. In a few years there will be impenetrable second growth. Nine out of ten trees must die to make way for the strongest, but in the end the forest always wins, if men will leave it alone, without fire, to its work of reproduction."[29]

Finally, Hutchison's view of the First Nations was not a great deal different from that of the long list of nineteenth-century travel writers who had preceded him. In the northern trading post of Hazelton, where "the stores are full of furs and trade goods and the smell of buckskin," one would find "no movie Indians or hangers-on to be dressed up for war dances on holidays," but "the same Indians who fought the white men because the white witchcraft had produced a fatal epidemic of measles." In the local graveyard, where the "dead houses" were "crowded together in a village of their own," Hutchison wrote, "there was a feeling of loneliness, of unseen presence and horror not described. Nothing Christian here, despite the crosses, no thought of Christian resurrection. It was the haunt of savages who would rise again in demon form."[30]

Even when his book first appeared, Hutchison's Canada was a country of the past with its picturesque farms, villages, and small towns, mostly inhabited by people of British and French origin (with a particular focus on gothic Acadian folk tales),[31] but with a nod to the Icelanders of Gimli, Manitoba as well as to "the men in sheepskin coats" in Saskatchewan and Alberta (the title of his chapter 14). Less welcome was British Columbia's Asian population, particularly the Japanese who – Hutchison claimed – had overcome immigration limits "by an unmatched capacity for reproduction,"[32] and who were then being expelled from the coast. As with George Grant's *Picturesque Canada* six decades earlier, the industrial landscape is largely ignored, even deplored by Hutchison, yet the number of farms in Canada had peaked by the time *The Unknown Country* appeared,[33] and villages and small towns were shrinking in number and population while cities rapidly expanded, thereby making Hutchison's portrait of Canadian society more than a little dated. It was, however, the deeply nostalgic tone that ensured the book's enduring success, as did the skilful writing and the comforting picturesque imagery with its roots in the country's earliest colonial travel narratives. Such narratives are far from complete or accurate representations of past societies but they do present us with a clear window onto the desires, motivations, beliefs, and prejudices of those who wrote them, and they did exert a profound influence upon the attitudes and perspectives of those who read them.

NOTES

1 The book was the result of a chance meeting Hutchison had with an executive from the New York publishing house, Coward-McCann. Vaughan Palmer, "Introduction to the Wynford Edition," in Bruce Hutchison, *The Unknown Country: Canada and Her People* (Don Mills, ON: Oxford University Press, 2010). The references in this chapter are to the first Canadian edition, published by Longmans, Green and Company.
2 Hutchison also wrote *Canada: Tomorrow's Giant* (Toronto: Longman's Green 1957); and *The Unfinished Country: To Canada with Love and Some Misgivings* (Vancouver: Douglas and McIntyre, 1985).
3 John Warkentin, *So Vast and Various: Interpreting Canada's Regions in the Nineteenth and Twentieth Centuries* (Montreal and Kingston: McGill-Queen's University Press, 2010).
4 See Hutchison's memoir, *The Far Side of the Street* (Toronto: Macmillan, 1976), 161–3.
5 Hutchison, *The Unknown Country*, 15–16.
6 Hutchison, *The Unknown Country*, 40.
7 Hutchison, *The Unknown Country*, 75.
8 Hutchison, *The Unknown Country*, 132.
9 Hutchison, *The Unknown Country*, 136.
10 Hutchison, *The Unknown Country*, 147.
11 Hutchison, *The Unknown Country*, 151.
12 Hutchison, *The Unknown Country*, 148–9.
13 Hutchison, *The Unknown Country*, 154.
14 Hutchison, *The Unknown Country*, 184.
15 Hutchison, *The Unknown Country*, 194.
16 Hutchison, *The Unknown Country*, 212.
17 Hutchison, *The Unknown Country*, 216.
18 Hutchison, *The Unknown Country*, 223.
19 Hutchison, *The Unknown Country*, 224.

20 Hutchison, *The Unknown Country*, chapter 15.
21 Hutchison, *The Unknown Country*, 315.
22 Hutchison, *The Unknown Country*, 312–13.
23 Hutchison, *The Unknown Country*, 325.
24 Hutchison, *The Unknown Country*, 332–3.
25 Hutchison, *The Unknown Country*, 341.
26 Leo Marx, *The Machine in the Garden: Technology and the Pastoral Ideal in America* (Oxford: Oxford University Press, 1964), 71, 113–14, 121–3, 150, 159–60.
27 Hutchison, *The Unknown Country*, 326.
28 Hutchison, *The Unknown Country*, 360.
29 Hutchison, *The Unknown Country*, 349.
30 Hutchison, *The Unknown Country*, 369–70.
31 See, for example, the story of the mute amputee Jerome, who had died "after a lifetime of silence and terror, watching the sea, they say, for his enemies to come and get him." *The Unknown Country*, 190–1.
32 Hutchison, *The Unknown Country*, 286–7.
33 "Canadian Farms Getting Bigger, but Rarer," http://www.cbc.ca/news/business/canadian-farms-getting-bigger-but-rarer-1.1244248. Viewed 25 May 2017.

Credits

An earlier version of chapter 1 was published as "'Like a fragment of the old world': The Historical Regression of Quebec City in Travel Narratives and Tourist Guidebooks, 1776–1913," *Urban History Review* 40, no. 2 (Spring 2012): 15–28.

An earlier version of chapter 2 was published as "Canadian Pastoral: Promotional Images of British Colonization in Lower Canada's Eastern Townships during the 1830s," *Journal of Historical Geography* 29, 2 (2003): 189–211.

An earlier version of chapter 3 was published as "West Coast Picturesque: Class, Gender, and Race in a British Colonial Landscape, 1858–71," *Journal of Canadian Studies* 41, no. 2 (2007): 5–41.

An earlier version of chapter 4 was published as "Scenic Tourism on the Northeastern Borderland: Lake Memphremagog's Steamboat Excursions and Resort Hotels, 1850–1900," *Journal of Historical Geography* 35, no. 4 (2009): 716–42.

An earlier version of chapter 5 was published as "Seeing Icebergs and Inuit as Elemental Nature: An American Transcendentalist On and Off the Coast of Labrador, 1864," in Ben Bradley and J.I. Little, eds, "Landscape, Nature, and Memory: Tourism History in Canada," special online issue of *Histoire sociale – Social History*, 49 (June 2016): 243–63.

An earlier version of chapter 6 was published as "Travels in a Cold and Rugged Land: C.H. Farnham's Quebec Essays in *Harper's Magazine*, 1883–89," *Journal of Canadian Studies* 47, no. 2 (Spring 2013): 215–45.

An earlier version of chapter 7 was published as "'A fine, hardy, good-looking race of people': Travellers, Tourism Promoters, and the Scots Identity on Cape Breton Island, 1829–1920," *Acadiensis* 44, no. 1 (Winter/Spring 2015): 20–35.

An earlier version of chapter 10 was published as "A Country Without a Soul: Rupert Brooke's Gothic Vision of Canada," *Canadian Literature* 219 (Winter 2013): 95–111.

Bibliography

Printed Primary Sources

Aberdeen, Countess of. *Through Canada with a Kodak*. Edinburgh: W.H. White and Co., 1893.

Alexander, Sir James Edward. *Transatlantic Sketches Comprising Visits to the Most Interesting Scenes in North and South America, and the West Indies*. London: R. Bentley, 1833.

The American House Traveller's Guide for River St. Lawrence, and the Cities of Montreal, Quebec & Ottawa. Montreal: D. Rose, 1868.

The Ancient City of Quebec. [place not identified]: Issued by the Canadian Pacific Railway Company; copyrighted by the Chateau Frontenac Co., 1894.

Bagshaw, Roberta L. *No Better Land: The 1860 Diaries of the Anglican Colonial Bishop George Hills*. Victoria, BC: Sono Nis Press, 1996.

Barrett-Lennard, Capt. C.E. *Travels in British Columbia*. London: Hurst and Blackett, 1862.

Barrows, Samuel J. and Isabel C. Barrows. *The Shaybacks in Camp: Ten Summers under Canvas*. Boston and New York: Houghton, Mifflin and Company, 1888.

Bartlett, W.H. and N.P. Willis. *Canadian Scenery Illustrated*, 2 vols. London: George Virtue, 1842.

Beautiful Memphremagog. Newport, VT, 1907. Reprint Ayer's Cliff, QC: Pigwidgeon Press, 1987.

Benjamin, S.G.W. "Cruising around Cape Breton." *Century Magazine* (July 1884): 352–64.

– *The Atlantic Islands as Resorts of Health and Pleasure*. New York: Harper and Brothers, 1878.

– *The Cruise of the Alice May in the Gulf of St. Lawrence and Adjacent Waters*. New York: D. Appleton and Company, 1885.

Bigsby, John J. *The Shoe and Canoe or Pictures of Travel in the Canadas*, vol. 1. London, 1850. Reprint New York: Paladin Press, 1969.

Bolles, Frank. *From Blomidon to Smoky and Other Papers*. Boston: Riverside Press, 1894.

Boston and Maine Railroad. *Lake Memphremagog and about There*. Boston, 1895.

Bourne, George. *The Picture of Quebec*. Quebec: D. and J. Smillie, 1829.

Bradford, William. *Photographs of Arctic Ice*. Photograph album held by the Library of Congress Prints and Photographs Division.

Brooke, Rupert. *Letters from America*. Toronto: McClelland, Goodchild, and Stewart, 1916.

Brown, James B. *Views of Canada and the Colonists Embracing the Experience of Eight Years' Residence*, 2nd ed. Edinburgh: Adam and Charles Black, 1851.

Brown, Robert. "The First Journey of Exploration across Vancouver Island." In H.W. Bates, ed. *Illustrated Travels: A Record of Discovery, Geography, and Adventure*. London: Cassell, Petter, and Galpin [n.d].

Browne, Charles F. *Artemis Ward: His Travels (1865)*. In Doyle, ed., *Yankees in Canada*.

Bryant, William Cullen Bryant, ed. *Picturesque America; or, The Land We Live In*, 2 vols. New York: D. Appleton and Company, 1872 and 1874.

Buchan, William F. *Remarks on Emigration: More Particularly Applicable to the Eastern Townships Lower Canada*, 2nd ed. Devonport and London: 1842.

Burt, Henry M. *The Wonders and Beauties of Lake Memphremagog: The Great Summer Resort of New England: How to Go There and What Is to Be Seen*. Springfield: New England Publishing Company, 1872.

Cameron, Wendy, Mary McDougall Maude, and Sheila Haines, eds. *English Immigrant Voices: Labourers' Letters from Upper Canada in the 1830s*. Montreal and Kingston: McGill-Queen's University Press, 2000.

Campbell, J.F. *A Short American Tramp in the Fall of 1864*. Edinburgh: Edmonston and Douglas, 1865.

The Canadian Tourist. Montreal and Toronto: Hew Ramsay, 1856.

Car Window Glimpses: En Route to Quebec by Daylight via Quebec Central Railway. New York: Leve and Aldent's Publication, 1887.

Chambers, E.T.D. *The Guide to Quebec*. [Quebec]: Quebec Morning Chronicle, [1895].

Chambers, William. *Things As They Are in America*, 1854. Reprint New York: Negro Universities Press, 1968.

Champness, W. "To Cariboo and Back: An Emigrant's Journey to the Gold Fields of British Columbia" (from the "Leisure Hour," 1862).

Chisholm's All Round Route and Panoramic Guide of the St Lawrence. Montreal: Chisholm and Co., 1867.

Cockloft, Jeremy. *Cursory Observations Made in Quebec Province of Lower Canada in the Year 1811*. Bermuda: Edmund Ward, n.d. Reprint Toronto: Oxford University Press, 1960.

Coke, E.T. *A Subaltern's Furlough: Descriptive Scenes in Various Parts of the United States, Upper and Lower Canada, New Brunswick, and Nova Scotia, during the Summer and Autumn of 1832*. London: Saunders and Otley, 1833.

Cornwallis, Kinahan. *The New El Dorado; or British Columbia*. London: Thomas Cautley Newby, 1858.

Cozzens, Frederick S. *Acadia: Or, A Month with the Blue Noses*. New York: Derby and Jackson, 1859.

Craig, Gerald M, ed. *Early Travellers in the Canadas, 1791–1867*. Toronto: Macmillan, 1955.

Dashwood, Richard Lewes. *Chiploquorgan, Or, Life by the Camp Fire*. London: Simpkin, Marshall and Co., 1872.

Daubeny, Charles. *Journal of a Tour Made through the United States and Canada*. Oxford: T. Combe, 1843.

Davison, G.M. *The Fashionable Tour: An Excursion to the Springs, Niagara, Quebec, and through the New England States*. Saratoga Springs, NY: G.M. Davison, 1828.

Dickens, Charles. *American Notes for General Circulation*, vol. 2. London: Chapman and Hall, 1842.

Dimock, Celia C. *Children of the Sheiling*. Sydney, NS: Lynk Printing, n.d.

Dix, John R. *A Hand Book for Lake Memphremagog*. Boston: Evans and Co., [1864].

Dixon, James. *Personal Narrative of a Tour through Part of the United States and Canada*. New York: Lane and Scott, 1849.

Doyle, James, ed. *Yankees in Canada: A Collection of Nineteenth-Century Travel Narratives*. Toronto: ECW, 1980.

Dufferin and Ava, Marchioness of. *My Canadian Journal, 1872–'78*. New York, D. Appleton and Company, 1891.

Duncan, John Morison. *Travels through Part of the United States and Canada in 1818 and 1819*, vol. 2. New Haven: Howe and Spalding; New York: W.B. Gilley, 1823.

Dwight, Theodore. *The Northern Traveller, and Northern Tour, With the Routes to the Springs, Niagara & Quebec, and the Coal Mines of Pennsylvania*. New York: J. and J. Harper, 1830.

Emmerson, John. *British Columbia and Vancouver Island: Voyages, Travels and Adventures*. Durham, UK, 1865.

Evans, Francis A. *The Emigrant's Directory and Guide to Obtain Lands and Effect a Settlement in the Canadas*. Dublin: William Curry; London: Simpkin and Marshall; and Edinburgh: Oliver and Boyd, 1833.

Extracts from Letters Written during a First Year's Residence in the Eastern Townships of Lower Canada. London: J.L. Cox and Sons, 1837.

Farnham, C.H. "A Winter in Canada." *Harper's New Monthly Magazine* 68 (February 1884): 392–408.

– "Canadian Voyageurs on the Saguenay." *Harper's New Monthly Magazine* 76 (March 1888): 536–56.

– "Cape Breton Folk." *Harper's New Monthly Magazine* 72 (December 1885): 607–25.

– "Labrador, First Paper." *Harper's New Monthly Magazine* 71 (September 1885): 489–502.

– "Labrador, Second Paper." *Harper's New Monthly Magazine* 71 (October 1885): 651–66.

– "Montreal." *Harper's New Monthly Magazine* 79 (June 1889): 83–98.

– "Quebec." *Harper's New Monthly Magazine* 76 (February 1888): 356–73.

– "The Canadian Habitant." *Harper's New Monthly Magazine* 67 (August 1883): 375–92.

– "The Lower St. Lawrence." *Harper's New Monthly Magazine* 77 (November 1888): 814–25.

– "The Montagnais." *Harper's New Monthly Magazine* 77 (August 1888): 379–94.

Farrell, Ella G. *Among the Blue Laurentians, Queenly Montreal, Quaint Quebec, Peerless Ste. Anne de Beaupré*. New York: Kenedy, [1912].

Fergusson, Adam. *Practical Notes Made during a Tour in Canada*. Edinburgh: William Blackwood; and London: T. Cadell, 1831.

Fergusson, C. Bruce, ed. *Uniacke's Sketches of Cape Breton and Other Papers Relating to Cape Breton*. Halifax, NS: Public Archives of Nova Scotia, 1958.

Fleming, Sandford. *The Intercolonial Railway. A Historical Sketch*. Montreal: Dawson Brothers, 1876.

Gingras, Eugène. *Guide de Québec*. Quebec: L.J. Demers et Frère, 1880.

Gosse, Philip Henry. *The Canadian Naturalist. A Series of Conversations on the Natural History of Lower Canada*. London: John Van Voorst, 1840. Reprint Toronto: Coles, 1971.

Gow, John M. *Cape Breton Illustrated: Historic, Picturesque and Descriptive*. Toronto: William Briggs, 1893.

Grande excursion d'été de Québec au Lac Memphremagog, Boston et New York, revenant par Montréal: une excursion de neuf jours toutes dépenses comprises, pour cinquante piastres seulement. N.p., 1881.

Grant, George Monro, ed. *Picturesque Canada: The Country As It Was and Is*, vol. 1 and 2. Toronto: Belden, [1882 and 1884?].

Grant, W. Colquhoun. "Description of Vancouver Island." *Journal of the Royal Geographical Society* 26 (1852): 268–320.

Gray, Hugh. *Letters from Canada, Written during a Residence There in the Years 1806, 1807, and 1808*. London: Longman, Hurst, Rees, and Orme, 1809.

Hall, Lieutenant Francis. *Travels in Canada and the United States, in 1816 and 1817*, 2nd ed. London: Longman, Hurst, Rees, Orme, and Browne, 1819.

Hamilton, Thomas. *Men and Manners in America*. Edinburgh and London: William Blackwood and Sons, 1843.

The Hand-book of Quebec. A Compendium of Information for the Use of Strangers Visiting the City and Its Environs. Quebec: T. Cary, 1850.

"Harry Guillod's Journal of a Trip to Cariboo, 1862." *British Columbia Historical Quarterly* 19 (1955): 187–232.

Hawkins's Picture of Quebec with Historical Recollections. Quebec: Neilson and Cowan, 1834.

Hazlett, William Carew. *The Great Gold Fields of Cariboo*, 1862. Reprint [Victoria?]: Klanak Press, 1974.

Henderson, Alexander. *Photographic Views and Studies of Canadian Scenery*. Montreal: [publisher not identified], 1865.

Heriot, George. *Travels through the Canadas*. London: Printed for Richard Phillips by T. Giller, 1807.

Howells, Annie Fréchette. "Summer Resorts on the St. Lawrence." *Harper's New Monthly Magazine* 69 (June–November 1884): 197–209.

Hunter's Panoramic Guide from Niagara Falls to Quebec. Boston: J.P. Jewett; Cleveland: H.P.B. Jewett, 1857.

Hunter, W.S., Jr. *Hunter's Eastern Townships Scenery, Canada East*. Montreal: John Lovell, 1860.

Hutchison, Bruce. *The Far Side of the Street*. Toronto: Macmillan, 1976.

– *The Unknown Country: Canada and Her People*. Toronto: Longmans, Green and Company, 1943.

Information respecting the Eastern Townships of Lower Canada. London: W.J. Ruffy, 1833.

Intercolonial of Canada. *A Ramble and a Rest: Pure Air, Sea Bathing, Picturesque Scenery; Summer of 1895*. Ottawa, Government Printing Bureau, 1895.

An Intercolonial Outing along the Shores of the Lower St. Lawrence and through the Provinces by the Sea. [St John, NB? 1893?].

"Iraneus Letters from the Lakes and the Hills." *New York Observer and Chronicle*, 17 August 1876.

Ireland, Willard, ed. "First Impressions: Letter of Colonel Richard Clement Moody, R.E., to Arthur Blackwood, February 1, 1859." *British Columbia Historical Quarterly* 15 (1951): 85–109.

James, Henry. *Portraits of Places*. Boston: Houghton, Mifflin and Company, 1883.

Johnson, R. Byron. *Very Far West Indeed: A Few Rough Experiences on the North-West Pacific Coast*. London: Sampson Low, Marston, Low, and Searle, 1872.

The Journal of Richard Henry Dana, Jr., ed. Robert F. Lucid (1968). In Doyle, ed., *Yankees in Canada*.

Keynes, Geoffrey, ed. *The Letters of Rupert Brooke*. New York: Harcourt, Brace and World, 1968.

Kipling, Rudyard. *A Book of Words: Selections from Speeches an Addresses Delivered between 1906 and 1927*. London: Macmillan, 1928.

– *Letters of Travel (1892–1913)*. London: Macmillan, 1920.

– *Something of Myself, for My Friends Known and Unknown*. Garden City, NY: Doubleday, Doran and Company, 1937.

Lambert, John. *Travels through Lower Canada, and the United States of North America, in the Years 1806, 1807, and 1808*. London: Richard Phillips, 1810.

LeMoine, J.M. *The Tourists' Notebook*. Quebec: F.X. Garant, 1876.

Lenman, Charles. *Adventures of an Angler in Canada, Nova Scotia and the United States*. London: R. Bentley, 1848.

Linton, J.J.E. *Letters from Settlers in the Huron District, C.W.* London: 1843.

Little, J.I., ed. *Love Strong as Death: Lucy Peel's Canadian Journal, 1833–36*. Waterloo, ON: Wilfrid Laurier University Press, 2001.

Lockett, E. *Cape Breton Hand-Book and Tourist's Guide, Containing in Addition Valuable Recipes, and Other Useful Information*. North Sydney and Sydney, n.d.

Lord, John Keast. *The Naturalist in Vancouver Island and British Columbia*. London: R. Bentley, 1866.

Lumsden, James. *American Memoranda by a Mercantile Man, during a Short Tour in the Summer of 1843*. Glasgow: Bell and Bain, 1844.

McLeod, Anne Burnaby and Pixie McGeachie, eds. *Land of Promise: Robert Burnaby's Letters from Colonial British Columbia, 1858–1863*. Burnaby, BC: City of Burnaby, 2002.

M'Gregor, John. *British America*, 2 vols. Edinburgh: William Blackwood; London: T. Caddell, 1832 and 1833.

Mack, W.G. *A Letter from the Eastern Townships of Lower Canada*. Glasgow: David Robertson, 1837.

Mackay, Robert W. Stuart. *The Strangers' Guide to the Cities of Montreal and Quebec*. Montreal: R. and A. Miller, 1852.

Mackenzie, Catherine Dunlop. "The Charm of Cape Breton Island. The Most Picturesque Portion of Canada's Maritime Provinces – A Land Rich in Historical Associations, Natural Resources, and Geographic Appeal." *National Geographic* 38, no. 1 (July 1920).

MacNeil, Neil S. *The Highland Heart in Nova Scotia*. New York: C. Scribner's, 1948.

Major Jones's Sketches of Travel: Comprising the Scenes, Incidents, and Adventures, in his Tour from Georgia to Canada (1848). In Doyle, ed., *Yankees in Canada.*

Mark, William. *Cariboo: A True and Correct Narrative.* Stockton: William Wright, 1863.

Mather, Frederic G. "A Summer at 'Magog' Lake." *The Continent: an Illustrated Weekly Magazine* 3, no. 21 (23 May 1883) [n.p.].

– "On the Boundary Line." *Harper's New Monthly Magazine* no. 291 (August 1874): 335–50.

Mayne, Commander R.C. *Four Years in British Columbia and Vancouver Island.* London: John Murray, 1862.

Montreal, Quebec and Ottawa: Three Interesting Cities in Canada. [place not identified]: Passenger Department, Grand Trunk Railway System, 1910.

Moodie, Susanna. *Roughing It in the Bush*, ed. Michael Peterman. New York: W.W. Norton, 2007.

Morgan, J.C. *The Emigrant's Notebook and Guide.* London: Longman, Hurst, Rees, Orme, and Brown, 1824.

My Canadian Sweetheart, or, Aunt Tabby's Summer Boarders: A Story of Lake Memphremagog. New York: Connecticut Valley and Passumpsic Railroads, 1885.

Myers, J.C. *Sketches on a Tour through the Northern and Eastern States, the Canadas and Nova Scotia.* Harrisonburg, VA: J.H. Wartmann, 1849.

Noble, Louis L. *After Icebergs with a Painter: A Summer Voyage to Labrador and around Newfoundland.* New York: D. Appleton and Company, 1861.

An Officer, *Travels through the Interior Parts of America: In a Series of Letters*, vol. 1. London: William Lane, 1789.

Oliver, Thos. J. *Holiwell's New Guide to the City of Quebec*, 6th ed. Quebec: C.E. Holiwell, 1888.

Owl's Head Mountain House Lake Memphremagog. [place and publisher not identified] , 1892.

Packard, Alpheus Spring. *The Labrador Coast: A Journal of Two Summer Cruises to the Region.* New York: N.D.C. Hodges, 1891.

Pinney, Thomas, ed. *The Letters of Rudyard Kipling, vol. 3, 1900–10.* London: Macmillan, 1996; *vol. 4, 1911-19.* Iowa City: University of Iowa Press, 1999; *vol. 5, 1920–30.* Houndmills, Basingstoke, Hampshire, UK: Palgrave Macmillan, 2004; *vol. 6, 1931–36.* Iowa City: University of Iowa Press, 2004.

Power, Tyrone. *Impressions of America; during the Years 1833, 1834, and 1835*, vol. 2. Philadelphia: Sherwood, Gilbert, and Piper, 1837.

Pritchard, Allan, ed. *Vancouver Island Letters of Edmund Hope Verney, 1862-65.* Vancouver: UBC Press, 1996.

Quebec, Canada. Quebec: Publicity Bureau of Quebec City, [1912?].

Quebec and Its Environs; Being a Picturesque Guide to the Stranger. [Quebec?]: Thomas Cary, 1831.

Quebec and Montreal Travellers' Free Guide: Containing Interesting Information for Tourists. Montreal: E. Senecal, 1872.

The Quebec Directory and Stranger's Guide to the City and Environs, 1844–5. Quebec: Printed for A. Hawkins by W. Cowan, 1844.

Rankin, D.J. *Our Ain Folk and Others*. Toronto: Macmillan, 1930.

Rattray, Alexander. *Vancouver Island and British Columbia, Where They Are; and What They May Become*. London: Smith, Elder and Co., 1862.

Report of the Court of Directors of the British American Land Company to the Proprietors, 19 June 1834. London: W.J. Ruffy, 1834.

Roberts, Charles G.D. *The Canadian Guide-Book: The Tourist's and Sportsman's Guide to Eastern Canada and Newfoundland*. New York: Appleton, 1891.

Roger, Charles. *Quebec: As It Was and As It Is, or, A Brief History of the Oldest City in Canada, from Its Foundation to the Present Time*, 5th ed. Quebec: printed for the proprietor, 1867.

Ross, John. *A Voyage of Discovery, Made under the Orders of the Admiralty*, vol. 1. London: John Murray, 1819.

Routhier, A.B. *Quebec. A Quaint Mediaeval French City in America at the Dawn of the XXth Century*. Montreal: Montreal Printing and Pub., ca 1904.

Rowan, John J. *The Emigrant and Sportsman in Canada. Some Experiences of an Old Country Settler*. London: Edward Stanford, 1876.

"The Saguenay." *Harper's New Monthly Magazine* 19 (June/November 1859): 145–60.

Sansom, Joseph. "Travels in Lower Canada, 1820." In Doyle, ed., *Yankees in Canada*.

Silliman, Dr Benjamin. *A Tour to Quebec in the Autumn of 1819*. London: Sir Richard Phillips and Co., 1822.

Sladen, Douglas Brooke Wheeton. *On the Cars and Off: Being a Pilgrimage along the Queen's Highway, from Halifax in Nova Scotia to Victoria in Vancouver's Island*. London and New York: Ward, Lock, [189?].

Small, H.B., compiler. *The Canadian Handbook and Tourist's Guide: Being a Description of Canadian Lake and River Scenery*. Montreal: M. Longmoore, 1866.

Smith, Dwight, ed. *A Tour of Duty in the Pacific Northwest: E.A. Porcher and H.M.S. 'Sparrowhawk,' 1865–1868*. Fairbanks: University of Alaska Press, 2000.

Smith, Theodore Clarke. "Camp by the Cliff," ch. 1 (1884–1889), (unpublished typescript kindly made available by John Scott).

Smyth, Eleanor. *An Octogenarian's Reminiscences*. Letchworth, Eng., 1916.

Snow's Hand-Book. Northern Pleasure Travel. Boston: Noyes, Snow and Company, 1878.

Souvenir, Union Meeting, Canadian Divisions, Brotherhood of Locomotive Engineers, Quebec, 18-20 June 1907.

Stewart, D.H., ed. *Kipling's America: Travel Letters, 1889-1895.* Greensboro, NC: ELT Press, 2003.

Sweetser, M.F. *The Maritime Provinces: A Handbook for Travellers.* Boston: James R. Osgood and Company, 1875.

Talbot, Edward Allen. *Five Years' Residence in the Canadas,* vol. 1. London: Longman, Hurst, Rees, Orme, Brown and Green, 1824.

Taylor, Frank H. "A Canadian Pilgrimage." *Harper's New Monthly Magazine* 63 (March 1881): 501–5.

Thoreau, Henry David. *A Yankee in Canada,* 1866. Reprint Montreal: Harvest House, 1961.

Tourists' Guide between Quebec and New England via Quebec Central Railway and Lake Memphremagog. Sherbrooke: [Quebec Central Railway?], 1885.

Townsend, James B. "Our Northern Lakes and Mountains." *Frank Leslie's Popular Monthly* 20, no. 1 (July 1885).

Travellers Hand-book of the City of Quebec and Its Environs. Quebec: G.T. Cary, 1857.

Trollope, Anthony. *North America.* New York: Alfred A. Knopf, 1951.

Tudor, Henry. *Narrative of a Tour in North America,* vol. 1. London: James Duncan, 1834.

Vernon, C.W. *Cape Breton at the Beginning of the Twentieth Century: A Treatise of Natural Resources and Development.* Toronto: Nation Publishing, 1903.

Warner, Charles Dudley. *Baddeck and That Sort of Thing,* 15th ed. Boston: Houghton, Mifflin and Company, 1892.

Wasson, D.A. "Ice and Esquimaux." *The Atlantic Monthly,* vol. 14, 15 (December 1864 – May 1865).

Weld, Isaac, Jr. *Travels through the States of North America and the Provinces of Upper and Lower Canada during the Years 1795, 1796, and 1797.* London: John Stockdale, 1799.

Wilkie, David. *Sketches of a Summer Trip to New York and the Canadas.* London: Berwick, 1837.

Williams, W. *Appleton's Northern and Eastern Traveller's Guide.* New York: D. Appleton, 1850.

Willson, [Henry] Beckles. *Nova Scotia: The Province That Has Been Passed By.* London: Constable and Co., 1911.

Withrow, W.H. *Our Own Country Canada: Canada, Scenic and Descriptive.* Toronto: W. Briggs, 1889.

www.ingramcontent.com/pod-product-compliance
Lightning Source LLC
LaVergne TN
LVHW090150080826
844660LV00013B/739/J

* 9 7 8 1 4 8 7 5 0 0 2 1 4 *